Multi-modal Competition and the Future of Mail

Multi-modal Competition and the Future of Mail

Edited by

Michael A. Crew

Rutgers, The State University of New Jersey, Newark, USA

and

Paul R. Kleindorfer

INSEAD, France and University of Pennsylvania, USA

ADVANCES IN REGULATORY ECONOMICS

Edward Elgar

Cheltenham, UK • Northampton, MA, USA

Published by
Edward Elgar Publishing Limited
The Lypiatts
15 Lansdown Road
Cheltenham
Glos GL50 2JA
UK

Edward Elgar Publishing, Inc.
William Pratt House
9 Dewey Court
Northampton
Massachusetts 01060
USA

A catalogue record for this book
is available from the British Library

Library of Congress Control Number: 2011936413

MIX
Paper from
responsible sources
FSC® C018575
FSC
www.fsc.org

ISBN 978 0 85793 581 6

Typeset by Servis Filmsetting Ltd, Stockport, Cheshire
Printed and bound by MPG Books Group, UK

Contents

List of sponsors vii
Preface and acknowledgements viii

1 Non-linear pricing, volume discounts and the USO under entry 1
Michael A. Crew and Paul R. Kleindorfer

2 Price differentiation: what is acceptable for a universal service provider? 18
Richard Eccles

3 Postal price regulation in a competitive environment 32
Ralf Wojtek and Martin Zauner

4 Failure to implement the Postal Directive in the EU and EEA: public and private enforcement of state liability 46
Alessandra Fratini and Mariacristina Bottino

5 Forecasting letter volumes: augmenting econometric baseline projections 60
Vance L. Martin, Chris Paterson and Jessie Xiaokang Wang

6 Uncertainty and projections of the demand for mail 77
Frédérique Fève, Jean-Pierre Florens, Leticia Veruete-McKay, Soterios Soteri and Frank Rodriguez

7 Do volume increases and decreases have the same effect on labor hours? 94
Michael D. Bradley, Jeff Colvin and Mary K. Perkins

8 A panel data analysis of inefficiency and heterogeneity in the postal sector 109
Catherine Cazals, Paul Dudley, Jean-Pierre Florens and Michael Jones

9 Affordability of postal services addressed to households 124
Claire Borsenberger, Denis Joram and Lise Martin

10 Towards a 21st century postal service 139
John C. Panzar

11 Privatization: could the benefits seen in other network industries be realized in postal industries? 150
Stuart Holder and Helen Smith

12 The confluence of the postal sector with the Internet economy and regulation 165
John Hearn

13 Allocating costs between universal services and services outside the scope of universal service 180
Heikki Nikali, Kari Elkelä, Pekka Leskinen, Päivi Rokkanen and Peter Karlsson

14 Price-cap regulation in the postal sector: single versus multiple baskets 195
Claire Borsenberger, Sébastien Bréville, Helmuth Cremer, Philippe De Donder and Denis Joram

15 Optimal pricing of mail in the transactional market and welfare for the wider communications market 206
Philippe De Donder, Helmuth Cremer, Paul Dudley and Frank Rodriguez

16 A market study of packets and parcels services 221
Stephen Gibson and Nancy Race

17 Defending mail markets against new entrants: an application of the defender model 236
Christian Jaag, Helmut Dietl, Urs Trinkner and Oliver Fürst

18 Liberalization and postal workers 247
Henrik B. Okholm and Anna Möller

19 Government use of the postal system: an ignored USO component 265
Michael J. Ravnitzky and J.P. Klingenberg

20 UPU terminal dues: winners and losers 278
James I. Campbell Jr, Alex Kalevi Dieke and Martin Zauner

21 On the use of reverse auctions to designate universal postal service providers 290
Carlos Costa

22 Priority and Non-Priority services: returning to the origins? 303
Filipa Silva

23 Understanding consumer preferences for paper and digital marketing channels 316
Kari Elkelä

24 Accounting for behavioral biases for non-biased demand estimations 331
Meloria Meschi and Carla Pace

Sponsors

Royal Mail
Deutsche Post DHL
Jersey Post
bpost
La Poste
R.R. Donnelley & Sons Company
United Parcel Service
ARCEP
Jersey Competition Regulatory Authority
Pitney Bowes
Siemens Industry – Mobility
US Postal Regulatory Commission
Posten AB
Postal Services Commission
Itella Corporation
Post Italiane
ANACOM
FedEx Express
FTI
KPMG LLP
LECG
NERA Economic Consulting
PostNL
Swiss Post
IBM Global Business Services
Oxera
Consumer Focus
SLS Consulting, LLC
Venable LLP
Bird & Bird LLP
Canadian Union of Postal Workers
Commission for Communications Regulation
Frontier Economics
International Post Corporation
London Economics
National Association of Letter Carriers
Accent
AlixPartners
An Post
Association of Postal Commerce
BIEK
Diversified Specifics
FratiniVergano–European Lawyers
K&L Gates LLP
Luis Jimenez Consulting LLC
New Zealand Post Limited
Swiss Economics

Preface and acknowledgements

This book is a result of the Center for Research in Regulated Industries' (CRRI) 19th Conference on Postal and Delivery Economics which was held on June 1–4, 2011 in St. Helier, Jersey. January 1, 2011 was an important year in the history of the postal sector in that postal markets for most countries in the European Union were fully opened up to competitive entry. This major change and the increasing impact of multi-modal completion, notably, email, social networks, and Internet advertising, are raising important questions about the future of mail. The conference and this book attempt to address some of the challenges resulting. They follow earlier conferences and workshops. In 1990, the first Conference on Postal and Delivery Economics was held at Coton House, Rugby, England, July 22–25, 1990, in honor of the 150th anniversary of the Penny Post and the contributions of Sir Rowland Hill. To date there have been 19 conferences, three workshops and now 18 edited volumes as part of CRRI's program on Postal and Delivery Economics.

The 2011 Conference was made possible by the support of its generous sponsors. We would like to thank sponsors not only for financial support, but also for their advice and encouragement, and for serving on the organizing committee. We would like to thank the following for their advice and comments: José Amado da Silva, Geoff Bickerton, Tim Brown, Lawrence Buc, Bernhard Bukovc, Philip Burns, Eduardo Cardadeiro, Gary Carroll, João Castro, Margaret Cigno, Julien Coulier, John Curran, Robert Curry, Bernard Damiens, Gene Del Polito, Paul Dudley, Richard Eccles, Charles Fattore, Stephen Ferguson, John Fletcher, Alessandra Fratini, Stephen Gibson, Ruth Goldway, Stefano Gori, Paul Hamilton, Robert Hammond, Greg Harman, John Hearn, Jan Bart Henry, Paul Hodgson, Stuart Holder, Derek Holt, George Houpis, Christian Jaag, Luis Jimenez, Denis Joram, George Kuehnbaum, David M. Levy, Martin Maegli, Walter Maschke, Leonardo Mautino, Heikki Nikali, Chris Osborne, Chris Paterson, Wolfgang Pickave, Leon Pintsov, Michael Ravnitzky, Ian Ridgway, Jim Sauber, Michael Scanlon, Gennaro Scarfiglieri, Rob Sheldon, Michael Shinay, Paul C. Smith, Nancy Sparks, Gregory Swinand, Joëlle Toledano, Urs Trinkner, Mark van der Horst, Joost Vantomme, Ian Volner, Sture Wallander, Tim Walsh, David Williams and Ralf Wojtek.

The host country plays an important role in these conferences. This year's conference, the 19th Conference on Postal and Delivery Economics, benefited greatly from the efforts of our host, Jersey Post. Gary Carroll and Ian Ridgway were gracious hosts. They and their colleagues provided both advice and assistance on numerous occasions and contributed greatly to the success of the event.

We would like to thank our distinguished dinner speakers, Ian Carr formerly of Jersey Post, Tim Brown of Postcomm, and Stephen Agar of Royal Mail. These speeches addressed current issues of regulation and postal reform against the background of increasing multi-modal competition in the postal sector, maintaining the conference tradition of stimulating presentations by distinguished leaders in the industry.

We benefited from the contributions of Francelis Montes de Oca. Francelis, Assistant Director of CRRI, provided outstanding administrative support for this conference, CRRI's other conferences and assisted us with the production of this book. We would like to thank all authors and participants of the conference, without whom the conference and this book would not have been possible. The usual disclaimers are applicable. In particular, the views expressed reflect the views of the authors and are not necessarily those of the sponsors.

Michael A. Crew and Paul R. Kleindorfer

1. Non-linear pricing, volume discounts and the USO under entry*

Michael A. Crew† **and Paul R. Kleindorfer**‡

1 INTRODUCTION

The inherent tensions between maintaining a Universal Service Obligation (USO) combined with full market opening (FMO) were recognized as postal markets began to become open to increased competition. These tensions are exacerbated by serious intermodal competition in the form of electronic substitution for both advertising and transactions mail. Indeed, the impact of electronic competition may be even more serious than the impact of direct competition from FMO, as illustrated by significant declines in mail volume for many major postal operators (POs) since 2008. Crew and Kleindorfer (2011a) demonstrated that retaining volumes for ultimate delivery by the universal service provider (USP) is fundamental to maintaining economies of scale and therefore the USO, and remaining financially viable. The purpose of this chapter is to review the role of price discrimination, especially quantity discounts, in maintaining volumes in the face of direct and electronic competition.

Price discrimination has been common in the postal sector for many years. Ramsey pricing is effectively a form of third-degree price discrimination, in which different prices are charged in different market segments, based on inverse elasticities, with low elasticity products having a higher markup. Quantity discounts, a form of second-degree price discrimination, have de facto been a feature of postal pricing in the form of worksharing discounts which have minimum volume requirements and may entail additional volume discounts. The purpose of this chapter is to provide a more formal analysis of price discrimination, especially the role of second-degree price discrimination or quantity discounts.[1] The chapter shows that quantity discounts have a major role to play as a competitive instrument and, therefore, as a means of retaining volume in the face of intermodal competition. Interestingly, this topic has received minimal attention in the literature on the postal sector. The analytical framework aims to provide a basis for competitive strategies by POs that is consistent with continued competition and maintaining the USO. Section 2 reviews briefly the nature of price discrimination. Section 3 concentrates attention on second-degree price discrimination (quantity discounts) in the postal sector and its potential for pricing innovations. The important preconditions for achieving the

† CRRI Professor of Regulatory Economics and Director of CRRI, Rutgers School of Business, Rutgers University.

‡ Distinguished Research Professor, INSEAD; and Anheuser-Busch Professor of Management Science, Emeritus, the Wharton School of the University of Pennsylvania.

benefits of quantity discounts are examined, including the necessity to prevent arbitraging away the benefits by paying such discounts only to originating mailers. Section 4 provides a discussion of the model and illustrative numerical results, with the detailed derivations provided in the Technical Appendix 1A. Section 5 concludes with the implications of the analysis focusing especially on the demand stimulating benefits of non-linear pricing and its role as a competitive tool when faced with electronic competition.

2 PRICE DISCRIMINATION AND PRICING INNOVATIONS

The origins of price discrimination go back many years to the early theory of monopoly. Discrimination requires different valuations by consumers and infeasibility of resale. In general, monopoly is not required for price discrimination to be employed profitably. Indeed, price discrimination is widespread but monopoly exists rarely outside of regulated energy utilities. However, to be profitable, price discrimination requires some degree of market power and some significant barriers to resale or transferability between consumers. Price discrimination, at its simplest, means that different consumers or classes of consumers pay different prices for essentially the same product. First-degree price discrimination is the most powerful form of price discrimination, where the price paid by each consumer is equal to his/her entire willingness to pay. It exists only in theory because in practice it requires that the monopolist have perfect knowledge of each and every consumer's demand function. Unlike first-degree price discrimination, second- and third-degree price discrimination do not require a monopoly but do require some degree of market power. They also require some ability to prevent arbitrage by making resale difficult.[2]

Second-degree price discrimination is non-linear pricing (NLP). Price multiplied by quantity is revenue, that is, $PQ = R$. Dividing R by Q gives a constant or linear price of P, which does not depend on Q. Contrast with a two-part tariff, where a subscription fee of F plus a price per unit of P are charged, resulting in a unit price of $F/Q + P$. Price clearly is a non-linear inverse function of Q with large consumers paying a lower (average) price than small consumers. The two-part tariff is a form of quantity discounting. Quantity discounts are synonymous with NLP.

Third-degree price discrimination is where the market can be segmented into two or more markets but the prices are linear in each market. In market 1, consumers pay the (linear) price of P_1 and pay P_2 in market 2. Second- and third-degree price discrimination may be combined. In market 1, a non-linear price might apply, while in market 2 a linear price or a different non-linear price from market 1 may apply. For example, non-profit mailers may pay a lower price than other bulk mailers for the same service with quantity discounts applying to either product.

Examples of price discrimination are numerous across the economy. As personal services cannot be resold, price discrimination is feasible in such markets. However, market power may be very small. For example, in the case of hair styling women are typically charged more for a haircut than men and children even though stylists have weak market power because of the very large number of suppliers. This is third-degree price discrimination reflecting differences in the demand elasticities. Other examples include airlines, where a sophisticated form of price discrimination, referred to as 'yield management', is employed. Market power arises from dominance of a hub and peak demands. Demand is further segmented by practices such as non-refundable tickets and change fees. Quantity discounts exist through special deals with large companies and are more widespread through frequent flyer programs. Such programs are normally considered loyalty programs, which are intended to increase demand and reduce price elasticity. They are similar to quantity discounts in that they introduce non-linearity into prices.

POs can benefit from the lessons of airlines and competitors in deriving pricing policies that make increased use of second-degree price discrimination. One result of second-degree price discrimination is that it will generally increase quantity demanded. In the postal contest, volumes will be greater under second-degree price discrimination than they would absent it. In view of the threats to volumes arising from electronic and direct competitors, second-degree price discrimination deserves special attention at this stage in the development of the postal sector. Retaining volumes means retaining scale economies in delivery and avoiding the higher average cost that arises from reductions in volume.

3 QUANTITY DISCOUNTS IN THE POSTAL SECTOR

Price discrimination is ubiquitous in modern economies and common in the postal sector as a result of the application of Ramsey pricing. Second-degree price discrimination is by no means as common. Some POs have quantity discount programs, for example, La Poste, bpost and the United States Postal Service (USPS). In all three cases they have come under scrutiny by regulators. The quantity discount programs of La Poste and bpost take the form of rebates for total annual volumes, with such rebates paid directly to the originating mailers.[3] In the case of the United States the Postal Regulatory Commission (PRC) has been critical of 'negotiated services agreements' (NSAs), as examined in Robinson et al. (2008) These take the form of discounts for large volume mailers, for example, large banks. The concern was that USPS was giving a discount that did not, in fact, increase volume. Interestingly, all the discussion of NSAs was at a time when the US economy was ripping along – to disaster as it turns out – and not when volumes were under considerable pressure as now. The case for the NSAs was made by Levy et al. (2006). The discussion is not surprisingly, given the forum, a restatement of the protagonists' positions. Now it is much less relevant because of the sea of change taking place in the postal sector as a result of rapidly declining volumes and loss of scope economies. The debate has now changed to what can be done to retain volume and less of a concern for the equity issues. So, for this reason the approach of La Poste and bpost is more interesting to today's problems because both aim at using quantity discounts as a device to make mail more competitive not just with entrants in the mail sector but much more importantly with the electronic competition that is making serious inroads into mail volume.

In applying quantity discounts to the postal sector, it is useful first to review the nature of second-degree price discrimination generally. Willig (1978) demonstrated the important result that any uniform price schedule unequal to marginal cost could be Pareto dominated by a non-linear outlay schedule (for example, one based on volume discounts). In other (non-technical) words, NLP would potentially make both the producer and its customers better off. However, for the benefits of NLP to be obtained, certain conditions need to be fulfilled.

First, it should be reiterated that NLP is a form of price discrimination as, by definition, the same price is not charged to all buyers. With NLP, larger-volume buyers receive a lower average price than smaller-volume buyers. It has long been recognized that price discrimination cannot operate effectively if arbitrage is allowed to occur and sellers in the lower-priced market are allowed to resell (arbitrage) to customers in the higher-priced market.[4] In the case of volume discounts, if arbitragers can resell the product bought at the volume discount the benefits of volume discounts (NLP) will be reduced or even lost entirely. In the postal sector, volume discounts (either to originators of mail or to worksharing providers) are an important example of NLP. Arbitrage in the postal sector can take the form of specious aggregation, in which a consolidator takes advantage of volume discounts by consolidating volumes across several mailers to achieve higher-volume discount thresholds without adding any value to the service. Moreover, under pure specious aggregation, the resulting volume discounts are entirely retained by the consolidator so that additional demand stimulation, the main objective of quantity discounts, is negligible. The only result under such specious aggregation is that the PO incurs an additional expense (namely paying the consolidator for a valueless service) leading ultimately to the need to increase prices to finance this additional expense, with associated declines in postal volumes. The resulting inefficient outcome is just the opposite of what is intended under NLP.[5]

NLP has a long history in applied microeconomic theory and in practice in the form of block tariffs and two-part tariffs in monopoly utilities, notably, electricity and gas. Economists have been interested in NLP in part because of its ubiquity in natural monopolies. Their interest was motivated by a desire to understand the reasons for its ubiquity and its success. The reasons relate very much to the features of natural monopolies. NLP functions successfully in natural monopolies because of the high fixed costs and the consequent dominant scale economies. The other important reason for its success is that electricity and gas companies are physically connected by a network, making resale impossible without the permission of the utility.

For POs, NLP has the potential to be successful. POs have strong scale economies in delivery. So, to the extent that NLP increases quantity consumed, POs' costs are lowered as a result of the reduction in unit costs with the increase in output. From the PO's point of view, the scale effect from the extra volume is a benefit. The other benefit, which is in fact enhanced by scale economies, is that NLP has the potential to make both the PO and its customers better off compared to a simple uniform or 'linear' price. NLP's ability to make customers and the firm better off has long been implicit in applied microeconomic theory but it was not formalized and codified until Willig (1978) showed that any uniform price greater than marginal cost was 'Pareto dominated' by a 'nonlinear outlay schedule' or NLP. This is just economist jargon to say that NLP has the potential to make both the firm and its customers better off. Consumers purchase a larger quantity and the PO makes a greater surplus. Willig's results apply to the situation faced by POs whose price is regulated and who are not currently employing quantity discounts. However, they would not necessarily apply to an unregulated monopolist, where NLP increases profits by less than the reduction in consumers' benefits.

The impact of NLP can be illustrated by means of a simple example of one consumer. (One of the important results derived by Willig is that this result applies for multiple consumers of varying types.) The consumer's demand is given by $x = 100 - 2p$.[6] If the consumer faces a simple uniform price of p = \$40, he/she consumes 20 units and derives net benefit of \$200, where net benefit is the consumer's total willingness to pay less what he/she actually pays. Now if the consumer faces the NLP of \$40 for the first 24 units and \$30 for the rest, he/she consumes 40 units and derives a net benefit of \$640. The PO is clearly better off with its revenue increasing from \$800 to \$1,440. Both the PO and the consumer are better off as a result of NLP. In this example, NLP clearly Pareto dominates uniform pricing. As shown by Willig, this result applies generally. In particular, it is always possible where the uniform price exceeds marginal cost to find an NLP (quantity discount) that can make all consumers better off and give the firm a greater profit. With scale economies the increase in output implied by NLP further increases the benefits.[7] In short, NLP, with scale economies, is a 'win–win' pricing policy!

NLP, then, is a powerful device for improving efficiency. It almost sounds too good to be true. In fact, all of the benefits claimed for NLP are true. This is not the problem. The problem is assuring the conditions necessary for the benefits from NLP to be attained. For an electric distribution company this is easy as it has a monopoly and the consumer is connected to its network by hardwire. There is de facto no opportunity for resale and consequent loss of the benefits of NLP to arbitragers. This is critical for the success of NLP. The other important condition for NLP to be Pareto dominating is that consumers have the choice of whether to take NLP or not. In the simple example above, the consumer can choose whether to take the NLP or not. Indeed, a smaller consumer might not find it worthwhile to purchase a sufficiently large amount to obtain the discount. These conditions are vital for the benefits of NLP to be achieved.

The application of NLP in the postal sector offers considerable promise of increased efficiency but implementation faces some major problems. The problems faced by POs in applying NLP are significantly greater than those faced by electric companies because, unlike electric companies, POs face serious problems of resale where arbitragers engage in specious aggregation and take the benefits of NLP away from the POs and their customers. It has long been recognized that the firm will lose the benefits of price discrimination if resale is possible. The same applies to NLP except that the benefits are not taken away solely from the firm but, based on Willig's insight, also from consumers as well as the firm or PO. Where a PO is employing quantity discounts and consolidators combine volumes from a number of small customers, the PO does not receive the benefit of demand stimulation unless consolidators pass on to their customers the income received from the PO in the form of quantity discounts. However, unless quantity discounts are actually traced through to originating mailers, there would be only minimal incentives for consolidators to share income they receive from the PO for aggregated quantity discounts.[8] The result, at the limit, is that the consolidator–arbitrager would retain all the benefit of NLP, with the PO and customers getting nothing. In practice, some sharing of quantity discount incentive payments between consolidators and originating customers might be expected, but it is likely that there would be minimal demand stimulation and a small benefit to consumers and the PO, but the overall pie would be reduced.[9] Under the case envisaged by Willig, the PO would get greater revenue and customers would benefit. As a result, demand would be stimulated and average costs would be reduced as a result of higher volumes and delivery scale economies. With consolidation and specious aggregation, the PO loses the contribution from NLP to the consolidator as well as facing higher unit costs from the reduced demand stimulation. A PO with a USO will find its revenue to fund the USO reduced by this loss of revenue and the increase in unit costs. It may have to raise prices, particularly for the USO customers, to cover the shortfall, resulting in a further erosion of volumes. Given the inefficiencies introduced by specious aggregation, we assume throughout this chapter that volume discounts are paid only to originating mailers.

There is another way in which consolidators contribute inefficiency apart from reduced revenue to the PO and lower benefits to customers. The consolidator–arbitrager is performing a service that does not add value. He/she just collects mail together in larger lots. Indeed, he/she may not even collect it, but may just take virtual credit for mail from several customers. Unlike the worksharing company that presorts and reduces the costs faced by the PO in other ways, all the pure consolidator does is aggregation. However, the consolidator does not operate at zero cost. He/she has his/her own variable and fixed expenses. These are much more a cause for concern than the transfer of surplus from the PO to the consolidator. In efficiency terms, these are arguably just a transfer if the size of the pie were not reduced in the ways described. However, the consolidator's expenses are what are known in economics as deadweight costs or losses. There are additional costs generated for the consolidator's activities that would not exist were it not for his/her activities. They represent a further reduction in the size of the pie.

The first lesson then in applying quantity discounts in the postal sector is that avoidance of losses from specious aggregation, arbitrage and the like is critical for the success of quantity discounts in the postal sector. Given that polices are put in place to safeguard against these problems, NLP provides an additional degree of freedom in the PO's competitive toolbox. This can be illustrated by the following examples, following the model in Appendix 1A.

4 ILLUSTRATIVE EXAMPLES

The appendix develops a model of NLP, which provides a per unit discount of δ per letter to originating mailers for annual volumes in excess of a specified threshold X^*. The discount applies to all letters sent to any address in the country. These quantity discounts are supplemental to applicable worksharing and access discounts. The key difference is that the latter are paid to worksharing providers and consolidators, while quantity discounts are paid to originating mailers.

For both the incumbent PO and (under bypass) the entrant(s), we assume a linear cost model as in Crew and Kleindorfer (2011a). Only the case of a single entrant and a single zone is considered here. (For the multi-zone case see the appendix.) The entrant and the PO have identical marginal costs, but the PO has greater fixed costs arising from the USO. Upstream unit costs for both the PO and the entrant are denoted C_u and delivery unit costs are denoted by C_d. Delivery costs are of the form $C_i(x) = F_i + C_d x$, $i = I, E$, where $F_I > F_E$ are the fixed cost of the PO and entrant.

There are both single-piece and bulk-mail customers. Single-piece customers purchase end-to-end (E2E) service only from the PO at E2E price PI. Bulk-mail customers are segmented into 40 segments indexed by their upstream mail preparation cost k. Worksharing discounts are assumed to be of the efficient component pricing rule (ECPR) form, so that customers with $k < C_u$ undertake worksharing, while those with $k > C_u$ purchase E2E

Table 1.1 Parameter values for examples

Postal operator's costs		Parameter	
Upstream cost		$C_u = 5$	
Downstream cost		$C_d = 15$	
PO fixed cost		$F_I = 100{,}000$; $F_E = 10{,}000$	
Demand	**Discount**	**Customer**	**Parameter values**
Undiscounted $\alpha = 0$	$D[P(k), k] =$ $h(k)*[\alpha - \beta*P_I(k,\delta)]$	Single-piece customers	$\alpha = 135$ or 150 $\beta = 2$ $h(k) = h(0) = 50$ $P_I(k, \delta) = P_I =$ PO's E2E price
	$D[P(k), k] = X*$ if $h(k)[\alpha - \beta P_I(k,\delta)] > X*$ $D[P(k), k] =$ $h(k)[\alpha - \beta*P_I(k,\delta)]$ if $h(k)*[\alpha - \beta*P_I(k,\delta)] \leq X*$ $X*$ = Discount threshold	Business/bulk customers	$X* = 50$ or 100 $\alpha = 135$ or 150 $\beta = 2$ $h(k) = h_0/(\lambda+k)$, $k = 1.0, 1.2, 1.4, \ldots, 10.0$ $\lambda = 0.1$; $h_0 = 15$ k = customer's upstream cost $P_I(k, \delta) = P_I - \delta - (C_uI - k)$ if $C_uI > k$ $P_I(k, \delta) = P_I - \delta$ if $C_uI \leq k$
Discounted $\delta > 0$	$D[P(k), k] =$ $h(k)[\alpha - \beta*P_I(k,\delta)] - X*$ if $h(k)[\alpha - \beta*P_I(k,\delta)] > X$ $D[P(k), k] = 0$ if $h(k)[\alpha - \beta*P_I(k,\delta)] \leq X$	Business/bulk customers	

service at price P_I (or P_E if they are served by the entrant). For volumes less than $X*$, the resulting E2E price for $k < C_u$ is therefore $P(k, \delta) = P_i - (C_u - k)$ and, for $k > C_u$, $P(k, \delta) = P_i$, where $i = I$ or E depending on whether I or E serves customer k. For volumes in excess of $X*$, the resulting E2E price for $k < C_u$ is $P(k, \delta) = P_i - \delta - (C_u - k)$ and, for $k > C_u$, $P(k, \delta) = P_i - \delta$, where $i = I$ or E depending on whether I or E serves customer k. It is assumed that larger customers have lower average costs of mail preparation, that is, the smaller k, the larger the demand of customer k. Each customer k chooses I or E as provider depending on which service provides the highest utility for the customer. Under these assumptions, the appendix shows that when the PO offers quantity discounts, all customers (in addition to single-piece customers) larger than a given threshold $k*$ choose the PO and all others choose the entrant, where $k*$ depends on the full price vector (P_I, δ, P_E). For the examples, demand and corresponding willingness-to-pay functions are assumed to be of the linear-quadratic form as described in Crew and Kleindorfer (2011a), with the I and E products perfect substitutes. Table 1.1 summarizes the cost and demand assumptions.

Tables 1.2–4 report some results for the parameter values given in Table 1.1. The base

Table 1.2 Results for base case (α = 150; no bypass)

	Welfare optimal	Ramsey uniform price	Ramsey NLP	Ramsey NLP
PO's E2E price P_I	20.0	24.3	24.8	26.3
Unit discount delta	0.0	0.0	0.7	3.5
Minimum qualifying volumes X^*	NA	NA	50.0	100.0
Demand for PO delivery	25,276	23,354	23,389	23,659
Demand qualifying for discount	NA	NA	16,067	14,191
Single-piece demand	5,500	5,071	5,023	4,868
Profit – PO	–100,000	20	5	5
Consumer surplus	713,397	609,268	609,399	610,000
Total welfare	613,397	609,288	609,404	610,005

Table 1.3 Results for intermodal competition case (α = 135; no bypass)

	Welfare optimal	Ramsey uniform price	Ramsey NLP	Ramsey NLP
PO's E2E price P_I	20.0	25.09	26.8	27.6
Unit discount delta	0.0	0.0	2.6	4.7
Minimum qualifying volumes X^*	NA	NA	50.0	100.0
Demand for PO delivery	21,915	19,633	19,764	20,113
Demand qualifying for discount	NA	13,092	13,398	11,527
Single-piece demand	4,750	4,241	4,066	3,986
Profit – PO	–100,000	1	5	0
Consumer surplus	536,428	430,615	430,993	431,959
Total welfare	436,428	430,616	430,998	431,959

case is shown in Table 1.2 where there are no entrants. Welfare optimality in all cases results in no entry and marginal cost pricing, with the PO's resulting loss equal to its fixed costs covered by the government. The Ramsey uniform price is where linear pricing is used. The last two columns show Ramsey prices with an initial block X^* (the minimum demand to qualify for discounts) of 50 and 100.[10] NLP results in higher welfare than uniform prices and the larger block of 100 results in the highest welfare. This pattern is apparent in Tables 1.3 and 1.4, which address entry. Table 1.3 is concerned with the impact of electronic competition in isolation, while Table 1.4 addresses both electronic and direct competition. In Table 1.3, intermodal competition is reflected in the drop in the intercept term, α, from 150 to 135, which reflects the drop in volume from electronic competition. Welfare drops as a result of the reduction in demand and the loss continues at the same level. The same pattern of increasing welfare from NLP continues. A higher single-piece price and a higher discount result in higher welfare. Indeed, comparing Tables 1.2 and 1.3, it is apparent from the larger values of optimal discounts in Table 1.3 that such demand-stimulating discounts become more important as intermodal competition decreases demand for traditional mail products.

Table 1.4 address intermodal and direct competition simultaneously. The first column

Table 1.4 Results for bypass and intermodal competition case ($\alpha = 135$)

	Ramsey no bypass	Pre-bypass scenario	Bypass scenario 1	Bypass scenario 2
P_I	27.6	29.0	29.0	29.0
P_E	NA	NA	27.0	27.0
Discount (delta)	4.7	3.0	3.0	4.0
Minimum qualifying volumes X^*	100.0	100.0	100.0	100.0
Demand for PO delivery	20,113	18,926	13,390	16,101
Demand – disc	11,527	10,477	7,940	9,651
Demand entrant	0.00	0.00	5,403	3,024
Household's demand	3,986	3,850	3,850	3,850
Profit – PO	0	38,910	–3,308	6,306
Profit entrant	NA	NA	27,823	11,169
Consumer surplus	431,959	387,202	390,733	399,655
Total welfare	431,959	426,112	415,247	417,131

is a repeat of the far right column from Table 1.3. The next column, the pre-bypass scenario, assumes that the PO is allowed to raise the single-piece price by the regulator but is also required to reduce the size of the discount.[11] The result is a substantial profit for the PO, which results in entry. Scenario 1 in the next column shows the effect of entry where the PO does not adjust its prices. The entrant makes a substantial profit and the PO now incurs a loss. The final column, Scenario 2, shows the impact of a response by the PO, which takes the form of an increase in the quantity discount and no change in the single-piece price.[12] Again the same important pattern emerges. The power of NLP in addressing the impact of intermodal and bypass competition is apparent.

5 IMPLICATIONS FOR POLICY AND FURTHER RESEARCH

This examination of NLP in the postal sector, while of a preliminary nature, reflects the increased interest in price discrimination not only by economists but also in practical applications, for example, airlines. It is apparent that NLP is an effective device for retaining large customers, and therefore volume, when facing electronic and direct competition. It provides assistance to POs where they are likely most vulnerable to losses in volume, namely, the large-customer segment. While, the potential of NLP for the postal sector as a device for addressing electronic and direct competition has been demonstrated, many unanswered questions remain. It is clear that NLP improves efficiency (welfare) for a PO facing electronic competition. However, the more complicated and more likely situation is for a PO to face both electronic and direct competition. Here numerous issues remain to be explored in policy and in economic theory. They include the role of regulation and quantity discounts. While this is not a settled issue, one implication of this chapter is that a hands-off approach to quantity discounts might be appropriate given the need to fund the USO and the increasing impact of electronic competition. NLP has not been extensively explored in oligopoly theory.[13] The nature of the market adjustment process between thee PO and entrants with NLP has not been explored in this chapter. Moreover, only the pure substitution case with homogeneous products has been considered here, while the reality of competition in postal markets will surely also encompass non-price factors such as quality of service and delivery frequency. In particular, developing oligopoly models where NLP is employed is a promising area for future research. This could include, for example, price leadership models with NLP. Research on the role NLP in the postal sector is timely and has potential in addressing the major problem of declining volume facing the postal sector.

NOTES

* The authors acknowledge the support of Royal Mail Group in the preparation of this chapter. The views expressed are solely those of the authors and do not necessarily reflect those of Royal Mail Group.

1. This chapter does not address the legal feasibility of price discrimination. However, Eccles (ch. 2 in this volume) and Wojtek and Zauner (ch. 3 in this volume) provide an interesting legal analysis of EU case law and principles that need to be respected by postal operators when designing and implementing quantity discount programs.
2. Interestingly, first-degree price discrimination does not require non-transferability. As the monopolist has perfect information resale is not an issue.
3. See Ambrosini and Klargaard (2006) and Crémer and De Donder (2010) for an extended discussion of the La Poste approach and its theoretical foundations.
4. For example, the literature of around a century ago was replete with discussions of this kind, which included the work of some famous economists of his day including Pigou (1920) and Robinson (1933). Wilson (1993) provides an extensive review and synthesis of the literature on non-linear pricing and its applications. Neoclassical price discrimination continues to be of interest to major economics journals, as illustrated by Aguirre et al. 2010.
5. The theoretical analysis of the need to prevent arbitrage is provided in Wilson (1993). The deleterious consequences of arbitrage for the postal sector are demonstrated in Cremer and De Donder (2010) and, for a model similar to that proposed in the appendix, in Crew and Kleindorfer (2011b). This concern did not underlie the debate over NSAs, where arbitrage and resale were not at issue. However, the concern for the USO customer was an issue for the PRC.
6. For purposes of computing consumer's surplus or willingness to pay, the area under the inverse demand function $p = 50 - 0.5x$ from 0 to the quantity demanded is used as computed in the appendix.
7. This simple example ignores scale economies and shows that, even without scale economies, NLP dominates uniform pricing.
8. The quantity discount would apply to all of the originating sender's mail, irrespective of whether it was E2E, access or workshared mail and irrespective of whether tendered directly or through an agent.
9. Various cases of sharing volume discounts between consolidators and originating mailers are analyzed, with accompanying examples, in Crew and Kleindorfer (2011b).
10. The values for PO profit for Ramsey computed by the spreadsheet are computed to be approximately zero, depending on the optimization tolerance. The actual values are reported.
11. A regulator might adopt a policy of this kind where the intent was to foster competition.
12. The last two columns are purely illustrative. They do not represent optimized or equilibrium results.
13. Wilson (1993) and Cremer and De Donder (2010) review existing results.

REFERENCES

Aguirre, Iñaki, Simon Cowan and John Vickers (2010), 'Monopoly price discrimination and demand curvature', *American Economic Review*, **100**(4), 1601–15.

Ambrosini, Xavier and Olaf Klargaard (2006), 'From theory to practice: vertical relations in the French postal market', in M.A. Crew and P.R. Kleindorfer (eds), *Liberalization of the Postal and Delivery Sector*, Cheltenham, UK and Northampton, MA, USA: Edward Elgar.

Cremer, Helmuth and Philippe De Donder (2010), 'Avantages et limites de la tarification non linéare: le contrat commercial dans le secteur postal', in F. Boldron, C. Borsenberger, D. Joram, S. Lecou and B. Roy (eds), *Libéralisation et Services Publics: Économie Postale*, Paris: Economica.

Crew, Michael and Paul R. Kleindorfer (2011a), 'Competitive Strategies under FMO and Intermodal Competition', in Crew and Kleindorfer (eds), *Reinventing the Postal Sector in an Electronic Age*, Cheltenham, UK and Northampton, MA, USA: Edward Elgar.

Crew, Michael and Paul R. Kleindorfer (2011b), 'Quantity discounts in the postal sector', Working Paper, INSEAD.

Levy, David, Joy Leong, Lawrence Buc and Michael Plunkett (2006), 'Benefit–cost regulation of negotiated service agreements', in M.A. Crew and P.R. Kleindorfer (eds), *Progress toward Liberalization of the Postal and Delivery Sector*, New York: Springer Science + Business Media, Inc.

Pigou, Arthur C. (1920), *The Economics of Welfare*, 4th edn, London: Macmillan.

Robinson, Joan (1933), *The Economics of Imperfect Competition*, London: Macmillan.

Robinson, Matthew, Margaret M. Cigno and J.P. Klingenberg (2008), 'Negotiated volume discounts in a regulated post', in Michael A. Crew and Paul R. Kleindorfer (eds), *Competition and Regulation in the Postal and Delivery Sector*, Cheltenham, UK and Northampton, MA, USA: Edward Elgar.

Willig, Robert D. (1978), 'Pareto superior nonlinear outlay schedules', *Bell Journal of Economics*, **9**(1), 56–69.

Wilson, Robert (1993), *Nonlinear Pricing,* Oxford: Oxford University Press.

APPENDIX 1A NONLINEAR PRICING, VOLUME DISCOUNTS AND THE USO

This appendix proposes the model for quantity discounts underlying the discussion and examples. It assumes that the PO sets a discount for total volumes consumed across all delivery areas (for example, on a quarterly or annual basis). The USP/PO delivers in n different zones in a country. A discount is offered for total volumes in all zones above a threshold. A uniform end-to-end (E2E) price throughout the country is assumed. The primary focus is on the no-bypass case, but some basic results are also presented for the case of competitive bypass.

Customers are designated/identified by their upstream cost per unit $k > 0$ of worksharing. The cumulative distribution of customers is denoted by $G(k)$, so that $G(k)$ represents the number of originating customers of mail with upstream preparation cost $< k$. It is assumed that larger customers have lower average costs of mail preparation, that is, the smaller k, the larger the demand of customer k.

Upstream unit costs for the PO are constant and denoted C_{UI}. Delivery zones are given by the set $N = \{1, \ldots, n\}$ and the PO's delivery cost is of the form $C_j(x) = F_j + C_{Dj}x$, where F_j is fixed cost, and C_{Dj} constant marginal cost, of delivery in zone $j \in N$. The incumbent PO is assumed to offer a unit discount $\delta > 0$ for all mail from a given customer that exceeds a given volume threshold X^*, no matter who prepares the mail and where in the country the mail is sent (as long as the PO makes the final delivery of the mail). Thus, denoting by P the PO's price of E2E service, the assumed non-linear outlay schedule (or bill), $B[P, \delta, X(k)]$ for any given customer k mailing the vector $\mathbf{X}(k) = [X_1(k), \ldots, X_n(k)]$ pieces of mail to zones $j \in N$ is:

$$B[P, \delta, X(k)] = P\left[\sum_{j \in N} X_j(k)\right] - \delta\left[\sum_{j \in N} X_j(k) - X^*\right]^+ \quad (1A.1)$$

where $x^+ = \max(x, 0)$. Thus, the price for E2E mail destined for zone $j \in N$ is P for total volumes less than X^*, and $P - \delta$ for incremental volumes once the threshold X^* is reached. The discounts that apply when the customer uses a consolidator or worksharing provider to perform upstream services rather than the PO are described more fully below.

No Bypass

Customer k's optimal choice rule for determining mail volumes in each zone $j \in N$ where the PO undertakes all final deliveries is first derived. For any demand vector $\mathbf{X} = (X_1, \ldots, X_n)$, price P and discount δ, customer preferences are assumed to be specified in the standard quasi-linear form:

$$V(X, P, \delta, k) = \sum_{j \in N} V_j(X_j, k) - B(P, \delta, X), \quad (1A.2)$$

where $V_j(X_j, k)$ is an increasing, strictly concave function representing customer k's willingness to pay for sending volume X_j to zone $j \in N$. The separable form of preferences

(1A.2) assumes independence of demand across zones $j \in N$, with the demand curve for customer k in zone $j \in N$ given by:

$$D_j(P, k) = \text{argmax}_{x \geq 0}\{V_j(x, k) - Px\}. \tag{1A.3}$$

For workshared mail tendered to the PO, it is assumed that the PO employs the retail-minus approach (or ECPR) for setting discounts, so that the PO's 'access price' for delivering workshared mail is $A = P - C_{UI}$. So, k utilizes worksharing rather than the PO's E2E service only if $k < C_{UI}$. Assuming this, the undiscounted price faced by customer k for E2E service provided by the PO is:

$$P(k) = P - (C_{UI} - k)^+ \tag{1A.4}$$

with a discount of δ per unit for volumes in excess of X^*. Thus, generalizing (1A.1) to allow for worksharing, if the customer registers all mail sent with the PO for delivery, then the total bill faced by the customer is:

$$B[P, \delta, X(k)] = P(k)\left[\sum_{j \in N} X_j(k)\right] - \delta\left[\sum_{j \in N} X_j(k) - X^*\right]^+. \tag{1A.5}$$

Consider now the consumer demand function when facing quantity discounts. This results from substituting (1A.5) into (1A.2). The problem is:

$$S(P, \delta, k) = \text{Max}_{x \geq 0}\left\{\sum_{j \in N}[V_j(x_j, k) - P(k)x_j] + \delta\left(\sum_{j \in N} x_j - X^*\right)^+\right\}. \tag{1A.6}$$

There are two continuous and strictly concave segments to the maximand in (1A.6), namely: (i) $0 \leq \Sigma_{j \in N} x_j \leq X^*$ and (ii) $\Sigma_{j \in N} x_j \geq X^*$. The solution to (1A.6) is therefore the greater of the maxima of these two segments, namely:

$$S(P, \delta, k) = \text{Max}\{S_u(P, k), S_d(P, \delta, k)\}, \tag{1A.7}$$

where the maxima of the undiscounted (u) and discounted (d) segment payoffs are given by:

$$S_u(P, k) = \text{Max}\left\{\sum_{j \in N}[V_j(x_j, k) - P(k)x_j]x \geq 0; \sum_{j \subset N} x_j \leq X^*\right\} \tag{1A.8}$$

$$S_d(P, \delta, k) = \text{Max}\left(\sum_{j \in N}\{V_j(x_j, k) - [P(k) - \delta]x_j\} + \delta X^* | x > 0; \sum_{j \in N} x_j > X^*\right). \tag{1A.9}$$

Denoting the optimal solutions to (1A.8)–(1A.9) by $X_u(P, k)$ and $X_d(P, \delta, k)$, then from (1A.6) and the strict concavity of $V(x, k)$, the Kuhn–Tucker conditions characterize the unique solutions to (1A.8)–(1A.9) as follows:

$$X_{uj}(P, k) = D_j[P(k) + \alpha, k]; \alpha \geq 0; \alpha\left\{X^* - \sum_{i \in N} D_i[P(k) + \alpha, k]\right\} = 0; \forall j \in N \tag{1A.10}$$

$$X_{dj}(P, \delta, k) = D_j[P(k) - \delta - \beta, k];\ \beta \geq 0;\ \beta\left\{X^* - \sum_{i \in N} D_i[P(k) - \delta - \beta, k]\right\} = 0; \quad \forall j \in N, \tag{1A.11}$$

where α and β are the Lagrange multipliers for the constraints in (1A.8)–(1A.9). Thus, denoting $X_j(P, \delta, k)$ as customer k's demand in zone $j \in N$ given (P, δ), from (1A.6)–(1A.11) the following solution for customer k's demand results:

$$X_j(P, \delta, k) = X_{uj}(P, k)\psi[S_u(P, k) - S_d(P, \delta, k)] + X_{dj}(P, \delta, k)\{1 - \psi[S_u(P, k) - S_d(P, \delta, k)]\} \tag{1A.12}$$

where $\psi(y) = 1$ if $y > 0$ and 0 else. Several properties of customer k's demand can be noted as follows.

Characteristics of customer demand response to NLP

For any customer $k \in K$, and any price vector (P, δ), customer demand (1A.12) satisfies the following:

1. $X(P, \delta, k)$ is decreasing in P;
2. $X(P, \delta, k)$ is increasing in δ;
3. $X(P, \delta, k)$ is decreasing in X^*;
4. the net consumer surplus $S(P, \delta, k)$ in (1A.7) is continuous in (P, δ).

These assertions follow from (1A.5)–(1A.12). In particular, (2) shows the demand stimulation effect of quantity discounts.

The Ramsey problem (welfare maximization subject to PO breakeven)

The Ramsey problem requires defining the welfare function and the PO profit function, as functions of the price vector (P, δ). All discounts are paid directly and only to originating mailers.[1]

Noting (1A.5) and (1A.12), the PO's profit function is:

$$\Pi(P,\delta) = \int_K B[P, \delta, X(P, \delta, k)dG(k)] - \sum_{j \in N}\left[C_{Dj}\int_K X_j(P, \delta, k)dG(k) + C_{UI}\int_{\hat{k}}^{\infty} X_j(P, \delta, k)dG(k)\right] - F, \tag{1A.13}$$

where $\hat{k} = C_{UI}$ is the smallest customer using third-party worksharing rather than the PO's E2E service.

Total welfare is aggregate willingness to pay across K minus total costs:

$$W(P, \delta) = \sum_{j \in N}\left\{\int_K V_j[X_j(P, \delta, k), k]dG(k) - C_{Dj}\int_K X_j(P, \delta, k)dG(k)\right\}$$

$$-\sum_{j\in N}\left[\int_0^{\hat{k}} kX_j(P,\delta,k)\,dG(k) + C_{UI}\int_{\hat{k}}^{\infty} X_j(P,\delta,k)\,dG(k)\right] - F, \tag{1A.14}$$

with the definition of $\hat{k} = C_{UI}$ as given above. Gross surplus $V(X, k)$ in (1A.14) could also be represented as the area under the inverse demand function $P_j(x, k)$ for k from 0 to X, where $P_j(x, k)$ is defined through (1A.5) by $D_j[P_j(x, k), k] = x,\ j \in N$.

The Ramsey problem is then given by:

$$\text{Max}_{P\geq 0, 0\leq\delta\leq P}\{W(P,\delta)\,|\,\Pi(P,\delta) \geq 0\}. \tag{1A.15}$$

It is straightforward to see that NLP weakly dominates uniform pricing for both the welfare optimal solution as well as all Ramsey solutions, including the pure profit-maximizing solution. This follows directly from the fact that any uniform price is a degenerate form of NLP in which $\delta = 0$ (so the maximizing solution over NLP tariffs has to be no less with NLP than with uniform pricing). Generally, the impact of NLP is to raise profits by stimulating demand, especially for larger customers. The potential benefits of NLP is directly related to the extent of scale economies. While this is evident and reflects the basic intuition of Willig (1978), the fact that the welfare optimal solution may entail a discount $\delta > 0$ is worth some additional explanation. The rationale for a positive δ in the welfare optimal solution can be understood on the basis of the following example.

Example Assume $N = \{1, 2\}$ with $C_{D1} < C_{D2}$, so that zone 2 is the high-cost zone. Suppose the set of customers K is partitioned into small customers K_S and large customers K_L, with $K = K_S \cup K_L$. Suppose further that all small customer demand occurs in the high-cost zone 2 and that all large customer demand occurs in the low-cost zone 1. Assume further that X^* is such that no small customer qualifies for the discount and all large customers qualify for the discount. Then the following solution is evidently the first-best solution:

$$P = C_{UI} + C_{D2};\ \ \delta = C_{D2} - C_{D1}. \tag{1A.16}$$

The solution (1A.16) corresponds to marginal cost pricing. While this example is artificial, it illustrates that there are potentially efficiency gains from NLP in the welfare-maximization case, beyond the additional profits NLP's through demand stimulation and retaining scale economies. This arises through the extra degree of freedom afforded by the discount δ.

One other important result concerning the importance of quantity discounts is in mitigating the impact of electronic competition. Given delivery scale economies, a secular decline in demand can be countered in part through quantity discounts. Formally, represent the WTP function defining demand in (1A.3) as $V_j(x_j, k, \theta)$, where θ is a demand shift parameter such that $\partial^2 V_j/\partial x_j\partial\theta > 0$, $\forall j, k$, that is, decreases in θ imply decreases in demand for all zones and customers. Given the cost assumptions, as the example in the text illustrates, a downward shift in demand leads to an increase in both the single-piece price and the optimal discount at the Ramsey solution.

Bypass

A single product provided by entrants is assumed with a uniform price P_E (identical for all entrants). The PO's product and the entrant's are perfect substitutes. The only difference between the PO and the entrant is that the incumbent PO uses quantity discounts, according to the price vector (P_I, δ) with discounts specified above. To avoid unnecessary notation, a single zone is assumed, corresponding to the case $N = \{1\}$ in the prior analysis. Given this assumption, the zonal subscript j is dropped.

This case is linked to the case of no bypass as follows. If customer k is served by the PO, then k's demand is $X(P_I, \delta, k)$ as specified in (1A.12); if k is served by E, then k's demand is $X(P_E, 0, k)$ as specified in (1A.12), with $X(P, \delta, k)$ given in (1A.12). The choice between I and E is determined by whichever gives rise to the greater net surplus. Formalizing this logic, the demand functions for customer $k \in K$ for I's and E's product are:

$$D_I(P_I, \delta, P_E, k) = X(P_I, \delta, k)\psi[\Delta(P_I, \delta, P_E, k)] \tag{1A.17}$$

$$D_E(P_I, \delta, P_E, k) = X(P_E, 0, k)\{1 - \psi[\Delta(P_I, \delta, P_E, k)]\}, \tag{1A.18}$$

where $\psi(y) = 1$ if $y > 0$ and 0 else, and where $\Delta(P_I, \delta, P_E, k)$ is the difference between customer k's net surplus when consuming I's product vs. E's product, that is,

$$\Delta(P_I, \delta, P_E, k) = \{V[X(P_I, \delta, k), k] - B[P_I, \delta, X(P_I, \delta, k)]\}$$
$$- \{V[X(P_E, 0, k), k] - B[P_E, 0, X(P_E, 0, k)]\}. \tag{1A.19}$$

The impact of quantity discounts under bypass can be seen as follows. From (1A.12), the function $\Delta(P_I, \delta, P_E, k)$ is given by:

$$\Delta(P_I, \delta, P_E, k) = \text{Max}_{x\geq 0}[V(x, k) - P_I x + \delta(x - X^*)^+] - \text{Max}_{x\geq 0}[V(x, k) - P_E x]. \tag{1A.20}$$

The following facts follow directly from (1A.20) and the assumption that $D(x, k)$ in (1A.3) is strictly decreasing in k:

1. If k would not qualify for the PO discount (because $X(P_I, \delta, k) < X^*$), then $\Delta(P_I, \delta, P_E, k) > 0$ if and only if $P_I < P_E$.
2. If k would qualify for the PO discount (because $X(P_I, \delta, k) > X^*$), then $\Delta(P_I, \delta, P_E, k) > 0$ implies $P_I - \delta < P_E$.
3. If $\Delta(P_I, \delta, P_E, k > 0$, then $\Delta(P_I, \delta, P_E, \tilde{k}) > 0$ for any $\tilde{k} < k$.

The net result of these facts is that for any (P_I, δ, P_E) there is a customer $\bar{k}(P_I, \delta, P_E) \in K$ such that $\Delta(P_I, \delta, P_E, k > 0$ for $k < \bar{k}$ and $\Delta(P_I, \delta, P_E, k) \leq 0$ for $k \geq \bar{k}$, so that $K_I = [0, \bar{k}(P_I, \delta, P_E)]$ and $K_E = [\bar{k}(P_I, \delta, P_E), \infty]$. Moreover, $\hat{k}(P_I, \delta, P_E)$ is decreasing in P_I and increasing in both P_E and δ. This also implies that the set of customers $k < \bar{k}$ who purchase the PO's product is decreasing in P_I and increasing in both P_E and δ. The demand functions (1A.18)–(1A.19) inherit these same properties. In particular, the basic rationale for NLP under bypass is present. NLP both acts to stimulate demand among the customers retained by the PO as well as increasing the set of customers the PO retains for final delivery of mail.

NOTE

1. As noted earlier specious aggregation is ruled out by this assumption.

2. Price differentiation: what is acceptable for a universal service provider?

Richard Eccles[†]

1 INTRODUCTION

The EU Postal Services Directive 97/67 as amended, most recently by Directive 2008/6 (the Directive) contains a strict obligation of the universal service provider (USP) not to discriminate as between services for businesses, bulk mailers or consolidators of mail whenever special tariffs for such services are applied. No distinction is made between worksharing discounts and purely commercial, volume discounts and, moreover, the provision has been interpreted strictly in individual cases by the European Commission and the European Court of Justice (ECJ).

By contrast, the French national regulatory authority, ARCEP, appears to have taken a competition-focused approach to the application of the provision by requesting an opinion from the Conseil de la Concurrence on the acceptability as a matter of competition law, of withholding purely commercial volume discounts as opposed to worksharing discounts from mail preparation firms. The Conseil concluded that mail originators were not in an equivalent position to mail preparation firms and therefore did not merit equal treatment as regards volume discounts.

It is important to USPs in a number of European countries to be able to apply volume discounts only to their own direct sender, mail originator customers, but not also to apply such discounts to intermediaries including mail preparation firms. However, USPs would be well advised to exercise caution in following the approach of La Poste as covered in the Conseil de la Concurrence Opinion without first taking into account this strictness of the European Commission and ECJ decisions under Article 12, fifth indent, of the Directive.

Section 2 of this chapter explains the relevant provisions of the Directive relating to price discrimination and Section 3 explains the key principles of EU competition law on price discrimination as abuse of dominance. Sections 4 and 5 deal with the 'meeting the competition' defense and volume discounts, respectively, under EU competition law. Section 6 addresses the issues of differential pricing as between intermediaries and end customers, from the perspective of the Directive, in particular, Article 12, fifth indent, by reference to the European Commission's approach in a specific case concerning German Postal Legislation and by contrasting the French *La Poste* case with the relevant European Court and European Commission cases. A summary and some conclusions are set out in Section 7.

† Partner, Bird & Bird LLP.

This chapter does not attempt a specifically economic analysis of price discrimination, though such analysis is undertaken by Crew and Kleindorfer (ch. 1 in this volume).

2 THE POSITION UNDER THE 2008 EU POSTAL SERVICES DIRECTIVE

The Directive requires USPs to set tariffs which are non-discriminatory and transparent (Article 12, fourth indent). It also requires that any uniform tariff obligation on the USP be limited to (basically) single-piece tariff mail, that is, mainly stamps and franked mail.[1] While a USP was always allowed by the Directive to charge lower prices in individual cases (subject to the non-discrimination obligation), the removal of the uniform tariff in respect of bulk mail and any other mail services other than the single-piece tariff mail, will allow increased pricing flexibility for USPs.

As regards the provision of any worksharing bulk-mail products and/or downstream access products, Article 12 (fifth indent) requires that USPs applying special tariffs, for businesses, bulk mailers or consolidators must avoid discrimination with regard to the tariffs and the associated conditions, both as between different third parties and as between third parties and the USP's own equivalent services. This provision has given rise to considerable debate as to the extent to which a USP is required to grant the same terms to intermediaries such as mail preparation firms as it grants to direct end customers (senders), as regards discounts not just for technical, worksharing activities, but also for volume-related discounts, respectively. This has been highlighted in the European Commission's announcement regarding German Postal Legislation (BdKEP case – restrictions on mail preparation) in 2004,[2] and the *Vedat Deniz* judgment[3] of the ECJ.

The issue was considered as a matter of EU and French competition law by the French Conseil de la Concurrence in the Opinion of 20 December 2007 concerning the application of EU and French competition law to La Poste's system of discounts under technical and commercial contracts, for worksharing activities and volumes (respectively). This was delivered pursuant to a request by the French national regulatory authority for electronic communications and postal services (ARCEP).[4] The substance of this Opinion was in effect upheld by the French courts, in particular by a court of first instance which rejected a claim by intermediaries (mail preparation firms) that La Poste's rebates were anti-competitive, and by the Court of Appeal which rejected an appeal by the intermediaries.[5]

More recently, in July 2011, the Belgian national regulatory authority has imposed a fine of €2.3 million on the Belgian incumbent postal operator, bpost, for infringing Belgian postal legislation by discriminating in the discounts offered to business customers and mail handlers, or intermediaries. The discrimination consisted of the fact that unlike the discounts given to business customers, the commercial discounts given to mail handlers were not based on the total volumes deposited with bpost, but only on the separate volumes of the various senders. As a result, mail handlers were not able to gain increased discounts by grouping volumes from various senders (Press release of the Belgian Institute for Postal Services and Telecommunications dated 27th July 2011).

Prima facie, the result of these cases appears to be that as a matter of EU law, the non-discrimination requirements of Article 12, fifth indent, of the Directive, must be applied strictly, while under EU competition law, at least as interpreted by the French civil courts, a refusal by the USP of commercial volume discounts to intermediaries and in particular mail preparation firms can be acceptable even if such discounts are granted to mail originators (senders).

3 EU COMPETITION LAW ON ABUSE OF DOMINANCE: THE NEED FOR A MATERIAL EFFECT ON COMPETITION

In order for discriminatory pricing between customers to constitute an abuse of dominant position, the pricing must relate to equivalent transactions, and must involve the unequal treatment of customers who are in a similar position, or possibly the equal treatment of different customers whose situations are markedly different. In any event, the EU and also UK case law shows that, in order for discriminatory conduct to be abusive, it is necessary that competition is harmed or distorted, and also that foreclosure of competition results. Article 102 of the Treaty on the Functioning of the European Union (TFEU) prohibits abuse of dominance, and provides (paragraph (c)) that abuse of a dominant position may consist in 'applying dissimilar conditions to *equivalent transactions* with other trading parties thereby placing them at a *competitive disadvantage*' (emphasis added). Most, though not all, of the EU cases on discriminatory conduct by dominant undertakings concern conduct by a vertically integrated dominant operator which benefits its own downstream business to the detriment of competitors.

In the 2007 Opinion concerning La Poste, the French Conseil de la Concurrence declared it acceptable as a matter of EU and French competition law that quantitative, volume discounts should be granted only to actual mail originator customers and not to intermediaries, while discounts specifically for worksharing are granted equally to both categories of customers, that is, mail originators and intermediaries. The conclusions regarding quantitative discounts were based on the finding that extending such discounts to intermediaries might distort the incentives needed to fulfill the objectives of growing and simulating demand from key sender customers and undermine the basis on which the pricing system was based, as La Poste might then only receive revenues corresponding to the maximum discounted rate.[6]

The Conseil de la Concurrence's conclusions were upheld by the Court of Appeal in its judgment (referred to above). The Paris Court of Appeal concluded that the mail preparation firms did not represent a true demand function as they were not the originators of the mail entrusted to them. Even if they were co-contractors in relation to La Poste in the sense of being depositories or holders of franking machines and recipients of technical services, they were not customers of La Poste in the sense of mail being sent solely on the customer's account. Moreover, mail preparation companies and mail originators are not active on the same market and no competitor relationship exists between them. The Court of Appeal drew attention to Article L2-1 of the Code of Postal Services and Electronic Communications, which distinguishes 'clients', parties contracting for the transport function, and intermediaries or consolidators which group together mail sent by several such customers. The Court of Appeal observed that only the mail originators are in a legal sense party to the postal services contract and the payers of the postal service. On this basis, the Paris Court of Appeal considered La Poste to be entitled as a matter of competition law and in particular the EU and French rules on abuse of dominance, to withhold volume discounts from mail preparation firms that are granted to mail originators.

In order for discriminatory pricing to be an abuse of dominance under EU competition law, it is further necessary that there be a materially harmful effect on competition, and moreover that competition be excluded or foreclosed. In the leading *British Airways* case,[7] the ECJ held that in order for there to be an abuse resulting from price discrimination, the discrimination must lead to a distortion of competition between business partners.[8] The case concerned loyalty rebates for travel agents and the ECJ based its conclusions on the analysis by the European Court of First Instance and the European Commission of the fidelity building effect of the rebate schemes and the finding that they could lead to exponential changes in the revenues of travel agents, thus affecting the ability of travel agents to compete.

In the *Clearstream* case,[9] the European Court of First Instance (now the European General Court) stated that the application to trading partners of different prices for equivalent services continuously over a period of five years by an undertaking having an effective monopoly on the relevant upstream market 'could not fail to cause' a competitive disadvantage.[10] In this case, the main competitor to the complainant in the downstream market for the provision of secondary clearing and settlement services for German registered securities, was part of the same group as the monopoly provider in the upstream market for primary clearing and settlement services for such securities. In effect, the Court allowed for what amounts to a presumption that the application by a de facto monopolist of different prices for equivalent services over a five-year period causes a competitive disadvantage to the victims of such differentiation, albeit in a situation where the discrimination directly benefited the relevant downstream business of that monopolist.

Price discrimination has in various cases been found to be abusive of a dominant position because it involved a dominant operator leveraging its market power into a downstream market.[11] In the *BdKEP* case, the Commission found that Deutsche Post[12] had abused its dominant position by discriminating against commercial mail preparation firms by denying them discounts off the normal postal tariff that were granted to direct bulk mailers in otherwise equivalent circumstances. The mail preparation firms were therefore at a competitive disadvantage as they were not allowed to qualify for quantity-based discounts, as direct bulk mailers could. The discrimination occurred as a result of the relevant provisions of the German Postal Law which the Commission found were contrary to EU law. Moreover, the Commission found that the refusal to grant quantity-based discounts to mail preparation firms induced Deutsche Post to extend its dominance on the market for basic postal services into the market for mail preparation services.[13]

The Commission's decision appears never to have been formally adopted, but it was published in draft in 2004 and has continued to be available on the website of the Commission's EC Competition in draft form. The Commission announced that it had made this ruling against Germany by means of a press statement dated 20 October 2004.[14] In any event, there can be little doubt that the continued presence of the 'draft' decision, on the Commission's website, means that it represents the position and thinking of the Commission, in particular DG Competition, on the issues covered.

4 'MEETING THE COMPETITION' AND THE EU COMPETITION RULES

It is a feature of the EU case law on abuse of dominance, that any price discrimination involved in selective price cuts by a dominant undertaking will not necessarily be considered to be an abuse of dominance, provided that the price cuts are undertaken as a defensive measure as a proportionate response to competition and that the prices remain above costs. By contrast, where a dominant undertaking cuts prices selectively so as to attract customers away from a specific competitor, this may well be seen as having an exclusionary effect and therefore as being an abuse of dominance, as shown for example by the *Irish Sugar* case.[15] In a case currently pending in the ECJ in the postal services sector,[16] Advocate General Paolo Mengozzi has concluded that it is an abuse of dominance for a dominant undertaking to grant selective price reductions to a level below its average total costs but above its average incremental costs, to the main customer of its principal or only competitor in the national market for distribution of unaddressed mail, where the selective pricing can be cross-subsidized by revenue from activities reserved to the USP.

The Commission has stated in its Discussion Paper on exclusionary abuses of dominance[17] that the 'meeting competition' defense can provide objective justification for behavior that would otherwise constitute a pricing abuse. The dominant company's behavior must be: first, only in response to a competitor rather than a new initiative; and second, proportionate and indispensable, such that the legitimate aim cannot be achieved to a similar extent by less anti-competitive alternatives and that the conduct is limited in time to the absolute minimum.

The Commission further stated that where prices are set below average avoidable costs, the meeting competition defense can normally not be applied, as '[P]ricing below average avoidable cost is in general neither suitable nor indispensable to minimize the dominant company's losses'.[18]

In the same vein, although much earlier than publication of the Discussion Paper, the Commission previously allowed Digital[19] to meet competitor prices as part of a series of undertakings to remedy the abuse of Digital's dominant position in the supply of hardware maintenance services for Digital computer systems. The undertakings *inter alia* allowed Digital to grant non-standard price reductions to meet competition. The price reductions were only to be granted on individual component services rather than a bundle of services, and Digital undertook to verify that they were proportionate and did not foreclose or distort competition.

Therefore EU competition law allows a degree of flexibility to dominant undertakings which cut prices selectively as a proportionate response to competitive entry. At least where the discounted price meets the competitor's price rather than significantly undercutting it and the dominant undertaking covers its total costs, the dominant undertaking may well be able to defend itself against allegations of discriminatory pricing.

5 VOLUME DISCOUNTS UNDER THE EU COMPETITION RULES

Discount systems, which are designed to ensure exclusive purchasing or quasi-exclusive purchasing by customers from a dominant operator, will normally be regarded as abuse of a dominant position. This will be the case where, for example, the customer receives discounts in return for purchasing all or a significant proportion of its requirements from the dominant undertaking. It can also be considered an abuse of dominance for specifically growth-related discounts to be offered, because such discounts have a tendency to incentivize the customer to direct all its new business to the dominant entity and away from competing suppliers. This was acknowledged as a possibility in principle in the postal services sector in relation to Royal Mail in Postcomm's decision, *Royal Mail's catalogue and advertising mail promotion scheme*.[20]

More difficult issues arise where a dominant undertaking offers volume discounts. Discounts linked to specified volume thresholds may, depending on the terms of the scheme and on the circumstances, constitute abuse. The principal test for the acceptability of rebates granted by a dominant undertaking is set out in the *British Airways* case: first, whether there is an exclusionary or foreclosure effect, and second, whether any such effects are outweighed by efficiency advantages which benefit consumers.

Volume discounts which are based on thresholds on an individualized customer basis (especially if they are retroactive), for example by reference to purchase levels in previous reference periods (*Michelin II*,[21] *British Airways*) or the customer's actual requirements for the relevant reference period (*Irish Sugar*[22]), are likely to be considered abusive. Rebates based on standardized volume thresholds are likely to be presumed to be acceptable provided that the thresholds are transparent to all customers, although the case law does not specifically establish any general rule that standardized volume-based discounts can be presumed to be based on cost savings as such.

The Commission states in its Discussion Paper on exclusionary abuses that a rebate system with a *standardized* volume threshold is less likely to have a loyalty-enhancing effect.[23] However, the Discussion Paper also indicates,[24] and, it is clear from the case law set out above, that if a standardized volume threshold is set at a level which equates to all or most of the requirements of a typical customer or definable group of customers, it will be regarded as abusive. Equally if the application of the discount is not transparent, it could have a loyalty-enhancing effect where the customer feels bound to continue purchasing from the dominant company. The Commission considers in its Discussion Paper[25] that a rebate system consisting of a grid of standardized volume targets may be indispensable to achieve cost savings. Cost savings are unlikely to be achieved with a rebate system where the threshold is set in terms of a percentage of total requirements of the buyer or an individualized volume target.

In addition to the above considerations, volume discounts should not result in the net price falling below costs; otherwise they can constitute abuse of dominance through predatory pricing. This could especially be the case where the resulting price is below-average variable costs or incremental costs. The European Commission referred to average total costs as the relevant benchmark in its Discussion Paper.[26] This said, by reference to the case law on predation, average variable cost or long-run average incremental cost would be more likely to be the relevant benchmark.[27] In the French Conseil de la Concurrence Opinion concerning La Poste's rebate system, the Conseil assessed La Poste's net prices at the highest range of the rebate by reference to the average variable costs in the distribution sector and the prices offered by competing operators. It found that the marginal price of the highest range of the rebate system was above the average attributable costs, both of La Poste and of one of its competitors. The Conseil therefore concluded that La Poste's rebate system did not foreclose distributors on the relevant mail distribution market.

In the postal services sector, under the equivalent national law rules to Article 102 TFEU, the Danish incumbent has been found by the Danish Competition Council to have abused a dominant position (in the national market for magazine mail) through a system of volume rebates involving individual target rebates and minimum thresholds for magazine mail.[28]

6 DIFFERENTIAL PRICING BETWEEN INTERMEDIARIES AND END CUSTOMERS

It is of considerable importance to incumbent postal operators in a number of European countries to be able to grant commercial discounts on a volume basis to end customers (as opposed to worksharing discounts under downstream access or bulk-mail contracts) without at the same time needing to grant the same such discounts to mail preparation firms and other intermediaries acting on behalf of several different end customers. In this respect, Article 12, fifth indent, of the EU Directive clearly requires equal treatment as between end customers and consolidators including mail preparation firms. Though capable of collecting together the same volume of mail overall, mail preparation firms do not in the same way generate or originate the mail. This is done by the end customers, and arguably it is they and not the mail preparation firms that merit such volume discounts. We have already seen how the French Conseil de Concurrence has decided that mail preparation firms are not equivalent operators to end customers because they do not generate the original demand for mail services, and therefore as a matter of competition law (under the EU and French rules on abuse of dominance) do not merit equal treatment as regards commercial, volume discounts as opposed to worksharing discounts. By contrast, the European Commission concluded in its (draft) decision in German Postal Legislation, that the refusal by Deutsche Post to extend volume and worksharing discounts to mail preparation firms that were provided for end customers, was an abuse of dominant position, in addition to being in breach of Article 12, fifth indent, of the EU Directive.

Article 12, Fifth Indent, of the EU Directive

Article 12 (fifth indent) of the Directive sets out the overriding requirement of strict non-discrimination, by requiring member states to ensure:

> [W]henever universal service providers apply special tariffs, for example for services for businesses, bulk mailers or consolidators of mail from different users, they shall apply the principles of transparency and non-discrimination with regard both to the tariffs and to the associated conditions. The tariffs, together with the associated conditions, shall apply equally both as

> between different third parties and as between third parties and universal service providers supplying equivalent services. Any such tariffs shall also be available to users, in particular individual users and small and medium-sized enterprises, who post under similar conditions.

It can clearly be inferred from this that equal treatment is required as between businesses, bulk mailers and consolidators, and these criteria are wide enough to cover mail preparation firms. (Recital 39 of the Directive also refers to 'all users' as including 'businesses, bulk mailers and consolidators of mail from different users'). The wording of Article 12, fifth indent, does not make expressly clear whether the equal treatment applies only to worksharing discounts or to volume discount elements. However, the requirement that the tariffs 'together with the associated conditions' must apply equally as between different third parties, is wide in scope. It implies that the volume criteria as well as worksharing or mail preparation specification criteria should apply equally as between all types of customers.

The Vedat Deniz case concerned German court challenges to an order by the German Federal Cartel Office to Deutsche Post not to refuse access to partial conveyance services (that is, downstream access services) to intermediaries, to the extent that it grants such downstream access to direct bulk mailers on a discounted basis. The Cologne Administrative Court referred the question to the ECJ for a preliminary ruling, as to whether a USP which applies special tariffs for business customers for submission of presorted postal items, is obliged to apply such special tariffs also to intermediaries on the same terms and conditions as business customers.

The ECJ stated that it was clear from the wording of Article 12, fifth indent, of the Directive, that if a universal postal service provider applies special tariffs, it must apply them equally as between third parties, stating (paragraph 28): 'whenever such a provider applies special tariffs to businesses and/or bulk mailers, consolidators of mail from different customers are entitled to enjoy the same tariffs under the same conditions'. The USP was protected, according to the ECJ, by the requirement then contained in Article 12, fifth indent (now moved to Recital 39 since the adoption of Directive 2008/6), that special tariffs 'shall take account of the avoided costs'. On this basis, the special tariffs can be set in such a way that they cover the specific costs linked to the provision of the universal postal service and do not differ from the normal tariffs except to the extent that the costs actually avoided are deducted from the full service tariff.

The ECJ concluded (paragraph 44) that the fifth indent of Article 12 is to be interpreted as

> precluding refusal to apply to businesses which consolidate . . . the special tariffs which the universal postal service grants . . . to its business customers for the deposit of minimum quantities of pre-sorted mail at its sorting offices.

The judgment of the ECJ in *Vedat Deniz* does not, however, expressly address the position where quantitative or volume discounts are separated from the worksharing or presortation discounts containing a minimum volume or quantity criterion. Rather, the minimum quantities which featured in the case appear to have been a minimum scale for the discounts for worksharing or presortation. However, in view of the clear language of the ECJ, the logic of the judgment leads to the conclusion that equal treatment for consolidators and intermediaries as compared with direct senders would still be required. The ECJ expressly stated that 'the associated conditions' are to apply equally as between third parties, having regard to the non-discrimination obligation on universal service providers contained in Article 12, fifth indent.[29]

The European Commission's Approach in the *German Postal Legislation (BdKEP – Restrictions on Mail Preparation)* Case

The European Commission decided against certain provisions in Germany's postal legislation, which prevented commercial mail preparation firms from earning equivalent discounts for presortation to those available to direct senders. The European Commission's conclusions were based both on EU competition law, in particular Article 106 TFEU (which concerns undertakings granted special or exclusive rights by the state) applied in conjunction with Article 102 TFEU (formerly Articles 86 and 82 EC, respectively) and also on Article 12, fifth indent, of the EU Directive.

Deutsche Post provided discount rates for the downstream submission of presorted mail at the relevant outbound or inbound sorting office, by reference to the number of items per mail category. The discounts were granted subject to the mail being prepared in compliance with certain quality requirements.[30] The quantitative discount element was an integral part of the discounts for the mail preparation requirements and was not separated as between presortation or worksharing discounts on the one hand and purely volume discounts on the other (as in the *La Poste* case).

The Commission found an infringement of the EU competition rules in Articles 106 and 102 TFEU through the following: first, a failure to grant quantity-based discounts to intermediaries or mail preparation firms for downstream access, which put such intermediaries at a competitive disadvantage as compared to Deutsche Post;[31] second, failure to treat self-provision intermediaries and major senders alike in relation to quantity-based discounts for downstream network access for similar volumes of mail.[32] The Commission considered that the failure to grant quantity-based discounts to intermediaries or mail preparation firms induced Deutsche Post to extend its market power on the market for basic postal services into the separate, upstream market for mail preparation services, and that Deutsche Post was also induced to discriminate between major senders and smaller business senders who did not meet the requirements individually, but who could do so in volume terms through consolidators.[33]

The Commission further stated that Deutsche Post's discounting policy was contrary to the EU Directive by reference to Article 12, fifth indent. It stated that where a member state decided to grant special tariffs for downstream access to a group of customers, it must apply equal tariffs and conditions to other groups of customers. The Commission further stated that the fact that the discrimination by Deutsche Post as between mail preparation firms and direct senders was in breach of the requirements of the Directive, itself meant that the discrimination was contrary to the EU competition rules on abuse, contrary to Article 82 (c).[34]

The Commission further concluded that the abusive conduct that it found on the part of Deutsche Post could not be justified by an exception for services of general economic interest under Article 106(2) TFEU (then Article 86(2) EC), because Article 12, fifth indent, of the Directive required that special tariffs granted in respect of downstream access under Article 12, fifth indent 'shall take account of the avoided costs, as compared to the standard service covering the complete range of features'.[35] The Commission considered that this wording ensured coverage of Deutsche Post's fixed network costs. The Commission also stated that even the switching of a sizeable share of Deutsche Post's business customers to competitors would have no impact on Deutsche Post's ability to perform the universal service. This is on the basis that the avoided costs tariff scheme was precisely designed to ensure the coverage of fixed network costs whatever proportion of customers use the option of downstream access.[36]

While the Commission clearly condemned an incumbent's system of discounts, which prevented quantitative discounts for direct senders being applied to mail preparation firms, in the *BdKEP* case, the Deutsche Post quantity or volume element of its discount structure was less separate and less distinct from the worksharing and presortation discounts than in the French *La Poste* case covered by the Conseil de la Concurrence Opinion. The quantitative discount element was an integral part of the discounts for the mail preparation requirements and was not separated as between the presortation worksharing discounts on the one hand, and the purely volume discounts on the other, as in the French *La Poste* case. Nonetheless, the Commission made clear in its (draft) decision that, under the German law, commercial mail preparation firms, whether acting as intermediaries for a sole originator or as a consolidator on behalf of several originators, were 'prevented from earning any quantity-based discounts' for handing over mail items at either outbound or inbound sorting centers and were also prevented 'from earning based discounts for downstream network access altogether'. Thus, the Commission's statement would seem to indicate that it would also have been opposed to a refusal to provide quantity-related discounts to mail preparation firms (that were available to direct senders) even if there had been a clearer separation between the presortation and quantity-related discounts. However, the issue did not arise in this way, and as a specific question it remains to be considered.

The French *La Poste* case contrasted with *Vedat Deniz* and *BdKEP* cases

It may be noted that the *La Poste* case concerned retail products whereas the *BdKEP* and *Vedat Deniz* cases concerned downstream access services. However, it is doubtful that this is in itself an explanation for the different results in the French and German cases. On the one hand Article 12, fifth indent, of the Directive appeared to apply equally to retail-based products involving worksharing and to downstream access services. Moreover, the French Conseil Opinion (and the related court judgments) were made mainly under EU and French competition law rather than the regulatory requirements emanating from the EU Directive, while the *BdKEP* (draft) decision of the Commission was based at least in part on Article 12, fifth indent, Directive and the *Vedat Deniz* judgment of the ECJ concerned mainly Article 12, fifth indent, of the Directive. The position taken by the French Conseil de la Concurrence Opinion could have been followed by regulatory intervention pursuant to Article 12, fifth indent, Directive, but this apparently has not happened. Therefore, since it was the French regulator, ARCEP, which requested the Opinion, it may be that it considers that competition law principles are a reasonable basis for limiting the strictness of Article 12, fifth indent, of the Directive to purely volume discounts.

The French Conseil de la Concurrence considered that La Poste was justified in limiting the quantitative discount to mail originators as opposed to mail preparation firms, because the two groups were not in an equivalent position as the mail preparation firms were not originating the demand for postal services. The objective of La Poste's discount structure, of growing and stimulating demand from key sender customers, would be undermined if it were extended to mail preparation firms, because the effects of the consolidation through such firms could be that La Poste might only receive revenues corresponding to the maximum discounted rate, and the desired incentive effects on end customers would be suppressed. It was a key feature of the La Poste system that the mail preparation work itself was remunerated under technical services contracts, under which the discounts were available equally to mail originators and mail preparation firms, while the quantitative discounts were contained in entirely distinct commercial contracts which were limited to direct senders (whose annual turnover realized with La Poste exceeded €0.8 million).[37] However, the sales figures eligible under the commercial contract and the resulting discount were identical whether or not the mail originator (the sender) had his mail her prepared by a mail preparation firm for purposes of a worksharing contract. Therefore, the existence of the commercial (volume) discount was considered not to result in any disincentive to using mail preparation services.[38]

It was also an important feature of the *La Poste* case that the commercial discounts were payable to originating senders irrespective of whether or not they used the services of a mail preparation firm. The French Conseil's Opinion states that there were three types of product and technical contracts with La Poste, contracts without a mail preparation firm (*Offres sans routeur*), contracts where the mail preparation firm was a contractor to the mail originator (*Offres avec routeur tireur*), but also contracts where the mail preparation firm manages the client's entire relationship with La Poste, entering into the product and technical contracts with La Poste on behalf of the mail originator. The Paris Court of Appeal referred to the mail originator as being in regulatory terms the customer and in a legal sense the only contracting party with La Poste. It appears that the mail preparation firms were agents of the mail originators, but the judgment of the Court of Appeal did not give any explanation as to whether or not mail preparation firms could nonetheless be regarded as customers for the purposes of Article 12, fifth indent, of the Directive.

The *La Poste* case does not address the situation, even as a matter of competition law, where the mail preparation firm enters into the contract with the USP, and the mail preparation firm does so acting in its own right, and not, in contractual terms, on behalf of the mail originators. In that situation, as regards Article 12, fifth indent, the *BdKEP* and *Vedat Deniz* cases show that volume discounts must be paid to mail preparation firms just as for direct senders.

In order for a system of commercial (volume) discounts to be defensible against regulatory intervention under Article 12, fifth indent, of the Directive, it may be necessary for an incumbent's discount to go further than La Poste apparently did by reference to the content of the Conseil de la Concurrence's Opinion. Arguably a system of volume discounts payable to mail originators but not mail preparation firms or intermediaries would be defensible in regulatory terms if it could be shown that the mail preparation firm acts as agent for the mail originators and that the discount is payable to any mail originator even where the contract holder or account holder with the incumbent is the mail preparation firm, rather than the mail originator, subject to confidentiality concerns being safeguarded. However, it would seem to be a key requirement of this approach that the mail preparation firm is operating in legal terms as agent for the mail originators, by reference to the Paris Court of Appeal's pronouncements in the *La Poste* case.

It would then be possible for the mail preparation firm or consolidator to specify the volumes posted on behalf of each end customer to enable any applicable volume discount to be paid by the incumbent direct to that mail originator in respect of its mail volumes transmitted to the incumbent by the mail preparation firm. In this way, all senders of mail would receive equal treatment in respect of a system of discounts which by their nature and definition would be applicable only to mail originators and not to intermediaries. The discounts would then be payable to the mail originator irrespective of whether the mail originator or its mail preparation firm holds the postal service contract with the incumbent. There is no indication in the Conseil de la Concurrence Opinion or in the Paris Court of Appeal judgment in the *La Poste* case that La Poste paid purely volume or commercial discounts directly to the relevant mail originators even in respect of mail that was channeled through mail preparation firms. It is possible that, as a matter of fact, such commercial discounts were so paid by La Poste direct to the relevant mail originators. However, as this was not stated in the Conseil de la Concurrence Opinion or in the Court of Appeal judgment, it cannot be regarded as part of the legal precedent established by the case. The present suggestion that such an approach should be acceptable is based only partly on the *La Poste* case, but also based on an analysis of principle by reference to Article 12, fifth indent, as well as competition law.

In view of the strictness with which Article 12, fifth indent, has been applied by the European Commission and ECJ in the *BdKEP* and *Vedat Deniz* cases, respectively, such a feature may be necessary in order to achieve an incumbent's objectives of confining commercial volume discounts to mail originators as opposed to mail preparation firms, in future cases. In any event, La Poste's discount structure was not examined in any detail under Article 12, fifth indent, of the Directive as opposed to competition law.

7 CONCLUSIONS

EU case law shows that foreclosure or exclusion of competition, not merely harm to competition, is a necessary feature in order for discriminatory pricing to constitute an abuse of dominant position. Moreover, many of the EU cases on discriminatory conduct by a dominant undertaking concern conduct by a vertically integrated dominant operator which benefits its own downstream business to the detriment of competitors. Thus the threshold for discriminatory conduct to be regarded as an abuse of dominant position is relatively high.

Under EU competition law, a serious competitive disadvantage to the victim of price discrimination must be shown, in order for such discrimination to be an abuse of dominance. Regulatory rules on discrimination are generally stricter, requiring compliance irrespective of whether or not anticompetitive effects result.

Article 12, fifth indent, does not distinguish between worksharing discounts and any purely commercial, volume-based discounts, but appears to apply equally to all such discounts. The strictness of Article 12, fifth indent, in this respect appears to be confirmed by the European Court judgment in the *Vedat Deniz* case and by the European Commission in the *BdKEP* case. By contrast, the French national regulatory authority, ARCEP, seems to take a purposive interpretation of Article 12, fifth indent, insofar as it was ARCEP that requested the opinion to be provided in 2007 by the Conseil de la Concurrence on the question of whether or not, on competition law principles, mail preparation firms and mail originators were in an equivalent position, for the purposes of receiving discounts. On the basis of the lack of equivalence of such intermediaries on the one hand and mail originators on the other, and in the absence of any subsequent intervention against La Poste by ARCEP pursuant to the Conseil de la Concurrence Opinion, it would seem that ARCEP has perhaps accepted the approach of the Conseil for purposes of the national implementation of the Directive (Article 12, fifth indent).

However, postal operators, in particular incumbent USPs, should be cautious about relying on the Conseil de la Concurrence Opinion concerning La Poste. The Opinion does not itself refer to the main issue of the scope and extent of the non-discrimination requirement under Article 12, fifth indent, of the Directive, being given primarily as an opinion under competition law. Moreover, the Conseil de la Concurrence Opinion cannot be relied upon in isolation, without full account being taken of the strict non-discrimination principles in Article 12, fifth indent, as interpreted and applied by the European Commission in the *BdKEP* case and by the ECJ in the *Vedat Deniz* case.

In order for an incumbent to be in a strong position to sustain a system of commercial volume discounts limited to mail originators (even where mail preparation firms are used), and which is defensible under Article 12, fifth indent, of the Directive, as well as under competition law, it is likely to be necessary for the incumbent to ensure the following. First, the system of commercial discounts should be maintained entirely separately, and under separate contracts from the worksharing discounts (which should be payable equally to intermediates). Second, the incumbent should ensure that the volume discounts are payable to the end customer irrespective of whether the originator has used the services of a mail preparation firm. Third, the volume discounts should be payable whether or not the holder of the contract with the postal incumbent is the mail originator or the mail preparation firm. Fourth, the mail preparation firms should in each case operate in legal terms as agent for the relevant mail originators (as appears to have been the case in the *La Poste* case).

Neither the Conseil de la Concurrence nor the Paris Court of Appeal stated in the *La Poste* case that purely commercial volume discounts were paid direct by La Poste to mail originators by reference to their mail volumes channeled through mail preparation firms, though La Poste may well have done so. The type of arrangement now put forward depends on the mail preparation firm acting as agent for the relevant mail originators and notifying the USP of the volumes posted on behalf of each end customer, to enable any applicable volume discounts to be paid by the incumbent direct to the mail originator (in respect of mail volumes transmitted via the mail preparation firm). On this approach only the originator, the sender, will be entitled to the volume discounts by virtue of the definition of the scope of the discount, irrespective of whether or not a mail preparation firm is involved, either in providing services to the sender or in acting as an intermediary (agent) for the sender. Such an approach seeks to reconcile the divergent themes of the French and EU case law, though it must be noted that overall the case law has not yet fully clarified the issues involved.

NOTES

1. Article 12, second indent, and Recital 38: member states may also maintain uniform tariffs for some other mail items in respect of general public interests, for example, newspapers and books.
2. Commission press statement IP/04/1254, 20 October 2004.
3. Joined cases C-287-06 to C-2-06, *Vedat Deniz & Others v Germany*.

4. Opinion No. 07-A-17 of 20 December 2007.
5. Case No. 05/24993, judgment of 26 March 2008.
6. See paras 180–82.
7. Case C/95/04P *British Airways v. Commission*, 15 March 2007.
8. Paras 144–5.
9. Case T-301/04 *Clearstream v Commission.*
10. Para 194.
11. For further details of cases of price discrimination in the postal services sector, for example 'Deutsche Post AG – interception of cross-border mail', OJ 2001 L331/40 and 'De Post – La Poste,' OJ 2002 L61/32, see Eccles and Kuipers (2008).
12. Commission Decision of 20 October 2004 (published in draft) 'BdKEP – restrictions on mail preparation'; see also IP/04/1254.
13. Paras 63, 70.
14. IP/04/1254: *The Commission acts against the discrimination of mail preparation service providers in Germany.* The reason why the decision was not formally adopted appears to be that, at the time, new German legislation was anticipated which would remove the infringement, and that this legislation was in fact introduced soon afterwards.
15. OJ (1997) L258/1, on appeal *Irish Sugar v Commission*, Case T-228/97, (1999) ECRII-2969 and Case C-497/99P, (2001) ECRI-5333.
16. Case C/209/10, *Post Danmark*, Advocate General's Opinion, 24 May 2011.
17. Commission Discussion Paper on the application of Article 82 to exclusionary abuses, December 2005, paras 81–2 and 132.
18. Para. 83.
19. Commission press release IP/97/868.
20. Postcomm decision dated 20 January 2005 – *Investigation into Royal Mail's Catalogue and Advertising Mail Promotion Scheme.*
21. Commission Decision of 20 June 2001 *Michelin II* (2002/405/EC).
22. Commission Decision of 14 May 1997 *Irish Sugar* (97/624/EC), see note 16, above.
23. Commission Discussion Paper on the application of Article 82 to exclusionary abuses, December 2005, para. 159.
24. Para. 159.
25. Commission Discussion Paper on the application of Article 82 to exclusionary abuses, December 2005, para. 173.
26. Para. 171.
27. *Deutsche Post AG*, Commission Decision of 20 March 2001, OJ 2001 L125/27; *Wanadoo*, Case T-340-03, 30 January 2007, *France Telecom v. Commission.*
28. Press release dated 22 December 2010.
29. Para. 43.
30. For example, presorted according to the first two digits of the post code, franked, machine readable and conveyed in bar-coded Deutsche Post-specific containers.
31. Paras 63, 75 and 85.
32. Paras 64, 65, 86 and 87.
33. Para. 86.
34. Para. 96.
35. This requirement was moved to recital 39 in Directive 2008/6.
36. Para. 113.
37. For a full explanation of the discount system operated by La Poste, see Geradin (2011).
38. See paras 115, 119 and 126.

REFERENCES

Eccles, Richard and Pauline Kuipers (2008), 'The proper scope of the rules on abuse of dominant position in a liberalized postal services market' in Michael A. Crew and Paul R. Kleindorfer (eds), *Competition and Regulation in the Postal and Delivery Sector*, Cheltenham, UK and Northampton, MA, USA: Edward Elgar.

Geradin, Damien (2011), 'Price discrimination in the postal services sector and competition law' in Michael A. Crew and Paul R. Kleindorfer (eds), *Reinventing the Postal Sector in an Electronic Age*, Cheltenham, UK and Northampton, MA, USA: Edward Elgar.

3. Postal price regulation in a competitive environment

Ralf Wojtek[†] **and Martin Zauner**[‡]

1 INTRODUCTION

With full liberalization of the postal markets the focus of price regulation shifts from *ex ante* price setting to detecting and preventing abuses in the liberalized market. While the dominant provider may still be subject to some price regulation, particularly with respect to consumers and the Universal Service Obligation (USO), it must be able to meet the new competition particularly in the field of business mail, parcels and express products. For this reason postal regulations in some countries, for example, Germany, have limited the *ex ante* price regulation to consumer mail whereas all other mail and all parcel products are subject only to *ex post* abuse control by the regulatory agency and the national and EU antitrust authorities.

Since the Universal Service Provider (USP) generally retains its dominant position even after full liberalization it is subject to the general constraints relating to the commercial behavior of a dominant undertaking. The main provision in this context is Article 102 TFEU (formerly the EC Treaty). As competition increases the special provision for public undertakings (Article 106 TFEU, formerly Article 86 EU) becomes of less importance if universal service – or a large part of it – is rendered not only by the USP but also by a number of its competitors.

As liberalization is progressing we observe more market-oriented pricing policies followed by the USPs, mostly in the areas of business mail and parcels. A typical tool employed by USPs is the widespread use of rebates. The use of rebates may appear to be the natural way for the ex-monopolist to defend its market share. In this regard the USP is subject to the same legal restrictions, which apply to every dominant provider. At the same time the Postal Directive provides for 'affordable' prices which shall be cost oriented with respect to the universal service. Tariffs must be transparent and non-discriminatory and common costs, which are necessary for the provision of both universal services and non-universal services, shall be allocated appropriately (Directive 2008/6/EC of 20 February 2008, Art. 12, the 'Third Directive'). Certain protective measures may be necessary in order to allow the new market entrants to establish a position in the newly opened market. In addition, the regulator has to make sure that the USP does not defend its market in non-regulated areas with advantages stemming from the remaining (legal or actual) monopoly. These very different and sometimes conflicting

† Attorney and Partner. Heuking Kühn Lüer Wojtek, Hamburg, Germany.
‡ Senior Economist, WIK, Bad Honnef, Germany.

considerations must be kept in mind in dealing with postal pricing strategies, especially the use of rebates.

The chapter proceeds as follows. Section 2 provides a typology of common rebates and their effects on competition. Section 3 discusses exemplary competition cases that deal with the application of rebates, predominantly in the postal sector. Section 4 summarizes our conclusions.

2 TYPES OF REBATES AND THEIR EFFECTS

Types of Rebates

Typically the following types of rebates can be found in the market:

1. *Quantity rebates* This rebate is a discount which is granted when the customer achieves a certain (minimum) volume. Usually, this type of rebate reflects economies of scale that come along with large quantities. Often, this kind of rebate is granted in network industries by two-part tariffs: such tariffs include a flat component (independent of volume) and a variable component (dependent of volume). The higher the demand, the lower is the average price paid arising from the spread of fixed costs over more units.
2. *Turnover-related rebates* The basis for this rebate is the seller's sales revenue received from each individual customer. Typically, the customer is required to realize a defined amount of revenue (which is usually determined *ex ante*) within a certain period (for example, one year) in order to get the rebate. This induces a 'pull effect', near the defined amount of turnover: if the customer's need is below this threshold, he/she has an incentive to expand demand above the threshold in order to get the rebate. As the rebate applies to every unit purchased, the average price for the entire purchase volume then falls below the average price applicable before the expansion of demand.
3. *Total turnover-related rebates* In addition to the turnover rebate described above, this type is granted on the entire turnover a customer has with different products of the selling company. In contrast to the turnover-related rebate, this rebate is related to all products that customers buy from the supplier rather than to one specific product. This induces an incentive for customers to demand products for which they usually have no need or high preference – or which they would generally buy from other companies. When buying all products from the same supplier, customers achieve a higher total rebate compared to buying a single product only. Thus, a company can leverage its market-dominant position into competitive market segments. This may be a particular concern with respect to incumbent postal operators wishing to expand their original business to neighboring markets.
4. *Fidelity rebates* Typically, this type of rebate focuses on the customers' entire demand of a product or service and not on a predefined volume. Customers receive a rebate only if they cover their total (or a high share of their total) need with the seller. This has an anticompetitive effect as the rebate ties the customer to the granting company. Furthermore, this kind of rebate can have a discriminatory effect:

customers with different needs get the same rebate even though their different volumes cause different economies of scale.

5. *Price reduction based on a reduced product or service* A typical case is 'worksharing' where part of the total service, such as collection and sorting, is done by customers themselves. This is not really a rebate but a reduced price based on a reduced service. Nevertheless, it has to be considered as a possible competition tool which may lend itself to abuse.
6. *Zonal pricing* Strictly speaking this is not a rebate either, but a price reduction based on – alleged or real – cost advantages such as higher density in metropolitan areas.

Some of the rebates discussed above may be offered in combination and different forms of rebates are also possible. In addition, it is important to differentiate if the rebate relates to all purchases starting with the first purchase (continuous rebate) or if the rebate applies once a certain threshold is passed (triggered rebate). In the second case the pull effect is higher than in the first case: the closer the customer comes to the threshold the greater is the incentive to purchase additional products and the smaller is the motivation to purchase from competitors. Once the threshold is passed the rebate is calculated on the entire volume. This has the same effect as if the purchases above the threshold are free: the rebate triggered by exceeding the threshold may be equal or even worth more than the costs of purchasing additional volumes needed to pass the threshold. Such an incentive leaves little room for smaller competitors.

Positive and Negative Effects of Rebates

A positive effect of a volume rebate is that it reflects economies of scale. If the customer purchases a higher volume, the seller has a better workload and, consequently, lower production costs. This advantage of lower costs is passed on to the customer by granting an adequate rebate. If the rebate corresponds with the economies of scale achieved and is granted to all customers in the same way, the rebate has no negative effects on competition.

However, rebates can have negative effects on competition, too. Market closure or exclusive dealing is such a negative effect. A market closure effect is typical for fidelity rebates where customers are required to cover their entire need (and not an absolute amount) exclusively from the granting company. Therefore, it is difficult for other companies to attract customers and volume and, thus, to enter the market. Another negative effect of rebates may be the discriminatory impact. A rebate is discriminatory if it is selectively granted only to certain customers. A discriminatory effect can also emanate from fidelity rebates.

Incumbent postal operators typically enjoy near-monopoly market positions in the mail market and sometimes also in the consumer-to-consumer (C2C) or business-to-consumer (B2C) parcel markets even after the fall of legal monopolies whereas competitors hold small market shares and usually offer only limited service portfolios. Therefore, the various effects of rebates as outlined above should be of particular concern from a regulatory point of view.

3 LEGAL CONSIDERATIONS

As a dominant provider the USP is subject to the general restrictions of Article 102 TFEU concerning the abuse of a dominant position, in particular the prohibition of discrimination. As Eccles (ch. 2 in this volume) properly points out, discriminatory pricing does not automatically constitute an abuse of dominant position under general competition rules; there must be the additional aspect of foreclosure or exclusion of competition, or other unfair practices in order to qualify for an 'abuse' within the meaning of Article 102 TFEU. The prohibition of competition is also addressed in Article 12 of the Third Directive. In addition, the Third Directive contains further constraints for the USP. Although these constraints are largely directed at the provision of universal services only they do influence the incumbent's choice of pricing strategies. For example, the incumbent must allocate common costs adequately to products within and outside the USO. In addition, the need to keep the prices of the universal service at affordable levels can make it necessary to allocate historical burdens not only on the USO part but also on new products and services outside the USO.[1]

Exclusionary Effect of Rebates and Bonuses

In a case involving agreements between British Airways and travel agents, the Court of First Instance (CFI) had to rule on the legality of bonuses linked to the growth in sales of airline tickets over a given period in comparison with a reference period.[2] The agreements with the airline provided for specific sales targets. Once the agent achieved the sales target, the agent qualified for a bonus calculated not only on the basis of tickets sold in excess of the target but for all tickets sold during the period in question. The economic impact on such a rebate scheme is much stronger than a rebate or bonus which applies only to products sold after the achievement of the particular target. As shown before, a quantity rebate that is triggered after the achievement of a specific target and is based on the entire turnover achieved with the dominant undertaking, tends to have a strong pull effect on the business partners of the dominant undertaking. In some cases the bonus may be the determining factor in making the business with the dominant provider a profitable one or not. Therefore, the business partners, who are subject to such a bonus scheme have an extremely high motivation to achieve the target. Conversely, their motivation to purchase the products or services from competitors is very low until the target value is achieved. Depending on the level of the target value, the bonus scheme may lead to a complete exclusion of competitors from business with purchasing companies that are subject to such bonus scheme.[3]

If the particular turnover target value is set in such a way as to cover the entire demand in products or services of a company which is subject to such a bonus scheme, the bonus has the effect of a 'fidelity bonus' or rebate, which ties the customer to the dominant provider. In that case the bonus or rebate scheme would be illegal since it would keep competitors out of the market and fortify the dominant position of the already dominant provider.

Even when the targeted turnover does not cover the entire demand of the purchasing company, the bonus relating to the entire turnover during a given period is questionable due to the described pull effect. As the CFI pointed out in the *British Airways* judgment, such a bonus scheme is particularly problematic where the undertaking holds a market share which is much larger than that of its competitors. In those circumstances the purchasing companies must buy the bulk of their product or services needs from the dominant provider, while competitors must basically wait until the purchasing companies have achieved their turnover targets before competing suppliers have a fair chance to sell their products to them. The CFI correctly concluded that a dominant undertaking – holding a significantly higher market share than its competitors – generally becomes an unavoidable business partner in the market. Therefore, the business partners of the dominant provider are also dependent on the cooperation with it – a situation which must not be exploited.

The *British Airways* case can well be used in the context of postal services: most USPs hold a dominant position which is far superior to the market share enjoyed by their competitors. Due to the former postal monopoly there usually is no single competitor that is able to cover the entire demand of the same range of products or services offered by the dominant provider. Therefore, any quantity-based rebates which are triggered after reaching a certain sales target and which include almost the entire turnover are highly problematic, as they tend to foreclose the market to competitors. The same is true if the rebate applies to the entire service portfolio. In such a case, there is a danger of expanding the original letter monopoly to new markets.

The relatively young history of competition in postal services shows a number of examples where the courts have found an abuse of this kind by the dominant provider.

The *Infopost Schwer* Case

In the year 2000 the German National Regulatory Authority 'Bundesnetzagentur' (BNetzA) had to rule on a rebate arrangement between the dominant postal provider Deutsche Post (DP) and two mail order companies for the transportation of catalogues.[4] The arrangement provided for linear rebates based on the total turnover, provided further that the mail order company had to ship all or nearly all of its catalogues through DP. The BNetzA classified the agreements as anticompetitive and found an abuse of a dominant position. In its ruling the BNetzA found that the rebates were not cost oriented but aimed at retaining the customer. Rather than relating to specific volumes, the rebates were dependent on reaching a certain share of the customer's demand. This was taken as a clear indication that the rebates did not reflect cost savings but were designed to exclude the competition.

Although the rebate schemes did not require that the mail order companies purchased their entire catalogue transportation volumes from DP, the exclusionary effect was still very strong. The BNetzA found that the potential loss of a bonus payment far exceeded the potential financial advantage resulting from a lower price offered by a competitor, who provided only 10 or 20 percent of the transportation services required by the mail order company.

Redmail vs. Österreichische Post

Another case involving a fidelity rebate is the case of the Austrian postal operator, *Redmail vs. Austrian Post* (the incumbent operator).[5] Due to the abolition of public subsidies the tariffs for delivery of newspapers in Austria has increased strongly since

2002. The sharp price increases made the market more attractive for competitors such as Redmail who offered to deliver newspapers as well. In order to mitigate the effect of the price increases, Austrian Post offered a multi-level transitional pricing to those customers who signed up at least 90 percent of their 2001 volumes with Austrian Post. If customers failed to ship the required 90 percent of the 2001 volume or if they withdrew from the contract, they had to pay a markup on the discounted tariff. This scheme worked like a penalty, especially where the customer had to pay more than 100 percent of the non-rebated price. The pricing scheme had the same effect as a fidelity rebate: customers had a strong incentive to stay with Austrian Post.

The Austrian High Court found that Austrian Post had abused its dominant position even though the customers had the – theoretical – possibility to ship a portion of their entire volume with the competitor, Redmail. The price scheme did not reflect economic cost savings due to higher volumes but was targeted to exclude Redmail from the market.

Hays vs. De Post–La Poste

In the case of Belgian postal operator De Post–La Poste, the European Commission had to deal with another exclusionary aspect of postal pricing.[6] A Belgian association of insurances (UPEA) had entered into an agreement with a private postal operator (Hays) which operated a document exchange service (business to business: B2B). In July 1998, De Post–La Poste approached UPEA and offered to provide a similar exchange service for UPEA. However, the prices offered by Belgian Post were higher than the Hays prices. Therefore, UPEA rejected the postal offer. As a consequence De Post–La Poste terminated an existing agreement with UPEA, which included preferential tariffs for other mail products (for example, B2C) which were still within the monopoly. At the same time, De Post–La Poste recommended that UPEA should reconsider its position regarding the document exchange service. Very soon thereafter UPEA and De Post–La Poste came to an agreement. The agreement on preferential tariffs in the monopoly area was renewed and extended, and subsequently the document exchange service was transferred to De Post–La Poste. The contract with Hays was terminated accordingly.

This case is an example of the exclusionary effect of a bundling agreement. The dominant provider, still enjoying a monopoly over business letters (B2C), made use of its dominant position in order to extend its dominant position to a new market segment outside the monopoly: the document exchange service (B2B).

The Commission decided that De Post–La Poste had abused its dominant position in order to squeeze out a competitor in the non-reserved area. The fact that the prices for the document exchange service operated by De Post–La Poste were less attractive than the prices offered by Hays shows that the effect of bundling may well lead to inefficiencies. In order to retain its favorable prices for business mail, UPEA had to accept a less attractive provider for its document exchange service. By contrast, the competitor Hays had no similar possibilities to counter De Post–La Poste's offer since the business mail (B2C) at that time was still subject to the postal monopoly. However, the same ruling would probably apply today when an (incumbent) operator would bundle products or services with a high market share with new and competitive services in order to push back a competitor.

Predatory Pricing

Another potential form of abuse designed to exclude competitors from the market is the use of predatory pricing. In the famous *AKZO* case the European Court of Justice (ECJ) established the principles of predatory pricing applying to dominant undertakings:[7]

1. prices below average incremental costs are generally assumed to be abusive because a dominant undertaking has no interest in offering such prices unless it aims to exclude its competitors from the market; and
2. prices below average total costs but above average incremental costs may be abusive if they are part of a plan to exclude a competitor.

France Télécom

The *France Télécom SA* case, decided by the ECJ on 2 April 2009, is a good example of the problems of predatory pricing in a highly monopolized market with only a few weak competitors.[8] France Télécom through its subsidiary Wanadoo offered Internet access services at prices below the variable costs of Wanadoo until August 2001. After August 2001 the prices covered the variable costs, but not the total costs. The Commission ordered Wanadoo to stop the violation of competition rules and imposed a fine of €10.35 million.

In its appeal to the ECJ, Wanadoo argued that it must be able to offer prices similar to those of its competitors in order to defend its market share.

The Court held that, generally speaking, even a dominant undertaking has the possibility to offer prices which are comparable to those of its competitors. However, this does not apply if the real objective of this price strategy is to strengthen or to abuse its dominant position.

The Court found sufficient indications in the circumstances of the case, which led to the conclusion that the price strategy employed by Wanadoo had the objective of strengthening the dominant position of Wanadoo and its parent company, France Télécom. The most important indication was the fact that the prices did not cover its variable costs and – after August 2001 – its total costs. The explanations given by Wanadoo for this pricing strategy did not satisfactorily prove a motivation other than to expand its market share from the telecommunications market to a neighboring market with the possible objective to recover the losses after destroying the competition.

The example exemplifies the problems which incumbents face in their endeavors to enter new markets.

European Commission vs. Deutsche Post AG

This case deals with rebates granted by the German postal operator DP to certain parcel customers.[9] DP used to have a very high market share particularly in the segment of mail order parcels. More than 90 percent of the volume shipped by mail order companies (except the volume shipped by Otto Versand, which used its own shipping company) were shipped through DP. In order to defend its market share, DP offered very high rebates. The Commission found that the resulting net prices were below average total costs and partly even below average incremental costs. The Commission concluded that these prices constituted an abuse of a dominant position. The Commission found proof for a plan to exclude competitors, particularly in the design of a rebate scheme which had the characteristics of a fidelity rebate.

From an economic point of view, the Commission used the concept of incremental costs. According to this concept a rebate is abusive if the turnover resulting from the sales of the specific product is lower than the additional costs of production of that product. In the opinion of the Commission there was little economic sense in offering a product at less than incremental cost unless the objective was to exclude the competition.

Price Discrimination

As mentioned earlier, most individual pricing schemes and particularly rebates include an element of discrimination. Price discrimination is not always prohibited. However, it is prohibited if it leads to a strengthening of the market share of the dominant undertaking. Different rebates which are not purely volume based may also lead to a distortion of competition among the customers of the dominant provider. Especially in the postal market where customers often have no choice but to use the incumbent, the discrimination aspect is relevant if mailing costs constitute a major element in the cost of production.

Quantity discounts necessarily contain an element of discrimination but are usually considered acceptable if they are applied evenly to all customers and do not contain hidden fidelity elements. Their purpose may be twofold: First, while they are usually designed to gain or retain large mailers by passing on economies of scale, there is the additional aspect of further strengthening the incumbent's dominant position thus leaving little room for new entrants. Second, there is the problem that the economic advantage of a discount might disappear if it is granted to large mailers and consolidators alike (Crew and Kleindorfer, ch. 1 in this volume). Limiting the discount opportunity to original mailers, however, may collide with the principle of non-discrimination.

ENTEGA

The German Supreme Court had an opportunity to spell out the particular limitations on price discrimination employed by a dominant undertaking – in this case of a household gas provider.[10] In this case the gas company had a quasi-monopoly in a certain area (region 1). In order to enter the market in the neighboring geographic area (region 2), the gas company used a subsidiary which offered lower prices for the same services in region 2 where another provider was the dominant undertaking. Unfortunately, there was an overlap of the two regions in a small town of region 1 which was covered by the dominant undertaking and where its subsidiary also offered the rates designed for region 2. A citizen of this town who was a customer of the dominant undertaking sued the gas company for damages because he paid a higher price than the customers of the subsidiary.

The Supreme Court found for the plaintiff and used the opportunity of the case to spell out the principles of price discrimination employed by a dominant undertaking. In region 1 where the defendant company was the dominant undertaking it was not allowed to charge different prices for the same services. It made no difference that the dominant undertaking had created a subsidiary, which offered the lower price. For the purpose of the application of competition rules the dominant undertaking and its subsidiary were to be considered as one and the same.

For region 2, however, the Court decided that the dominant undertaking should be able to offer lower prices if that was necessary in order to enter a new geographical market where another company was the dominant undertaking. The Court interpreted the competition rules to encourage competition even if this leads to different prices in different geographical areas, provided that the different prices are used only in order to enter a new market. Predatory pricing was not an issue in this case. The court, therefore, did not have to deal with the question if the prices charged in region 2 were at least cost covering.

European Commission/Conseil de la Concurrence vs. La Poste

In this case, the French postal operator La Poste granted special rebates to certain large customers and to its own subsidiary, Datapost, using La Poste's downstream access.[11] Other customers and competitors offering consolidation services did not get the same rebates. In addition, La Poste used different access conditions thus making it more difficult for competitors, as compared to preferred customers and Datapost, to make use of rebates.

The Commission found that the different treatment of its customers and particularly of competitors compared to its own subsidiary constituted price discrimination and an abuse of a market dominant position. The Commission and the French Conseil de la Concurrence also criticized the discriminatory access conditions, such as minimum volumes, which were set arbitrarily and not geared to costs. As a result of this access and pricing strategy of La Poste the number of consolidators benefiting from the rebate decreased by about 50 percent while Datapost was not affected by these rules since its consolidation volume was far higher than the minimum volumes set by La Poste. The Commission considered saved handling costs for La Poste, economies of scale, and the added value achieved by La Poste as acceptable criteria. However, arbitrary increases of the minimum volume required for preferential tariffs – instead of an increase according to the cost saved – was considered as an indication of abuse. The arbitrary access conditions to preferential tariffs worked to the advantage of La Poste's subsidiary, thus strengthening the dominant market position.

Worksharing Prices

Although worksharing prices reflect the lower costs of a reduced service the pricing strategies involved may also lend themselves to abuse of a dominant position, as the *La Poste* case (above) shows. It was the aspect of price discrimination, which led the German Federal Cartel Office (FCO) to force the German postal operator DP to offer consolidation services and access conditions, including access prices, not only to its large customers but also to competitors or potential competitors. The FCO did not, however, determine the appropriate access price. For the purposes of the FCO it was sufficient to stop the dominant undertaking from discriminating among customers and competitors asking for the same kind of access to the postal network.

When the national regulatory authority BNetzA looked at the problem, it had to determine the proper access price taking into consideration the reduced cost of a reduced service. Since large customers and consolidators collect their own mail and, after sorting it, hand it over at large mail centers, the dominant provider saves the cost of collecting and presorting the mail. At the same time, however, there may be new and additional costs created by the need to accept the letters at a mail center.

In its decision of 15 September 2000, BNetzA determined that a rebate of 21 percent on standard letters was appropriate to reflect the reduced costs of the product.[12]

In 2008, however, after full liberalization went into effect, DP increased the rebate voluntarily by 5 percentage points although there was no change in the services offered.

When in 2010 the preferential value-added tax (VAT) treatment of letters shipped by DP was abolished and mail services of DP and its competitors had to compete on the same VAT basis, this was hailed as the breakthrough for competition. Under the new VAT law most of the business mail and all worksharing products are now subject to full VAT. As a response, DP decided to increase its worksharing rebates again in order to retain its large customers, this time to 38 percent of the standard letter price.

At the request of competitors, BNetzA reviewed the new rebates and, after an investigation, concluded that the net price charged by DP for the worksharing product was still adequate to cover DP's costs. Therefore, BNetzA concluded that there was no abuse of DP's dominant position. The decision left many competitors unhappy, particularly because they felt that the repeated increase of rebates was triggered by the opening of the market and not by cost savings. It remains to be seen whether the price strategy used in the worksharing case will lead to a further strengthening of the dominant position of DP. In any case, the result of the investigation shows that under antitrust and regulatory rules the incumbent still has considerable room to devise its own pricing strategies as long as the principles of non-discrimination and coverage of costs are observed.

Zonal Pricing

Zonal pricing is another form of price discrimination. It may constitute an abuse but it may also be justified, depending on the effect and the goal of the pricing strategy. In the case of *Postcomm vs. Royal Mail* (Postal Service Commission, 2008, p. 17), the British regulator, 'Postcomm', had to consider an application of Royal Mail for special prices limited to high density zones, such as London. The tariffs to be charged in these zones would differ, among others, on business density and the level of wages. In its review of the application, Postcomm did not completely reject the idea of zonal pricing, provided that the postal provider demonstrates that the prices are revenue neutral, cost-reflective, do not cause unacceptable changes for customers, and meet the requirements of the Third Postal Directive. A central argument of Postcomm's critique of the application was the effect of discrimination between customers, which was considered to be contradictory to the requirements of the Third Postal Directive. In addition, Postcomm found that the costs indicated by Royal Mail differed from its own calculation. Furthermore, Postcomm found that certain zones were subject to different rebates although their costs were the same. The discrimination among users within the Greater London zone seemed unjustified as the delivery costs in this zone and in the remaining part of London were identical. In addition, Postcomm noted that the new zonal price scheme was likely to increase customers' costs because they would have to execute complex calculations in order to determine their costs of mailings.

Royal Mail withdrew its application before a final decision was taken.

The considerations made by Postcomm in the zonal price application are most interesting from the point of view of the development of postal markets:

1. on the one hand there is the positive effect of using cost-based prices;
2. on the other there is the potential discrimination among customers; and
3. the potential impact on the total costs of the universal service if the zonal price is not cost neutral.

Following the considerations of Postcomm in that case, a zonal price structure which reflects actual costs and does not discriminate among customers, which is cost neutral for the universal service and which does not exclude competition, appears to be possible from a regulatory standpoint as long as the pricing scheme does not create unreasonable burdens for customers. However, the problems of zonal prices are evident particularly where revenues resulting from cost advantages in high-density areas are used to offset higher costs in low-density areas. Considering the 'affordable price' requirement of the universal service, a regulator may have to reject a cost-based zonal price if this would lead to unaffordable prices in other areas. The lack of definition of 'affordable price' does not make the regulator's task easier. From a competition law aspect, geographic price differentiation remains problematic as it leads to discrimination among customers of the same dominant undertaking. As the *ENTEGA* decision (see above) suggests, there must be special circumstances to justify the discrimination. These may not be limited to the development of new markets as in the *ENTEGA* case. However, the case suggests that price discrimination is subject to stricter controls in a market which is characterized by a near-monopoly than in other markets where customers may easily choose among several suppliers.

Combination of Predatory Pricing and Discrimination

On June 14, 2011 BNetzA concluded an investigation against a subsidiary of Deutsche Post (First Mail) and its parent company DP concerning the use of predatory pricing strategies.[13] As a result of its investigation, BNetzA found that the prices charged by First Mail were substantially below the prices of DP itself and even below the worksharing prices charged by DP to large customers and competitors for presorted letters.

On the basis of its investigation, which included an analysis of the cost structure of First Mail, BNetzA determined that the prices charged by First Mail were predatory and abusively compromised the business opportunities of competitors. In addition, BNetzA found that by offering different prices to different customers First Mail and DP were in violation of the obligation not to discriminate. With respect to DP itself, BNetzA found that DP had violated its obligation not to discriminate by allowing First Mail to offer discriminatory prices. First Mail must change its prices in accordance with the guidelines outlined in the decision, until August 31, 2011. This includes a minimum price floor for worksharing at €0.341/standard letter (the same price as the access price charged by DP), plus costs of additional services such as handling, pick-up and stamping. The price changes must be documented and presented to BNetzA by September 7, 2011.

The decision, which is still subject to appeal, contains a number of important points from a regulatory viewpoint. DP had tried to justify the use of its subsidiary First Mail with the argument that (i) First Mail is not subject to the same regulatory constraints as the incumbent itself, (ii) First Mail operated with a lower cost structure than DP because all general services such as marketing, personal, legal were rendered by DP, (iii) DP had no choice but to create a low-cost entity in order to beat the competition and (iv) the activities of First Mail were limited to high-density areas in Germany.

With respect to the first argument, BNetzA ruled that DP itself together with its subsidiaries must be considered as one and the same economic entity. In this respect the decision is in the same line as the case of *France Télécom* (see above). Therefore, First Mail is subject to the same regulatory constraints as the incumbent itself. The subsidiary First Mail is a 100 percent subsidiary and had run losses ever since it had been taken over by DP. All management functions were delegated to DP, which maintained the liquidity of its subsidiary. Consequently, First Mail was considered to be under the same regulatory and competition law restrictions as the incumbent itself.

The lower-cost argument was rebutted on the basis of the argument that First Mail's costs, as presented by DP, did not include general overhead costs and costs for services rendered by DP itself. BNetzA found that First Mail would be operating at a loss of 30 percent. According to BNetzA, DP itself and its 100 percent subsidiaries must be considered as an economic unit which makes it necessary to allocate the same overhead costs to the subsidiary as to DP itself. BNetzA applied the incremental cost test as outlined by Bradley et al. (2004) which includes the general overhead, the use of the capital employed, and reasonable profit.

DP's argument that the use of a low-cost entity was necessary in order to beat the competition, was rejected, too. The same argument was used unsuccessfully by Wanadoo in the *France Télécom* case. BNetzA found that – just like DP itself – First Mail was bound to the prohibition of predatory pricing as well as to the obligation not to discriminate. Since the prices charged by First Mail did not cover its long-term incremental costs, BNetzA, in applying the 'AKZO Test', looked for, and found, evidence of an intention to destroy the competition.[14] One of those signs was the fact that ever since First Mail was taken over by DP it had been running losses. Furthermore, BNetzA concluded that on the basis of its business model First Mail hardly had any chance to ever recover its losses. Most importantly, however, BNetzA concluded that the establishment and use of a secondary delivery network by DP did not make any economic sense other than to destroy the competition. First Mail had been established in an area of highest density where the competition was particularly intense. Furthermore, DP had argued that its own delivery network suffered because competitors were taking away volumes. BNetzA concluded that the use of First Mail did not generate any synergies but, on the contrary, reduced the productivity of DP's original delivery network. As demonstrated by Geradin and Henry (2010) there is no justification for foreclosure if the measures employed by the incumbent do not improve efficiency sufficiently to avoid harm to consumers.

Finally, with respect to DP's last argument, BNetzA rejected the idea of regional pricing, especially as it was targeted at those areas where the competition was strongest. In the opinion of BNetzA, DP was discriminating among its customers by allowing customers in those areas where First Mail was active to make use of low tariffs, whereas in all other areas customers had to pay DP's higher prices. DP's general argument of lower costs in areas where its subsidiary First Mail was active was not supported by any facts or figures. BNetzA ruled that DP cannot escape its obligation not to discriminate by the use of different subsidiaries. In this regard the ruling follows the *ENTEGA* judgment (see above).

4 CONCLUSIONS

The postal market is still characterized by the strength of one dominant undertaking within each national territory and the comparative weakness of competitors there. The general competition rules applying to pricing strategies of dominant undertakings also apply to postal operators. In particular, courts and regulatory authorities are sensitive with respect to any pricing strategies that have an exclusionary effect on new competition. Any strategy which aims at binding customers by fidelity rebates or other measures with similar effect is completely prohibited. The same applies to bundling strategies by which the dominant undertaking expands its dominant position in one market to a neighboring market.

Pricing strategies discriminating among customers are prohibited unless there is a good reason, such as the creation of new competition in a neighboring market. There may be other good reasons for price differentiation such as cost savings and economies of scale. However, the cases suggest that such reasons must be carefully scrutinized with respect to their potential impact on users and the development of competition in the postal market. The case law seems to imply that postal incumbents are subject to particular constraints in applying different prices except where they reflect saved costs only as, for example, in worksharing. The non-discrimination rule also applies to quantity discounts reflecting economies of scale: quantity rebates must be transparent, not arbitrary, and must reflect cost advantages.

Although there may be an economic argument for a different treatment of original senders with large mail quantities as compared to consolidators as outlined by Crew and Kleindorfer (ch. 1 in this volume), the case history seems to suggest that regulatory concerns prevail in the postal market requiring equal treatment of original senders and consolidators. If consolidation is an integral part of the liberalization process, as the inclusion of consolidation services in the Third Directive suggests, the regulatory authorities must keep that in mind and give room to consolidation. Even if a different treatment may appear acceptable under general competition rules, as pointed out by Eccles (ch. 2 in this volume), postal regulation requires a stricter interpretation of the concept of discrimination.

Another regulatory concern relating to quantity discounts for postal services is the problem of (hidden) fidelity effects if the thresholds are designed so as to protect the dominant market position of the incumbent. If it is an objective of market liberalization and postal regulation to reduce the dominant position of the incumbent, pricing strategies which would normally be acceptable under general competition law may not be acceptable from a regulatory point of view. Therefore, pricing strategies designed to defend its market share are highly questionable if employed by an incumbent.

Regulatory concerns are of particular importance with respect to zonal pricing which may have an adverse impact on the cost of universal service in non-metropolitan areas if cost advantages in one area are needed in order to offset cost disadvantages in other areas.

At the present stage of the development of competition in the market for postal services it is not sufficient to rely on the power of competition and competition rules in order to achieve a well-functioning market for postal services. It is the regulator's task to assist in the development of a functioning market for postal services. Competition law and regulation are not in opposition but, on the contrary, complement each other. In applying competition rules to the postal services market it is necessary to ensure that the regulatory goals are observed as laid down in the Third Directive. The concurrent application of competition rules and regulatory objectives makes postal services a special subject of legal and economic research. Further exploration of this field is required as the market for postal services is about to become an integral part of the larger market for general services.

NOTES

1. See EU Commission, decision of 12.IX.2007, C (2007) 4144, in the matter of State Aid (C 36/2007) Germany Deutsche Post AG (sections 4.1 and 7.4), requiring a reasonable contribution to the fixed costs if a postal network is used for commercial activities of the incumbent.
2. Case C-95/04 P *British Airways*.
3. In the case of travel agents, this kind of rebate encourages the agent not to act in the interests of the principal, the traveling public.
4. Bundesnetzagentur, BK5 99-014-1n, decision of 16 August 2000.
5. Oberster Gerichtshof, 16 Ok 46/05, judgment of 27 February 2007.
6. COMP/37.859, decision of 5 December 2001.
7. C-62/86, judgment of 3 July 1991.
8. C-202/07 P, judgment of April 2009.
9. European Commission, Comp/35.14, decision of 20 March 2001.
10. BGH 23.06.2009 Az. KZR 21/08 and KZR 22/08, WRP 2009, 1402.
11. European Commission, EU 2002/344, decision of 23 October 2001.
12. BK5b-10/013, decision of 15 September 2010.
13. *BNetzA vs. First Mail* (DP), BK5b-11/018, decision of 14 June 2011.
14. ECJ, C-62/86; decision of 3 July 1991 (*AKZO*); ECJ, C-333/94P; decision of 14 November 1996 (*Tetra Pak*).

REFERENCES

Bradley, M., J. Colvin and M. Perkins (2004), 'Testing for anti-competitive behavior in public enterprises', in M. Crew and P.R. Kleindorfer (eds), *Competitive Transformation of the Postal and Delivery Sector*, Boston, MA: Kluwer Academic Publishers.

Geradin, D. and D. Henry (2010), 'Abuse of dominance in the postal sector: the contribution of the Guidance Paper on Art. 82 EC', in M. Crew and P. Kleindorfer (eds), *Heightening Competition in the Postal and Delivery Sector*, Cheltenham, UK and Northampton, MA, USA: Edward Elgar.

Postal Services Commission (2008), *Annual Report 2007/08*, London.

4. Failure to implement the Postal Directive in the EU and EEA: public and private enforcement of state liability*

Alessandra Fratini† and Mariacristina Bottino‡

1 INTRODUCTION

The Postal Directive (Directive 2008/6/EC),[1] as all EU directives, contains a timetable for its implementation: to be transposed into national laws by 31 December 2010 or 31 December 2012 for those member states who have secured a two-year extension.[2] Any failure to do so on time or in a correct manner would lead to infringement proceedings. In January 2011 the European Commission indeed activated the infringement procedure provided for in Arts 258 and 260(3) of the Treaty on the Functioning of the European Union (TFEU)[3] against five of the 16 member states that were required to transpose the Postal Directive into their domestic law by 31 December 2010.[4]

Moving from the current implementation status of the Postal Directive, this chapter will address member states' liability and other possible consequences of a lack of transposition of the Directive in the context of both public and private enforcement. Section 2 reviews the relevant categories of infringement under EU law and then provides an overview of the 'public enforcement' remedies available to the Commission and to fellow member states for infringement of EU law. Section 3 refers to the innovative tool introduced by the Lisbon Treaty under Art. 260(3) TFEU while Section 4 reviews the defenses that a member state can put forward in this respect.

Section 5 further addresses the 'private enforcement' of state liability for failure to implement the Directive. With respect to those provisions that appear to have 'direct effect' under EU law (*in primis*, full market opening), it will discuss the mechanisms available to private parties willing to enforce their rights under the Directive, absent its transposition into national law, and it will briefly survey the applicable case law (for example, *Francovich*[5] and *Brasserie du Pêcheur*[6]).

Since the Postal Directive will be incorporated into the European Economic Area (EEA) Agreement, Section 6 investigates what steps might be taken, should any of the three European Free Trade Association (EFTA) countries exercise the right to veto the Directive under the EEA Agreement, to ensure the proper functioning of the internal postal market. The decision on what measures should be taken, if any, has no precedents to be relied upon and presents an indisputable political dimension. Finally, Section 7 concludes.

† Partner, FratiniVergano, European Lawyers, Brussels.
‡ Attorney, FratiniVergano, European Lawyers, Brussels.

2 THE INFRINGEMENT PROCEEDING

Under Art. 17(1) EU, as 'guardian of the Treaties', the EU Commission is entrusted with the exclusive role to ensure the application of the Treaties and of the measures adopted by the institutions pursuant to them, and to oversee the application of EU law under the control of the Court of Justice of the EU (CJEU). The Commission enforces this role by way of infringement proceedings pursuant to Arts 258 and 260 TFEU,[7] whenever it is of the opinion that a member state is in breach of its obligations under EU law.

Pursuant to Art. 258, first indent, TFEU (*ex* Art. 226 EC), if the Commission considers that there may be an infringement of EU law that warrants the opening of an infringement procedure, it addresses a 'letter of formal notice' to the member state concerned, requesting that it submit its observations by a specified date. This pre-litigation administrative phase aims at enabling the member state to conform voluntarily to the requirements of the Treaty, thus facilitating a settlement of the dispute '*à l'amiable*'.

In the light of the reply or absence of a reply from the member state, the Commission may also decide to address to it a 'reasoned opinion'. This clearly and definitively sets out the reasons why it considers that there has been an infringement of EU law and calls upon the member state to comply within a specified period. The reasoned opinion must provide a coherent and detailed statement, based on the letter of formal notice, of the reasons that have led the Commission to conclude that the member state has failed to fulfill one or more of its obligations under the Treaties or secondary legislation.

If the member state fails to comply with the reasoned opinion, the Commission may decide – and it enjoys a wide discretion – to bring the case before the CJEU.[8] The referral to the CJEU opens the judicial phase of the procedure. Under Art. 260(1) TFEU, if the CJEU finds in its judgment that the member state has failed to fulfill an obligation under EU law, the offending member state is required to take the necessary measures to comply with the judgment.

In the event that, after it has been sentenced for the first time by the CJEU pursuant to Art. 258 TFEU, the offending member state continues not to fulfill its obligations under EU law, the Commission may open a new infringement proceeding, this time pursuant to Art. 260(2) TFEU. This may lead the CJEU to find that the state is not compliant with the previous judgment (it has committed a 'breach on breach') and to impose a lump-sum and/or a penalty payment, as requested by the Commission.[9]

Formally introduced by the Maastricht Treaty in order to ensure the enforcement of judgments against persistent infringements, the procedure pursuant to Art. 260(2) TFEU has been modified by the Lisbon Treaty. The pre-litigation phase has been removed and Art. 260(2), first indent, TFEU no longer requires that the Commission issues a reasoned opinion before the (second) referral to the CJEU. This will in practice speed up the procedure and reduce its average duration.

Each member state is responsible for the implementation of EU law within its own legal system. Three types of infringement can be envisaged with respect to EU directives: (i) failure to adopt implementing measures (and/or to communicate those) before the specified deadline; (ii) failure to implement correctly and/or apply the directive; and (iii) failure to cooperate with the Commission in the transposition. CJEU case law shows that most of the infringement proceedings fall within the first type, that is, lack of implementation of directives, by way of a delay in transposition and notification to the Commission of national implementing measures.[10]

In this case, once the deadline for transposition has expired, the infringement procedure is automatically initiated by the Commission, following a systematic monitoring of notification of national implementing measures. In this respect, the Lisbon Treaty has introduced an important tool which could play the function of a strong deterrent to further infringements and 'correct' the member states' 'bad trend' concerning the widespread problem of late transposition of directives.[11] While maintaining all the procedural steps laid down in Art. 258, first indent, TFEU (letter of formal notice, reasoned opinion, referral to the CJEU), Art. 260(3) TFEU allows the Commission to immediately propose pecuniary sanctions when referring a member state to the CJEU. Previously, this possibility was only available following a judgment of the CJEU.

The second instance concerns a substantive infringement of EU law, as a result of national legislation not compatible with the directive. The Commission may be made aware of national implementing measures that are not in line with the directive concerned either as a result of investigations by its own departments or via complaints. This type of infringement is one the most serious categories of failure to comply with EU law and it attracts priority attention by the Commission due to the significant threats to the uniform application of EU law arising from non-conformity of national legislation to directives.[12]

As to the third type, an infringement procedure may be initiated for failure to facilitate the achievement of the Commission's tasks, in particular where the member state concerned is reluctant to cooperate in infringement proceedings. A manifest and persistent unwillingness to cooperate on the part of a member state would infringe the principle of sincere cooperation under Art. 4(3) TEU.[13]

According to the case law, under this provision member states are under a duty to facilitate the achievement of the Commission's tasks. Member states are required, in particular, to cooperate in good faith, by facilitating the Commission's enquiries pursuant to Art. 258 TFEU and providing all information requested for that purpose.[14] Therefore, the Commission may introduce an infringement procedure if, despite the contacts made, a member state does not forward any information, so as to frustrate the Commission's efforts to uncover the facts vital to a detailed examination of the case.

3 INFRINGEMENT PROCEEDINGS FOR FAILURE TO NOTIFY TRANSPOSITION MEASURES OF THE POSTAL DIRECTIVE

As mentioned above, on 31 December 2010 the period for transposing the Postal Directive came to an end without all of the member states concerned having notified the national measures necessary to comply with it. The Commission thus initiated infringement proceedings against the failing member states, notably Finland, Ireland, Italy, Portugal and the United Kingdom. These infringement procedures fall into the first of the abovementioned categories regarding the enforcement of EU directives.[15] In the letters of formal notice, the Commission referred to the new instrument under Art. 260(3) TFEU, pointing out the lump-sum or penalty payment that it may suggest, should it bring a case before the CJEU on the grounds that the member state concerned had failed to fulfill its obligation to notify measures transposing the Postal Directive.

These are among the first cases in which the new provision is being applied and they are interesting insofar as they will enable the Commission to develop its policy by building upon the 2010 Communication on the implementation of Art. 260(3) TFEU ('the Communication').[16]

The Communication highlights the criteria that should guide the *discretionary power* of the Commission in giving application to the new procedure and, more generally, the proper approach of the Commission when seeking a daily penalty payment or a lump sum from a non-compliant member state.

In line with settled case law, the Communication confirms that the Commission can have recourse to the new possibility provided by Art. 260(3) TFEU 'when it deems appropriate' and as a matter of principle in all cases of failure to fulfill an obligation covered by Art. 260(3): this includes both the total failure to notify any measure to transpose a directive adopted under a legislative procedure and the partial notification of transposition measures.[17]

The Communication also clarifies the method used to determine the amount of the sanctions provided for by Art. 260(3). Overall, the sanctions must be geared to the instrument's essential objective, which is to ensure that EU law is transposed in good time and to prevent a repetition of this type of infringement. Three fundamental criteria will be taken into account by the Commission: the seriousness of the infringement, its duration, and the need to ensure that the sanction itself is a deterrent to further infringements.[18] From the point of view of the effectiveness of the penalty, the Communication insists that the amounts shall be fixed so as to be appropriate in order to ensure the deterrent effect of the sanction. The imposition of purely symbolic penalties would indeed render the new instrument useless.[19]

In the context of Art. 260(3), the date on which the obligation to pay the penalty payments takes effect is the day on which the judgment is handed down: this means that the daily penalty payment runs from the day on which the judgment is delivered by the CJEU.

In addition, unlike the procedure for non-compliance with a previous judgment under Art. 260(2) TFEU, the amount set by the Commission will bind the CJEU, which cannot impose a penalty exceeding the requested amount.[20]

Finally, the Communication outlines the narrow scope for a settlement, which is conditional upon the member state having notified the transposition measures required to put an end to the infringement, provided that the Commission has proposed only a penalty payment and not a lump-sum penalty. In fact, according to the logic underlying the penalties, in cases where a member state rectifies the infringement after the CJEU is seized and before the judgment is delivered, the Commission does not withdraw its action for that reason alone. While the CJEU cannot impose a penalty payment for continuing infringement because such a decision has lost its purpose, it can nevertheless impose a lump-sum payment penalizing the duration of the infringement up to the time the situation was rectified, because this aspect of the case has not lost its purpose.[21]

It follows that, once the Commission has initiated infringement proceedings and the case is referred to the CJEU, a member state will have little room to escape financial sanctions. Unless it notifies the transposition measures required to put the infringement to an end, it will incur an obligation to pay a penalty sanction.

At the time of writing (in July 2011), the procedures initiated against Finland and Italy were to be closed following the notification of the implementing measures adopted by the Finnish and Italian authorities, respectively, on 9 and 23 March 2011.[22] The proceedings concerning Ireland, Portugal and the United Kingdom are still ongoing.

A brief overview of the CJEU case law shows that member states involved in the infringement proceedings have few arguments to rely upon in order to excuse their failure to notify the relevant implementing measures.

4 MEMBER STATES' DEFENSES

The case law on member states' failure to implement directives offers an interesting overview of the variety of defensive arguments that member states involved in infringement procedures usually put forward to justify their conduct.

Arguments relying on technical, financial or administrative difficulties are systematically rejected by the CJEU.[23] The latter has also rejected arguments that justified the lack of cooperation by referring to provisions, practices or circumstances related to the member states' own internal legal systems, such as the dissolution of a national assembly or an overloaded parliamentary timetable.[24]

Indeed, it is a 'fundamental principle' constantly repeated by consolidated case law that a member state may not plead situations relating to its internal legal order in order to justify a failure to comply with its obligations under EU law.[25] In particular, a member state cannot rely on difficulties caused by the federal nature of its constitutional order in order to excuse a failure to cooperate with the Commission.[26] Similarly, the fact that the fulfillment of a particular EU law obligation is the responsibility of a semi-autonomous local body, rather than that of the central state administration, does not exonerate a member state from its obligations towards the EU.[27]

Furthermore, neither the shortness of the period of transposition,[28] nor the direct effect of the directives is an admissible argument to justify failure to transpose.[29] The narrow margin that member states are granted in order to excuse a failure to implement a directive also applies to instances of *force majeure*. While the CJEU appeared willing to accept the argument of *force majeure* as an excuse for failing to implement a directive, the notion of *force majeure* is so narrowly circumscribed, that no member state has ever successfully excused an infringement under this argument.[30]

Also the argument of reciprocity, which is typical of international law does not play any role in EU law. Any default on the part of other member states in performing obligations imposed by EU law, such as a delay in transposing a directive, may not be invoked by a member state in order to justify its own, even temporary, failure to perform its obligations. The rationale behind this reasoning is the need for a uniform application of EU law. As clarified by the CJEU, the EU treaties did not merely create reciprocal obligations between the various subjects to whom the treaties apply, but also established a new legal order which governs the powers, rights and duties of the said subjects, as well as the procedures necessary for the purposes of having any infringement declared and punished.[31] Similarly, and for the same reasons, the CJEU never considered as an acceptable member state's defense an argument based on the inactivity of the EU institutions.[32]

Finally, a controversial defense is based on the invalidity of the EU measure to be implemented. Rejected in principle by the CJEU,[33] this argument is admitted 'only if the measure at issue contained such particularly serious and manifest defects that it could be deemed non-existent'.[34]

In the light of this brief overview, it may reasonably be concluded that the interested member states have limited chances to escape the judicial phase of the infringement proceedings initiated against them because of their failure to transpose the Postal Directive.

In fact, the only solution for the member states concerned is to accelerate the adoption of transposition measures, at the latest, within the deadline fixed by the Commission's reasoned opinion. In doing so, the member states may also avoid the risk of incurring damages due to claims brought in national courts by individuals who have suffered losses as a result of a failure to transpose the Postal Directive. In fact, since *Francovitch*,[35] the CJEU asserted the possibility for an individual to seek reparation of damages suffered as a result of an infringement of EU law by a member state.[36]

5 REMEDIES OF PRIVATE ENFORCEMENT: DIRECT EFFECT OF THE POSTAL DIRECTIVE AND ACTION FOR DAMAGES

Not envisaged in the treaties, the notion of direct effect was developed by the CJEU to allow individuals to rely directly on EU law before their national courts. The CJEU devised the theory of direct effect for the first time in *Van Gend & Loos*,[37] then extended it to the rights conferred by directives on individuals in *Van Duyn*[38] and later systematized this principle further in *Ratti*[39] and *Becker*.[40]

The CJEU wisely placed the emphasis on the function of a directive and its binding nature and held that, in order for direct effect to be relied on, a directive must be unconditional and sufficiently precise, no national measures must have been adopted within the prescribed period, or the national legislation must be incompatible as a result of defective or inadequate transposition.[41] Accordingly, individuals are able to support their rights, while the effectiveness of EU law is protected and not impaired by any failure to implement a directive, or by the incorrect transposition of a directive.[42]

As a directive is binding in nature for the member states, individuals may only claim the rights conferred by directives against the state, or an emanation of the state, and not against other individuals. This is defined as the 'vertical' direct effect (that is, *vis-à-vis* the state) of directives[43] and prevents individuals from claiming rights under the directive against other private actors (that is, the 'horizontal' direct effect).

However, the CJEU developed some expedients in order to neutralize as far as possible the negative consequences arising from the limited direct effect of a directive. It has primarily admitted a broad interpretation of the doctrine of direct effect against state action, clarifying that a directive may be relied on against all organs of the administration, including decentralized and public authorities, regardless of the capacity in which these are acting.[44] Another 'antidote' to the ban on horizontal enforcement of the direct effect of directives is the principle of consistent interpretation, that is, the obligation for national judges to interpret a national law consistently with the provision of directives. Where the principle of consistent interpretation does not help, the last resort is a claim for damages against the defaulting member state.

Regarding the Postal Directive, it cannot be ruled out that some of its provisions have direct effect. In particular, Art. 7, which abolishes the so-called 'reserved area', appears to meet all the conditions required for direct effect. On the one hand, by imposing that 'member states shall not grant or maintain in force exclusive or special rights for the establishment and provision of postal services', it is sufficiently clear and precise.[45] On the other hand, the obligation imposed on member states to remove any special or exclusive right is not subject to any condition.

While there is no doubt as to the direct effect of Art. 7 (that is, there is *de iure* no more reserved area even in the absence of transposition measures), this provision shall be read in conjunction with Art. 9(2) of the Postal Directive. The latter provision confers upon member states the *faculty* to introduce authorization procedures, including individual licences, to the extent necessary in order to guarantee compliance with the essential requirements, and to ensure the provision of the universal service. Art. 9(2) states that authorizations may: (i) be made subject to universal service obligations; (ii) if *necessary and justified*, impose requirements concerning the quality, availability and performance of the relevant services; and (iii) *where appropriate*, be subject to an obligation to (a) make a financial contribution to the sharing mechanisms referred to in Art. 7(3)(b); (b) be subject to an obligation to make a financial contribution to the national regulatory authority's operational costs; and (c) be made subject to or impose an obligation to respect working conditions laid down by national legislation.[46]

If, on one hand, the wording of Art. 9(2) seems to be clear and precise, on the other, it is far from being unconditional insofar as the implementation of the provision is subject to the member states' discretionary power to introduce authorization procedures. It follows that while Art. 7 of the Postal Directive can be relied upon against the unfulfilling member state to support the right to provide postal services that under national law still fall within the abolished reserved area, an interested operator will still need to go successfully through the authorization procedure before being able to exercise its right.[47]

Interested parties can still bring legal proceedings against the member state in order to obtain reparations of their rights according to the case law concerning state liability.

Formulated for the first time in *Francovich*[48] as *inherent* in the system of the treaties,[49] the principle whereby a state must be liable for loss and damage caused to individuals as a result of breaches of EU law for which the state can be held responsible is recognized as an essential requirement in order to ensure the full effectiveness of EU law and the protection of the rights which it grants individuals.[50] The right to obtain redress from the member state is recognized by the CJEU as essential where the full effectiveness of EU rules are subject to prior action on the part of the state and where, consequently, in the absence of such action, individuals cannot enforce the rights conferred upon them by EU law before the national courts.

Under this principle, for the state liability to apply three conditions shall be met, namely: the infringed provisions vest individuals with rights, the breach is sufficiently serious and there is a direct causal link between the breach of the law and the loss sustained.[51]

In the case of the Postal Directive, it appears that all the conditions under which state liability may be claimed could easily be met. Since its earlier case law, the CJEU has admitted a presumption of existence of a serious breach where a member state has failed to achieve a result sought by a directive within the period it lays down.[52] To this purpose, a mere omission is sufficient to establish liability, due to the fact that neither a fault nor negligence on the part of the organ of the state to which the infringement is attributable is required for engaging its liability.

Therefore, it is reasonable that the assessment of liability in such a case shall not raise particular doubts for the competent national court. In addition, the task of the latter should be greatly facilitated where the breach of EU law has already been established by the CJEU at the end of the procedure discussed above. Although the infringement proceedings is not a necessary prerequisite to action for damages, the CJEU decision that, at the end of such a procedure, finds a member state in breach of EU law makes it easier to assess the state liability.

In light of the foregoing, failure to implement the Postal Directive may be considered a breach *sufficiently serious*, which entails the grant of rights to individuals who have suffered losses and damages. Lack of implementation clearly deprives interested operators of the right to fully access the internal market of postal services, ultimately depriving individuals of the benefits of a dynamic and open postal market.

This situation appears to justify the actions for damages to obtain reparations according to the case law concerning state liability. The actual reparation for damages is, however, subject to national law. As clarified by an established case law,[53] since EU law imposes no specific criteria for the various heads of damage, it is for the national court to rule on those heads of damage in accordance with the domestic law which it applies, subject to the principles of equivalence and effectiveness laid down in the *Rewe* and *Comet* case law.[54]

6 THE IMPLEMENTATION OF THE POSTAL DIRECTIVE IN THE EEA

The Postal Directive is relevant for the EFTA countries which are part of the EEA, that is, Iceland, Liechtenstein and Norway (hereinafter 'EEA EFTA states'). Pursuant to the EEA Agreement, the EEA EFTA states participate in the internal market on the basis of their application of the relevant *acquis*. In particular, whenever the EU adopts or amends an act related to the internal market, the contracting parties assess its EEA relevance with a view to amending the applicable Annex to the EEA Agreement, in order to bring the Agreement as close as possible to EU legislation. This permits the harmonious development of law in the EEA, that is, both within the EU and the EEA EFTA states.

The EEA Agreement does not transfer any legislative powers from any of the contracting parties and therefore does not impose any direct effect of EU legislation on the EEA EFTA states. The adoption of EEA rules thus takes place in the EEA institutions established by the Agreement and the EEA EFTA states then implement the EEA rules at the national level.

More specifically, whenever one legal act (for what matters here, a directive) is amended in the EU or a new one is adopted, a corresponding amendment should be made to the relevant annex of the EEA Agreement. Formally, such a change occurs in that the EEA Joint Committee (JC)[55] decides to insert a reference to the new/amended act in the relevant annex to the EEA Agreement.

Therefore, similarly to any EU legislative act, the Postal Directive shall be incorporated into the EEA Agreement[56] further to a decision made by the JC. Only such a decision triggers the obligation for EEA EFTA states to transpose the directive into national law by the set time limit, even if it is left to each EEA state to choose the form and the method of implementation.

Art. 102 of the EEA Agreement lays down the general principles governing the adoption and entry into force of necessary amendments of the Agreement. In order to guarantee legal security and the homogeneity of the EEA, the JC is to take a decision concerning an amendment of an annex as closely as possible to the adoption by the EU of the corresponding new EU legislation.

According to Art. 102, the JC shall, in particular, make every effort to find a mutually acceptable solution. If an agreement on an amendment of an annex to the EEA Agreement cannot be reached, the JC shall examine all further possibilities to maintain the good functioning of the EEA Agreement and take any decision necessary to this effect, including the possibility to take notice of the equivalence of legislation. Such a decision shall be taken at the latest at the expiry of a period of six months from the date of referral to the JC by the EU Council or, if that date is later, on the date of entry into force of the corresponding EU legislation.

The decision inside the JC is a result of an agreement between the EU on the one hand and the EEA EFTA states, 'speaking with one voice', on the other. It is the unanimity requirement that allows each of the EEA EFTA States to have a 'reservation' right (commonly referred to as a 'veto') on any new EU act.

In this regard, Art. 102 provides that if, at the end of a time limit of six months, the Contracting Parties fail to reach an agreement in the JC to amend an annex, the 'affected part is regarded as provisionally suspended', unless the JC takes a decision to the contrary. Such a suspension shall take effect up to six months after the end of the period referred before, but in no event earlier than the date on which the corresponding EU act is implemented in the EU.[57]

The practical consequences of the provisional suspension should be discussed in the JC, which is charged with finding any possible solution in order to limit the potential negative effects linked to it. However, in no event can the suspension affect the rights and obligations which individuals and economic operators have already acquired under the EEA Agreement. This is made clear by Art. 102(6) and it is further specified by the final act of the Agreed Minutes of the Negotiations. Finally, the Contracting Parties shall, as appropriate, decide on the adjustments necessary due to the suspension.

The right of reservation has not been used to date.[58] Should any of the EEA EFTA states disagree with the incorporation of the Postal Directive into the EEA Agreement, this would open a number of questions the reply to which, while being legal in nature, has an inevitable political dimension. The issue is far from being theoretical, as it is likely that Norway will exercise the reservation right and oppose the incorporation of the Postal Directive into the EEA Agreement.[59]

As to the consequences of the exercise of the reservation right, the absence of any precedent to be relied upon leaves many of the issues open to interpretation. While a political assessment falls outside the scope of this chapter, we shall limit our review to the legal implications of such an occurrence.

To begin with, from a legal point of view, it is clear that, being expressly provided by the EEA Agreement,[60] the exercise of the reservation right does not constitute in itself a violation of the EEA Agreement. However, it is also apparent that such an exercise would produce, as a result, a deviation from one of the main objectives of the EEA Agreement, namely the dynamic consistency between the rules in the EU and the EEA.

It is worth noting at the outset that any decision to put the reservation clause into effect will be taken by the EEA EFTA states 'speaking with one voice'. This means that the consequences of a (possible) Norwegian reservation[61] will also apply to the other EEA EFTA states, notably Liechtenstein and Iceland.

Under Art. 102(5) of the EEA Agreement, if the JC has not taken a decision on an amendment of an annex, 'the affected part of the Annex is regarded as provisionally suspended'. Despite the apparently uncomplicated wording, this provision raises some questions in connection with the scope and the timing of the suspension to be applied.

As for the scope, the question arises as to which 'part' of Annex XI shall be regarded as being 'affected' under Art. 102(5) of the EEA Agreement. The previous Postal Directives (Directives 97/67/EC and 2002/39/EC) are currently listed in the 'Postal Services' section of Annex XI, named 'Electronic communication, audiovisual services and information society' and are actually the only two acts included therein.

Leaving aside the formalistic discussion on whether 'part of the Annex' refers to a section or to individual acts therein, it is reasonable to argue that there shall be a concrete assessment of the parts that are *directly* affected. In this respect, it can be convincingly maintained that those parts of the Annex that have been amended by the Postal Directive are 'affected' by it (that is, Directives 97/67/EC and 2002/39/EC). While some commentators speculated that the exercise of the reservation right would imply the further suspension of the entire Annex XI,[62] such an interpretation does not appear to be persuasive. In fact, having the reservation clause an exceptional character, the corresponding provision of Art. 102 shall be interpreted narrowly. In other words, it seems appropriate to assume that only those parts of the Annex that are *directly* affected may be suspended, not being sufficient instead that a part of the Annex is *indirectly* affected. For the same reason, it is questionable that the exercise of the reservation right would involve and 'freeze' even Annexes VIII and XIV, which concern the 'Right of establishment' and 'Competition', respectively, as announced in the media.[63]

As to the timing, the relevant question concerns the effective date from which any suspension would start to run. According to Art. 102(4) and (5), as mentioned above, the affected part of Annex XI should be suspended 12 months after the referral to the JC but in no event earlier than the date on which the Postal Directive is implemented in the EU.

At the time of writing, it appears that the Postal Directive has so far not been referred to the JC, thus the 12-month deadline has not yet commenced. As regards the directive's implementation date, the Postal Directive provides for two implementation deadlines (notably, 31 December 2010 under Art. 2(1) and 31 December 2012 under Art. 3). Should the latest one be deemed relevant, on the ground that the directive can be considered implemented only when the last EU member state has actually transposed it, the exercise of the reservation clause could trigger a situation of uncertainty which could last for a long time. In addition, the notion of implementation may be interpreted in the sense of complete and correct implementation: this would mean that, for the Postal Directive to be 'implemented' in the EU, any infringement proceedings for lack of – or incorrect – transposition shall be successfully terminated.

It is true that, in order to understand the real extent of the reservation clause, the EU and the EEA EFTA states may request the CJEU to give an interpretation of Art. 102

as provided by Art. 111(3). According to the latter, in fact, if a dispute regarding the interpretation of the EEA Agreement has not been settled within three months after it has been brought before the JC, the Contracting Parties can agree to request the CJEU to give a ruling on interpretation.

However, as observed by some authors,[64] 'while the ruling by the European judges would be binding as to its legal interpretation, it would leave the Contracting Parties free to decide upon the political conclusion to be drawn thereof'. It will thus remain up to both parties (the EEA states on the one hand and the EU on the other) to find a suitable compromise in order to overcome the impasse created by a Norwegian reservation and to prevent a confusion of practical effects that such situation will create.

Indeed, it is difficult to foresee the impact of the suspension of Annex XI and predict the specific content of the substantial rules that would apply, should Norway 'veto' the Postal Directive. What does the suspension mean in practice? Does it imply a suspension of the previous Postal Directives and therefore the 're-emerging' of pre-liberalization national rules, or does it simply mean that the entry of the Postal Directive into Annex XI is provisionally suspended, leaving the previous legislative framework unchanged? Will the EU member states apply the reciprocity clause under Art. 3(3) of the Directive and refuse to grant (or withdraw, where they have been granted already) authorizations for services within the abolished reserved area to Norwegian postal operators (and their subsidiaries) that still benefit from the reserved area?[65]

The answer to these interrogatives will come to light following the outcome of discussions in the JC and at a higher political level. In any case, it is worth recalling that, with a view to limiting pathological effects related to the right of reservation, the Contracting Parties have drawn it as a tool having an exceptional and temporary character.[66]

7 CONCLUSION

It is the member states' responsibility to bring into force the laws, regulations and administrative provisions necessary to comply with the Postal Directive within the set deadline. Failure to do so will result in infringement proceedings being initiated, be it for lack of notification, non-conform transposition or lack of cooperation. In the case of lack of notification, the new tool introduced under Art. 260(3) TFEU allows the Commission to request penalty sanctions.

Answering a parliamentary question on postal services,[67] the Commissioner for the Internal Market recently confirmed the intention of the Commission to pursue the implementation of the Postal Directive. This intention is validated by the infringement proceedings initiated by the Commission against the member states that failed to notify national implementing measures, and by the concrete possibility that proceedings for non-correct implementation and lack of cooperation be initiated in the future.

The above overview showed that lack of transposition of the Postal Directive may entail further consequences for the member state concerned in the context of private enforcement, including direct effect and damages.

The state's responsibility for lack of transposition bears wider significance in the context of the implementation of the Postal Directive in the EEA, where the exercise of the reservation right by any of the three EEA EFTA states may affect the maintenance of the internal postal market within the EEA and create complex political consequences in the relation between the EU and the EEA EFTA member states.

NOTES

* Alessandra Fratini is the author of sections 1, 3, 6 and 7. Mariacristina Bottino is the author of sections 2, 4 and 5.

1. Directive 2008/06/EC of the European Parliament and of the Council of 20 February 2008 amending Directive 97/67/EC with regard to the full accomplishment of the internal market of Community postal services, OJ L 52, 27.2.2008, p. 3.
2. According to Art. 3 of the Postal Directive, by derogation to Art. 2, the following member states may postpone the implementation of the Directive until 31 December 2012: Czech Republic, Greece, Cyprus, Latvia, Lithuania, Luxembourg, Hungary, Malta, Poland, Romania and Slovakia.
3. See Art. 260 TFEU, as modified after the entry into force of the Lisbon Treaty and the recent Commission Communication concerning the Implementation of Art. 260(3) TFEU of 11 November 2010, OJ C 12, 15.1.2011, p. 1.
4. Notably Finland, Ireland, Italy, Portugal and the United Kingdom. For an overview of infringement proceedings opened against member states, see http://ec.europa.eu/eu_law/eulaw/decisions/dec_20110126.htm#.
5. Joined cases C-6/90 and C-9/90, *Francovich*, [1991] ECR I-5357.
6. Joined cases C-46/93 and C-48/93, *Brasserie du Pêcheur*, [1996] ECR I-1029.
7. The right to initiate an action for failure to fulfill obligations is not an exclusive prerogative of the Commission. A member state may also bring an action against another member state for an alleged infringement of an obligation under the treaties. This initiative is subject to a preventive request to the Commission, who must deliver an opinion within three months.
8. It is established case law that the Commission has discretionary power in relation to infringements and is the sole judge of when to bring proceedings concerning the application of EU law. See, *ex multis*, Case C-317/92, *Commission v Germany*, [1994] ECR I-2039; Case C-422/92, *Commission v Germany*, [1995] ECR I-1097.
9. Art. 260(2), second indent, TFEU.
10. The last report from the Commission on monitoring the application of the EU law (2009), COM (2010) 538 confirms that late transposition continues to constitute a widespread, systematic problem undermining the attainment of the EU's objectives.
11. The new tool should contribute to reducing the 51 percent average of the late notification of transposition measures which, according to the 27th annual report on monitoring the application of EU law (2009), was registered in 2009.
12. The Commission Communication, 'Better monitoring of the application of Community Law' (COM (2002) 725 final/4), refers to this type of infringement as one of the most serious categories of failure to comply with EU law. The Communication also mentions infringements that undermine the foundations of the rule of law and infringements that undermine the smooth functioning of the Community legal system.
13. For an example of an infringement procedure under Art. 4(3) TEU (formerly Art. 10 EC and previously Art. 5 EEC), see Case C-82/03, *Commission v Italy*, [2004] ECR I-6635.
14. In this perspective see, *inter alia*, Case C-478/01, *Commission v Luxembourg*, [2003] ECR I-2351, para. 24.
15. Although to date the Commission has initiated only infringement proceeding for failure to notify transposition measures of the Postal Directive, this does not exclude the possibility that the Commission initiates in the future the infringement proceedings for incorrect implementation.
16. Commission, Communication 'Implementation of Art. 260(3) of the Treaty', OJ C 12, 15.1.2011, p. 1.
17. According to Communication (point 19), partial notification occurs either where the transposition measures notified do not cover the whole territory of the member state or where the notification is incomplete with respect to the transposition measures corresponding to a part of the directive.
18. See points 12–14 and 23–28 of the Communication.
19. See point 15 of the Communication.
20. According to the wording of Art. 260(3), the Court retains the discretional power to dismiss a Commission proposal regarding sanctions. Indeed, '[i]f the Court finds that the member state concerned has not complied with its judgment it may impose a lump sum or penalty payment on the member state concerned *not exceeding the amount specified by the Commission*' (italics added).
21. See point 11 of the 2005 Communication.

22. The Commission closed the infringement proceedings initiated against Italy on 16 June 2011.
23. See, for example, Case C-42/89, *Commission v Belgium*, [1990] ECR I-2821.
24. See Case 100/77, *Commission v Italy*, [1978] ECR 175, para. 9.
25. See, in this regard, Case C-274/98, *Commission v Spain*, [2000] ECR I-2823, paras 19 and 20; Case C-236/99, *Commission v Belgium*, [2000] ECR I-5657, para. 23.
26. See Case C-22/02, *Commission v Italy*, [2003] ECR I-9011, para. 9.
27. The CJEU has consistently held that 'the fact that a member state has conferred on its regions the responsibility for giving effect to directives cannot have any bearing on the application of Art. [258 TFEU]'. In fact, '[w]hile each member state may freely allocate internal legislative powers as it sees fit, the fact remains that it alone is responsible towards the Community under Art. [258 TFEU] for compliance with obligations arising under [EU] law'. See, to that effect, *inter alia*, Case C-298/97, *Commission v Spain*, [1998] ECR I-3301, paras 13 and 14; Case C-326/97, *Commission v Belgium*, [1998] ECR I-6107, paras 6 and 7; Case C-87/02, *Commission v Italy*, [2004] ECR I-5975.
28. See Case C-8/70, *Commission v Italy*, [1970] ECR 961, para. 8.
29. See Case C-177/04, *Commission v France*, [2006] ECR I-02461 and Case 102/79, *Commission v Belgium*, [1980] ECR 1473.
30. Case 101/84, *Commission v Italy*, [1985] ECR 2629.
31. See Case 52/75, *Commission v Italy*, [1946] ECR 277, para. 11 and Case 232/78, *Commission v France* [1979] ECR 2729.
32. See Case 90/63 and 91/63, *Commission v Luxembourg and Belgium*, [1964] ECR 1217.
33. See Case 226/87, *Commission v Greece*, [1988] ECR, 3611, para. 14.
34. See ibid., para. 16.
35. Joined cases C-6/90 and C-9/90, *Francovich* (cited above, n. 5).
36. In the case of directives this possibility was recognized as a compensation for lack of transposition of directives not having direct effect.
37. Case 26/62, *Van Gend & Loos*, [1963] ECR 1.
38. Case 41/74, *Van Duyn*, [1974] ECR 1337.
39. Case 148/78, *Ratti*, [1979] ECR 1629.
40. Case 8/81, *Becker*, [1982] ECR 53.
41. See also Case C-266/07, *Flughafen*, [2008] ECR I-5999, para. 23; and Case C-138/07, *Cobelfret*, [2009] ECR I-731, para. 58.
42. See the Opinion of Advocate General Ruiz-Jarabo Colomer in joined cases C-152/07, C-153/07 and C-154/07, *Arcor*, [2008] ECR I-5959.
43. Case 152/84, *Marshall I*, [1986] ECR 723, para. 47.
44. See Case C-356/05, *Alaine Farrell*, [2007] ECR I-3067.
45. See Art. 7(1), first statement, of the Postal Directive.
46. See Art. 9(2) of the Postal Directive.
47. One may draw the same conclusion about Art. 7(3) concerning financial mechanisms to compensate the net costs of universal service obligations.
48. Joined cases C-6/90 and C-9/90, *Francovich* (cited above, n. 5).
49. Ibid., para. 35.
50. Ibid., para. 33, where the CJEU ruled that the full effectiveness of EU law would be impaired and the protection of the rights which it grants would be weakened if individuals were unable to obtain redress when their rights are infringed by a breach of EU law for which a member state can be held responsible.
51. Such conditions are considered exhaustive by the CJEU. See joined cases C-6/90 and C-9/90, *Francovich* (cited above, n.5); joined cases C-46/93 and C-48/93, *Brasserie du Pêcheur*, [1996] ECR I-1029; case C-224/01, *Köbler*, [2003] ECR I-10239, para. 51.
52. See joined cases C-178/94, C-179/94, C-188/94, C-189/94 and C-190/94, *Dillenkofer*, [1996] ECR I-484.
53. See joined cases C-46/93 and C-48/93, *Brasserie du Pêcheur* (cited above, n. 51), paras 83–90.
54. Respectively, Case 33/76, *Rewe*, [1976] ECR 1989 and Case 45/76, *Comet*, [1976] ECR 2043.
55. The EEA JC is responsible for the management of the EEA Agreement and typically meets seven to eight times a year.
56. See Art. 7(b) of the EEA Agreement, which states that an act corresponding to an [EU] directive shall leave to the authorities of the Contracting Parties the choice of form and method of implementation.
57. See Art. 102(5) of the EEA Agreement.
58. The use of the reservation right by Norway has been demanded on several occasions (in connection with the directives on food additives, bio-patents, the gas market and, most recently, data retention).
59. Following the Norwegian Labour Party's vote, at their 63rd national convention in early April 2011, all the parties in the current government coalition support Norway's exercise of the reservation right in connection with the Postal Directive (see, for instance: http://eurodale.eu/2011/04/11/an-era-ends-for-the-efta-and-the-eea/).

60. In this respect see Norberg et al. (1993, p. 144).
61. At the time of writing (in July 2011), the Norwegian government was yet to formally communicate its position on the reservation clause.
62. See, for example: http://eurodale.eu/2011/04/11/an-era-ends-for-the-efta-and-the-eea/.
63. See, for instance, the article available at: http://eurodale.eu/2011/04/11/an-era-ends-for-the-efta-and-the-eea/.
64. Norberg (1992, p. 1194).
65. Under Art. 3(3) of the Postal Directive, 'member states that abolish their reserved area by 31 December 2012 may, between 1 January 2011 and 31 December 2012, refuse to grant the authorisation provided for in Art. 9(2) of Directive 97/67/EC for services within the abolished reserved area in question to postal operators providing services within the scope of the universal service, as well as companies controlled by them, which are granted a reserved area in another member state'.
66. However, the suspension remains in effect until the question loses its relevance, for example, because the EEA accepts the act or the EU accepts the necessary changes or the parties agree to bring it to closure.
67. See answer to question No. 1823/2011 on the European Parliament's website at: http://www.europarl.europa.eu/sides/getDoc.do?pubRef=-//EP//TEXT+WQ+E-2011-001283+0+DOC+XML+V0//EN&language=EN.

BIBLIOGRAPHY

Amalfitano, Chiara (2007), 'I procedimenti di "doppia condanna" a carico degli Stati membri dell'Unione europea: la prassi giurisprudenziale', *Diritto dell'Unione europea*, **12** (4), 865–72.

Condinanzi, Massimo and Roberto Mastroianni (2009), *Il Contenzioso dell'Unione europea*, Turin: Giappichelli.

Craig, Paul (2009), 'The legal effect of directives: policy, rules and exceptions', *European Law Review*, **34** (3), 349–77.

Emerson Michael, Marius Vahl and Stephen Woolcock (2002), *Navigating by the Stars: Norway, the European Economic Area and the European Union*, Brussels: Centre for European Policy Studies.

Kilbey, Ian (2010), 'The interpretation of Article 260 TFUE (ex 228 EC)', *European Law Review*, **35** (3), 370–86.

Lenaerts, Koen and Piet Van Nuffel (2011), *European Union Law*, London: Sweet & Maxwell.

Naalsund, Thomas G. (2010) 'Oversikt over mulige konsekvenser av norsk reservasjon mot eus tredje postdirective', available at: http://www.regjeringen.no/upload/SD/Vedlegg/Post/Kluge_utredning_reservasjonsrett.pdf (accessed 7 July 2011).

Norberg, Sven (1992), 'The Agreement on a European Economic Area', *Common Market Law Review*, **29** (6), 1194–8.

Norberg, Sven, Karin Hökborg, Martin Eliasson and Lucien Dedichen (1993), *EEA Law: A Commentary on the EEA Agreement*, Stockholm: Fritzes.

Prete, Luca and Ben Smulders (2010), 'The coming of age of infringement proceedings', *Common Market Law Review*, **47** (1), 9–61.

Tridimas, Takis (1994), 'Horizontal effect of directives: a missed opportunity', *European Law Review*, **19**, 621–36.

5. Forecasting letter volumes: augmenting econometric baseline projections[1]

Vance L. Martin[†], Chris Paterson[‡] and Jessie Xiaokang Wang[§]

1 INTRODUCTION

In recent times postal authorities around the world have had to contend with two major elements of uncertainty, each of which have created substantial difficulties in understanding and forecasting letter volumes. The first stems from the threats inherently residing within the postal industry itself that give rise to an increasingly dynamic landscape. These threats include those presented by substitution, rationalization, consolidation and competition. A second area of uncertainty has arisen from the fact that domestic economies operating within a more integrated world economy are becoming increasingly susceptible to contagion effects as substantial shocks in one country are being transmitted to other economic systems with greater effect than ever before. These shocks then impact upon domestic postal industries via a number of channels. Income effects suppressing domestic demand act to reduce the number of transactions and hence soften bill payment and presentment mail growth. Additionally, as company profits begin to fall so too does the availability for discretionary spending to stimulate promotional mailings. Certainly, in a climate where business confidence is low, advertisers will also be conscious of diminishing response rates to a direct mail campaign. Confounding the problem for the postal industry further is an acknowledgement that these twin dangers are not mutually exclusive. As the level of economic activity begins to decline as a result of the transmission of external shocks and the economic climate begins to deteriorate, behavioral shifts surrounding senders tend to gain further momentum. In darker times these agents develop a greater propensity to rationalize their cost base and in doing so look towards alternatives to the traditional letter as a mechanism for achieving their own objectives. Therefore, they are then more likely to engage actively in substitution, rationalization and consolidation practices.

These dynamics characterizing the landscape of the industry can create enormous difficulties when attempting to model and develop a set of *ex ante* letter volume forecasts. This chapter provides a framework to best deal with these inherent dynamics and utilizes the Australian postal industry as a salient example. Many studies in this field have long acknowledged the futility of attempting to model aggregate mail volumes without

[†] University of Melbourne.
[‡] Director, Diversified Specifics, Australia.
[§] University of Melbourne.

first delving into the characteristics underlying the different types of mail. Indeed, difficulties in aggregating the drivers themselves have been discussed more recently by Nikali (2011) relating to any attempt to develop a holistic measure of substitution. The need for delineation across different letter volume segments then suggests that the process of accurately forecasting segmented small letter volumes should crucially involve two stages. First, the establishment of an econometric baseline incorporating observed and dynamic historical associations sets a sound foundation for the forecasts. This chapter utilizes vector error correction modeling (VECM) techniques to generate such a baseline. The VECM procedure provides a general and flexible framework in which to capture the dynamics of letter volume fluctuations. The key feature underpinning this class of models is that it decomposes segmented letter volumes into their long- and short-run components.

For over a decade now however, it has become increasingly apparent that associations governing future letter volume fluctuations are unlikely to mirror empirical movements fully across the forecast period as there may be a number of one-off events and emerging trends that will also impact upon actual volumes. That is, the combined effects of substitution, consolidation and rationalization are likely to place significant downward pressures on future letter volume growth rates yet are difficult to isolate and quantify within an econometric framework using historical data given their recent emergence. Indeed, obtaining a set of tractable data points on such trends can also be problematic. Therefore, the second stage in generating segmented *ex ante* letter volume baseline forecasts requires an augmentation of the econometric result with further statistically sound internal and market-based intelligence. It is the combination of these two components to the methodological approach that ensures the practical applicability of the *ex ante* forecasts.

The forecast augmentation methodology presented in this chapter relates to the recent work by Fève et al. (2010), where a Bayesian approach using a Kalman filter is adopted to identify the relative importance of informational updates. To demonstrate the approach, forecasts of letter volumes in Australia are augmented in the presence of the recent Federal election by using updated information from Australia Post that provides a more detailed breakdown of letter volumes over the sample period. Alternatives for treating significant short-run shocks such as the global financial crisis are also discussed in an attempt to isolate whether or not these impacts result in a one-off structural shift in demand as against acting as a catalyst for an accelerated decline in letter volumes. If the latter scenario is indeed relevant this will require further observations to assess fully, however the question nonetheless still remains very relevant as the behavioral mindset of senders may alter in the periods during and after the occurrence of such a shock. Any intelligence to this effect should necessarily be incorporated within the final set of *ex ante* forecasts either econometrically or via the process of augmentation.

This chapter proceeds as follows. The proposed line of research is placed in the context of previous studies in Section 2. In Section 3 the methodological framework used to generate the baseline econometric model and forecasts is discussed. This framework is applied to small letter volumes in Australia in Section 4, with Section 5 containing some brief concluding remarks.

2 PREVIOUS STUDIES

There is a widespread use of econometric techniques for forecasting purposes by national postal operators (NPOs) and understanding their limitations is a crucial component when attempting to generate such letter volume projections. For a comprehensive review of various studies, see Robinson (2006), and for a more general discussion of econometric forecasting methods, see Hendry and Ericsson (2001). Fève et al. (2010) acknowledge that significant changes in the external environment must be attended to by some form of *ex post* parameter adjustment based upon a posterior distribution that evolves as new information becomes available. Such information, they suggest may emanate from stated preference studies, internal institutional knowledge and cross-country research comparisons. Their process involves the continual updating of econometric models as new volume data become available, and melding the model outcomes with findings from relevant alternative market-based information sources.

It is important at this stage to emphasize how integral it is that NPOs' internal data channels must be geared towards quantifying both short- and long-run letter volume demand shifts and trends. Cazals et al. (2008) also attempt to modify econometric letter volume forecasts where structural market uncertainties exist within postal markets. Indeed, they suggest that expert knowledge is one means of achieving this modification. Although all hypotheses, data channels and research undertakings must be underlined by a solid scientific methodological framework and robust quantifications. In a later study, Cazals et al. (2010) highlight how market surveys may also be used to provide insight regarding letter mail content type, and stipulate that letter mail econometric forecasts related to markets where significant uncertainties exist, such as future impacts of electronic substitution, should be augmented with what is referred to as 'off-model additional net trend adjustments' (ANTAs).

The outcome versus projection analysis specified by Fève et al. (p. 8) involves a validation of forecasts against realized values to act as a basis for the augmentation of the prevailing parameters. Such a technique attempts to tackle the emergence of short-run substitutive or competitive trends not directly discernible in an econometric framework. However, what also requires consideration is the forward impact of any one-off events that are reasonably likely to affect letter volumes in the forecast period. Structural break analysis does become important here, however, as there is also a need to assess the ongoing impact of the event. For example, the event might not result in an ongoing change in all parameter estimates and therefore fall outside the realm of a pure structural break yet still might have an impact upon future letter volumes inside the forecast period.

Significant differences among postal markets worldwide are also emerging and the principal argument of research conducted by Nikali (2011) focuses on one aspect of these divergences by suggesting that it is almost impossible to define let alone measure substitution of letter volume demand in an aggregate sense. Rather, the Nikali approach conceptualizes a corrugated substitution diffusion curve against a backdrop of a Finnish bill payments environment that is very similar to the Australian case. On the other hand, paper bill presentment mail in Finland is 83 percent of total invoices, while in Denmark the proportion of paper-based invoices rests at 32 percent. This leads Nikali to highlight that between 2000 and 2009, letter volumes decreased by 29 percent in Denmark as compared to 9 percent in Finland; see Elkelä (2011) for an excellent discussion of further cross-country comparisons. Technological diffusion inconsistencies such as these combined with changing mailer behavioral dynamics further reiterate the need for augmentation. The augmentation of *ex ante* forecasts undertaken in this chapter therefore utilizes post-forecast period internal volume data as an illustrative example of how the econometric baseline forecasts might be validated and then enhanced accordingly.

3 MODELING FRAMEWORK

In the determination of an appropriate commencement date for each of the letter volume segments, a timeframe is chosen with the aim of minimizing potential structural breaks in the long-run associations over the sample period in which the model is estimated. Data availabilities on the most relevant letter volume drivers might also restrict the timeframe over which the model is to be constructed and assist in determining the initial observation point if there exists no appropriate proxies.

Having identified the number of cointegrating equations this information is then used in the next step to build error correction models. In this phase a dynamic multivariate model of letter volumes may be developed based upon a VECM framework. This class of models integrates both the aforementioned long-run dynamics of the process with the short-run response functions. The technique was employed by Trinkner and Grossman (2006) to analyze aggregate postal volumes. However, it is applied in this undertaking to generate models for individual letter volume segments. Each of the preferred dynamic models must then be subjected to a battery of robustness checks to determine lag structures in addition to examining its properties under differing deterministic specifications, with or without a time trend and intercept. Where conjecture still remains as to the most appropriate model given the presence of a number of candidate models remaining from the aforementioned tests, *ex post* forecasting assessments of the root mean square error (RMSE) may then be utilized to resolve the preferred VECM.

The long- and short-run components of the VECM are defined formally as follows. Letting $VOLUME_t$ represent the volume of letters at time t and X_t represent a set of drivers determining letter volumes also at time t, the relationship between $VOLUME_t$ and X_t is given by:

$$VOLUME_t = \beta_0 + \beta_1 X_t + u_t, \tag{5.1}$$

where β_0 and β_1 are parameters and u_t is a disturbance term. Under the condition that $VOLUME_t$ and X_t are both nonstationary integrated processes of order one, these variables represent a cointegrated system provided that u_t is a stationary process. In this scenario $\beta_0 + \beta_1 X_t$ represents the level of letter volumes in the long run as deviations from this relationship are transitory by definition, as measured by the stationary component u_t.

The short-run component is a dynamical multivariate system whereby each variable in the long-run model in (5.1) in general adjusts towards the long-run equilibrium. Assuming for simplicity that X_t is a scalar, the VECM is:

$$\Delta VOLUME_t = \alpha_1 u_{t-1} + \phi_{1,1}\Delta VOLUME_{t-1} + \phi_{1,2}\Delta X_{t-1} + v_{1,t}$$

$$\Delta X_t = \alpha_2 u_{t-1} + \phi_{2,1}\Delta VOLUME_{t-1} + \phi_{2,2}\Delta X_{t-1} + v_{2,t}, \tag{5.2}$$

where $v_{1,t}$ and $v_{2,t}$ are disturbance terms. The choice of the lag structure is chosen for simplicity to be one-quarter, but longer lags can easily be entertained. The parameters α_1 and α_2 are the error correction parameters which control the speed and the direction of the system towards the long run in the next period following a shock to the long run, as given by u_{t-1}. The parameters $\phi_{i,j}$ allow for additional short-run characteristics as the process equilibrates towards the long run, such as oscillatory behavior for example.

The adoption of the VECM framework to generate baseline forecasts of letter volumes has several advantages over other forecasting methodologies. First, it provides a natural framework in which to decompose letter volumes into short- and long-run movements. Second, the establishment of a long-run association imposes parameter restrictions on the vector autoregression (VAR) thereby providing a more parsimonious representation to the standard unrestricted VAR. Third, as the VECM is a multivariate system, it provides a convenient method for generating *ex ante* baseline forecasts of all variables within the system.

4 APPLICATION TO AUSTRALIAN SMALL LETTER VOLUMES

Small Letter Volumes

Small letter volume data over the July 1995 to September 2010 timeframe were supplied by Australia Post. The total amount of small letters sent within Australia was delineated into two segments: Other and PreSort Barcoded volumes. The Other small letter volume segment consists of full-rate business mail, cheque payments and other consumer correspondence that satisfies the relevant small letter category size and weight requirements; the major products categories are Ordinary letters and Clean Mail. The PreSort Barcoded small letter volume segment consists of bulk (300+) lodgments of (i) Business Transactional letter volumes such as bills, statements, share notices and letters advising customers of price increases, policy changes, and so on; and (ii) Direct Mail including promotional letters, brochures and other addressed promotional material that satisfies the relevant small letter category size and weight requirements. The dominant category within this segment is PreSort Transactional letters.

Figure 5.1 shows that since the financial year 1995/96 the volume trends pertaining to each of these two letter volume segments has altered considerably due to their diverse underlying characteristics, where a financial year in Australia is defined from July to June of the next year. Over this period the Other small letter volume segment tends to be characterized by a declining trend attributable primarily to a behavioral change by mailers when engaging in bill payment activities. Moreover, Australian private consumers and business (small and medium-sized enterprises: SMEs, and large enterprises) developed an increasing propensity to engage in telephone and Internet bill payment media at the expense of the traditional single-piece mail item that formerly comprises a larger proportion of cheques and money orders within that letter volume segment.

Conversely, sustained high rates of economic activity within Australia, largely due to a resources boom, resulted in high rates of growth in PreSort Barcoded small letter volumes

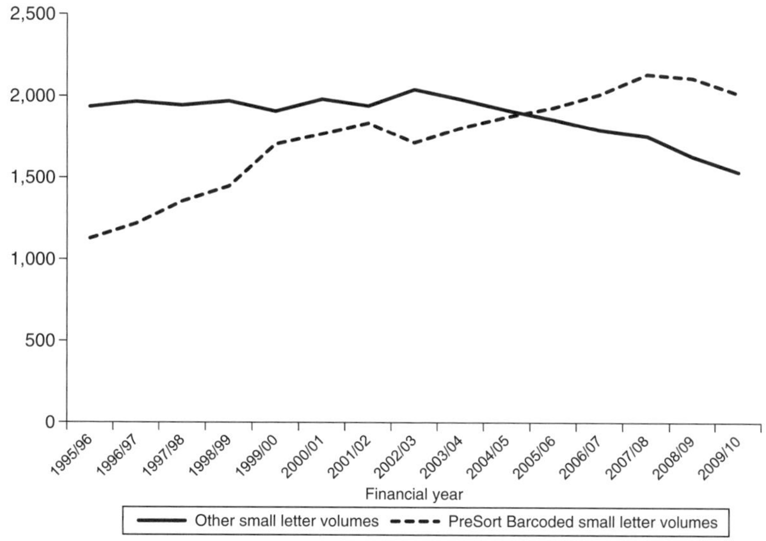

Figure 5.1 *Other vs. PreSort Barcoded small letter volumes, 1995/96 – 2009/10 (financial year, millions)*

over that same timeframe. Historically, on the bill presentments side of a transaction, there was no strong signal to indicate that the consumer had accepted an online relationship with the biller in the same manner that manifested itself in terms of the bill payments component of a transaction. A lack of incentives for the bill receiver, such as greater convenience or offers of an interest free settlement period, limited the penetration of an alternative platform for bill presentment type mail. As a result, with no appetite for change away from the traditional mail item, this letter volume segment continually performed well. In very recent times, however, initial movements towards consolidation, rationalization and substitution of these bulk small letter volumes have begun to raise questions and challenge the nature of this traditional association that links PreSort small letter volume growth to the number of transactions within the domestic economy. For these reasons there is a need to incorporate other information such as that from stated preference cross-sectional studies or panel data, in order to capture any of these effects not discernible from long-run empirical trends when generating a reliable set of letter volume forecasts.

In Table 5.1, each of the letter volume segments are aligned with fluctuations in the level of Australian non-farm GDP and highlight the lower levels of economic growth prevalent in 2008/09 and 2009/10. From 2008/09 as the level of economic activity slowed the long-run upward trend in PreSort Barcoded small letter volumes dissipated as, simultaneously a more pronounced decline in Other small letter volumes began to emerge. The key factor in explaining this slowdown has been the impact of the global financial crisis although the extent to which this event has acted as a one-off structural break as against acting as a catalyst for accelerated movements towards consolidation, rationalization and substitution practices on behalf of mailers remains to be seen.

Again this calls in the importance of the augmentation process to overlay upon the existing econometric results. In the case of Other small letters over the entire examinable

Table 5.1 Small letter segment volume growth %, per annum.

Year	Other	PreSort Barcoded	Australian non-farm GDP growth
2003/04	–2.93	5.23	3.75
2004/05	–3.41	3.82	2.93
2005/06	–2.93	3.02	3.09
2006/07	–3.45	4.21	4.00
2007/08	–2.08	6.15	3.77
2008/09	–7.12	–1.07	1.13
2009/10	–5.81	–4.57	2.30

timeframe fluctuations in the level of GDP do not register as a statistically significant volume driver. Instead, apart from real price changes, it has been the effects of substantive movements to substitutive technologies that have crowded out any influences by other drivers since the year 2000. During this time the buoyancy of the Australian economy prevented an assessment of how Other small letter volumes responded to very low rates of economic growth. The magnitude of the post-2008/09 declines, however, suggests that there have been some letter volume declines associated with the lower rates of economic growth. Intuitively, this makes sense as the number of transactions declined substantially leading to a large reduction in the number of bills and the feasible amount of bill payments.

Other Small Letter Volume Model

Efforts to model Other small letter volumes commences with an acknowledgement of the underlying characteristics of this product segment which primarily consists of bill payments transactional mail from individuals in addition to SME mailings. For over a decade a range of hypotheses were generated in concert with management at Australia Post, international research and robust economic theory. The most important of these hypotheses was the substitutive effects that arise via the proliferation and uptake of various platforms that facilitate bill payments via media that do not include the traditional mail item, such as phone and the Internet. Direct observations on the number of bills settled via these alternative media remain extremely difficult to quantify. Until the Reserve Bank of Australia began quantifying cheque volumes in 2002, there was no direct measure of bill payments via the post. As a result of this data limitation early incarnations of the model, developed through the late 1990s and early 2000s, utilized credit cards as a proxy for these substitutive effects. The availability and uptake of personal credit combined with an increasing perception surrounding its convenience and security as a viable means for settling a transaction meant that the credit card acted as an enabler of these alternative technologies. As credit cards proliferated so too did phone and Internet banking increase and the use of credit card numbers appeared to be a sound proxy for substitutive movements away from the traditional letter. With the global financial crisis, however, it became increasingly obvious that personal credit began to follow its own path as growth in this variable began to slow not because of a decline in substitution away from the traditional mail item, but rather through the propensity for personal credit cards to plateau given

Table 5.2 Johansen cointegration test of the Other small letter volumes model

Hypothesized no. of cointegrating equations	P-value
None	0.029
At most 1	0.197
At most 2	0.134

that the level of economic activity itself became stagnant. By contrast, traditional forms of bill payments such as cheque volumes continued to slide. Given that cheque volumes represent a more direct measure of declines in bill payments via the traditional mail item due to substitution, whereas credit cards were more of an enabler or conduit, the model presented in this chapter incorporates this variable directly to capture substitutive pressures for Other small letters.

Another statistically significant driver of Other small letter volumes is fluctuations in real price. The real price decreases at an annual average rate of 0.26 percent between 2000/01 and 2008/09, however nominal price has increased in 2008/09 and again at the commencement of 2010/11. Given the importance of this variable, any tendency for increasingly frequent nominal price increases is likely to alter both the trend and the elasticity as mailers' behavior changes when faced with successive, or indeed a series of, price increases. Given the initial investigation of the drivers the key variables included in the VECM for Other small letter volumes consists of:

1. *OTHER* Other small letter volumes, natural logarithms, seasonally adjusted;
2. *CHEQUE* Cheque volumes, natural logarithms, seasonally adjusted; and
3. *PRICE* real price of Other small letters, natural logarithms, seasonally adjusted.

To allow for the two lags in the VECM together with the data being defined in quarterly changes, the estimation period begins in December 2004 and ends in September 2010, in line with cheque volume data availability from the Reserve Bank of Australia. Tests of nonstationarity of these variables based on the Dickey–Fuller unit root test illustrate that all three variables are integrated processes of order one.

To test for a long-run relationship among these variables, the results of the Johansen cointegration test are presented in Table 5.2. In performing this test the lag length of the VAR is set equal to 3, which is determined optimally using a range of information criteria. Adopting a 5 percent significance level, the cointegration test shows that there is one long-run relationship among the variables. Choosing Other small letter volumes as the dependent variable, the long-run relationship is estimated with standard errors in parentheses, as:

$$OTHER_t = 0.036 + \underset{(0.017)}{0.495}CHEQUE_t - \underset{(0.089)}{0.310}PRICE_t + \hat{u}_t, \tag{5.3}$$

where u_t is the residual. Both drivers of Other small letter volumes in the long-run are statistically significant at conventional levels. In particular, the long-run is characterized by a positive relationship between Other small letter volumes and Cheque volumes with an elasticity of 0.495. There is also an inverse relationship between Other small letter

Table 5.3 Diagnostic tests of the VECM Other small letter volumes

Statistic	*OTHER*	*CHEQUE*	*PRICE*
R-squared	0.632	0.311	0.224
S.E. equation	0.018	0.020	0.027
Log likelihood	87.929	84.798	74.315

volumes and price whereby a 1 percent increase in price results in a fall of 0.310 percent in Other small letter volumes.

The short-run estimated model consists of three equations corresponding to the three variables in the long-run equation. Some diagnostics are given in Table 5.3. The short-run estimated model for Other small letter volumes (*OTHER*) with standard errors in parentheses, is:

$$\begin{aligned}\Delta OTHER_t = & -\underset{(0.008)}{0.029} - \underset{(0.290)}{1.189}\hat{u}_{t-1} + \underset{(0.164)}{0.182}\Delta OTHER_{t-1} - \underset{(0.129)}{0.063}\Delta OTHER_{t-2} \\ & -\underset{(0.224)}{0.563}\Delta CHEQUE_{t-1} - \underset{(0.211)}{0.219}\Delta CHEQUE_{t-2} \\ & -\underset{(0.163)}{0.182}\Delta PRICE_{t-1} + \underset{(0.152)}{0.085}\Delta PRICE_{t-2} + \hat{v}_{1,t}.\end{aligned} \quad (5.4)$$

The estimate of the error correction parameter of –1.189 is statistically significant, showing that Other small letter volumes adjust following shocks that push the system of the long-run. This parameter estimate is also negative which is consistent with the presence of cointegration as positive shocks ($u_{t-1} > 0$) which immediately push small letter volumes above their long-run level, resulting in a fall in letter volumes over time towards the long-run.

The short-run estimated model for Cheque volumes (*CHEQUE*) is:

$$\begin{aligned}\Delta CHEQUE_t = & -\underset{(0.009)}{0.045} - \underset{(0.320)}{0.813}\hat{u}_{t-1} + \underset{(0.180)}{0.266}\Delta OTHER_{t-1} + \underset{(0.142)}{0.071}\Delta OTHER_{t-2} \\ & -\underset{(0.247)}{0.599}\Delta CHEQUE_{t-1} - \underset{(0.233)}{0.502}\Delta CHEQUE_{t-2} \\ & +\underset{(0.179)}{0.144}\Delta PRICE_{t-1} + \underset{(0.167)}{0.024}\Delta PRICE_{t-2} + \hat{v}_{2,t}.\end{aligned} \quad (5.5)$$

As the error correction parameter estimate of –0.813 is statistically significant, Cheque volumes also act as an equilibrating mechanism to restore long-run equilibrium.

The short-run estimated model for real price of Other small letters (*PRICE*) is:

$$\begin{aligned}\Delta PRICE_t = & +\underset{(0.012)}{0.002} + \underset{(0.444)}{0.280}\hat{u}_{t-1} - \underset{(0.250)}{0.221}\Delta OTHER_{t-1} + \underset{(0.197)}{0.284}\Delta OTHER_{t-2} \\ & +\underset{(0.342)}{0.157}\Delta CHEQUE_{t-1} - \underset{(0.323)}{0.160}\Delta CHEQUE_{t-2}\end{aligned}$$

$$- \underset{(0.249)}{0.099}\Delta PRICE_{t-1} + \underset{(0.232)}{0.026}\Delta PRICE_{t-2} + \hat{v}_{3,t}. \tag{5.6}$$

In contrast to the $OTHER_t$ and $CHEQUE_t$ short-run models, the insignificant error correction parameter estimate in the short-run model of $PRICE_t$ shows that prices are weakly exogenous and do not respond to shocks which force the system off the long-run. Moreover, the lack of insignificance in the parameter estimates on the other lagged variables in this equation, suggest that this variable is strongly exogenous with its dynamics being determined outside of the specified VECM.

PreSort Barcoded Model

As illustrated in Figure 5.1, PreSort Barcoded small letter volumes exhibit an upward overall trend from 1995/96. PreSort Barcoded small letter volumes return to negative annual growth on only two occasions since 2003/04 – see Figure 5.1 – and both of those declines have occurred in the most recent two financial years. Domestic non-farm economic activity is the key statistically significant driver within the model and is positively associated with PreSort Barcoded small letter volumes. The number of traditional mail item bill presentments, reflected by bulk periodic letter volumes (for example, bills and statements) from the major mailers, tends to be greater in times of higher economic activity and softer during times of slower economic activity. Growth in the domestic economy is statistically a key element of PreSort Barcoded small letter volume model. Given its transactional and promotional based characteristics the slowdown in the Australian economy in line with the global financial crisis has been a significant factor associated with this letter volume decline. Such an association with the declining GDP is immediately evident from the figures reported in Table 5.1.

The importance of the promotional component of the PreSort Barcoded small letter volume segment is also reflected through the statistical association with the health of the Australian advertising industry. The Australian Stock Exchange's Consumer Discretionary Index is utilized as a forward predictor of discretionary spend, which in turn has an impact on the level of company-specific promotional spend available. Direct mail is assumed to constitute an important part of marketers' overall promotional tools. A stagnant or declining advertising industry is assumed to dampen demand for PreSort Barcoded small letter volumes.

The variables in the VECM for PreSort Barcoded small letter volumes consist of:

1. *PRESORT* PreSort Barcoded small letter volumes, natural logarithms, seasonally adjusted;
2. *GDP* Australian non-farm GDP, natural logarithms, seasonally adjusted; and
3. *SP200* S&P Top 200 ASX discretionary index, natural logarithms, seasonally adjusted which is used as a proxy for Advertising Industry Health Measure.

Also included is a dummy variable *BARCODE* to take into account the introduction of barcoding technology in October 1999 to enhance the processing of PreSort letters. Accompanying the introduction of such technology were product changes, the most important of which included a reduction of the minimum lodgment requirement to qualify for the PreSort discount, to 300 letters. This change was hypothesized to be

Table 5.4 Johansen cointegration test of the PreSort Barcoded small letter volumes model

Hypothesized no. of cointegrating equations	P-value
None	0.001
At most 1	0.129
At most 2	0.264

Table 5.5 Diagnostic tests of the VECM PreSort Barcoded small letter volumes model

Statistic	*OTHER*	*CHEQUE*	*PRICE*
R-squared	0.297	0.005	0.144
S.E. equation	0.042	0.009	0.106
Log likelihood	106.249	197.383	51.369

negatively associated with Other small letter volumes. The modification in lodgment requirements created a greater propensity for mailers to switch, at the margin, from sending Other small letter volumes to a PreSort equivalent. This variable is included in the short-run component of the VECM, but not in the long-run section.

The estimation begins in March 1996 and ends in September 2010 to take into account the inclusion of one lag in the VECM and that the variables are expressed in quarterly changes. Tests of nonstationarity of these variables based on an augmented Dickey–Fuller unit root test show that all three variables are integrated processes of order one. The results of the Johansen cointegration test are presented in Table 5.4. The lag length of the VECM is 1, which is determined optimally using a range of information criteria.

The long-run estimated model of PreSort Barcoded small letter volumes is estimated with standard errors in parentheses, as:

$$PRESORT_t = \underset{(2.076)}{-\ 5.784} + \underset{(0.102)}{0.752}GDP_t + \underset{(0.039)}{0.175}SP200_t + \hat{u}_t, \tag{5.7}$$

where $\hat{u}_t$ is the residual. Both drivers of PreSort small letter volumes in the long-run are statistically significant at conventional levels. The long-run relationship between PreSort small letter volumes and GDP is positive with an elasticity of 0.752. A test of the hypothesis that this relationship is one to one is not rejected at the 5 percent level. The relationship between PreSort small letter volumes and advertising is also positive with an elasticity of 0.175.

The short-run estimated model consists of three equations corresponding to the three variables in the long-run equation. Some diagnostics are given in Table 5.5. The short-run estimated model for PreSort Barcoded small letter volumes (*PRESORT*) with standard errors in parentheses, is:

$$\Delta PRESORT_t = \underset{(0.071)}{-\ 0.228}\hat{u}_{t-1} - \underset{(0.116)}{0.313}\Delta PRESORT_{t-1} + \underset{(0.689)}{0.273}\Delta GDP_{t-1}$$

$$- \underset{(0.053)}{0.021}\Delta SP200_{t-1} + \underset{(0.008)}{0.004}BARCODE_t + \hat{v}_{1,t}. \quad (5.8)$$

The estimate of the error correction parameter is statistically significant with a t-statistic of 0.228/0.071 = –3.223, showing that PreSort small letter volumes adjust to the presence of disequilibrium shocks which force the system out of long-run equilibrium. As with Other small letter volumes, this parameter estimate is also negative whereby positive shocks ($u_{t-1} > 0$) which push PreSort small letter volumes above their long-run level, are followed by falls in letter volumes over time towards the long-run.

The short-run estimated model for Australian non-farm GDP (GDP) is:

$$\Delta GDP_t = -\underset{(0.015)}{0.061}\hat{u}_{t-1} + \underset{(0.025)}{0.042}\Delta PRESORT_{t-1} - \underset{(0.147)}{0.195}\Delta GDP_{t-1}$$

$$- \underset{(0.011)}{0.014}\Delta SP200_{t-1} + \underset{(0.002)}{0.006}BARCODE_t + \hat{v}_{2,t}. \quad (5.9)$$

These results show that GDP is not weakly exogenous as the error correction parameter estimate is statistically significant.

The short-run estimated model for Advertising Industry Health Measure as proxied by the S&P Top 200 ASX discretionary index (*SP200*) is:

$$\Delta SP200_t = \underset{(0.180)}{0.055}\hat{u}_{t-1} - \underset{(0.294)}{0.078}\Delta PRESORT_{t-1} + \underset{(1.746)}{3.028}\Delta GDP_{t-1}$$

$$+ \underset{(0.135)}{0.228}\Delta SP200_{t-1} - \underset{(0.020)}{0.028}BARCODE_t + \hat{v}_{3,t}. \quad (5.10)$$

These results show that *SP200* is weakly exogenous as the error correction parameter estimate is statistically insignificant. This variable is also strongly exogenous as none of the lagged variables is statistically significant on the other variables in the equation.

Forecast Augmentation

When contrasting the econometric forecasts to actual small letter volumes in the September quarter of 2010 the Federal election is an example of a significant one-off event that may have inflated volumes beyond the models projections. The September 2010 quarter witnessed in excess of 34 million addressed articles generated through election type mailings across the two small letter volume segments discussed in this chapter. The danger in interpreting the econometric forecasts at face value is that once positive and negative factors outside the model are discounted for, then it reveals the emerging threats to mail that may be beginning to suppress volumes beyond that anticipated econometrically. Table 5.6 suggests that although the econometric forecast underestimates actual volume growth for the September quarter, once election-related mailings are added to the econometric baseline the augmented forecast, in the final column, reduces the gap for Other small letters and overshoots the actual volumes considerably for PreSort Barcoded small letters, the latter of which is represented graphically in Figure 5.2. Although election mail is included within the augmented econometric forecast for PreSort Barcoded small letter volumes, the result is otherwise based upon its historical associations and it 'misses' very recent trends towards consolidation, rationalization and bill presentment substitution. This is the X-factor as depicted in the lower portion of Figure 5.2 that

Table 5.6 Small letter growth comparisons

Small letter volume	Percentage growth on previous quarter (s.a.)		
	Actual volumes	Econometric forecast	Augmented forecast
Other	–0.07	–2.41	–1.73
PreSort Barcoded	5.34	1.22	7.22

requires a second round of augmentation to better quantify these emerging trends. The dashed line in the lower portion of the figure illustrates that actual volumes (530 million) minus the extra PreSort Barcoded small letter volumes emanating from the Federal election (32 million) indicates the econometric baseline does not account for the emerging threats of consolidation, rationalization and substitution.

It is important to note that a number of Federal elections have occurred throughout the timeframe over which the VECM has been estimated and therefore account in some part for the resultant characteristics of the model through the parameter estimates and standard errors. The difference with the most recent election is the availability of quantifiable letter volumes specifically associated with this event. This provides additional information that can act as the basis for the augmentation conducted in this chapter. The absence of similar measurements for previous elections is not the only barrier in incorporating these political events into the VECM framework. Differences in election-related mailings can occur due to a number of factors. First, the mix between the promotional channels utilized to communicate with the electorate can alter. Estimates dating back to 2004 indicate a substantially lower number of addressed (as against unaddressed) election mail when contrasted to its most recent counterpart. Second, the lead time into an election and timing of promotional mailings associated with an election are also variable and can be determined by factors including the tightness of the campaign, specific events and changes in mailing strategies across various elections. For these reasons, crude attempts to model elections as a set of homogeneous events via the construction of dichotomous variables can result in outcomes that are ill conceived. This was verified by re-estimating the VECM and including election-related dummy variables to deliver statistically insignificant parameter estimates.

Global Financial Crisis

To investigate the impact of the global financial crisis on the estimated model results and the effect on letter volumes in general, dichotomous variables are introduced into the estimated VECMs presented above. As the sample period of Other small letter volumes is relatively short, the analysis now focuses on PreSort small letter volumes.

The initial approach to capture the global financial crisis is to specify a dummy variable capturing the whole of the crisis period, beginning in September 2007 and ending at the end of the sample period, September 2010. Another approach is to introduce a smooth adjustment term by specifying a non-linear error correction model following van Dijk and Frances (2000). Including this variable as an exogenous variable into the VECM means that the dummy variable enters the three short-run equations in (5.4) and (5.5).

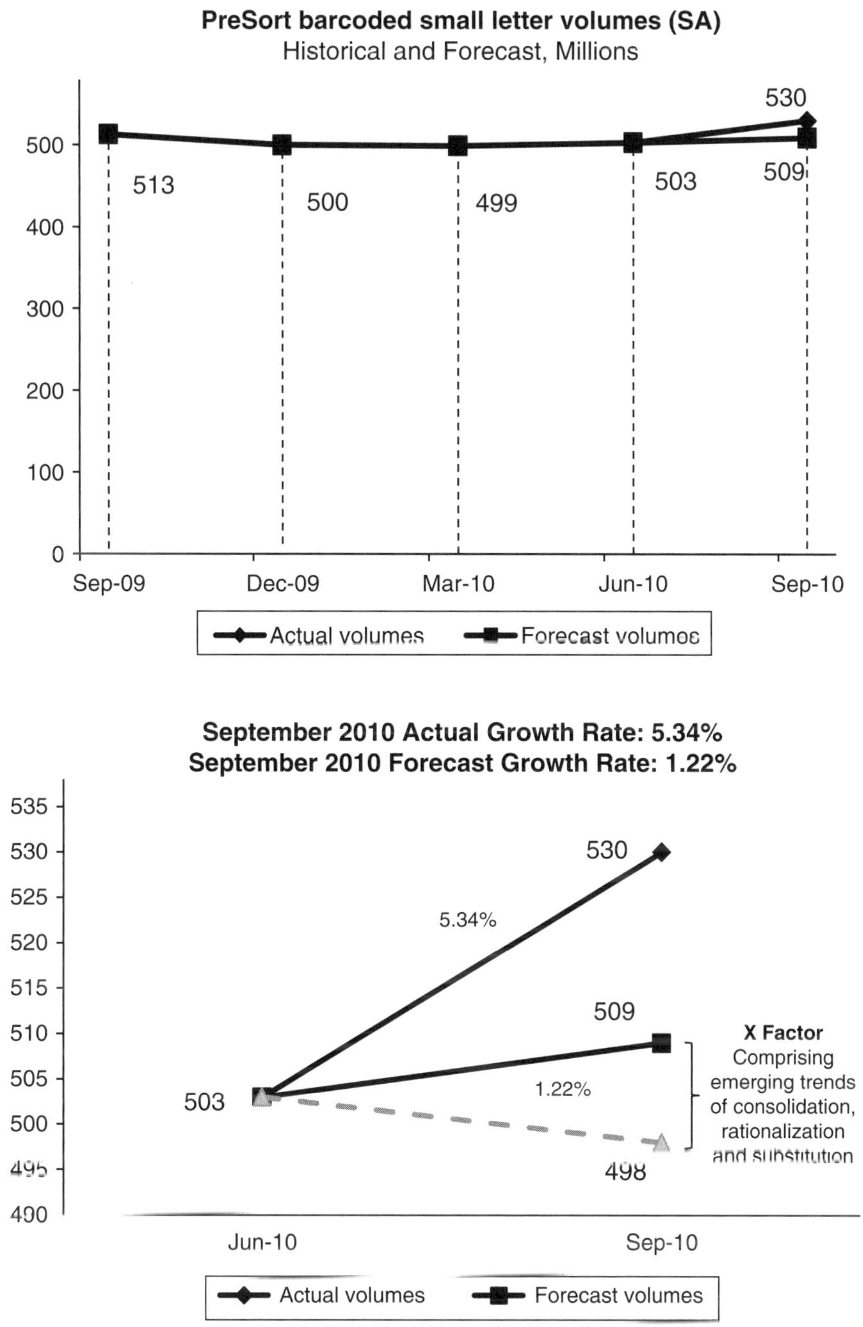

Figure 5.2 Other small letter volumes forecasts

The empirical results show that the parameter estimates associated with the variable are all statistically insignificant (results not presented).

The finding of no strong impact of the global financial crisis on the model results may reflect that the impact of the event may change over time. To account for this a range of dummy variables corresponding to each quarter of the global financial crisis beginning September 2007 are specified. However, to take into account potential losses of degrees of freedom, statistically insignificant dummy variables are excluded from the estimated model. The final estimated model for small letter volumes contains two dummy variables corresponding to the September and December quarters of 2008. Given the timing of these dummy variables this would suggest that these variables are capturing the bankruptcy of Lehman Brothers in particular. The estimated long-run model of PreSort small letter volumes is:

$$PRESORT_t = \underset{(2.670)}{-\ 6.095} + \underset{(0.182)}{0.775}GDP_t + \underset{(0.068)}{0.180}SP200_t + \hat{u}_t, \tag{5.11}$$

while the three short-run equations are:

$$\begin{aligned}\Delta PRESORT_t = & \underset{(0.061)}{-\ 0.167}\hat{u}_{t-1} - \underset{(0.121)}{0.330}\Delta PRESORT_{t-1} + \underset{(0.755)}{0.424}\Delta GDP_{t-1} \\ & - \underset{(0.057)}{0.020}\Delta SP200_{t-1} + \underset{(0.009)}{0.011}BARCODE_t \\ & - \underset{(0.047)}{0.017}GFC_t^{08:Q3} - \underset{(0.045)}{0.001}GFC_t^{08:Q4} + \hat{v}_{1,t},\end{aligned} \tag{5.12}$$

$$\begin{aligned}\Delta GDP_t = & \underset{(0.012)}{-\ 0.051}\hat{u}_{t-1} + \underset{(0.023)}{0.038}\Delta PRESORT_{t-1} - \underset{(0.146)}{0.208}\Delta GDP_{t-1} \\ & - \underset{(0.011)}{0.020}\Delta SP200_{t-1} + \underset{(0.002)}{0.005}BARCODE_t \\ & + \underset{(0.009)}{0.012}GFC_t^{08:Q3} - \underset{(0.008)}{0.022}GFC_t^{08:Q4} + \hat{v}_{2,t},\end{aligned} \tag{5.13}$$

$$\begin{aligned}\Delta SP200_t = & \underset{(0.142)}{0.069}\hat{u}_{t-1} + \underset{(0.284)}{0.124}\Delta PRESORT_{t-1} + \underset{(1.775)}{3.387}\Delta GDP_{t-1} \\ & + \underset{(0.135)}{0.131}\Delta SP200_{t-1} - \underset{(0.021)}{0.019}BARCODE_t \\ & + \underset{(0.112)}{0.178}GFC_t^{08:Q3} - \underset{(0.105)}{0.222}GFC_t^{08:Q4} + \hat{v}_{3,t}.\end{aligned} \tag{5.14}$$

The empirical results in (5.11) to (5.14) are qualitatively very similar to the empirical results presented in (5.7) to (5.10) which do not contain the two global financial crisis dummy variables, denoted *GFC*. The immediate impact of the global financial crisis is a negative impact on both *GDP* and *SP200* in the short-run. Interestingly, there is no direct impact of the dummy variables on letter volumes in the short-run as the parameter estimates of the dummies in the *PRESORT* short-run equation are all statistically insignificant. This suggests that the main impact of the global financial crisis on letter volumes is through an indirect channel via the impact of the crisis on *GDP* and *SP200*, which, in turn, impact upon letter volumes.

The empirical results from including the effects of the global financial crisis suggest that the negative effect of the crisis on letter volumes is cyclical with letter volumes falling directly in line with the fall in national output. This also suggests that as the economy improves over time so should letter volumes. In contrast, there is no strong statistical evidence showing changes in short- and/or long-run elasticities as a result of substitution effects and the adoption of new technologies arising from the crisis.

5 CONCLUSIONS

The past decade has seen a significantly different domestic and international postal landscape due to a series of emerging trends in substitution, price, rationalization and consolidation. Movements towards rationalization and consolidation are endemic to the PreSort small letter volume segment and quantifiable time-series data on these phenomena are difficult to source and therefore embed within an empirical examination that is solely econometric. Where it is not possible to proxy consolidation, rationalization and substitution for PreSort small letter volumes, this methodology reveals their combined magnitude. Future extensions should aim at monitoring this gap, or X-factor, over time with any widening signifying a significant threat to the future of bill presentment type mail. It would then be possible to utilize alternative research techniques in these areas to act as a second stage in the augmentation process.

With regard to Other small letter volumes, substantial and pervasive uptake of both telephone and online banking to pay bills which were once the domain of the traditional mail item have declined dramatically in the past decade. In addition, stagnant nominal price movements within the 1990s are no longer applicable and result in long-run price elasticities that are effectively redundant. Future studies should focus on how volumes respond to successive price increases and whether the accelerating volume declines are linked to increasing costs incurred by the senders.

Indeed, econometric models tracing back to the mid-1990s in Australia had no means by which to analyze how such volumes react to a slowdown in economic activity prior to the global financial crisis. Furthermore, Transactional and promotional PreSort Barcoded small letter volume growth rates have, additionally, been affected by deteriorating levels of domestic economic activity and discretionary spend. Although movements in PreSort Barcoded small letter volumes have shown a statistically strong association with these factors since 1995/96, a behavioral change among the major mailers or the emergence of a viable and widely accepted platform for bill presentments would significantly threaten this association. That is, should the increasing rates of small letter rationalization and consolidation be accompanied by a sustained growth in electronic substitutive practices on the bill presentment side of a transaction, then PreSort Barcoded small letter volumes would be exposed to a significant downside threat regardless of the level of economic or promotional activity within Australia. It is crucial that any explanatory or forecasting model account for all of these factors, given the characteristics of this rapidly changing landscape.

NOTE

1. The authors wish to thank the following individuals and organizations for their analysis, suggestions and recommendations that have assisted in improving the methodological approach over the past decade: Mark Pollock, Heikki Nikali, Chris Koo, Hartmuth Scholz, Qiubang Li, Sandra Mills, Tony Medic, Paul Kleindorfer, Michael Crew, Matthew Harding, Australia Post, The Australian Competition and Consumer Commission & Frontier Economics.

REFERENCES

Cazals, C., J.P. Florens, F. Rodriguez and S. Soteri (2008), 'Forecast uncertainty in dynamic models: an application to the demand for mail', in M.A. Crew and P.R. Kleindorfer (eds), *Competition and Regulation in the Postal and Delivery Sector*, Cheltenham, UK and Northampton, MA, USA: Edward Elgar, pp. 63–73.

Cazals, C., J.P. Florens, L. Veruete-McKay, F. Rodriguez and S. Soteri (2010), 'UK letter mail demand: a content based time series analysis using overlapping market survey statistical techniques', Toulouse School of Economics Working Paper Series, 10–170.

Elkelä, K. (2011), 'Invoicing in 16 European countries', in M.A. Crew and P.R. Kleindorfer (eds), *Reinventing the Postal Sector in an Electronic Age*, Cheltenham, UK and Northampton, MA, USA: Edward Elgar.

Fève, F., J.P. Florens, F. Rodriguez and S. Soteri (2010), 'Forecasting mail volumes in an evolving market environment', in M.A. Crew and P.R. Kleindorfer (eds), *Heightening Competition in the Postal and Delivery Sector*, Cheltenham, UK and Northampton, MA, USA: Edward Elgar.

Hendry, D.F. and N.R. Ericsson (eds) (2001), *Understanding Economic Forecasts*, Cambridge, MA and London: MIT Press.

Nikali, H. (2011), 'Does the level of price elasticity change with the progression of substitution?', in M.A. Crew and P.R. Kleindorfer (eds), *Reinventing the Postal Sector in an Electronic Age*, Cheltenham, UK and Northampton, MA, USA: Edward Elgar.

Robinson, A. (2006), 'A review of price elasticity models for postal products', Background Paper No. 22, Pitney Bowes.

Trinkner, U. and M. Grossman (2006), 'Forecasting Swiss mail demand', in M.A. Crew and P.R. Kleindorfer (eds), *Progress towards Liberalization of the Postal and Delivery Sector*, New York: Springer Science+Business Media, Inc.

van Dijk, D. and P.K. Frances (2000), 'Nonlinear error-correction models for interest rates in the Netherlands', in Barnett, W.A., D.F. Hendry, S. Hylleberg, T. Terasvirta, D. Tjostheim and A. Wurtz (eds), *Nonlinear Econometric Modeling in Time Series Analysis*, Cambridge: Cambridge University Press.

6. Uncertainty and projections of the demand for mail*

Frédérique Fève[†], Jean-Pierre Florens[‡], Leticia Veruete-McKay[§], Soterios Soteri[¶] and Frank Rodriguez[††]

1 INTRODUCTION

Projections of the demand for mail are an important driver of business decisions in the postal sector. Such projections, for example, support investment decisions, help determine the nature and scope of regulatory controls and represent a key variable in business valuations. However, given the long-term nature of such decisions and, in many instances, their 'irreversibility', it is important that postal operators assess and manage appropriately the risks and uncertainties inherent in projecting mail volumes over the medium and long terms. While much has been published on the principles of forecasting and there is also a substantial literature examining factors driving the demand for mail historically, there are relatively few papers that consider specifically the important area of the forecasting of mail volumes.[1] Until relatively recently the results from modeling historical data using time-series econometric techniques could then be used to project forward prospects for mail volumes. More recently, however, significant structural change in the mail market has made such forecasting more complex and subject to considerable levels of uncertainty.

We have explored these issues from a theoretical perspective in two previous papers. In Fève et al. (2010) we set out a methodological framework in which, in an evolving market environment where there is a lack of historical data, an integral part of the forecasting process for future levels of demand is to follow a Bayesian approach and incorporate informative priors. In addition to outputs from a time-series econometric model, information for a forecast made in period T may be obtained from a variety of sources, including business expert opinion and data from other markets. Such information can then be updated after each period to revise and improve a forecast made in the next period, $T + 1$, and subsequent periods as a recurring process. However, it may be that projections made at a point in time to inform a particular decision cannot be revised after that decision has been made and so, in such circumstances, are irreversible. In a changing market

† Researcher, Toulouse School of Economics (IDEI), University of Toulouse Capitale.
‡ Professor, Toulouse School of Economics (IDEI), University of Toulouse Capitale.
§ Senior Economist, Royal Mail Group.
¶ Head of Economic Forecasting, Royal Mail Group.
†† Associate, Oxera.

environment differences between projections and outcomes (or errors) can become large but there may be no opportunity to revise the projection. In Cazals et al. (2008) we considered the potential scale of errors that might arise over the long term both from within an estimated time-series model derived using historical data and also as a result of structural change in future levels of demand. Potentially, such errors can become very large if the initial projection cannot be updated.

In this chapter we draw together insights from both of these papers and develop two areas. First, we set out a general approach to projecting the demand for mail over the long term where it is not possible to update that projection because it has been made to support a specific decision at time *T* which itself is irreversible.[2] However, uncertainty is inherent in any long-term projection and it is important to understand the potential range of possible demand outcomes which can become very wide. So, in the second area considered in the chapter, we provide an empirical example of the potential for divergence between projections and outcomes. We do this through a case study of projections prepared by Royal Mail Group and draw implications from this for the future application of our framework for projecting the demand for mail over the long term. Given that outcomes may differ significantly from projections, such uncertainty is unavoidable and the costs of differences between outcomes and projections may be high, a key conclusion is that it is essential to manage *ex ante* the possible consequences of a wide range of possible demand outcomes so that such costs can be minimized.[3]

The remainder of the chapter is structured as follows. Section 2 contains a case study of long-term projections for the demand for mail prepared by Royal Mail Group. Section 3 draws implications from the case study for preparing mail volume projections. Our general approach to projecting the demand for mail is set out in technical form in Appendix 6A. We draw on the appendix extensively throughout Sections 2 and 3 and this is an integral part of the overall chapter.

2 A CASE STUDY: PROJECTIONS MADE FOR UK PRICE CONTROL REVIEW

Context and Framework for Projections

We consider a number of theoretical and methodological issues associated with the forecasting of mail volumes over the medium to long term through a case study of projections prepared by Royal Mail Group. The appendix to this chapter outlines more fully the theoretical and methodological framework underpinning this forecasting approach. The context for this set of projections is that, under the terms of its licence, the company is subject to price controls which are set by its regulator, Postcomm.[4] For the price control period starting in April 2006, Postcomm began its review in 2004 and required Royal Mail Group to provide it, in January 2005, with a detailed set of financial year volume projections up to and including 2010/11.[5] The projection was therefore one of 7 years with the last observed outcome year being 2003/04, although some traffic data were available for the first half of 2004/05 given that the projections were prepared between October and December 2004. The projections were to be reviewed by Postcomm and its intention was to use the projections submitted or an amended or alternative set as one of the key components in setting the regulatory framework and controls on Royal Mail Group's prices to come into effect in April 2006.[6] The controls covered about £6 billion of revenue in 2006/07, over 80 percent of the company's revenue from its mail products in that year.

The forecasting framework adopted by Royal Mail Group in 2004 to construct long-term volume projections contained two components. First, a set of data-based forecasts was produced using time-series econometrics modeling techniques. The construction of data-based forecasts using such techniques is outlined in the appendix (first subsection). Second, further information was used to augment the data based forecast to allow for the potential impact of additional effects from e-substitution over the projection period. The role and use of such information is outlined in the appendix (second subsection) which discusses the concepts of Bayesian informative priors and the use of non-identified models. These are key elements of our general approach and relate, in particular, to the treatment of the possible future impact of unobservable variables or potential structural changes in the mail market environment that are not, and cannot be, included in the data-based model forecasts.

The data-based forecasting model used by Royal Mail Group to prepare projections of its mail volumes for the price control review was its Inland Letter Traffic Model (ILTM), a time-series econometric model used to help project addressed inland mail volumes. The version of the ILTM used for the projections was estimated using data over the period from 1976Q1 to 2003Q2. Table 6.1 reports estimated coefficients, diagnostic tests and long-run elasticities from the model. The model contains three equations, each in error correction form, for First Class non-presort mail, Second Class non-presort mail and Other (mainly presort) mail. Traffic in each of the equations (expressed as traffic per household per working day) is dependent on (a letter demand weighted measure of) economic activity (y) and at least one of a set of letter prices ($p1$, $p2$, $p3$). Additionally, a measure of quality of service is significant in the Second Class equation and advertising prices in the Other (mainly presort) equation. All three equations also contained 'unexplained' trend terms which were negative for First and Second Class traffic and positive for Other (mainly presort) traffic. The long-run (volume-weighted) economic activity elasticity for total traffic per household was approximately unity (1.02) while the 'unexplained' net trend at the end of the estimation period was slightly negative (at –0.6 percent per annum). The diagnostic tests reported in Table 6.1 suggest that the model was well specified and robust, and the predictive failure test results indicate that there was no evidence that the equations were beginning to break down.

In preparing projections in 2004 to run forward to 2011, however, it seemed likely that the effects of e-substitution would become more marked than had been apparent in the UK up to 2003Q2. There was an anticipation and perhaps some early signs that changes in the environment, notably the expansion of Internet usage and broadband, would impact negatively on mail volumes in excess of the effects incorporated in the ILTM. As discussed in the second subsection of the appendix, where there is an expectation that factors that are likely to impact in the future are not contained in full or even in part in an existing model then it is important to try and reflect such potential impacts in developing projections even though such a larger construction of the model may be non-identified. A set of *ex ante* Bayesian informative priors were included in the form of additional net trend adjustments to the effects of explanatory variables in the equations

Table 6.1 Addressed inland letter traffic model (ILTM): estimated coefficients and diagnostic tests

First Class non-presort[1]			Second Class non-presort[1]			Other traffic (mainly presort)[1]		
Dependent variable $\Delta(q_{1t}–h_t)$			Dependent variable $\Delta(q_{2t}–h_t)$			Dependent variable $\Delta(q_{3t}–h_t)$		
Estimation method least squares			Estimation method least squares			Estimation method least squares		
	Estimated coefficients	*T*-value		Estimated coefficients	*T*-value		Estimated coefficients	*T*-value
ECT1*$_{t-1}$	–0.46	–5.0	ECT2*$_{t-1}$	–0.52	–7.6	ECT3*$_{t-1}$	–1.01	–9.3
Trend[2]	–	–	Trend[2]	–0.007	–6.6	Trend[2]	0.013	9.2
T87[2]	–0.004	–4.2	T87[2]	0.004	4.7	T97[2]	–0.010	–7.8
p_{1t-1}	–0.34	–2.8	p_{1t-1}	0.29	2.2[3]			
p_{2t-1}	0.25	2.9	p_{2t-1}	–0.24	–2.2			
			qos_{t-1}	0.25	3.0			
Δy_t	0.70	1.9	Δqos_t	0.22	3.9	Δy_t	1.69	3.1
Δy_{t-2}	0.51	1.3						
Δp_{1t-2}	0.33	2.4						
$\Delta(q_1–h)_{t-1}$	–0.21	–2.2						
$\Delta(q_1–h)_{t-1}$	–0.14	–1.7						
R^2 adj.	0.88		R^2 adj.	0.93		R^2 adj.	0.83	
Reg. SE	0.026		Reg. SE	0.036		Reg. SE	0.031	
Durbin Watson	1.9		Durbin Watson	2.2		Durbin Watson	2.0	
Estimation period 76 Q3–03 Q2			Estimation period 76 Q1–03 Q2			Estimation period 83 Q2–03 Q2		
ECT1* = $q_{1t}–h_t–1.37y_t$			ECT2* = $q_{2t}–h_t–0.44y_t$			ECT3* = $q_{3t}–h_t–1.15y_t–0.32(pa_t–p_{3t})$		
Diagnostic tests[3]		P-values	Diagnostic tests[3]		P-values	Diagnostic tests[3]		P-values
Serial correlation		0.18	Serial correlation		0.45	Serial correlation		0.90
Heteroskedasticity		0.43	Heteroskedasticity		0.16	Heteroskedasticity		0.23
Normality		0.86	Normality		0.61	Normality		0.26
Predictive failure		0.83	Predictive failure		0.14	Predictive failure		0.99

Variable	Long-run elasticities			
	First Class (non-presort)	Second Class (non-presort)	Other (mainly presort)	Total traffic
Economic activity, y	1.37	0.44	1.15	1.02
First Class letter price, p	–0.72	0.55	na	–0.03
Second Class letter price, p_2	0.53	–0.47	na	0.00
Other letter price, p_3	na	na	–0.32	–0.16
Quality of service, *qos*	ns	0.49	na	0.12
Price of non-mail advertising, *pa*	na	na	0.32	0.16
Estimated total time trends impact per auum in 2003 Q2 (%)	–3.0	–2.0	1.3	–0.6

Notes:

1. Definition of variables (lower-case denotes natural logarithm): q_i index of volume of product stream i (i = 1, . . . 3, where 1 = First Class non-presort, 2 = Second Class non-presort, 3 = Other (mainly presort)); p_i, index of price of product stream i (i = 1, ..., 3) deflated by all items Retail Prices Index (RPI), where the Other traffic letter price, p_3, is proxied by the p_2 index price under the assumption that the discount rate applied to presorted products was broadly constant over time and that nearly all presorted traffic is non-First Class; h, number of households; ECT, Error Correction Term; y, Gross Value Added weighted by each sector's contribution to letter demand; *pa*, price of non-mail advertising deflated by RPI; *qos*, quality of service for First Class; Δ, change operator. The estimated models also include deterministic variables such as constant, seasonal dummy and time trends, which were statistically significant at the 5% level.
2. Trend refers to a time-trend variable starting in the first calendar quarter of the estimation period. T87 refers to a time-trend variable equal to: 1 in 1987Q1, 2 in 1987Q2, . . . and 66 in 2003Q2 and equal to zero for all other quarters. Similarly, T97: 1 in 1997Q1, . . .
3. The reported diagnostic tests undertaken to the residuals were the following:
   the Serial Correlation test is a Lagrange multiplier (LM) test of up to 4th order autocorrelation.
   the Normality test is the Jarque–Bera test for normality in the residuals;
   the Heteroskedasticity test is White's test based on the regression of squared residuals on fitted values;
   the predictive failure test is Chow's test with a breakpoint set at 1999Q2.

in Table 6.1. This approach is consistent with that summarized by equation (6A.2) in the appendix.[7]

Another methodological issue considered in the appendix is the importance of undertaking sensitivity or scenario analysis around a central projection of the long-term prospects for mail. 'High'- and 'low'-volume scenarios were developed by considering two possible sources of uncertainty. The first of these related to economic growth. A second source of uncertainty considered the possibility that future e-substitution impacts not incorporated explicitly in the explanatory variables in the model could differ from the central assumptions on additional net trend adjustments.[8]

The assumptions for the values of the explanatory variables used in the projections were based mainly on external sources. An average rate of economic growth to 2010/11 of 2.7 percent was based on published information from the Bank of England and HM Treasury. The high- and low-volume cases applied sensitivities whose annual averages over the years to 2010/11 were 3.0 and 2.1 percent, respectively, but the two volume scenarios retained the assumptions for all other variables from the central volume case. The projection for household growth (0.7 percent per annum) was sourced externally while prices were assumed to move approximately in line with the overall price control in the then current period (RPI – 1 percent per annum).[9] The assumptions for the Bayesian-style adjustment factors anticipating a possible structural break were to reduce the net trend elements from the ILTM and to do so by a larger amount each year up to and including 2010/11. The cumulative effect of these adjustments was a reduction of about 12 percent in total over the whole period. These values were lowered by a half in the high-volume sensitivity and increased by a half for the low scenario.

Projections and Sources of Differences

Table 6.2 summarizes the projections made in 2004, outcomes over the period to 2010/11 and the sources of differences between them using the framework in the appendix. We report results for both the central case and the low-volume scenario. The data-based forecast component of the projection is recorded in line 1. From Table 6.1, the key variable driving this part of the forecast was economic activity. As this was assumed to grow broadly in line with its historical average so too was traffic. For the central case, this component of the projection implied growth of 24 percent in volumes and 19 percent in the low projection. The second element of the projection sought to anticipate the structural break in traffic (line 2). The projection adopted by Royal Mail Group, which included both elements, was for traffic growth of 12 percent over the 7 years to 2010/11 (line 3). In the low scenario projection, volumes were approximately at their 2003/04 levels. Volumes in fact fell by 22 percent by 2010/11 compared with 2003/04 (line 7).

As discussed in the first subsection of the appendix, differences between the projected and outcome traffic volumes can be ascribed to five potential sources of error: errors in forecasting model input variables; revisions to past observations of variables used to estimate the model; errors in the estimation of parameters; random model error; and structural breaks. First, there was a significant error from the forecasting of future values of the explanatory variables in the model. To estimate this impact we applied the long-run elasticities and time-trend coefficients reported in Table 6.1 to estimates of outcomes for each of the variables and calculated the difference in the forecast to that produced in 2004

Table 6.2 Projections, outcomes and sources of differences, 2003/04 to 2010/11

Component of projection/ outcome	Volume growth 2003/04 to 2010/11,%			
	Central case		Low scenario	
	Volume growth	of which due to:	Volume growth	of which due to:
Ex ante projection in 2004				
1. Data-based forecast using time-series econometric model and forecasts for input variables in 2004[1]	24		19	
+2. Adjustments anticipating structural break[2]	–12		–17	
=3. *Projection adopted by Royal Mail Group*	*12*		*2*	
Ex post projection				
+4. Impact of errors in forecasting input variables (mainly UK recession, 2008-09)[3]		–14		–9
+5. Impact of: errors in past observations of variables and in estimation of parameters; and from random model errors[4]		–2		–2
+6. Impact of unanticipated part of structural break (mainly additional effects of e-substitution and Internet)[5]		–18		–13
=7. *Outcome*	–22		–22	

Notes:

1. Forecasts in line 1 are derived from the econometric model reported in Table 6.1, using 2004 input driver assumptions for the period 2004/05 to 2010/11.
2. The magnitude of the structural break that was anticipated, as reported in line 2, is equal to the cumulative impact of the additional net trend adjustments assumed in 2004.
3. Line 4 is estimated as the difference between the projections derived in note 2 and projections using reported outcome input driver data available in May 2011, where the impact of the outcome data is estimated using the long run elasticities and coefficients from the econometric model reported in Table 6.1.
4. Line 5 is the sum of two calculations. The first provides the estimate jointly of the impact of errors in past observations of variables and in the estimation of parameters. This is estimated as the difference between the projections derived in note 3 and projections using the same input driver variables as in note 3 but based on updated econometric estimates for the long run coefficients for all variables except the time trends contained in Veruete-McKay et al. (2011) (this accounted for less than 1½%). The second calculation is for the impact of random model error and this is estimated as the difference between the projections using the full econometric model reported in Veruete-McKay et al. and the observed outcome (this accounted for less than ½%).
5. Line 6 is estimated as the difference between the projections derived in note 4 and projections using the full econometric model reported in Veruete-McKay et al. with input driver variable reported outcomes available in May 2011, including updated time trend coefficients and additional variables contained in that version of the model. Note that the latter variables were not included in the version of the econometric model used to construct the projections in 2004.

using the forecast values for the input variables at that time. Strictly, this provides an estimate of the extent to which the projection would have been closer to the outcome if the input variables in the model had been forecast perfectly. Additionally, however, the ILTM has been re-estimated subsequently with data extending to 2008Q1 (see Veruete-McKay et al., 2011). The estimated parameter values and long-run elasticities for economic activity, prices and quality of service remained close to those reported in Table 6.1 and the new version of the model forecasts well up to and including 2010/11. We therefore consider that using the 2004 model to assess errors from the forecasting of input variables also reflects accurately the impact of these variables on the demand for mail to 2011.

Nearly all of the error arising from the forecasting of the explanatory variables in the model was due to the recession in the UK during 2008–09. UK economic output fell by about 5 percent over the two years rather than rising by about 5 percent in line with trend as was assumed in the data based forecast.[10] Jointly these impacts are estimated to have adversely affected mail volumes by about 14 percent over the period compared with the central case projections, predominantly during the recession in 2008–09, and by about 9 percent compared with the low-volume scenario projection (line 4).

The second and third sources of errors (revisions to past observations of variables and errors in model parameter estimates) are considered together. To estimate their impact we have used information from the ILTM model re-estimated with data extending up to 2008Q1[11] and updated estimates of the long-run elasticities for the variables included in the earlier model reported in Table 6.1. The joint impact of these effects is estimated to be less than 1½ percent (see Table 6.2, note 4). The fourth source of error, which is that associated with model random error, is estimated to be under ½ percent and is calculated as the difference between the projections using the full econometric model reported in Veruete-McKay et al. and the observed outcome. Our total estimate then of these three sources of error jointly is small at –2 percent (line 5).

The fifth source of error arises from the unanticipated component of the structural break for the demand for mail and is very significant. We have estimated this by using results from the full equations in Veruete-McKay et al., which include further updated estimates for the time-trend coefficients in the model and also other variables, most notably a variable measuring internet advertising expenditure as a proportion of total advertising expenditure[12]. Our estimate for the central case projection for this source of error is –18 percent and –13 percent for the low-volume scenario (line 6). Note that the use of adjustments reflecting Bayesian informative priors here reduced, although only in part, the extent of the total error in the projection arising from the structural break.

3 IMPLICATIONS

In this section we draw a number of key implications from our case study for the future application of our general framework for preparing long-term projections of mail volumes. These implications relate mainly to the case where a set of projections is prepared to inform a particular decision which, once made, cannot be revised. The case study in Section 2 relating to a price control review is an example of this type.

1. *Assessment and re-estimation of data-based models.* The analysis of outcomes versus projections (OVP) is an effective way to undertake an ongoing assessment of the model used to prepare the data-based forecast. Where differences between outcomes and projections are relatively small, random and unbiased the model in place is likely to remain satisfactory for future projections that may be required. However, where OVP analysis begins to highlight systematic and substantial bias in errors, this suggests that a structural break may be emerging and points to the likely

need to re-estimate the model itself.[13] Where, of course, a set of projections has been prepared for a particular purpose, the projections themselves cannot be changed and are irreversible.

In practice, such a process of assessment and re-estimation is not instantaneous. There may be a lag of a few quarters before reliable outcome data allow the impact of a structural break to be identified satisfactorily using econometric techniques. Concern that such a change is unfolding may come about more quickly. During a period of transition there is considerable uncertainty regarding the time profile, form and full final extent of the structural break. For example, in the case study in Section 2, there was a structural break in the dynamics of the UK mail market which began to become evident from OVP analysis during 2005 and 2006. However, the earliest that it would have been possible to begin to identify the impact of the structural break econometrically was probably in the second half of 2006 using time-series data up to 2006Q1.[14]

2. *Forecasting of input variables* A second set of issues relates to the forecasting of input variables in the data-based component of the projections. As noted in Section 2, this is one of the main potential sources of error and, as shown by our case study, a significant part of the error in the forecasts was due to the forecasting of input variables linked primarily to the UK recession in 2008–09. Since economic growth remains one of the prime drivers of mail volumes (see Veruete-McKay et al., 2011) it seems prudent to incorporate the possibility of a recession when constructing long-term volume projections. The observed outcome for economic growth over the period from 2004/05 to 2010/11 was around 1 percent per annum and for the UK economy, at least, an average of about 1 percent appears appropriate for a long-term downside scenario. However, with inflation targeting in place in the UK (and many other countries), there is an asymmetry around a central forecast for economic growth. It is less likely that this will be well in excess of its trend rate over a significant period due to the use of monetary policy to curb inflationary pressures. This suggests strongly that assumptions for economic growth in an upside scenario might be expected to be closer to the central forecast than assumptions for a downside scenario which reflect the possibility of a recession.
3. *Sensitivity analysis and Monte Carlo simulations* This raises the issue more broadly of the use of sensitivity analysis in the consideration of uncertainty in projections. The first subsection of the appendix discusses the approach to this through resampling techniques such as Monte Carlo simulations. Approaches of this type have indicated wide margins of possible outcomes around a central forecast for mail volumes.[15] The case study in Section 2 included sensitivities for economic activity and the adjustments anticipating increased impacts from e-substitution during the projection period. However, as shown in Table 6.2, the downside projection proved to be insufficiently pessimistic given the combination of a severe recession and a major structural break in the demand for mail. The sensitivities were not incorporated into a set of Monte Carlo simulations and specified only high and low values. The experimental studies cited indicate the clear value of adopting a more comprehensive approach to the treatment of uncertainty when undertaking scenario-based business analysis.

Such simulations should be applied both to the data-based component of the model as well as to Bayesian informative priors in the non-identified part of the projection. A simulation approach with probabilistic specification of input variables would be likely to result in a significantly wider range of possible outcomes and a more comprehensive reflection of the uncertainty surrounding a central set of forecasts. The distribution of outcomes from these simulations would assist in defining downside and upside cases more fully, for example from percentiles of the distribution of modeled outcomes, and would provide additional information to assist in the management of the consequences of volume uncertainty. Specific scenarios could also be undertaken as part of business analysis of the long-term prospects for the demand for mail and then assessed, with respect to their likelihood, within a Monte Carlo framework.

4. *Importance of non-identified part of the overall model* Where there is an expectation of a structural break, a data-based forecast is likely to prove insufficient. Section 2 illustrated the important role of the non-identified part of the model in making projections. The approach adopted there, with adjustments to projections in anticipation of possible additional effects from e-substitution, was fairly simple and largely deterministic rather than probabilistic in form reflecting Royal Mail Group's initial and only partly developed application of the full approach set out in the current chapter. Nevertheless the adjustments moved the projections in the direction of the final outcomes by about 12 percent in the central case by the end of the 7 years of the projections and by 17 percent in the low volume scenario. The principle of applying such adjustments to data-based forecasts appears to us to be established firmly both in terms of a theoretical methodological framework, as outlined in the appendix, and also empirically through our case study in Section 2. With regard to future projections, the difficult issue that arises is the size of the Bayesian-style adjustment that should be made which is inherently subject to a substantial degree of uncertainty.

An updated version of the ILTM was re-estimated (with data to 2008Q1) and forecast satisfactorily for a further three-year period to 2010/11. This could be interpreted erroneously as suggesting that, as the model appears to have been well identified up to 2011, any adjustments to the data-based forecast should be set to zero. First, there is continuing structural change in the postal market from the impact of e-substitution. The time profile of this process can be depicted as a 'large corrugated s-curve' (Nikali, 2008) where structural change is non-linear and implies that potential adjustments to a data-based forecast should be considered explicitly. Second, there may be non-identified effects other than e-substitution. An example could be the possibility, say due to a change in government policy, of recipients of direct mail being required to opt in to receive direct mail rather opting out. Overall, adjustments to the data-based forecast to reflect non-identified effects related to e-substitution or other factors could be negative or positive depending on whether these effects might be expected to strengthen or moderate relative to those incorporated in the data-based model estimated from historical data.

Accordingly, there is a need to continue to develop the non-identified parts of the model for projecting mail volumes to augment the data-based model. This part of the overall framework should take account of impacts from e-substitution and other factors that differ by segment of traffic whether by product stream or content type.[16]

The specifics of the development of the non-identified part of the model for forecasting mail volumes are outside the scope of the current chapter but we consider this to be an important strand of work that should accompany the use of historical data analyzed with econometric techniques. This joint approach is summarized in equation (6A.2) in the appendix.[17]

5. *Managing the implications of uncertainty in long-term projections* During a period of continuous structural change in the demand for mail, any long-term projection of mail volumes is inherently very uncertain however well structured and researched its preparation. At the same time, commercial, planning, operational and regulatory imperatives generate requirements for such projections. A key issue here is that many of these applications require projections to inform decisions made at a specific point in time that cannot be reversed. As a result there is no opportunity for the projections underpinning a decision to be revised and, hence, the projections that support this decision also are irreversible. Requirements for such sets of projections are unlikely to diminish not least because of continuing public policy objectives relating to the provision of universal service in the postal sector. It is essential, therefore, that the high level of uncertainty inherent in the long-term prospects for the demand for mail and the costs associated with errors in long-term forecasts are recognized explicitly in the commercial and regulatory use of such projections.

   In a regulatory context this involves *ex ante* putting in place a framework that underpins robustly the provision of universal service across a very wide range of possible demand outcomes such that the Universal Service Obligation can be met on a continuing basis. As an example, the regulatory framework that was developed in the UK and operated from 2006 introduced mechanisms which attempted to manage the impact of uncertainty in volume outcomes whether above or below a central projection.[18] The specifics of such frameworks lie outside the scope of the current chapter. However, whether in the UK or elsewhere, it remains essential that a proactive approach be followed to manage the consequences arising from the uncertainty inherent in projecting the future demand for mail.

NOTES

* The analysis contained in this chapter reflects the views of the authors and are not necessarily those of Royal Mail Group. We would like to thank Marion Frederick for her extensive work on the production and physical preparation of the chapter.

1. An extensive literature exists on forecasting. For example, Clements and Hendry (1998) provide a general presentation and the *Journal of Forecasting* publishes internationally refereed papers on forecasting.
2. Our overall approach is in line with the methodology set out in Fève et al. (2010).
3. One area where this is particularly important is in the design of regulatory frameworks which *inter alia* seek to safeguard the provision of universal service in the postal sector.
4. See Condition 21 of Royal Mail Group's licence prior to 1 October 2011. The Postal Services Act 2011 replaced Postcomm, as the company's regulator, by Ofcom.
5. This reflected the possibility of the regulator setting a control for up to a five-year period (that is, from 2006/07 to 2010/11). Royal Mail Group's financial year runs from April to March so that the first year of the new control period was 2006/07.
6. It should be noted that the price control used an amended set of projections, based on those reported here, which were provided to Postcomm in September 2005. The amended projections were close to those

provided in January 2005, not least because they were prepared using the same versions of the models. However, the January projections represent the outputs from a full forecasting round rather than an update as in September and so provide a better source for our case study.

7. These adjustments, which by their very nature must be judgmental, were based on an assessment of information gathered as part of the re-estimation process for successive versions of the ILTM, from outcome versus projection analysis and from econometric evidence of trend movements in mail volumes in the USA.
8. At the same time, Royal Mail Group noted that it was possible for its future mail volumes to move outside a range defined by the 'high' and 'low' volume scenarios and that this had implications for the structure of the price control to be set by Postcomm (see Section 3).
9. This assumption was solely for the purpose of the projection and clearly did not pre-empt the setting of the price control itself. The all items Retail Prices Index (RPI) is a measure of consumer price inflation used in the UK for price controls applied to regulated utility companies including Royal Mail Group.
10. Output growth was below trend also in 2010/11 and additionally there were less adverse effects on other variables in the model including lower prices for non-mail advertising.
11. As contained in Veruete-McKay et al. (2011).
12. See Soteri et al. (2009) for a detailed discussion of this variable.
13. Standard statistical measures and tests would be applied in making such an assessment. In a situation where a model was to be updated each period, we would follow the process set out in Fève et al. (2010).
14. See Soteri et al. (2009). This was well after the time such a model could have been adopted for the projections required for price control review purposes.
15. See Cazals et al. (2008) and Fève et al. (2010).
16. There is an important dimension to this also in terms of sender–recipient categories and factors affecting changes to preferences for sending and receiving mail in a disaggregated analysis (for example, Elkelä, 2011).
17. Our theoretical framework has some similarities with approaches that focus primarily on non-identified models but with a data-based component to the forecast. An example is BCG (2010) which projects mail volumes in the USA to 2020. Our approach, however, emphasizes the requirement, first, for a well-specified econometric model and the role of a data-based forecast from this to which, second, should be added a non-identified part of the projection evaluated by prior distributions.
18. See Condition 21.14 of Royal Mail Group's licence prior to 1 October 2011.

REFERENCES

Boston Consulting Group (BCG) (2010), 'Projecting US mail volumes to 2020: compendium', available at: http://www.prc.gov/(S(4fn3sp553yb4dm45gbfebc55))/Docs/68/68381/NALC.T2.Q.5.BCG.Projection.pdf (accessed 6 August 2010).

Cazals, C., J.P. Florens, F. Rodriguez and S. Soteri (2008), 'Forecast uncertainty in dynamic models: an application to the demand for mail', in M.A. Crew and P.R. Kleindorfer (eds), *Competition and Regulation in the Postal and Delivery Sector*, Cheltenham, UK and Northampton, MA, USA: Edward Elgar, pp. 63–73.

Clements, M. and D. Hendry (1998), *Forecasting Economic Time Series*, New York: Cambridge University Press.

Elkelä, K. (2011), 'Invoicing in 16 European countries', in M.A. Crew and P.R. Kleindorfer (eds), *Reinventing the Postal Sector in an Electronic Age*, Cheltenham, UK and Northampton, MA, USA: Edward Elgar, pp. 20–35.

Fève, F., J.P. Florens, F. Rodriguez and S. Soteri (2010), 'Forecasting mail volumes in an evolving market environment', in M.A. Crew and P.R. Kleindorfer (eds), *Heightening Competition in the Postal and Delivery Sector*, Cheltenham, UK and Northampton, MA, USA: Edward Elgar, pp. 116–34.

Florens, J.P., V. Marimoutou and A. Peguin-Feisolle (2007), *Econometric Modelling and Inference*, New York: Cambridge University Press.

Florens, J.P., M. Mouchart and J.M. Robin (1989), *Elements of Bayesian Statistics*, New York: M. Dekker.

Nikali, H. (2008), 'Substitution of letter mail for different sender-receiver segments', in M.A.

Crew and P.R. Kleindorfer (eds), *Competition and Regulation in the Postal and Delivery Sector*, Cheltenham, UK and Northampton, MA, USA: Edward Elgar, pp. 89–106.
Postcomm (2006), 'Licence Granted to Royal Mail Group Limited on 23 March 2001' (as amended subsequently on May 25, 2006), available at: www.psc.gov.uk (accessed 25 May 2006).
Soteri, S., F. Fève, J.P. Florens and F. Rodriguez (2009), 'Internet advertising and direct mail: trends and analysis for the UK', in M.A. Crew and P.R. Kleindorfer (eds), *Progress in the Competitive Agenda in the Postal and Delivery Sector*, Cheltenham, UK and Northampton, MA, USA: Edward Elgar, pp. 209–22.
Veruete-McKay, L., S. Soteri, J.C. Nankervis and F. Rodriguez (2011), 'Letter traffic demand in the UK: an analysis by product and envelope content type', *Review of Network Economics*, **10** (3).

APPENDIX 6A FORECASTING THEORY AND METHODOLOGICAL FRAMEWORK

Economic phenomena are difficult to forecast because they are generated by non-stationary mechanisms containing important elements of uncertainty. In contrast to observations in the natural sciences which are usually assumed to be reproducible because they are generated by time-invariant laws, economic events are 'unique': for example, the conditions under which GDP is generated in the UK differs across different time periods and are specific to each observation. The regularity in the generation of economic phenomena cannot come from the complete explanation of these phenomena but may follow only from the relations between the different components of the event. This is the reason why econometric models usually take the form of relations between variables and regularity is investigated through the stability of the parameters of these relations. These econometric equations ('regression functions' or 'cointegration relations') involve only a limited number of variables even if the total understanding of the phenomena needs a large number of elements. The absence of numerous variables is then compensated by the introduction of random unobservable elements introducing a degree of uncertainty in the model. Non-stationarity and uncertainty explain why economic forecasting is extremely difficult and why the analysis of forecasting errors is important.

In order to discuss the forecasting problems in economics relevant to modeling the demand for mail we distinguish between two levels of techniques. First we consider what we call 'data-based forecasting' and in a second step analyze data and 'expert-based forecasting'. Note that in both cases we consider model-based forecasting and assume that the models used are not *ad hoc* tools only justified by the data but represent economically interpretable relations (demand or supply functions typically).

Data-based Forecasting

The forecasting challenge may be expressed as follows: we are at date T and wish to forecast one or several variables k periods ahead. Where we denote by Y_{T+k} the unknown future values of these variables and by $\hat{Y}^T_{T+k}$ their forecasts made at time T. To realize this objective we have an 'information set' containing variables observed for different time periods (for example, from 1 to T) and denote by X_t the observed variables at time $t = 1, \ldots, T$. We assume the variables of interest Y_t are part of X_t and denote by Z_t the other observed variables ($X_t = (Y_t, Z_t)$).

If X_T represents the history of X_t, $\hat{Y}^T_{T+k}$ is a function of elements of X_T only. Note that the larger X_T is the better the forecasts we have. Even if some information may be irrelevant it cannot decrease the quality of the forecast. However the size of the information set is limited by constraints on its tractability. The way to forecast Y in this context is the following. First, we specify a set of relations between Y and Z (and possibly past values of these variables plus some deterministic elements such as a trend). Typically these relations have an economic interpretation and depend on unknown parameters θ, which is a vector containing α, β, γ, δ, and involve a random unobservable component U_t. For example, we may consider a linear relation:

$$Y_t = \alpha + \beta Y_{t-1} + \gamma Z_t + \delta t + U_t, \qquad (6A.1)$$

which is linear, dynamic (due to Y_{t-1}) and contains a linear trend δt and a random white noise term U_t

Next, this relation is estimated using the information set to yield: estimated values of the parameters ($\hat{\alpha}$, $\hat{\beta}$, $\hat{\gamma}$, $\hat{\delta}$); information about the precision of this estimation; and an evaluation of the magnitude of errors (the variance of U_t). This relation can then be tested by examining: the stability of the parameters; the functional form of the relation; exogeneity of the variables; and the normality of the statistical noise, among others.

Forecasting is then undertaken in two steps. First, the Z variables are forecast by $\hat{Z}^T_{T+k}$. Then the model explaining Y as a function of Z is used for forecasting: Z is replaced by $\hat{Z}^T_{T+k}$, the estimated equation generates $\hat{Y}^T_{T+k}$ and the residuals are set to 0. In practice, several forecasts are prepared for several future periods ($T + k$ to $T + k + s$).

From a statistical viewpoint a good forecasting method should be evaluated *ex ante* (before the realizations of the future values) and satisfy two properties. First, there should be no systematic error in the forecast. Given the information available at time T, the forecast error $Y_{T+k} - \hat{Y}^T_{T+k}$ (the difference between true and forecast values) should have a zero mean (at least if the information set is large). Note that the available information should contain the forecast of the explanatory variables Z if they do not come from the information set. This does not mean that the statistician had used all the relevant information but rather that the available information was used correctly (in particular that the parameters were correctly estimated).

Second, there should be a correct evaluation of the uncertainty surrounding the forecast. This is formalized by the estimation of the variance of the forecast error $Y_{T+k} - \hat{Y}^T_{T+k}$ which should be used to construct confidence intervals for the prediction. For example, 'fan charts' can be constructed using Monte Carlo simulations, as in Cazals et al. (2008), to depict confidence intervals at many different percentage values. Usually such confidence intervals increase with the forecast time horizon. If the model remains identical the fan chart is located around 0, but if the model changes in a non-anticipated way by the econometrician, the chart is centered around systematic errors. A naive analysis of the evaluation of this variance reduces to a consideration of the variance of the unobservable components. As has been illustrated in Cazals et al., this computation can underestimate considerably the error's variance, which may arise from many sources (see Clements and Hendry, 1998).

First, forecast errors may arise from the explanatory variables $Z(Z_{T+K} - \hat{Z}^T_{T+k})$. Second, the errors could be due to past observations (for example, recent observations of GDP are only estimates that may be revised at a later date). Another possibility is that forecast errors relate to parameter estimates and a fourth source may be associated with random model error (that is, U_t, in equation (6A.1)). Finally, non-stability of the model could arise even if it is well estimated and explains perfectly the past as a structural break may occur in the future which modifies the dynamics of Y.

The first four sources of forecast errors identified above may be taken into account by statistical techniques (mainly based on resampling methods such as Monte Carlo or bootstrap). However, the last one (future breaks in the model) cannot be determined solely by historical data and should be derived from information coming from other sources. In order to control for possible changes in the model the best strategy is to update it in the light of new information as it becomes available. Analyses of outcomes versus projections (OVP) should be undertaken on a regular basis, and where there is evidence of systematic errors, this would point to a requirement to re-specify and re-estimate the model. This strategy is an efficient means to detect structural breaks in the model. If a new observation is out of the confidence interval of the prediction, a change in the data-generating process may be suspected (for example, a modification of the slope of a trend). For short-term forecasting, this may be neglected if the break has a relatively low magnitude but should be incorporated into the model for longer-term forecasting.

Forecasting with Non-identified Models Using Information from Several Sources

The main characteristic of the data-based approach to forecast variables outlined above is to consider a statistical model which is assumed to be identified; that is, a model where all the unknown parameters may be estimated using the dataset (even with possibly large errors). We next consider a larger model construction which may be non-identified; that is, a model where the available statistical observations do not contain information on all the parameters (as, for example, in a linear model with collinear explanatory variables).

Why is analysis of this larger model of interest? The first reason is that it is more relevant to economics modeling which is likely to contain unobservable variables. For example, a demand model for mail should incorporate the impact of the use of email and other forms of electronic communications. However, our knowledge of the use of these technologies is not complete and a model which is extended to electronic mail will have several unobservable variables. A second reason is to incorporate in the model the possibility of regime changes in the future or of structural breaks in the model. These elements of the model are, by their very nature, unobservable and make the model non-identified. The standard way to introduce unobservable variables in a model is to assume that they are generated by a statistical model depending on parameters but that these parameters may be non-identified (for a summary of problems arising from unobservable components in a model, see Florens et al., 2007, ch. 18).

Non-identified models cannot be used directly for forecasting using the data set X_T as they need to be completed by information on the non-identified parameters. This information may be deterministic (the value of the parameter is fixed) but it is better to specify a probability distribution on the non-identified parameters (for example, a normal distribution). This probabilistic information is then viewed as a prior information in the statistical terminology. We consider the model as a Bayesian model where the prior information may be vague on the identified parameters and precise on the non-identified parameters. Indeed the data will give information on identified parameters but the prior will be unchanged by the sample for the non-identified parameters. The concepts of non-informative and informative priors have been studied extensively in Bayesian statistics (see, for example, Florens et al., 1989). The main interest in probabilistic specification of the prior information (compared to deterministic) is for the prior to be revised and updated when new data and information become available (see Fève et al., 2010).

The main question is how to derive informative prior distributions. Usually they are informed by other models (perhaps using observations of mail demand in other countries which may be assumed to be 'in advance' of a country under study) but are not immediately treated as data generated by the model. They may also be informed from different data sources, such as opinion surveys. If such quantitative information exists it should be used by experts to form informative priors on the non-identified parameters of the model. For example, consider equation (6A.1) but assume that after period T (the last observed period) the equation is modified into:

$$t > T \qquad Y_t = \alpha + \beta Y_{t-1} + \gamma Z_t + \delta t + \Lambda_t + U_t, \tag{6A.2}$$

where Λ_t is a new element acting on the variable Y. For instance Λ_t may be equal to $\lambda\zeta_t$, where ζ_t is a new variable (not observed before T) and λ is a parameter. The Bayesian model will put a prior distribution on λ (for example, a mean value and measurement of uncertainty) and will introduce a model generating the future values of ζ_t. This model will involve parameters provided also by a prior distribution. In this example the first part of equation (6A.2), $\alpha + \beta Y_{t-1} \gamma Z_t + \delta t$, represents the data-based component of the forecast and Λ_t the non-identified part of the forecast evaluated by prior distributions.

7. Do volume increases and decreases have the same effect on labor hours?*

Michael D. Bradley[†], **Jeff Colvin**[‡] **and Mary K. Perkins**[§]

1 INTRODUCTION

The overwhelming majority of postal costs are labor costs and the study of the response of labor hours to volume changes has been a major focus of postal costing analysis. It has been the central topic of a number of previous papers across the range of postal functions. Studies have examined the responsiveness of hours to volume changes in various activities and in many cases found cost elasticities significantly lower than one (see Bradley and Robinson, 1988; Bradley and Colvin, 1995, 1999; Cazals et al., 2001; Gazzei et al., 2002). However, this result is most pronounced in studies of delivery costs (such as Cazals et al., 2004a, 2004b; Bradley et al., 2006; Farsi et al., 2006). Indeed, the notion that hours would increase more slowly than volume accords well with one's intuition regarding the delivery activity. However, how do workhours behave when mail volume is falling rather than increasing? Intuition suggests that hours would fall more slowly than volumes, but by how much? Is there a symmetric response in hours to volume increase and decreases? Until recently it has not been possible to answer this question empirically, since no observations, or very few, existed for falling volumes.

With the end of the era of persistently rising volume many posts now face the possibility of ongoing volume declines arising from a mixture of long-term trends (electronic diversion) and stagnation. This raises the question as to whether the cost studies performed in an era of ever-increasing volume are still appropriate in an era of flat or declining volume, a question of high interest to postal analysts and postal management, as cost measurement remains of key importance to policy decisions. Informal analysis suggests the need for more attention to this issue, as there are a variety of reasons why reducing hours in response to volume declines may not be as easy as adding hours in response to volume growth. These include job tenure restrictions associated with union contracts, the need to maintain universal service at existing levels, simultaneous growth in the number of delivery points as volume declines, and the productivity characteristics of manual labor in network industries. If indeed labor hours are materially less responsive to falling volumes than increasing ones, a number of important policy questions need to be investigated. For example, if labor is sufficiently inflexible with respect to volume declines,

† Professor of Economics, George Washington University.
‡ Manager of Cost Attribution, United States Postal Service.
§ Associate Professor of Economics, Howard University.

owing to the basic nature of a network and/or to the institutional arrangements governing labor relations, it might not be possible to finance the Universal Service Obligation (USO) in the face of volume declines without significant changes to the regime in which a given post operates.

It is not our goal to address these policy issues in this chapter, as there have been initial investigations into the policy implications of asymmetric cost responses, sometimes drawing upon simulated data (see, for example, Harman et al., 2010). In contrast, there has been little or no empirical work investigating the presence and degree of cost asymmetries. Thus, the objective of this chapter is to produce evidence useful for evaluating the existence of and measuring such an asymmetry. To do this, we employ a battery of empirical models including a threshold model, a rolling regression model, and a regime-switching model. Each of these models can contribute to our understanding of how delivery costs behave during the period of volume declines. For example, we can test the assumption of a symmetric response in hours to volume changes by estimating non-linear switching models for the outside and inside carrier activity. These models have the ability to estimate separate responses in hours to volume increases and decreases and provide formal tests of the hypothesized equality of those responses. As described below, we use historical data from the United States Postal Service to estimate the models.

The remainder of the chapter is structured as follows. In Section 2, we provide a brief description of the Postal Service's delivery network and describe the data we shall be using. Sections 3, 4, and 5 present the models that we shall be using to investigate asymmetry as well as the empirical results generated by estimating those models. They are a threshold model, a rolling regression model and a switching model, respectively. Section 6 concludes and discusses future research issues.

2 BACKGROUND AND DATA

We use data from the United States Postal Service's city carrier delivery network. City carriers deliver mail primarily in urban and suburban locations and the Postal Service has approximately 150,000 city carrier routes that deliver mail to about 90 million delivery points. The direct wage cost of operating the city carrier network was over $15 billon in the Postal Service's most recent fiscal year. When indirect costs such as supervision, building maintenance and benefits are included the cost rises to almost $21 billion per year. This is nearly 28 percent of the Postal Service's total annual cost.

The dataset consists of weekly observations on delivered volume, hours spent in the office by city carriers and hours spent on the street by city carriers. The data cover five fiscal years from FY 2006 through FY 2010. The Postal Service's fiscal year starts on October 1, so the dataset covers the period from October 1, 2006 through September 30, 2010. During this period, the average weekly delivered volume on the city carrier network fell from 2.8 billion pieces to 2.1 billion pieces. But this decline was not uniform. As Figure 7.1 shows, volume was steady or increasing in 2006 and 2007, fell sharply in 2008 and 2009 and then started to recover in 2010. As a result, the period includes many weeks during which volume increased and many weeks during which volume decreased.

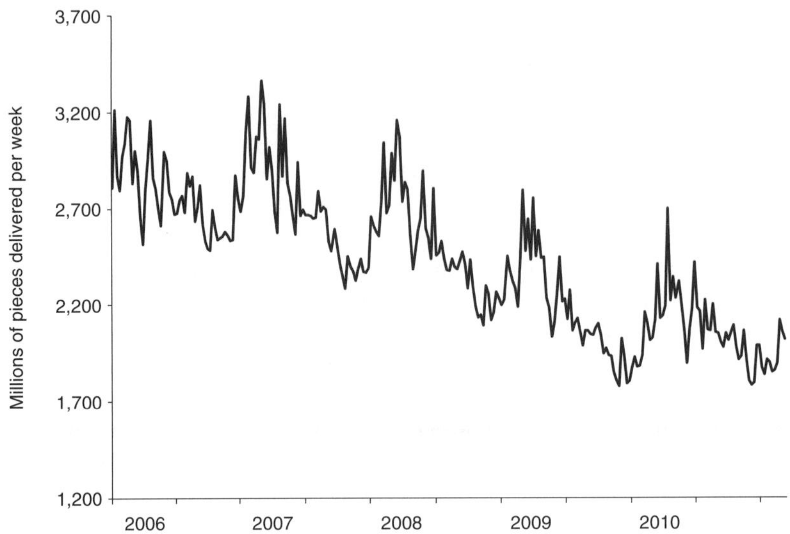

Figure 7.1 Volume delivered on the city carrier network

Figure 7.2 Weekly city carrier office hours

While volume was falling, the Postal Service also reduced its city carrier office hours (Figure 7.2) and city carrier street hours (Figure 7.3). The decline in office hours appears to have started sooner and to be a more pronounced downward trend than the decline in street hours.

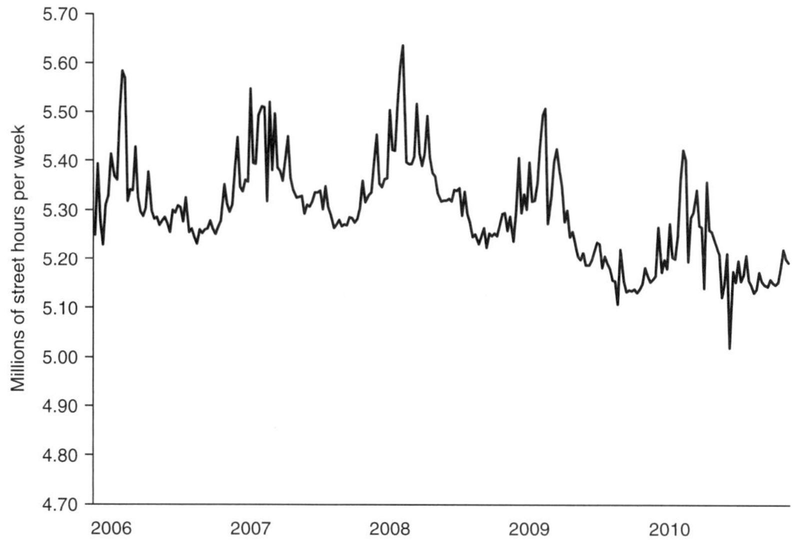

Figure 7.3 *Weekly city carrier street hours*

3 USING A THRESHOLD MODEL TO EXAMINE ASYMMETRIES IN OFFICE AND STREET HOURS

In this section, we use a threshold autoregressive (TAR) model to investigate the adjustment in hours through time and test whether that adjustment process asymmetric. That is, we test whether it is different during periods of volume decline from during periods of volume increase. A TAR model specifies (at least) two sets of dynamics for the variable of interest, y, with the regime switch dependent upon the value of a 'transition' variable, labeled z (see Hansen, 1997 and Tsay, 1989). The threshold model can be written as:

$$y_t = a_0 + \sum_{i=1}^{p} \alpha_i y_{t-i} + \left(\sum_{i=1}^{p} \beta_i y_{t-i}\right)\delta_t + \varepsilon_t,$$

where:

$$\delta_t = \begin{cases} 0 \text{ if } z_{t-d} \leq c \\ 1 \text{ if } z_{t-d} > c \end{cases}$$

In the threshold approach the behavior of the variable y_t is a pth order autoregressive model governed by the coefficients α_i when the transition variable z_{t-d} is below the threshold value, c. When the transition variable is greater than the threshold value, the behavior of the variable y_t is an autoregressive model governed by the coefficients $\alpha_i + \beta_i$. Thus the variable y_t changes behavior depending on the relationship between the transition variable and the threshold.

The transition variable is the observable state variable we mentioned above. Changes in this variable lead to changes in the behavior of y_t. The transition variable has a subscript

Table 7.1 Selecting the lag length for street hours

Lags	AIC	SIC
2	–6.47919	–6.3669
3	–6.49784	–6.3695
4	–6.59436	–6.4500
5	–6.65123	–6.4908
6	–6.64199	–6.4655
7	–6.63241	–6.4399

$t–d$ to indicate that it is a lagged value, and d is an integer value which is non-negative. The parameter d is known as the 'delay,' and indicates the delay between changes in the transition variable and changes in the behavior of y_t.

The TAR model seems simple, with an indicator variable δ switching from zero to one as the transition variable crosses a threshold value. This is a step function, with δ zero when z_{t-d} is on one side of the threshold and one when z_{t-d} is on the other side. Yet, despite this simplicity, the TAR model has proven useful as a model to capture non-linear behavior. For applications of threshold models see Bradley and Jansen, 2002, 2004 and 2011.

In this instance, we shall model separately the dynamics for street hours and office hours. The threshold variable will be the change in volume. Specifically we shall separate periods in which volume is rising from periods in which volume is falling, so the z variable will be the change in volume and the c parameter will be zero. We do this by setting the delay equal to zero so we are examining a possible switch in response that begins with the contemporaneous change in volume.

Note that the transition variable just defines when the alternative dynamics would begin and a contemporaneous transition variable does not imply that hours are responding contemporaneously to volume changes. The response in hours will take time and we capture this with a lagged adjustment mechanism in our model. Based upon our understanding of the Postal Service adjustment process, we allow for two types of adjustment. First, we specify that current period hours could be determined, in part, by the value from the same period last year (SPLY). This reflects a longer-term planning and adjustment process. In addition, we allow within-year adjustment. This reflects a shorter-term reaction to volume changes. This process is less well defined and we use the data to determine its length by allowing it to be as long as 26 weeks and then using formal statistical tests to determine its actual length.

The first step in specifying the threshold autoregressive model is to identify the appropriate lag length for the dynamic model. The lag structure was chosen by application of the Schwarz Information Criterion (SIC) although the results were confirmed by the Akaike Information Criterion (AIC). As Table 7.1 shows, the information criteria indicate that five lags are appropriate.

In addition, the model includes seasonal dummies and the value of street hours from the same period in the previous years.[1] This latter term was included to test whether there is any stickiness in the delivery network in which current hours are dependent upon the previous year's hours, regardless of any changes in current conditions, like a fall in volume. With these additions the TAR model estimated for street hours (SH) is:

Table 7.2 TAR Model for street hours

Variable	Coefficient	*t*-statistic	*p*-value
Constant	–0.8469	–0.870	0.385
SH(–1)	0.4192	3.648	0.000
SH(–2)	0.1173	1.439	0.152
SH(–3)	–0.0009	–0.011	0.992
SH(–4)	0.0805	0.824	0.411
SH(–5)	0.3252	3.489	0.001
SH(–52)	0.1211	1.615	0.108
Q2	–0.0110	–3.548	0.001
Q3	–0.0068	–2.429	0.017
Q4	–0.0067	–2.310	0.024
SH(–1)*δ	–0.0647	–0.447	0.656
SH(–2)*δ	0.0960	0.822	0.412
SH(–3)*δ	–0.1155	–0.931	0.353
SH(–4)*δ	0.1637	1.305	0.194
SH(–5)*δ	–0.1727	–1.426	0.156
SH(–52)*δ	0.2154	2.187	0.030
Q2*δ	0.0047	1.175	0.241
Q3*δ	0.0059	1.475	0.138
Q4*δ	0.0104	2.537	0.013
Adjusted *R*–squared	0.846171		
F–statistic	60.929		
Wald statistic *F*(10,188)	4.0145		

$$SH_t = \alpha_0 + \sum_{i=1}^{5} \alpha_{t-i} SH_{t-i} + \alpha_6 SH_{t-52} + \sum_{k=2}^{4} \theta_k Q_k$$

$$+ \left(\sum_{i=1}^{5} \beta_{t-i} SH_{t-i} + \beta_6 SH_{t-52} + \sum_{k=2}^{4} \varphi_k Q_k \right) \delta_t + \varepsilon_t,$$

where:

$$\delta_t = \begin{cases} 0 \text{ if } DV_t \geq 0 \\ 1 \text{ if } DV_t < 0. \end{cases}$$

Note that the dynamics for street time are defined by the α coefficients in times of volume growth but by the sum of the α and β coefficients in times of volume decline. To the extent that the β coefficients are different from zero, then the behavior of street hours during volume declines is different from the behavior during times of volume increases. A Wald test of the null hypothesis that the β coefficients are jointly equal to zero is rejected at any level of significance. The estimated model is presented in Table 7.2.

A comparison of the estimated coefficients from the two regimes provides some insights into how the two periods differ (Table 7.3). Two results are of note. The coefficient on the first-order term is smaller when volumes are falling. This indicates that street hours are less flexible during these periods. In other words, if an increase in volume caused an

Table 7.3 Estimated coefficients from the two regimes

	DV > 0	DV < 0
SH(–1)	0.4192	0.3546
SH(–2)	0.1173	0.2133
SH(–3)	–0.0009	–0.1164
SH(–4)	0.0805	0.2442
SH(–5)	0.3252	0.1525
SH(–52)	0.1211	0.3365

increase in street hours in a previous period, that effect is more likely to be transmitted to subsequent periods than if a decline in volume caused a decline in street hours in a previous period. Note also that this not just a case in which the responsiveness is delayed to later periods. Examination of the sum of the coefficients on the remaining four terms, from lag 2 through lag 5 shows it to be 0.52 during positive volume growth periods and just 0.49 during periods of volume decline. This means that the total response in positive growth periods exceeds that in the negative growth periods.

This finding of more sluggish dynamics in negative growth periods is reinforced by the fact that the estimated coefficient on values of street hours from the previous year is nearly three times as large during periods of volume declines. This means that during periods of volume declines current period hours are more likely to reflect hours for the same period in previous year than during periods of volume increases. This is because there is less adjustment of hours on a year-over-year basis during periods of volume declines.

The estimation of a TAR model for office hours follows the same procedures as described above. The specification of the lag structure indicated that just two lags are appropriate for an autoregressive model for office hours but, unlike street hours, a time trend is also appropriate. The office hour (OH) threshold model thus has the following specification:

$$OH_t = \alpha_0 + \sum_{i=1}^{2}\alpha_{t-i}OH_{t-i} + \alpha_3 OH_{t-52} + \alpha_4 t + \sum_{k=2}^{4} + \theta_k Q_k$$

$$+ \left(\sum_{i=1}^{2}\beta_{t-i}OH_{t-i} + \beta_3 OH_{t-52} + \beta_4 t\sum_{k=2}^{4}\varphi_k Q_k\right)\delta_t + \varepsilon_t,$$

where:

$$\delta_t = \begin{cases} 0 \text{ if } DV_t \leq 0 \\ 1 \text{ if } DV_t < 0. \end{cases}$$

Unlike the results for street hours, the results for office hours provide no evidence of asymmetry in the dynamics. For example, the Wald test fails to reject the null hypothesis that the coefficients are the same during increases and decreases in volume. This suggests that the dynamics of the adjustment in office hours is quite a bit different from than the dynamics of adjustment in street hours. While these threshold models do not produce any evidence as to why the dynamics of the two activities differ, consideration of their operational differences suggests that the results are intuitive.

First and foremost, street activities have a substantial network component that is largely independent of the delivery workload. Every day, carriers must perform a variety of functions, such as driving to the first stop on the route or driving between delivery points, which must be done regardless of the amount of mail delivered. These types of activity are slow to adjust and would be expected to remain in place even when volume was falling. This would reduce the degree of dynamic adjustment to an external shock such as a fall in volume. Office time has a much smaller network component. Second, the method of adjustment is much easier for office time than it is for street time. When office time increases or decreases, the carrier just goes to the street either later or sooner. This can ultimately lead to an adjustment in routes but that is typically done through reorganizing street time. The large degree of network fixity in street activities suggests that street hours are more difficult to adjust. Street delivery is most efficiently accomplished in 'sections' of similar delivery points and this creates an inherent lumpiness in delivery workload. That lumpiness, in turn, makes it more challenging to 'fine tune' delivery hours and makes them less flexible.

The threshold models provide evidence that the dynamics of street hours are different, in a manner consistent with limited network adjustment, during periods of volume decline. However, we are specifically interested in examining whether the relationship between volume and street hours varies between volume increases and volume decreases. We examine this relationship in two ways, first with rolling regressions and second with a switching model.

4 USING ROLLING REGRESSIONS TO EXAMINE THE IMPACT OF DECLINING VOLUME ON THE HOURS ELASTICITY

While the TAR model indicated that the dynamic adjustment in hours has changed, it did not explicitly estimate the relationship between hours and volume. In this section, we use a rolling regression model to investigate whether that relationship has been stable or whether it has been changing as volume declines have become persistent.

A straightforward way to measure the relationship between hours and volume is to estimate the elasticity of hours with respect to changes in volume. One way to examine the impact of volume declines on the relationship between hours of street time and volume is to investigate what has happened to that elasticity during the period of volume decline. We have a dataset of weekly observations on the Postal Service's delivery hours and volume from FY2006 through FY2010, a period over which the Postal Service experienced sharp declines in volume.

A useful way of investigating whether or not there has been any impact on the elasticity of hours with respect to volume is to estimate a set of rolling regressions. A rolling regression model is defined as:

$$y_t(n) = X_t(n)\beta_t(n) + \varepsilon_t(n), t = n, \ldots, T.$$

In this equation, $y_t(n)$ is the vector for the dependent variable, $X_t(n)$ is the matrix of explanatory variables, $\beta_t(n)$ is the vector of regression parameters and $\varepsilon_t(n)$ is the vector

Table 7.4 Initial estimation of street hours model

Variable	Coefficient	t-statistic	p-value
Constant	13.70404	7104.581	0.0000
Volume	0.085991	8.586450	0.0000
Volume^2	–0.068563	–1.041978	0.2984
Delivery Points	0.078703	0.401330	0.6885
Delivery Points^2	–138.3467	–4.420871	0.0000
Volume * Delivery Points	–3.160335	–1.211640	0.2268
Q2	–0.001670	–0.854247	0.3938
Q3	–0.011528	–5.284849	0.0000
Q4	–0.012407	–5.546630	0.0000

Table 7.5 Final estimation of street hours model

Variable	Coefficient	t-statistic	p-value
Constant	13.69782	10959.16	0.0000
Volume	0.109305	11.37150	0.0000
Volume^2	–0.079991	–2.762060	0.0062
Delivery Points	0.727939	4.042463	0.0001
Q3	–0.008243	–4.366994	0.0000
Q4	–0.008953	–4.601409	0.0000

of error terms. The observations on $y_t(n)$ and $X_t(n)$ are of fixed length for any regression and represent the n periods immediately preceding period t. For example, the last regression estimated would cover the periods from $T - n + 1$ through T.

The model we shall be estimating is a basic translog in volume and delivery points including seasonal dummy variables (Q2, Q3 and Q4) to control for seasonal variations in mail volume. It is given by:

$$\ln (SH_t) = \beta_0 + \beta_1 \ln\left(\frac{Vol_t}{\overline{Vol}}\right) + \beta_2 \ln\left(\frac{Vol_t}{\overline{Vol}}\right)^2 + \beta_3 \ln\left(\frac{DP_t}{\overline{DP}}\right) + \beta_4 \ln\left(\frac{DP_t}{\overline{DP}}\right)^2$$

$$+ \beta_5 \ln\left(\frac{Vol_t}{\overline{Vol}}\right) * \ln\left(\frac{DP_t}{\overline{DP}}\right) + \sum_{k=2}^{4} \mu_k Q_k + \varepsilon_t.$$

However, estimation of this model was initially disappointing because of the lack of significant coefficients (Table 7.4).

Investigation revealed that these results reflect the fact that delivery points change very little from week to week so the first-order delivery point term, the second-order delivery point term and the cross-product term are all highly collinear. In addition, the coefficient on the quarter two dummy is insignificant. Dropping the superfluous higher-order terms in delivery points and the quarter two dummy yields more reliable results (Table 7.5). The model produces a short-run elasticity of about 11 percent. This is lower than the elasticity of street time found using cross-sectional data of about 37 percent[2] but is consistent with previous work on short-run elasticities using daily data.[3]

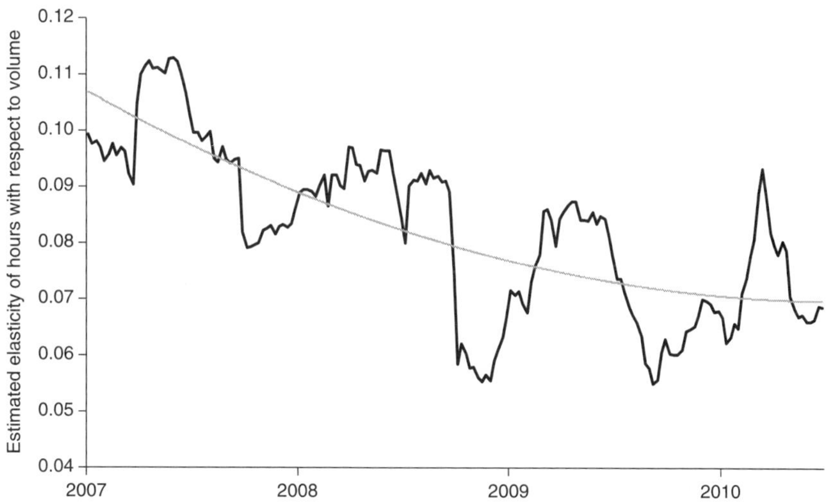

Figure 7.4 Rolling regression results: 1.5-year window

We can now estimate the model using the rolling regression approach. Ideally, one would like the window to be as small as possible to permit investigation of changing coefficients, as long as the window is not so small that the results are unstable. We found that the smallest window that we could use was 1.5 years or 78 observations.[4] Figure 7.4 presents the results for estimating the street time equation using a 78 observation window.

While this shows a fair amount of movement in the estimated hours elasticity, it also shows a marked downward trend. This reflects the fact that the responsiveness of hours to volume has been falling as volume has been falling. Estimation of the trend shows that it is negative and significant. Let μ be the elasticity of street hours with respect to volume. Then a trend equation for the elasticity yields:

$$\mu_t = \underset{(48.11)}{10.7\%} + \underset{(-7.19)}{-0.0405\,t} + \underset{(3.65)}{0.0001\,t^2}. \quad R^2 = 0.75, \;\; 82 \text{ obs.}$$

Note that the t-statistics are presented in the parentheses.

This result is confirmed when the window is extended to two years. Extending the window has both benefits and costs. On the benefit side, it has the advantage of providing more stable results – with more observations used to estimate the equation, the potential impact of an anomalous observation is reduced. On the cost side, it may make it more difficult to identify changes in the structure of the model. This is for two reasons. First, extending the window pushes back the starting date for the analysis and thus reduces the data available that might be generated by differing structures. In our case, extending the window by 26 weeks means that there is no separate rolling regression analysis for 2007. This could be important if the structural change started in this period. Second, extending the window prolongs the influence of historical data in estimating the hours elasticity. For example, the final estimated elasticity will include data from the first half of 2009 under a two-year window, whereas only the second half of 2009 would be included under a year-and-a-half window. If the relationship between hours and volume is stable, this

Figure 7.5 Rolling regression results: 2-year window

should not matter, but if that relationship is indeed changing, a longer window may have a greater difficulty in picking up the changes.

Figure 7.5 presents the results of estimating the rolling regression with a two-year window. As expected, the longer window generates smoother results than the year-and-a-half window, reflecting the potential benefit of greater stability. On the other hand, the larger window precludes identifying the higher elasticities that occurred early in the period of analysis and is not sufficiently granular to pick up the leveling-off effect that occurred in 2010 as the decline in the elasticity appeared to stabilize. Nevertheless, it provides strong confirmation of the key point that the elasticity of street hours with respect to volume was falling during the recent periods of volume decline.

The visual result is confirmed by estimation of the underlying trend which is both negative and statistically significant:

$$\mu_t = \underset{(73.70)}{9.45\%} + \underset{(-2.25)}{-\ 0.0085\,t} + \underset{(-3.11)}{-\ 0.0001\,t^2}. \quad R^2 = 0.87, \ 156 \text{ obs.}$$

The second way we can examine the relationship between street hours and volume during a period of volume declines is through a switching regression and that analysis is presented in the next section.

5 USING A SWITCHING REGRESSION TO INVESTIGATE AN ASYMMETRIC RESPONSE OF STREET HOURS TO VOLUME

Previous evidence indicates that the behavior of street hours with respect to volume differs in periods of volume decline from the behavior during periods of volume increases. In this section, we attempt to directly measure directly the degree of difference by estimating a model that explicitly allows for a different response during volume

Table 7.6 Estimated switching model for street hours

Variable	Coefficient	*t*-statistic	*p*-value
Constant	13.6970	12052.36	0.000
ln(Volume)	0.1102	11.448	0.000
ln(Delivery Points)	0.5699	2.970	0.003
Q3	–0.0086	–4.519	0.000
Q4	–0.0097	–4.895	0.000
ln(Volume)*δ	–0.0369	–2.404	0.017
R-squared	0.6617		
S.E. of regression	0.011239		

declines. This extends and formalizes the rolling regression results by providing a formal statistical test of regime change and a distinct measure of the size of that change. Thus, to estimate the switching regression model we use the final specification from the rolling regression that eliminates the unneeded higher-order terms and the insignificant seasonal dummy variable:

$$\ln(SH_t) = \beta_0 + \beta_1 \ln\left(\frac{Vol_t}{\overline{Vol}}\right) + \beta_2\delta \ln\left(\frac{Vol_t}{\overline{Vol}}\right) + \beta_3 \ln\left(\frac{DP_t}{\overline{DP}}\right) + \sum_{k=3}^{4}\mu_k Q_k + \varepsilon_t,$$

where:

$$\delta_t = \begin{cases} 0 \text{ if } DV_t \geq 0 \\ 1 \text{ if } DV_t < 0 \end{cases} \text{ and } DV_t = Vol_t - Vol_{t-1}.$$

The null hypothesis that there is no difference in the responsiveness of street hours to changes in volume during periods of volume declines is $\beta_2 = 0$. This is tested with a standard *t*-statistic test on the coefficient. The estimated model is presented in Table 7.6. The estimated coefficient on the switching variable is negative indicating that street hours are less responsive to volume during periods of volume decline. The *t*-statistic for testing the null hypothesis is –2.043, implying rejection of the hypothesis of a symmetric response to volume increases and decreases.

The elasticity of street hours to a volume change during periods of volume increase is just over 11 percent. The elasticity of street hours to a volume decline during periods of volume decline is the sum of that coefficient and the coefficient on the switching variable. Adding those coefficients together yields an elasticity of just 7.3 percent. This means that street hours are one-third less responsive to volume changes during volume declines than volume increases.

Estimation of a switching regression for office hours shows that, in general, office hours are much more responsive to volume than are street hours. The results also fail to reject the null hypothesis of a symmetric response. While the coefficient on the switching variable is negative, the associated *t*-statistic is just –0.7305.

The results from the switching model are consistent with, but do not duplicate, the results of the previous two models. Recall that the threshold model investigates the dynamic adjustment in hours through time and demonstrates that the dynamics of street hours are different, in a manner consistent with limited network adjustment, during

Table 7.7 Estimated switching model for office hours

Variable	Coefficient	*t*-statistic	*p*-value
Constant	12.8394	4242.395	0.000
Ln(Volume)	0.7057	27.529	0.000
ln(Delivery Points)	–7.0937	–13.882	0.000
Q3	–0.0194	–3.806	0.000
Q4	–0.0072	–1.369	0.172
Ln(Volume)*δ	–0.0299	–0.730	0.466
R-squared	0.9651		
S.E. of regression	0.029931		

periods of volume decline. While this approach provides important insight into the nature of the hours adjustment process, it does not explicitly estimate the relationship between volume and hours. The second two models are required for investigating this causal nexus and each provides different, though complementary, insights. The rolling regression model provides important evidence on how the relationship between hours and volume has evolved, as volume declines have become persistent. This is important not only for determining that a change has occurred but also for providing a basis for future investigation of why that change has occurred. The rolling regression results thus provide an important part of understanding the impact of volume declines on the delivery network, but they do not provide a formal test of a structural shift and do not provide a distinct measure of the size of that shift. These important measurements are provided by the regime switching model (Table 7.7).

6 CONCLUSION

We produce empirical evidence on the existence of an asymmetric response in delivery time to increases and decreases in volume in recent years. To our knowledge, this is the first time such evidence has been produced. We use a battery of econometric techniques to examine United States Postal Service data over the last five fiscal years. We find strong evidence in favor an asymmetry for outside or 'street' hours but find no evidence of an asymmetry in inside or 'office' hours. Moreover, our empirical evidence suggests that the asymmetry is substantial with the hours elasticity of street time being a third less during periods of volume decline than it is during periods of volume increase. To the extent that the postal industry is facing a period of secular volume decline, we suggest that policy makers should be aware of this important result. While it is beyond the scope of this chapter, we also suggest that future research on the implications of this asymmetry would be important and enlightening. Among other areas of interest, it would be useful to decompose the effects of volume changes on hours. As noted above, the asymmetric response in hours is likely related to at least two factors: the fundamental network characteristics of street delivery and restrictions stemming from labor market inflexibility. Each of these sources raises important policy issues. To the extent that the asymmetric response is duc to network characteristics, policy analysis would focus on making delivery operations more flexible.[5] For example, if it were possible to develop a delivery system which greatly reduces or eliminates fixed routes, then perhaps carriers could be deployed according to the daily arrival profile. This would require very rapid dissemination and analysis of the information on each day's volume by destinating address. It is clear, in addition, that the presence of a USO-related requirement that carriers pass each residence each day would increase the difficulty of instituting such a system.

On the other hand, if the asymmetry is more related to labor market inflexibility, then policy analysis would require an entirely different approach and would focus on the elements of the labor contracting process that bring about the inflexibility. For example, the contract could be restructured to developed incentives to enhance flexibility. Naturally, the two causes are by no means mutually exclusive. Because our results indicate that the asymmetry is material, knowing the extent of each impact would be useful for policy considerations.

NOTES

* The views expressed in this chapter are solely those of the authors and should not be construed to represent the views of the United States Postal Service, or any other institution. The authors thank Lawrence G. Buc, Michael Crew, Paul Kleindorfer, and Sture Wallender for helpful comments on an earlier draft.

1. The seasonal variation in Postal Service volume occurs at the quarterly frequency, with volume being highest in the first quarter of the fiscal year (October through December) and lowest in the fourth quarter of the fiscal year (July through September). Accordingly, we define each seasonal dummy variable so that it takes the value of one during the quarter of interest and a value of zero in all other quarters.
2. See, Docket No. ACR2010, USPS-FY10-2, FY 2010 Public Cost Segments and Components Reports.
3. See, Response of the United States Postal Service to Question 9 of Chairman's Information Request No.3, Docket No. R2010-1, May 2010.
4. When the number of observations was reduced to 78, the second-order term in the log of volume was no longer significant. Consequently we estimated the rolling regressions for a first-order term in volume, a first-order term in delivery point, and two seasonal dummies.
5. We thank Paul Kleindorfer for this point.

REFERENCES

Bradley, Michael D. and Jeff Colvin (1995), 'An econometric model of postal delivery', in M.A. Crew and P.R. Kleindorfer (eds), *Commercialization of Postal and Delivery Services*, Boston, MA: Kluwer Academic Publishers.

Bradley, Michael, D. and Jeff Colvin (1999), 'Productivity and technical change in a public service enterprise', in M.A. Crew and P.R. Kleindorfer (eds), *Emerging Competition in Postal and Delivery Services*, Boston, MA: Kluwer Academic Publishers.

Bradley, Michael D., Jeff Colvin and Mary K. Perkins (2006), 'Measuring scale and scope economies with a structural model of postal delivery', in M.A. Crew and P.R. Kleindorfer (eds), *Liberalization of the Postal and Delivery Sector*, Cheltenham, UK and Northampton, MA, USA: Edward Elgar.

Bradley, Michael D. and Dennis W. Jansen (2000), 'Are business cycle dynamics the same across countries? Testing linearity around the globe', *Studies in Nonlinear Dynamics and Econometrics*, **4** (2), 51–71.

Bradley, Michael D. and Dennis W. Jansen (2004), 'Forecasting with a nonlinear dynamic model of stock returns and industrial production', *International Journal of Forecasting*, **20**, 321–342.

Bradley, Michael D. and Dennis W. Jansen (2011), 'Forecasting asset prices using nonlinear models', in Matthew Higgins (ed.), *Advances in Economic Forecasting*, Kalamazoo, MI: W.E. Upjohn Institute.
Bradley, Michael, D. and Alan R. Robinson (1988), 'Determining the marginal cost of purchased transportation', *Journal of Transportation Research Forum*, **30** (1).
Cazals, Cathérine, Pascale Duchemin, Jean Pierre Florens, Bérnard Roy and Oliver Vialaneix (2001), 'An econometric study of cost elasticity in the activities of post office counters', in M.A. Crew and P.R. Kleindorfer (eds), *Postal and Delivery Services: Pricing, Productivity, Regulation and Strategy*, Boston, MA: Kluwer Academic Publishers.
Cazals, Cathérine, Frédérique Fève, Jean-Pierre Florens and Bérnard Roy (2004a), 'Delivery costs II: back to parametric models', in M.A. Crew and P.R. Kleindorfer (eds), *Regulatory and Economic Challenges in the Postal and Delivery Sector*, Boston, MA: Kluwer Academic Publishers.
Cazals, Cathérine, Jean-Pierre Florens and Soterios Soteri (2004b), 'Delivery costs for postal services in the UK: some results on scale economies with panel data', in M.A. Crew and P.R. Kleindorfer (eds), *Regulatory and Economic Challenges in the Postal and Delivery Sector*, Boston, MA: Kluwer Academic Publishers.
Farsi, Mehdi, Massimo Filippini and Urs Trinkner (2006), 'Economies of scale, density and scope in Swiss Post's mail delivery', in M.A. Crew and P.R. Kleindorfer (eds), *Liberalization of the Postal and Delivery Sector*, Cheltenham, UK and Northampton, MA, USA: Edward Elgar.
Gazzei, Duccio S., Carla Pace and Gennaro Scarfiglieri (2002), 'On the output elasticity of the activities of post office counters in Italy', in M.A. Crew and P.R. Kleindorfer (eds), *Postal and Delivery Services: Delivering on Competition*, Boston, MA: Kluwer Academic Publishers.
Hansen, B.E. (1997), 'Inference in TAR Models', *Studies in Nonlinear Dynamics and Econometrics*, **2**, 1–14.
Harman, Greg, Wim Koevoets, Alejandro Requejo, Erik van der Merwe and Navin Waghe (2010), 'The effect of falling volumes on traditional efficiency analysis', in M.A. Crew and P.R. Kleindorfer (eds), *Heightening Competition in the Postal and Delivery Sector*, Cheltenham, UK and Northampton, MA, USA: Edward Elgar.
Tsay, R. (1989), 'Testing and modeling threshold autoregressive processes', *Journal of the American Statistical Association*, **84**, 231–40.

8. A panel data analysis of inefficiency and heterogeneity in the postal sector*

Catherine Cazals[†], Paul Dudley[‡], Jean-Pierre Florens[§] and Michael Jones[¶]

1 INTRODUCTION

The analysis of efficiency is of great interest for policy decision makers, particularly for businesses and regulators. Many methods may be applied to estimate inefficiencies of production units. These methods include deterministic or stochastic methods and parametric or non-parametric methods, applied on cross-sectional or panel data. However the most often used in the applied literature is the parametric stochastic frontier analysis (SFA), for which a particular form for the studied efficiency frontier (production or cost) is specified and some particular distribution for inefficiencies is assumed. Different specifications and assumptions may be more appropriate in some applications than others, and this may depend on the structure of the dataset and the policy questions involved for the sector in question. The present chapter examines these questions concerning the appropriate SFA method and specification to apply to delivery office data in the postal sector.

The delivery offices in the postal sector are particularly suited to frontier and efficiency estimation. First, there are numerous operational offices, each fulfilling a similar purpose and function, and thereby providing a sizeable dataset for comparison. Second, the operational office functions, particularly in delivery, are highly labor intensive, thereby creating scope for the practice and efficiency of one office to differ from that of another.

In previous research within the postal sector, the SFA has been applied to a single year of data in cross-sectional analysis of delivery offices and mail centers (Horncastle et al., 2006; Moriarty et al., 2006). In this analysis, the number of delivery offices, over 1,300 in the UK, contributed to the SFA being successfully applied to establish the gap between outturn costs and an estimated efficiency frontier, and between noise and inefficiency in respect to that gap.

The monitoring of throughput and cost over time might be expected to yield additional information about the current efficiency of delivery offices, as well as the degree to which the efficiency frontier moves over time. Indeed, Horncastle et al. and Moriarty et al. both referred to the potential for further insight to be gained from attaining similar datasets over multiple years, and applying SFA to panel data.

† Professor, Toulouse School of Economics (IDEI & GREMAQ).
‡ Head of Regulatory Economics, Royal Mail Group.
§ Professor, Toulouse School of Economics (IDEI & GREMAQ).
¶ Regulatory Advisor, Royal Mail Group.

In the standard form the SFA model is formulated as a 'composed error' model, with an error term decomposed into two components: inefficiency and 'noise'. In cross-sectional (CS) SFA the comparison of the production units is made over a single year. In standard panel SFA the comparison is made over multiple years. The models usually considered are fixed effects model or random effects models, with the inefficiency either time varying or time invariant. We focus here on the random rather than the fixed effects approach so that both time-varying and time-invariant regressors can be analyzed. (Moreover it is the approach which is most often employed in empirical literature on inefficiency.)

An approach named the 'true random effect model' was developed by Greene (2004, 2005) to conduct panel stochastic frontier estimation in the presence of unobserved heterogeneity (relating to missing or unobservable variables). The model adds a third component in the error term in order to take into account unobserved heterogeneity and then distinguishes it from inefficiency and noise. This model assumes that inefficiency and noise terms are time-varying independent and identically distributed (iid), and unobserved heterogeneity is time invariant. In this chapter, we extend this true random effects model in order to take into account a time-varying inefficiency term that is not iid but with a specification developed originally by Battese and Coelli (1992) (denoted BC time-varying specification in what follows). A true random effects model assuming a time-invariant inefficiency has been developed by Cazals et al. (2011).

The time-invariant inefficiency is often thought to be more appropriate when dealing with a short time period and/or efficiency is thought unlikely to vary much over time. Cazals et al. compared standard SFA panel and cross-section analysis to a simulated dataset and then to a real delivery office dataset. It showed that the standard SFA panel models were prone to overestimate the inefficiency in the presence of unobserved heterogeneity and noise, and that this was consistent with results obtained from its application to postal data. It also showed that the time-invariant true random effects model performed well in simulated data assuming time-invariant inefficiency and unobserved heterogeneity, and reasonably well for the real delivery office data.

In this chapter we apply a variety of standard (random effects) and non-standard (true random effects) SFA models, as identified above, to panel datasets that are simulated under different assumptions relating to the inefficiency term – namely time-invariant, time-varying iid and time-varying BC specifications. This extends the analysis of Cazals et al. to include analysis of time-varying inefficiency. We use this to compare and contrast the performance of various models in estimating the true inefficiency. We then use these results as context when applying these models to real multi-period data of delivery offices in the UK where the distribution of inefficiency is unknown. This enables us to gain some further insights on the real data, such as whether a hypothesis of an iid time-varying inefficiency term is or is not reasonable.

Section 2 sets out the theoretical basis of SFA estimation and estimation method for a random effects model with unobserved heterogeneity. Section 3 undertakes a simulation of data with and without unobserved heterogeneity, and different assumptions relating to the noise and inefficiency, to assess the accuracy of standard SFA and random effects with unobserved heterogeneity estimations under alternative environments. Section 4 undertakes a similar analysis on actual data of UK delivery offices. Section 5 concludes.

2 ESTIMATION METHODOLOGY FOR STOCHASTIC FRONTIER ANALYSIS

SFA can analyze the production frontier where, for a given level of input, we search for the production unit which produces the maximum output or the cost frontier where, for a given level of output, we search for the unit which produces a minimal cost. We focus here on the cost frontier.

Standard Methods

We consider a sample of N production units for which we observe the cost, denoted by C, the quantity of outputs, denoted by the vector Y, and some environmental variables describing observed heterogeneity, denoted by the vector Z. For the analysis of delivery offices in the postal sector, N is the number of delivery offices, Y includes the volume of mail delivered per number of delivery points and Z includes other factors of cost such as the number of delivery points and proportion of business mail delivered by the delivery office.

The cost frontier model for the stochastic frontier is then written as follows:

$$C = f(Y, Z)\exp(v) = f(Y, Z)\exp(u + \varepsilon),$$

where $v = u + \varepsilon$, and u is the standard random disturbance term and $\varepsilon \geq 0$ represents the cost inefficiency term. It means that the observed cost (C) may be different from the efficient cost due to a random noise and inefficiency. In this case, a measure of the efficiency score is provided by:

$$EF = \frac{C}{f(Y, Z)\exp(u)} = \exp(\varepsilon).$$

This is the ratio of observed to 'stochastic' frontier cost and is then greater or equal to 1 (a unit value meaning 'cost efficiency' for a particular production unit). In most applications, the variables (C, Y and Z) are transformed into logarithm and Cobb–Douglas or Translog functional forms are considered for the function $f(\cdot)$.

When the information about the sample of production units is available for a single point in time, we deal with cross-section data. When we can observe the same production units at different dates, we deal with panel data. In the case of cross-section data, all the variables in the previous model are indexed by i, $i = 1, \cdots, N$, which identify each production unit. If we simplify the model for ease of presentation, by considering only one output and one environmental variable (that is Y and Z each have only one component), and a simple linear form in the logarithm of the variables (that is a Cobb–Douglas form for the function $f(\cdot)$), then the econometric specification of a cross-sectional model is:

$$c_i = \alpha + \beta y_i + \delta z_i + u_i + \varepsilon_i, \tag{8.1}$$

where c_i, y_i and z_i represent the logarithms of C_i, Y_i and Z_i, respectively.

Usually in the standard SFA applications, it is assumed that (i) the random noise u_i is iid $N(0, \sigma_u^2)$, (ii) the one-sided term for inefficiency ε_i is iid $N^+(0, \sigma_\varepsilon^2)$ (that is half normally distributed),[1] (iii) these two terms are independent, and moreover (iv) u_i is assumed to be independent of y_i and z_i.

The most commonly used and most efficient estimation method for this model is the maximum-likelihood method.[2] The log-likelihood function is:

$$l(\theta, \sigma, \lambda) = \text{constant} - N\text{Ln}\sigma + \sum_{i=1}^{N}\text{Ln}\Phi\left(\frac{v_i\lambda}{\sigma}\right) - \frac{1}{2\sigma^2}\sum_{i=1}^{N} v_i^2, \quad (8.2)$$

where $\theta = (\alpha, \beta, \delta)$, $v_i = u_i + \varepsilon_i$, $\sigma^2 = \sigma_u^2 + \sigma_\varepsilon^2$, $\lambda = \sigma_\varepsilon/\sigma_u$, and $\Phi(\cdot)$ is the standard normal cumulative distribution function.

We obtain estimates for parameters and then also an estimate for residuals $\hat{v}_i$, $i = 1,\ldots, N$, which contain information on the inefficiency $\hat{\varepsilon}_i$. We use the conditional distribution of ε given v to estimate the production unit specific inefficiency (Jondrow et al., 1982). We have:

$$E(\varepsilon_i|v_i) = \sigma_*\left[\frac{\phi(\frac{v_i\lambda}{\sigma})}{1 - \Phi(-\frac{v_i\lambda}{\sigma})} + \frac{v_i\lambda}{\sigma}\right], \quad (8.3)$$

where $\sigma_* = (\sigma_\varepsilon^2\sigma_u^2)/\sigma^2$, and the inefficiency for the production unit i is $EF_i = \exp[-E(\varepsilon_i|v_i)]$.

An alternative estimator of the inefficiency term, given by Battese and Coelli (1988), is:

$$E[\exp(\varepsilon_i)|v_i] = \left[\frac{1 - \Phi(\sigma_* - \frac{\mu_{*i}}{\sigma_*})}{1 - \Phi(-\frac{\mu_{*i}}{\sigma_*})}\right]\exp(-\mu_{*i} + 0.5\sigma_*^2) \quad (8.4)$$

where $\mu_{*i} = (v_i\sigma_\varepsilon^2)/\sigma^2$. These two measures can be different since the exponential is a non-linear function $(\exp[E(\varepsilon_i|v_i)] \neq E[\exp(\varepsilon_i)|v_i])$. (See Kumbhakar and Lovell, 2000 for more technical details.)

In the case of panel data, all the variables in the model are now indexed by i, $i = 1, \ldots, N$, and also by t, $t = 1, \ldots, T$, which identify the date of observation. In this case, the simplified model is written (for logarithms of variables) as:

$$c_{it} = \alpha + \beta y_{it} + \delta z_{it} + v_{it}, \quad (8.5)$$

where $v_{it} = u_{it} + \varepsilon_{it}$ for time-varying inefficiency or $v_{it} = u_{it} + \varepsilon_i$ for time-invariant inefficiency.

In the case of a model with time-invariant inefficiency, assumptions about the distributions of the error components are similar to the one made for the cross-sectional model, that is: u_{it} are iid $N(0, \sigma_u^2)$ and ε_i is iid $N + (0, \sigma_\varepsilon^2)$. The two main specifications for a panel model are 'fixed effects' or 'random effects' models. In a fixed effects specification, the model is reinterpreted by considering $\alpha_i = \alpha + \varepsilon_i$ as a firm-specific inefficiency term. No distributional assumptions are needed for inefficiency and this model may be estimated by the least squares dummy variables (LSDV) method. However, this specification has the drawback that time-invariant regressors may not be accommodated. The most often used specification is the random effects model, and so we focus on this model in what follows.

The estimation of a random effects model specified as in equation (8.5) is performed using the maximum-likelihood estimation method, as it is more efficient than generalized least squares (GLS) method. The log-likelihood for a sample of N production units observed for T periods is (see Pitt and Lee, 1981):

$$l = \text{const} - \frac{N(T-1)}{2}\text{Ln}\sigma_u^2 - \frac{N}{2}\text{Ln}(\sigma_u^2 + T\sigma_\varepsilon^2) + \sum_i \text{Ln}\left[1 - \Phi\left(-\frac{\mu_{*i}}{\sigma_*}\right)\right] - \left(\frac{v'v}{2\sigma_u^2}\right) + \frac{1}{2}\sum_i \left(\frac{\mu_{*i}}{\sigma_*}\right)^2, \tag{8.6}$$

where $\mu_{*i} = T\sigma_\varepsilon^2 \bar{v}_i/(\sigma_u^2 + T\sigma_\varepsilon^2)$, $\sigma_*^2 = \sigma_u\sigma_\varepsilon/(\sigma_u^2 + T\sigma_\varepsilon^2)$, and $\Phi(\cdot)$ and $\phi(\cdot)$ are the standard normal cumulative and density functions. The efficiency score is then computed using estimated parameters and a formulae close to the one given in equations (8.3) or (8.4) (see Khumbakar and Lovell, 2000 or Greene, 2008 for a detailed presentation). The case where the inefficiency is assumed to be time varying is addressed by some modifications in the notation and writing of log-likelihood in equation (8.6) (see Battese and Coelli, 1995 or Greene, 2008).

True Random Effects Models with Unobserved Heterogeneity

There is a growing literature considering the effect of unobserved heterogeneity for SFA panel estimation. For example, Greene (2004, 2005) and Farsi et al. (2005) added an extra stochastic term in random effects models with an iid time-varying inefficiency term. The model is similar to equation (8.5), but with a composed error written as: $v_{it} = u_{it} + w_i + \varepsilon_{it}$. This model is the 'true random effects model' defined by Greene (2004, 2005).

Cazals et al. (2011) developed and applied an estimation method for a random effects model with unobserved heterogeneity and a time-invariant inefficiency term by considering the model described by equation (8.5), where:

$$v_{it} = u_{it} + w_i + \varepsilon_i, \tag{8.7}$$

where w_i represents time-invariant unobserved heterogeneity, and is assumed to be normally distributed $(N(0, \sigma_w^2))$. The estimation technique for the parameters of the model is based on the simulated maximum likelihood. The individual efficiency scores are obtained using estimated parameters, simulations for random terms and non-parametric regression to obtain estimates for $E[\exp(\varepsilon)|v]$. This is the true random effects model with time-variant inefficiency.

In this chapter, we propose an extension of the previous model in order to consider inefficiency with a BC specification – that is, a model where the composed error term is assumed to be:

$$v_{it} = u_{it} + w_i + \varepsilon_{it}, \tag{8.8}$$

where w_i represents time-invariant unobserved heterogeneity, and is assumed to be normally distributed $(N(0, \sigma_w^2))$, and ε_{it} is the time-varying inefficiency term specified as follows:

$$\varepsilon_{it} = \exp[\beta \cdot (t - T)] \cdot \varepsilon_i, \tag{8.9}$$

where ε_i is iid $N+(0, \sigma_\varepsilon^2)$, and T is the number of observation periods. We apply the same estimation method as the one described in Cazals et al. after an adaptation of the likelihood function in order to integrate the additional parameter β. As in the previous model, after the estimation of main parameters, individual inefficiencies are obtained by simulation and non-parametric regression. This is the true random effects model with a BC time-varying specification of inefficiency.

3 SIMULATED DATA ANALYSIS

We apply a variety of standard (random effects) and non-standard (true random effects) SFA models to panel datasets that are simulated under different assumptions relating to inefficiency term – namely time-invariant, time-varying iid and time-varying BC specifications. We consider each without and with unobserved heterogeneity. We use this to compare and contrast the performance of various models in estimating the true inefficiency.

For the simulation of time-invariant inefficiency, the data-generating process is described by the following model, similar to equation (8.6) (where to simplify we consider only one exogenous variable):

$$c_{it} = \alpha + \beta y_{it} + u_{it} + w_i + \varepsilon_i, \tag{8.10}$$

with $i = 1, \ldots, N$ and $t = 1, \ldots, T$, c and y representing the cost and the output, respectively, ε_i is iid $N^+(0, \sigma_\varepsilon^2)$ and represents the inefficiency term, assumed to be time invariant, u_{it} are iid $N(0, \sigma_u^2)$ and represent the standard statistical noise, and w_i represents some time-invariant unobserved heterogeneity assumed to be iid $N(0, \sigma_w^2)$. We assume that these three components are distributed independently of each other, and of the regressors.

We assume $N = 200$, $T = 6$ and generate 50 panel data samples. The variable y_{it} is generated from:

$$y_{it} = 1.2 + 0.986 y_{i,t-1} + \zeta_{it}, \text{ where } \zeta_{it} \sim N(0; 0.5),$$

where the coefficients of (8.10) are assumed to be: $\alpha = -3.7$ and $\beta = 0.9$ and the variance $\sigma^2 = \sigma_u^2 + \sigma_w^2 + \sigma_\varepsilon^2$ such that $\sigma^2 = 0.05$. If we denote $\sigma_\varepsilon^2 = a_\varepsilon \sigma^2$, $\sigma_u^2 = a_u \sigma^2$, and $\sigma_w^2 = a_w \sigma^2$, we can consider the case where there is no unobserved heterogeneity in the true (unknown) model when $a_w = 0$, and another where there is unobserved heterogeneity in the true (unknown) model when $a_w \neq 0$. For our simulation we consider the case of $a_\varepsilon = 0.7$ such that without unobserved heterogeneity $a_u = 0.3$, and with unobserved heterogeneity, $a_u = 0.1$ and $a_w = 0.2$. These values are purely illustrative and are not calibrated to reflect observed values.[3]

For the simulation with a model of time-varying iid inefficiency, we use the same model and values of parameters as previously but ε_i in equation (8.10) is replaced by ε_{it} and assumed to be iid $N^+(0, \sigma_\varepsilon^2)$. And finally for the simulation with a model of time-varying

Table 8.1 Standard panel SFA (random effects models) efficiency scores using simulated data without and with unobserved heterogeneity

True model		Without unobserved heterogeneity			With unobserved heterogeneity		
		Time-invariant inefficiency	iid time-varying inefficiency	BC time-varying inefficiency	Time-invariant inefficiency	iid time-varying inefficiency	BC time-varying inefficiency
		$a_e = 0.7$; $a_u = 0.3$	$a_e = 0.7$; $a_u = 0.3$	$a_e = 0.7$; $a_u = 0.3$	$a_e = 0.7$; $a_u = 0.1$; $a_w = 0.2$	$a_e = 0.7$; $a_u = 0.1$; $a_w = 0.2$	$a_e = 0.7$; $a_u = 0.1$; $a_w = 0.2$
RE_ti		1.303	1.016	1.361	1.447	1.142	1.508
RE_tv	*t*1	1.305	1.025	1.416	1.448	1.145	1.569
	*t*2	1.304	1.021	1.390	1.447	1.143	1.539
	*t*3	1.303	1.019	1.365	1.447	1.142	1.511
	*t*4	1.302	1.018	1.342	1.446	1.141	1.485
	*t*5	1.302	1.018	1.321	1.446	1.140	1.460
	*t*6	1.301	1.020	1.301	1.446	1.140	1.437
Estimate		Good	Under	Good	Over	Under	Over

BC specification, we assume $\varepsilon_{it} = \exp[\beta \cdot (t - T)] \cdot \varepsilon_i$ with ε_i iid $N^+(0, \sigma_e^2)$ and $\beta = -0.05$.

For each sample, we estimate using standard maximum-likelihood or simulated maximum-likelihood methods, the models referred to above as: (i) a standard random effect model with time-invariant inefficiency (RE_ti); (ii) a standard random effect model with time-varying BC inefficiency (RE_tv); (iii) a standard CS models; (iv) a true random effect model with time-invariant inefficiency (TRE_ti); (v) a true random effect model with iid time-varying inefficiency (Greene's model), denoted (TRE_tv); and (vi) a true random effect model with time-varying BC specification for inefficiency (TRE_tvbc).

We compare the mean of estimated efficiency scores between these different methods, and to the mean value for the 'true' (unknown) inefficiency which is equal to 1.303 for $a_\varepsilon = 0.7$ when the inefficiency term is time invariant or iid time varying in the true model. For the simulation the model with a time-varying BC specification for inefficiency the true inefficiencies for $a_\varepsilon = 0.7$ are higher and range from 1.398 in the first period (*t*1) to 1.300 in the final period (*t*6), and therefore decrease over the period.[4]

The results for the average of the mean of individual efficiency scores over the 50 samples are given in Tables 8.1–3.

Table 8.1 shows the results obtained using standard panel SFA, without unobserved heterogeneity in the true model in the first three columns of figures and with unobserved heterogeneity in the last three columns. In the absence of unobserved heterogeneity, the standard estimation methods for panel SFA provide a good estimate of the true inefficiency when that inefficiency is time invariant or time varying with a BC specification in the true model (this result was expected as these estimation methods were developed for these cases), but not when the inefficiency is time varying iid. In this last case, indeed, the time-varying iid inefficiency term is not correctly distinguished from the noise term in the estimation method (most inefficiency is considered as noise).

Table 8.2 Cross-section SFA efficiency scores using simulated data without and with unobserved heterogeneity

True model		Without unobserved heterogeneity			With unobserved heterogeneity		
		Time-invariant inefficiency	iid time-varying inefficiency	BC time-varying inefficiency	Time-invariant inefficiency	iid time-varying inefficiency	BC time-varying inefficiency
		$a_e = 0.7$; $a_u = 0.3$	$a_e = 0.7$; $a_u = 0.3$	$a_e = 0.7$; $a_u = 0.3$	$a_e = 0.7$; $a_u = 0.1$; $a_w = 0.2$	$a_e = 0.7$; $a_u = 0.1$; $a_w = 0.2$	$a_e = 0.7$; $a_u = 0.1$; $a_w = 0.2$
CS	*t*1	1.308	1.309	1.421	1.309	1.302	1.425
	*t*2	1.305	1.309	1.393	1.308	1.310	1.400
	*t*3	1.290	1.310	1.353	1.298	1.318	1.363
	*t*4	1.300	1.306	1.337	1.306	1.305	1.346
	*t*5	1.309	1.304	1.328	1.305	1.307	1.325
	*t*6	1.296	1.298	1.296	1.302	1.294	1.302
Estimate		Good	Good	Good	Good	Good	Good

In the presence of unobserved heterogeneity, the standard panel SFA overestimates the true inefficiency when that inefficiency is time invariant or time varying with a BC specification, but underestimates the true inefficiency when that inefficiency is time-varying iid. Indeed, again in the estimation method, when the true model has a time-invariant unobserved heterogeneity component, iid noise term and time-varying iid inefficiency term, most of the inefficiency is not correctly identified and is considered as noise, explaining the observed underestimation for inefficiency. In the case of time-invariant inefficiency (or BC specification), the unobserved heterogeneity component is not correctly identified and here considered for a large part as inefficiency, explaining the observed overestimation for inefficiency. We conclude as expected that the standard panel SFA does not estimate well in the presence of unobserved heterogeneity – a conclusion also reached in Cazals et al. (2011) (absent the BC time-varying inefficiency).

Table 8.2 shows the results obtained using cross-section SFA, without unobserved heterogeneity in the 'true' model in the first three columns of figures and with unobserved heterogeneity in the last three columns. Whether in the absence of or presence of unobserved heterogeneity, the cross-sectional SFA provides a good estimate of the 'true' inefficiency when that inefficiency is time invariant and when the inefficiency is time-varying iid. This is also the case or the BC time-varying inefficiency. We conclude that the cross-sectional SFA estimates well in the presence of unobserved heterogeneity – a conclusion also reached in Cazals et al. (2011) (absent the BC time-varying inefficiency).

Table 8.3 shows the results obtained using non-standard panel SFA (true random effects models that take into account unobserved heterogeneity), without unobserved heterogeneity in the true model in the first three columns of figures and with unobserved heterogeneity in the last three columns. The results show that each of the three methods makes a good estimate for the specification of inefficiency for which the model was designed – whether time-invariant, time-varying iid or time-varying BC. The TRE_ti (true random effects model for time-invariant inefficiency) method, developed in Cazals

Table 8.3 True random effects model efficiency scores using simulated data without and with unobserved heterogeneity

True model		Without unobserved heterogeneity			With unobserved heterogeneity		
		Time-invariant inefficiency	iid time-varying inefficiency	BC time-varying inefficiency	Time-invariant inefficiency	iid time-varying inefficiency	BC time-varying inefficiency
		$a_e = 0.7$; $a_u = 0.3$	$a_e = 0.7$; $a_u = 0.3$	$a_e = 0.7$; $a_u = 0.3$	$a_e = 0.7$; $a_u = 0.1$; $a_w = 0.2$	$a_e = 0.7$; $a_u = 0.1$; $a_w = 0.2$	$a_e = 0.7$; $a_u = 0.1$; $a_w = 0.2$
TRE_ti		1.295	Non-convergence	1.348	1.303	Non-convergence	1.356
TRE_tv	*t*1	Non-convergence	1.299	Non-convergence; close to 1 for some units	Non-convergence	1.301	Non-convergence
	*t*2		1.305			1.302	
	*t*3		1.303			1.301	
	*t*4		1.303			1.300	
	*t*5		1.298			1.303	
	*t*6		1.301			1.300	
TRE_tvbc	*t*1	1.298	Non-conver gence	1.406	1.300	Non-conver-gence	1.411
	*t*2	1.301		1.384	1.302		1.388
	*t*3	1.300		1.360	1.303		1.364
	*t*4	1.300		1.338	1.302		1.342
	*t*5	1.299		1.316	1.302		1.320
	*t*6	1.299		1.297	1.303		1.301
Estimate		Dependent	Dependent	Dependent	Dependent	Dependent	Dependent

et al., provides good estimates not only for time-invariant inefficiency, but also for a time-varying BC specification of inefficiency as the estimated inefficiency is close to the mean value of true inefficiency over the 6 periods. However, the TRE_tv method (Greene's method for iid time-varying inefficiency) does not converge when the specification for the inefficiency is time-invariant or time-varying BC. The TRE_tvbc method does not converge when the specification for the inefficiency is time-varying iid, but gives good estimates for time-varying BC inefficiency (as expected) and also for time-invariant inefficiency. The simulation results suggest then that Greene's model only yields good inefficiency estimates when the true (unknown) inefficiency is time-varying iid (that is the model for which it is designed), with or without unobserved heterogeneity in the true model, and the two other methods yield good inefficiency estimates when the true inefficiency is time-invariant or time-varying BC, with or without unobserved heterogeneity in the true model.

We first observe that, when true inefficiency is time invariant and unobserved heterogeneity is present in the data, application of standard random effect methods (that do not take into account unobserved heterogeneity) leads to overestimation of inefficiency.[5] In this case, Greene's model (TRE_tv) does not work as many convergence problems arise in the estimation procedure and it gives almost all individual inefficiencies close to 1, with no dispersion. However, true random effect models taking into account the unobserved heterogeneity for time-invariant inefficiency (TRE_ti) perform well, and this is also the case for time-varying BC inefficiency (TRE_tvbc). The cross-sectional model is robust to this specification as it also provides good results.

Second, when the inefficiency is time-varying iid and unobserved heterogeneity is present in the data, standard random effect models (RE_ti and RE_tv) underestimate inefficiency and this is also the case even when no unobserved heterogeneity is present in the data. The TRE_tv model performs well (with or without heterogeneity) as expected, but the TRE_ti and TRE_tvbc models do not converge. The cross-section estimates are good.

Third, when the inefficiency has a time-varying BC specification, the two standard random effects models perform well when no unobserved heterogeneity is present in the data (as expected), but overestimate the inefficiency when there is unobserved heterogeneity. The TRE_tv model does not converge whatever the case for unobserved heterogeneity, and the TRE_ti and TRE_tvbc models perform well. In this case, cross-section estimates are also good.

4 APPLICATION OF SFA TO REAL DATA FOR DELIVERY ACTIVITY IN THE POSTAL SECTOR

In this section we apply the SFA methods previously mentioned to a real dataset of delivery offices in UK. More precisely we use a dataset for 1,334 delivery offices observed for 6 years between 2003/04 and 2008/09 – a period over which delivered volumes reduced year on year. For each delivery office, we have information about the number of hours worked (which represents the cost, denoted *C*), the volume of delivered mail (denoted *Y*), and some environmental variables: the number of delivery point (denoted *DP*), the area surface of the delivery zone denoted *AR*, the proportion of business delivery points (denoted *pbus*) and an indicator of the type of delivery area (denoted urban, suburb or rural, equal to 1 if the delivery office is in the corresponding area, 0 otherwise, and the reference variable is 'city' representing a deep urban area).

We consider then the following model

$$\mathrm{Ln}C = \alpha + \beta \mathrm{Ln}(Y/DP) + \phi \mathrm{Ln}(DP) + \delta \mathrm{Ln}Z + v,$$

where **Z** is the vector with the environmental variables (*AR*/*DP*, prop. bus, and dummies for the type of delivery area). As in the models presented in the Section 2, the random term *v* is a composed term, with a statistical noise assumed to have a normal distribution, an inefficiency term, assumed to have a half-normal distribution, and potentially an unobserved heterogeneity term assumed to have a normal distribution. These various terms are assumed to be independent of each other and of regressors.

This model is then estimated using the panel structure of data, for which we apply standard random effects models and 'true random effects models', and also for each year separately, that is for cross-sectional data. The estimation methodologies applied here are the maximum-likelihood or simulated maximum-likelihood methods as described in Section 2.

In Table 8.4 we give the average of estimated individual efficiency scores for the period

Table 8.4 Efficiency scores obtained from alternative methods on real data

	RE_ti	RE_tv	TRE_tv	TRE_tvbc	TRE_ti	CS
Average	γ	From γ +0.03 to γ	Around $\gamma - 0.27$	From $\gamma - 0.13$ to $\gamma - 0.25$	$\gamma - 0.14$	Between $\gamma - 0.20$ and $\gamma - 0.17$
Estimate	High	High	Low	Medium	Medium	Medium

expressed relative to the result for RE_ti of γ (whereby a value equal to 1 means efficiency and then the more the value is greater than 1 the greater the inefficiency). The scale of the score relative to those of the cross-sectional results is stated as low, medium or high in the final line of the table. The results from the real data have interesting parallels with the simulated results.

First, results appear to reflect the presence of unobserved heterogeneity. Indeed, in the simulated exercise, when no unobserved heterogeneity is present in the data, panel standard random effects models (RE_ti and RE_tv) give results close to the cross-section model results, and the TRE_ti and TRE_tvbc true random effects models, except in the iid time-varying case where inefficiency is underestimated with random effects models and then lower than in the cross-section case. The high efficiency scores obtained here for the standard panel SFA models in comparison to the scores obtained in cross-section models are consistent with the simulated results where there was unobserved heterogeneity.

Second, the results seem to indicate that the case of iid time-varying inefficiency (from the TRE_tv model) may be discarded. Indeed, the simulation exercise showed that in the case of time-varying iid inefficiency, results for inefficiency in standard panel methods (RE_ti and RE_tv) were underestimated and much lower than cross-section results, and moreover, the simulated results from Greene's model (TRE_tv) were close to the results obtained with cross-section models. The configuration of results obtained from actual data is different from the simulated results with time-varying iid inefficiency.

Third, the true random effects model with a time-varying BC inefficiency term yields an efficiency score of $\gamma - 0.13$ in the first period that reduces to $\gamma - 0.25$ in the final period. In contrast, the true random effects model with a time-invariant inefficiency term yields a single estimate of $\gamma - 0.14$ for the whole period. The results from cross-sectional models yield an efficiency score that increases from $\gamma - 0.20$ to $\gamma - 0.17$ in the first 4 years and then decreases to $\gamma - 0.19$, and application of standard random effects model with BC time-varying inefficiency gives decreasing inefficiency. These results, compared to results obtained in the simulation exercise, seem to reflect the presence of some time-varying BC inefficiency rather than time invariant inefficiency. Indeed, in the simulation exercise we see that when the true inefficiency is time invariant, standard random effects model with time-varying inefficiency (RE_tv), CS models and true random effects models with time-varying BC inefficiency (TRE_tvbc) yield estimates of inefficiency that are time invariant over the period: this is not the case in our application on real data.

We also observe that in the simulation exercise, for the model with time-varying BC inefficiency and unobserved heterogeneity, the application of TRE_ti gives a value for inefficiency corresponding to the mid-value for the range of inefficiency obtained by application of TRE_tvbc or CS models. We are not exactly in the same configuration for the postal data – it seems that the shape of evolution of inefficiency over the period is not monotone as in the case of the simple BC specification.

For illustration, the estimated equations for the true random effects model with time-varying BC inefficiency (TRE_tvbc) and equations for the cross sectional model are included in Appendix 8A. In general, the cost functions are dominated by two variables: the number of delivery points and volume per delivery point. Their coefficients are broadly similar across the panel models, while the coefficient on the volume per delivery point variable is considerably lower than in the cross-sectional model. While refinements to the equations could change the specific efficiency scores presented in Table 8.4 and the appendix, we would not expect them to change significantly the relative results reported above.

5. CONCLUSIONS

In this chapter we have reviewed the SFA methods used for efficiency estimation for simulated and real postal sector data. This is a development from Cazals et al. (2011) which drew attention to the problem of the presence of unobserved heterogeneity when applying stochastic frontier estimation within the postal sector.

More specifically we have looked at the performance of efficiency estimation for standard panel SFA with the inefficiency either time varying in a random effects model (RE_tv) or time invariant in a random effects model (RE_ti); for a CS SFA model; and for non-standard, true random effect models with the inefficiency in a time-invariant (TRE_ti) model, a time-varying iid (TRE_tv) model or a time-varying BC specification (TRE_tvbc) model. We reviewed the performance of efficiency estimation for these models using simulated data for three different assumptions about the inefficiency term: time invariant, time varying iid and time varying with a BC specification. We did so in the absence and then in the presence unobserved heterogeneity.

We confirmed the finding of Cazals et al. that the standard SFA panel models do not perform well in the presence of unobserved heterogeneity. We also found that the true random effects Greene model performs well only for the specific assumption about inefficiency for which it is designed, that is iid time-varying inefficiency. Then we use the true random effects model for time-invariant inefficiency developed in Cazals et al. and extend it to the case of time-varying BC inefficiency and found that each performs well for these two specifications of inefficiency, but not for iid time-varying inefficiency.

This simulation exercise mainly shows the error (sometimes very large) that can be made in estimating the value for inefficiency if we apply a 'bad' estimation method. A key lesson to be learned from this exercise is that any empirical analysis of inefficiency using panel data should begin with a review of results obtained from estimation of different models in order to detect possible unobserved heterogeneity, with the resulting implications for choosing a particular specification for modeling inefficiency.

When we applied the models to real delivery office data from the UK we found that they all converged. The simulated data results provided insights into what might be happening with the real data. The results appear to reflect the presence of unobserved heterogeneity – the high efficiency scores for the standard SFA models were consistent with the simulated results where there was unobserved heterogeneity. They also suggest the presence of some time-varying inefficiency with a BC specification. Moreover, if we consider the time-varying BC model to identify a range of inefficiency estimates (by taking the first and final period estimates, whereby the former is close to the time-invariant estimate), we also observed that the cross-section model estimates fell within this range and noted that potential further refinements to the assumptions of the time-varying BC model could yield even closer results to those of the cross-section model.

In the light of these results, it is not possible to recommend a single preferred true random effects model of panel SFA for application to the UK delivery office data. However, the true random effects (TRE) model with a time-varying BC inefficiency term appears to perform well and is robust to several environmental conditions.

Hence TRE is superior to RE and so further research as to the appropriate specification for SFA for the postal sector should be in TRE. In order to be more confident about the most appropriate model specification for the real dataset, it may be appropriate to consider further the effect of misspecifications for other important assumptions in SFA such as the functional form of the frontier, the distributional assumptions for the terms of the composed error, or other specifications for evolution in time for inefficiency.

NOTES

* The analysis contained in this chapter reflects the views of the authors and may not necessarily be those of Royal Mail Group. Further refinements to the equations could change the results presented in this chapter using actual data, but we would not expect them to change significantly the relative results of the different methods.

1. Other distributions may be considered for the inefficiency term as, for example, truncated normal or exponential.
2. For technical details about estimation for stochastic frontier see, for example, Aigner et al. (1977); Meeusen and Van den Broeck (1977); Battese and Coelli (1995); Cornwell and Schmidt (1996); Kumbhakar and Lovell (2000); Fried et al. (2008); Greene (2008).
3. Some sensitivity analysis is included in Cazals et al. (2011).
4. We also note that a lower value of a_ε narrows the range and lowers the average inefficiency.
5. Indeed, Cazals et al. (2011) show that the gap is largest when the part of unobserved heterogeneity increases.

REFERENCES

Aigner, D.J., K. Lovell and P. Schmidt (1977), 'Formulation and estimation of stochastic frontier production function models', *Journal of Econometrics*, **6**, 21 37.

Battese, G. and T. Coelli (1988), 'Prediction of firm level efficiencies with a generalized frontier production function and panel data', *Journal of Econometrics*, **38**, 387–99.

Battese, G. and T.J. Coelli (1992), 'Frontier production function, technical efficiency and panel data: with application to paddy farmers in India', *Journal of Productivity Analysis*, **3**, 153–69.

Battese, G. and T. Coelli (1995), 'A model for technical inefficiency effects in a stochastic frontier production function for panel data', *Empirical Economics*, **20**, 325–32.

Cazals, C., P. Dudley, J.-P. Florens and M. Jones (2011), 'The effect of unobserved heterogeneity in stochastic frontier estimation: comparison of cross-section and panel with simulated data for the postal sector', submitted to the *Network Review of Economics* following presentation of the paper at the Toulouse Postal Conference, March 2010.

Cornwell, C. and S. Schmidt (1996), 'Stochastic frontier analysis and efficiency estimation', in L.

Matyas and Sevestre (eds), *The Econometrics of Panel Data: A Handbook of the Theory with Applications*, Boston, MA: Kluwer Academic Publishers.
Farsi, M., M. Filippini and M. Kuentzle (2005), 'Unobserved heterogeneity in stochastic cost frontier models: an application to Swiss nursing homes', *Applied Economics*, **37**, 2127–41.
Fried, H., K. Lovell and S. Schmidt (2008), *The Measurement of Productivity Efficiency and Productivity Growth*, Oxford: Oxford University Press.
Greene, W. (2004), 'Distinguishing between heterogeneity and inefficiency: stochastic frontier analysis of the World Health Organization's panel data on national health care systems', *Health Economics*, **30**, 959–80.
Greene, W. (2005), 'Reconsidering heterogeneity in panel data estimators of the stochastic frontier model', *Journal of Econometrics*, **126**, 269–303.
Greene, W. (2008), 'The econometric approach to efficiency analysis', in Fried et al. (eds).
Horncastle, A., D. Jevons, P. Dudley and E. Thanassoulis (2006), 'Efficiency analysis of delivery offices in the postal sector using stochastic frontier and data envelopment analysis', in M.A Crew and P.R. Kleindorfer (eds), *Liberalization of the Postal and Delivery Sector*, Cheltenham, UK and Northampton, MA, USA: Edward Elgar, pp. 149–64.
Jondrow, J., I. Materov, K. Lovell and P. Schmidt (1982), 'On the estimation of technical inefficiency in the stochastic frontier production function model', *Journal of Econometrics*, **19** (2/3), 233–8.
Kumbhakar, S. and K. Lovell (2000), *Stochastic Frontier Analysis*, Cambridge: Cambridge University Press.
Meeusen, W. and J. Van den Broeck (1977), 'Efficiency estimation from Cobb–Douglas production functions with composed errors', *International Economic Review*, **18**, 435–44.
Moriarty, R., S. Yorke, G. Harman, J. Cubbin, M. Meschi and P. Smith (2006), 'Economic analysis of efficiency of Royal Mail units and the implications for regulatory policy', in M.A. Crew and P.R. Kleindorfer (eds), *Liberalization of the Postal and Delivery Sector*, Cheltenham, UK and Northampton, MA, USA: Edward Elgar, pp. 165–82.
Pitt, M. and L. Lee (1981), 'The measurement and sources of technical inefficiency in Indonesian weaving industry', *Journal of Development Economics*, **9**, 43–64.

APPENDIX 8A ESTIMATED EQUATIONS FOR POSTAL DATA

The estimated equations for the cross-sectional model and true random effects model with time-varying BC inefficiency for postal data are shown in Tables 8A.1–2, where: Y = volume of delivered mail; DP = number of delivery point); AR = area surface of the delivery zone; *pbus* = proportion of business delivery points and an indicator of the type of delivery area (denoted urban, suburb or rural, equal to 1 if the delivery office is in the corresponding area, 0 otherwise, and the reference variable is 'city' representing a deep urban area).

Table 8A.1 Cross-section model for 1st year (2003/04)

	Coefficient	Standard error	*t*-ratio
constant	–2.2291	0.1435	–15.53
urban	0.0267	0.0292	0.91
suburb	–0.0289	0.0297	–0.97
rural	–0.0519	0.0338	–1.53
Ln DP	1.0418	0.0063	165.58
Ln Y/DP	0.6070	0.0185	32.82
Ln DP/AR	–0.0575	0.0057	–10.13
pbus	1.3026	0.1374	9.48
Variance e	0.0119		
Variance u	0.0199		

Table 8A.2 True random effects model: time-varying BC inefficiency

	Coefficient	Standard error	*t*-ratio
constant	1.5261	0.1215	12.56
year	0.0069	0.0009	7.68
urban	–0.0070	0.0044	–1.56
suburb	–0.0065	0.0059	–1.09
rural	–0.0083	0.0093	–0.89
Ln DP	0.8420	0.0100	84.17
Ln Y/DP	0.3059	0.0069	44.17
Ln DP/AR	–0.0233	0.0034	–6.89
pbus	0.6568	0.0887	7.41
beta	–0.1801	0.0112	–16.11
Variance e	0.0075		
Variance u	0.0027		
Variance v	0.0320		

9. Affordability of postal services addressed to households*

Claire Borsenberger[†], Denis Joram[‡] and Lise Martin[§]

1 INTRODUCTION

Price affordability is a general principle, common to many services of general economic interest (SGEIs). In practice, social policies dealing with affordability in the telecom, water or energy sectors are aimed at lower-income consumers and are implemented through subsidies and various forms of price regulation including price ceilings and uniform pricing.

In the postal sector, affordability is one of the characteristics of the universal service. The European Directive (97/67/CE) requires that member states 'ensure that the tariffs for each of the services forming part of the universal service shall be affordable', but does not specify what an affordable tariff is and how affordability is measured. The subsidiarity principle applies on this topic, leaving this to member state discretion. However, this is not a trivial issue. The affordable or non-affordable feature of a product or a service should be reflected in its unit price and the ability of customers to pay for a given level of consumption.

Some studies measured affordability by calculating the number of minutes of work required to afford a particular service (see, for example, Copenhagen Economics, 2010 and Deutsche Post, 2010). Except for these contributions, the affordability issue has not been studied in depth in the postal sector yet. This could be explained by the small part of the typical household budget dedicated to postal services. However, the direct impact of postal prices on the budget of households is only one aspect of the problem, as emphasized by Frontier Economics (2005). A large part of postal services is used as input in the production of many other goods consumed by households. So, prices of postal services have indirect impacts on household budgets through the price of final products using postal services as intermediary inputs. This aspect should not be neglected when assessing the impact of changes in the tariff structure and the affordability of postal prices.

In the second section of this chapter, we shall attempt to define the affordability principle by examining works done in other sectors (such as water, energy) and examine how the European Postal Directive requirements on affordability have been transposed into national law. In Section 3, we shall review studies done in the postal sector to

† Economist, European and National Regulation Division, La Poste.
‡ Chief Economist, European and National Regulation Division, La Poste.
§ Economist, European and National Regulation Division, La Poste.

measure affordability. To go further, in Section 4, we shall focus on household spending on postal services in France, and in Section 5 we shall consider not only the direct effect but also the indirect effect – through the consumption of other goods using postal services as input – of postal price variations on French household budgets. Section 6 concludes.

2 THE AFFORDABILITY PRINCIPLE AND DEFINITION

As stated in the Green Paper on services of general interest (European Commission 2003), the concept of affordability was developed in the context of the regulation of telecommunications services. Subsequently, it was also introduced into many fields, such as housing, energy, water, health care, insurance and postal services worldwide (see, for instance, Quigley and Raphael, 2003; Barrantes and Galperin, 2008; Gan and Hill, 2008; Smets, 2008; Kleindorfer et al., 2009; Yang et al. 2010). This concept relies on the principle that an SGEI or an essential good (which has no substitute and whose consumption is mandatory) should be offered at an affordable price in order to be accessible for everybody. Application of this principle helps to achieve economic and social cohesion within countries.

From the general interest point of view, the affordability or economic accessibility of a good could be defined as the ability to pay for the 'relevant' or 'socially desirable' consumption level (and not necessarily the real consumption level, which could be quite different) regarding the household's size and composition. Arguably, postal services or more broadly communication services do not meet a vital need such as water, health or energy. However, they contribute to the social integration of citizens and as such are an essential service that must be accessible to all, both from a physical point of view (access to the network of points of contact)[1] and an economic one (affordability). Lack of access to postal services (for budgetary reasons) could be harmful to households that have no other means to communicate. In this context, the Postal Directive encourages member states to take measures to ensure that the tariffs for each service included in the universal service comply with some principles.[2] Article 12 stipulates that 'prices shall be affordable and must be such that all users, independent of geographical location, and, in the light of specific national conditions, have access to the services provided'.

In a competitive market, prices are oriented towards costs. The free game of competition guarantees that economic efficiency is achieved but does not guarantee that price is 'affordable'. The higher the cost to produce a good, the higher the risk that the good is unaffordable, at least for low-income people. As stated in the Green Paper on services of general interest (European Commission, 2003, p. 38), 'affordability should not be confused with, and does not necessarily equate to, cost orientation. Indeed, the best the market could offer is a price oriented towards cost. But if this cost is not judged to be affordable, the State may choose to step in to ensure that everybody has affordable access'.

To achieve affordability objectives, public authorities generally put in place subsidy mechanisms, such as social or reduced tariffs and uniform tariffs. In the postal sector, designing a price cap is also a way to limit the increase of the average price of universal service products and to reach the affordability objective. For example, in France, the national regulatory authority (NRA) could suspend or modify the tariff evolution planned by the universal service provider (USP) if the universal principles (including affordability) are not met. Implementing the affordability principle raises at least two questions: affordability for whom and for what goods?

In some cases, affordable measures are designed for everyone but in general they are designed to help low-income households ('persons that depart from those provided under normal commercial conditions' as stated in the Green Paper). This is the case in France in the energy and telecom sectors where 'social' tariffs can be obtained under restrictive income conditions. In the postal sector, application of a uniform tariff is a way to provide more affordable postal services to those households that are most costly to serve, that is to say, in general, households living in rural areas. However, this uniform tariff increases the cost of the service for households living in areas less expensive to serve, whatever their income level (including the most disadvantaged).

Despite the fact that the 'affordability' principle is largely spread and supported by governments through social politics, there is no common and well-defined measure of the affordable character of a good or a service. This could be explained by the fact that affordability is related to the price of the good consumed and to the consumer's income and other obligations determined by the consumer's social circumstances, in other words to his/her ability to pay. Under such a general approach, everyone would have his/her own affordable price level.

Perhaps the simplest measure of affordability would be an index comparing the price paid by a household to its income. A good with a price P is deemed affordable for a household with gross income X if P/X is less or equal to an 'affordable limit'. For example, the Royal Bank of Canada (2010) measures the housing affordability by the proportion of median pre-tax household income required to service the cost of mortgage payments (principal and interest), property taxes and utilities for several types of housing. Typically, a part of gross annual income devoted to 'mortgage expenses' higher than 30 or 35 percent is considered as unaffordable. In the field of health, according to Yang et al. (2010), the World Health Organization assesses affordability by calculating the number of days' income required for patients to purchase any of the selected 16 generic medicines for the eight different designated types of disease, taking the lowest-paid government worker as the baseline. In general, treatments that cost one day's income or less are considered affordable. In the energy sector, the UK government considers that households are in 'fuel poverty' if more than 10 percent of their income is spent on heating (Barrantes and Galperin, 2008).

In the postal sector, the European legislation does not specify the criteria for determining affordable prices. In theory, these criteria must be defined by the member states. Relevant criteria could be linked, for example, to the penetration rate or to the price of a basket of basic services related to the disposable income of specific categories of customers. Particular attention should be paid to the needs and capacities of vulnerable and marginalized groups. Finally, once an affordable level has been set, the member states should ensure that this level is effectively offered, by putting in place a price control mechanism (price cap, geographical averaging) and/or by distributing subsidies to the persons concerned (Green Paper, p. 18).

3 A SURVEY OF STUDIES ON AFFORDABILITY IN POSTAL SECTOR

Since 2001, Deutsche Post has published an annual survey on letter prices in Europe. Among other information,[3] Deutsche Post calculated the number of minutes of work needed to buy a standard D+1 letter stamp (see Figure 9.1). The calculation is based on the hourly wage rate of an industrial worker established by the Institut der Deutschen Wirtschaft. In Bulgaria, a worker needs to work almost 16 minutes to earn the postage fee for a standard letter, while in the Netherlands it is around 1.08 minutes. On average, in Europe a worker needs to work for 3.33 minutes to earn the amount to afford a standard letter.

Copenhagen Economics (2010) also examined price affordability of postal services by calculating how many minutes of work (before tax) were required in 2009 to afford two standard mail products: a single letter of 20g (see Figure 9.2) and a single parcel of 1kg. As a proxy for wages, the Copenhagen Economics Institute used the average hourly labor cost statistics from Eurostat. On average, it took 1.7 minutes of work to afford a 20g letter, less than the estimation made by Deutsche Post. The countries with the greatest affordability (the smallest number of minutes worked) were Iceland, Luxembourg, and the United Kingdom followed by the Netherlands and Switzerland. All these countries required less than one minute of work to afford a 20g tariff letter. The least affordable were Bulgaria (8.2 minutes working time) and Latvia (more than 6 minutes).

Comparing these results, we see significant differences: the Copenhagen Economics estimates of working time required to afford a stamp are significantly less than those of Deutsche Post, and countries are ranked differently. This emphasizes the difficulty in estimating the affordable character of a good or service and the importance of the proxy used to measure affordability.

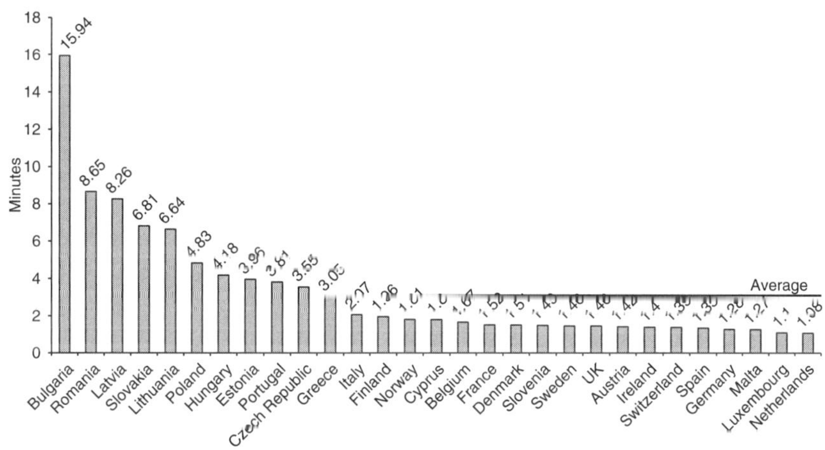

Source: Deutsche Post (2010).

Figure 9.1 Minutes of work required to afford a 20g letter

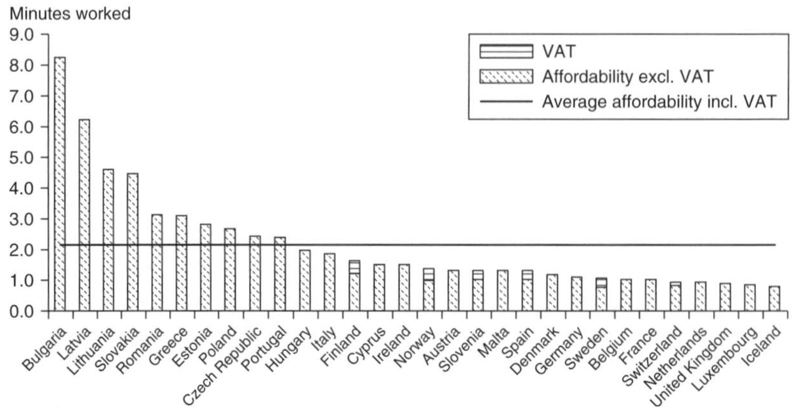

Source: Copenhagen Economics (2010).

Figure 9.2 Number of minutes of work necessary to afford a 20g tariff letter, 2009

4 HOUSEHOLD SPENDING ON POSTAL SERVICES

The Situation in Europe

In all European countries, postal services (purchase of stamps, pre-paid envelopes, parcels, and so on) are not a large budget item for households. The average amount spent on postal services in EU27 in 2005 was €26, corresponding to 0.11 percent of the average annual household consumption expenditure (see Figure 9.3). Note that this figure includes both purchase of products belonging to the scope of universal service (US) and products outside this scope. This last category of products is not subject to an affordability constraint. So, the US affordability issue concerns an even lower amount of expenditure and represents a lower share in household budgets.

According to the Eurostat (2005) Household Budget Survey (HBS), Germany had the highest average annual expenditure amount on postal service, with €64[4] (using the purchasing parity standard: PPS) representing a share of 0.22 percent of consumption expenditure, followed by Malta (with €42 PPS spent on postal services; 0.15 percent of consumption expenditure) and the Netherlands (€38 PPS or 0.13 percent of consumption expenditure). The lowest spenders on postal services are Bulgaria, Lithuania and Portugal with respectively €1, €2 and €3 spent on postal services in 2005, representing 0.01 or 0.02 percent of household consumption expenditure.

The French Case

According to the 2006 'Family budget' survey from the French national statistical institute (INSEE), postal services (inside and outside the scope of US) represent on average 0.11 percent of consumption expenditure of French households, or €31 per year.

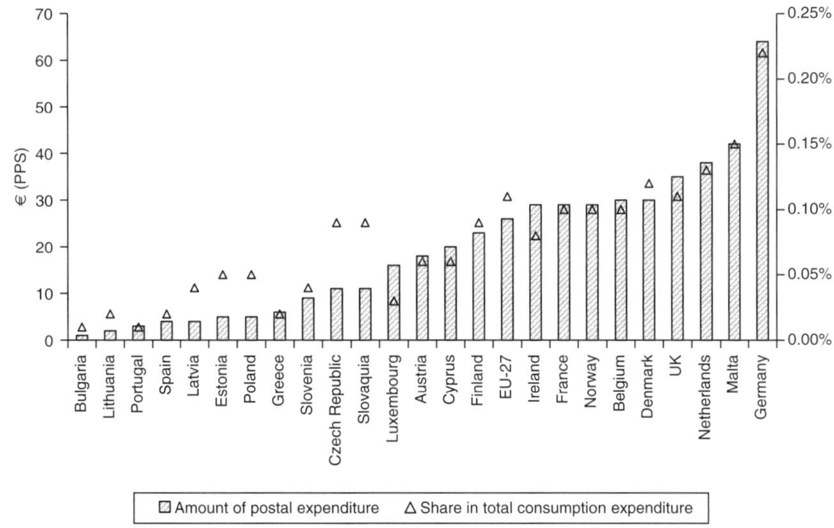

Source: Eurostat (2005).

Figure 9.3 Household consumption expenditure in postal services (2005)

Postal services are what economists call a 'normal' good and a 'necessity' good: the consumption of postal services in absolute value tends to rise with income but the budget share devoted to postal services tends to decrease with disposable income (Engel curve). Despite lower postal expenditure in absolute value (households belonging to the first income decile spent an average €19 against €41 for the richest households) the poorest households devote a slightly higher share of their consumption expenditure to postal services. Excluding the 7th decile, we can observe in Figure 9.4 that the share of postal services in household consumption expenditure declines as income increases. Thus, while households belonging to the second and third deciles spend the same amount of money on postal services, the affordability problem is more 'sensitive' for households belonging to the second decile because of their lower income. A similar situation is observed for households belonging to the fourth and sixth deciles.

The Engel curves for goods such as energy and telecommunications (Figure 9.5) are steeper and these goods represent a larger share in French household budgets. Increases in the price of these goods have a priori greater effects on affordability than those associated with postal services.

5 THE IMPACT OF A GENERAL INCREASE OF POSTAL PRICES ON HOUSEHOLD BUDGETS

All postal operators in Europe are experiencing a fall in mail volume. Recently TNT Post announced a decline in the volume connected to the US by 33 percent in 2010 compared to the volume handled in 2004.[5] In France, the volume of letters has declined by 8.7 percent since 2005.[6] Experts expect an average mail volume decline of 22 to 26 percent

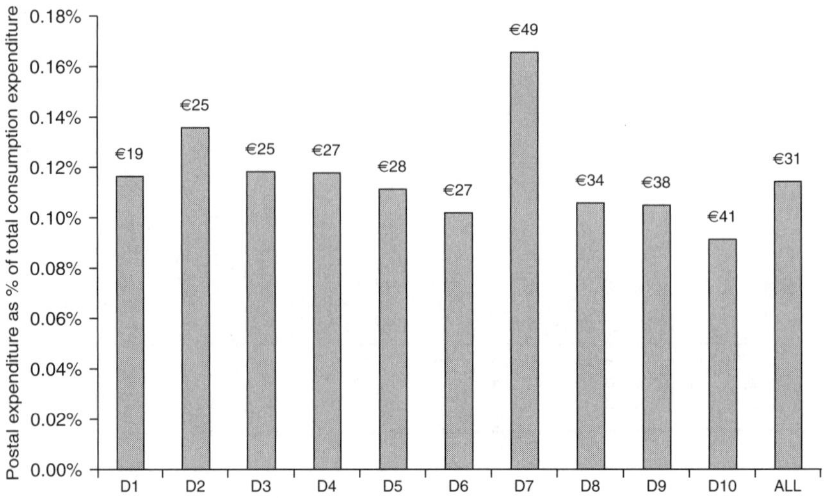

Source: INSEE: 2006 Family Budget Survey.

Figure 9.4 Share of postal services in the annual consumption expenditure of French households by decile of income (2006)

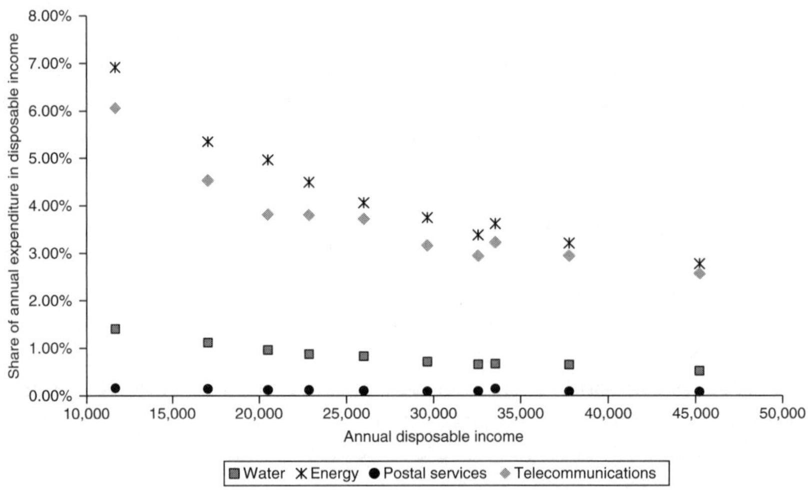

Source: INSEE.

Figure 9.5 Engel curves for utilities in France (2006)

over the next 10 years.[7] In this context, postal operators could plan to finance the necessary reorganization of postal infrastructure with price increases in order to counterbalance the increase in unit costs associated with falling volumes. A question then arises: would postal services remain affordable for households, notably for the poorest?

The Invisible Side of the Affordability Issue

Due to the character of postal services as an intermediate good offered to businesses, the study of the impact of price changes for postal services on households should not be limited to the observation of the evolution of the price of products bought by households. The direct effect of a variation of prices paid by households is only the 'first-round' effect of the story. Household budgets may indeed be indirectly affected by price changes experienced by businesses that use postal services to produce their final goods (such as banks, insurance, and mail order). Insofar as the markets in which businesses operate are competitive, they have an incentive to pass through a share of their cost savings to households via lower final prices.[8] In the case of an increase of postal input price, they have an incentive to pass through less than 100 percent of their cost increase in their final price. We could even go further and consider an additional round of responses to changes in postal price on the price of products using postal input which may generate variations in the consumption of these products and have an impact on the consumption of inputs. We ignore these 'third-round' effects here; they are likely to be minimal in any case.

This indirect/second-round effect is particularly relevant in the postal sector where the share of intermediate demand in total consumption of postal services is high. In 2008, 89 percent of the global demand for postal services (final and intermediate) in the UK came from British companies who use these services as input in their production. In addition, 84 percent of intermediate demand for postal services came from 20 sectors. The major consumers of postal services as input were the insurance industry and the banking and finance sector. In France, the national statistical institute does not provide detailed data on this issue: data on the intermediate consumption of postal services are aggregated with those of telecommunication services.[9] According to an internal and non-public study, the prime users of postal services in France belong to the financial sector, public administrations and retailing, as in the UK.

Volume and Turnover Data

For our purposes, we need to distinguish two price elasticities: the reaction of household demand to price variation and that of business customers. Results of elasticity estimates[10] generally agree that non-urgent mail (Second Class, advertising mail) and bulk mail (presorted mail) have higher price elasticity than First Class and priority letters. In other words, business customers are more sensitive to price variations than households.[11] In the present study, we shall assume that the price elasticity of demand is equal to –0.3 for households and –0.5 for businesses.

According to the annual report of the French observatory of postal activities, in 2009 15,347 million correspondence items were delivered in France which generated revenues of €7,837 million. Households and small and medium-sized enterprises (SMEs)[12] sent 2,611 million items (17 percent of the total volume) and businesses 12,736 million (83 percent of the total volume). Data are summarized in Table 9.1. Note that French households and SMEs spent on average €73 per year on postal services.[13] One can assume that the gap between this amount and that given by the French statistical institute (€31) corresponds to the postal expenditure of SMEs. French households (including SMEs) received an average of 156 direct mails and 294 other correspondence items over the year and sent

Table 9.1 Initial setting

	Price elasticity	Volume (million items)	Turnover (million euros)	Average unit price (€)
Households and SMEs/ single-piece mail	–0.3	2,611	1,891	0.72
Businesses/bulk mail	–0.5	12,736	5,946	0.47
Total		15,347	7,837	0.52

Source: Annual report of the French observatory of postal activities (ARCEP, 2010).

Table 9.2 Final setting

Change in products price (%)	Single-piece mail price	Household volume (million items)	Revenues from households (€m)	Change in household expenditure (%)	Bulk-mail price	Business volume (million items)	Revenues from business (€m)	Change in business expenditure (%)
+2	0.73	2,595	1,906	+0.8	0.48	12,609	6,045	+1.7
+5	0.76	2,572	1,944	+2.8	0.49	12,418	6,128	+3.1
+10	0.80	2,533	2,006	+6.1	0.52	12,099	6,255	+5.2

92 letters. In the remainder of this chapter, we shall study the impact of an increase in the price of all products included in this basket on the household budget.

Estimation of the Direct Impact of an Increase in Single-piece Mail Price on Household Budgets

We assume that the prices of products offered to households increase by 2 percent, 5 percent and 10 percent, all things being equal (notably household income). Knowing the price elasticities, we can easily calculate the new volume of products consumed and the additional direct postal expenditure borne by households and businesses (see Table 9.2).

Considering the French average expenditure in postal services (€31.19 in 2006), households would directly spend on average for postal services €31.44 if price increases by 2 percent, €32.07 if price increases by 5 percent and €33.08 if price increases by 10 percent. Assuming that the price elasticity of demand is the same for each income group, the expenditure of households belonging to the first decile would directly increase, respectively, by €0.15, €0.53 and €1.14 per year.

Estimation of the Indirect Impact of an Increase in Bulk-mail Price on Household Budgets

To estimate the indirect impact of an increase in bulk-mail price on household budgets, we made several assumptions. First, we assume that the extra-costs burden by businesses is distributed between economic sectors according to their shares in the intermediate consumption of postal services. To do this, we use figures for the UK for 2008 (see Appendix 9A for the distribution of postal extra costs between economic sectors).

A share of each industry's cost increase is passed on to households, depending on the degree of competition in the industry: the more competitive the industry, the less the share of cost increase businesses will pass through in the retail price of their final good. For the purpose of this study, we use the markup estimates made by Molnar and Bottini (2008) in service industries for European members of the OECD over the 1993–2006 period.[14] The most competitive sectors, users of postal services in France, were wholesale, motor vehicle and retail distributions; the least competitive were market research and management consultancy. We then assume that the rate of cost increase passed through to households' final prices is equal to 50 percent in the most-competitive sectors and 75 percent in the less-competitive ones. Moreover, when we do not get information on the competitive intensity of a given economic sector, in order not to minimize and underestimate the indirect effect on households of an increase of bulk-mail price, we assume that any increase in the cost of production is totally passed through in final prices to households. With all these assumptions, the rate of cost increase passed through to households in final price of goods produced with postal services is equal to 81 percent (see Appendix 9A).

Finally, to estimate the indirect effect of a price change for businesses on households, we need to distribute the passed-through cost increase among the different deciles of households in proportion to their consumption of the given final good. Not doing this could distort results, overstating the negative impact of the second-round effect for lower-income households since it is likely that higher-income groups consume proportionately more of some goods, such as financial services, for instance. The difficulty of this exercise lies in the imperfect compatibility between the input–output tables and the items of expenditure in the household expenditure survey. We need to make some assumptions to match the two classifications. For instance, we associated the items 'Food, Drink, Tobacco' and 'Clothing & Footwear' from the household expenditure survey with 'Retail and Wholesale distributions' from the input–output table. Then we distribute the business costs increase over household income deciles, according to their consumption.

Under all these assumptions, the yearly expenditure of the first decile income group would increase indirectly by €1.99 if bulk-mail price increases by 2 percent, €3.67 if bulk-mail price increases by 5 percent, €6.24 if bulk-mail price increases by 10 percent. The total annual consumption expenditure of the low-income group would indirectly increase by, respectively, 0.012, 0.023 and 0.039 percent if the bulk mail price increases by 2, 5 or 10 percent.

On average, these bulk-mail price increases would generate an indirect increase of households' annual spending of €3.11 if the bulk mail price increases by 2 percent (0.011 percent of the global yearly consumption budget), €5.74 if bulk-mail price increases by 5 percent (0.021 percent of the global yearly consumption budget) and €9.75 if bulk-mail price increases by 10 percent (0.036 percent of the global yearly consumption budget).

The Global Impact of Postal Price Increases

In the case of a simultaneous increase of single-piece and bulk-mail prices of 2, 5 or 10 percent, the total impact on households' annual expenditure is represented in Figure 9.6. On average, French households would spend €0.25 more per year to send mail (direct

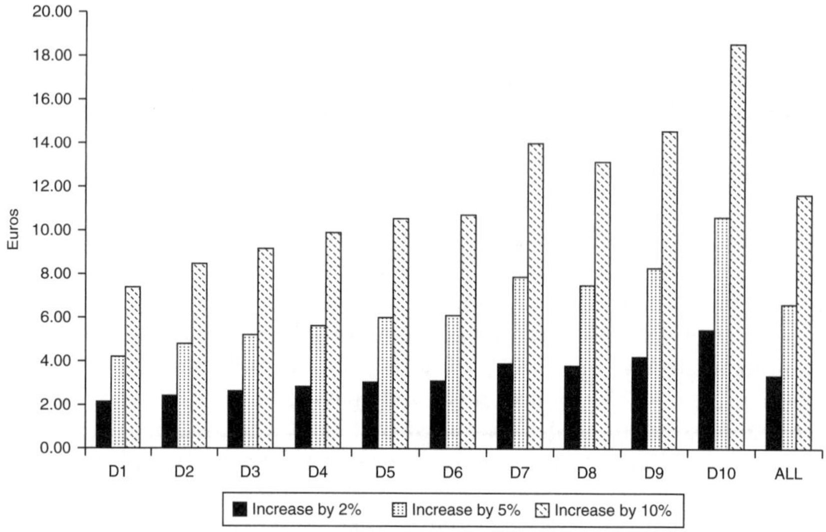

Figure 9.6 Additional annual expenditure for households due to a general increase of postal tariffs (single piece and bulk mail) (€)

purchase of postal products) and €3.11 more per year due to the bulk-mail price increase (additional expenditure on products using postal service as input) if postal prices increase by 2 percent. In the case of a 5 percent increase, these figures are, respectively, €0.88 and €5.74. And in the case of a 10 percent increase, €1.89 and €9.75.

For the poorest households, a global increase of 2, 5 and 10 percent in postal prices would induce an additional expenditure of €0.15, €0.53 and €1.14 for sending mail and an additional spending of €1.99, €3.67 and €6.24 in other products (using postal services as input). In percentage of annual budget devoted to consumption expenditure, these increases represent for households belonging to the first decile of income, respectively, 0.013, 0.026 and 0.046 percent.

Regarding these figures and taking into account that initial prices are considered as affordable by the regulator, the affordability of postal services seems not to be challenged by price increases, unless postal tariffs would increase by a disproportionate amount. Moreover, all these estimates are made under an 'all-things-being-equal' assumption, notably the level of demand. However, we could expect a decrease in postal demand following price increases. In other words, the all-things-being-equal assumption tends to overestimate the impact of a postal price increase on household budgets.

6 CONCLUSION

Affordability of postal services is one of the main characteristics of US as stated in the postal European Directive. However, it is very difficult to define what an affordable tariff is. From the general interest point of view, the affordability or economic accessibility of a good could be defined as the ability to pay for the 'relevant' or 'socially desirable' consumption level, based on household characteristics, and could be measured by an index comparing the price paid by a household to its income.

To achieve the affordability objective, public authorities could use different tools. In the postal sector, affordability is reached through price-cap mechanisms (sometimes with several baskets of products) and tariff regulation. However, few studies have yet been done on this topic. This could be explained by the rather low share of the household consumption budget devoted to postal services in Europe and perhaps the complexity of this issue.

Indeed, reducing the affordability issue to the study of direct expenditure of households could be restrictive, notably when this product or service is an important input in the production function of other firms. The main users of postal services as input are the insurance, banking, finance and public administration sectors in the UK and presumably in most developed countries.

This is why in this chapter, we go further and, as in Frontier Economics (2005), consider the indirect impact of postal tariffs faced by businesses in their global expenditure of consumption. To illustrate our comments, we consider a global increase of postal tariffs in France (both on single piece and bulk mail) – by 2, 5 and 10 percent. Note that these initial prices are considered affordable by the regulator. Making several assumptions on price elasticity and on the passed-through ratio of costs increases to final prices, we showed that an increase of 2 percent of all postal prices has a very small impact on the consumption budget of the poorest households (+€2.14 per year representing 0.013 percent of total expenditure). Even a 10 percent increase of postal prices seems not to be challenging for the affordability character of postal tariffs in France (the annual expenditure of the poorest households would increase by €7.38). Moreover, these estimates do not take into account the likely negative effect of price increases on demand, which could reduce the share of budget devoted to postal services despite the price increase.

Such an analysis should be made in all countries to deal with the affordability issue. The most challenging difficulty is to collect the required data since in most national accounting systems statistics on postal services are aggregated with those of telecoms and furthermore, the structure of the input–output table needed to deal with postal intermediate consumption does not match exactly with household budget survey items. This induces approximate results when calculating the indirect effect of business tariff changes on household expenditures.

NOTES

* The opinions expressed in this chapter are those of the authors and do not necessarily reflect the positions of the Groupe La Poste.

1. For a review of the degree of physical accessibility to postal networks, see Borsenberger et al. (2011).
2. The scope of universal service among member states varies greatly from a small range restricted to single-piece letters and basic parcels to a larger definition including bulk mail and bulk parcels, direct mail, periodicals, and non-priority letters.
3. Deutsche Post compares each year the nominal price of domestic and cross-border (within Europe) fastest letter mail (with D+1 target) and the evolution of prices since 1999 (adjusted by inflation).
4. According to the German Statistical Office, German households spent on average €3.36 per month for letters and postcards and €0.88 for parcels (€50 per year).

5. TNT Newsletter, Issue 12, April 2011.
6. ARCEP (2010).
7. IPC (2010).
8. As demonstrated by Frontier Economics (2005), in the framework of a tariff rebalancing consisting in increasing the price of single-piece mail (weakly competitive, even monopolistic, market) and decreasing the price of bulk mail (competitive or contestable market), the price increases borne by households may be partially offset by a decrease in the price of goods and services produced with postal inputs.
9. We encounter the same problem with Eurostat data.
10. See Robinson (2007) and Visco Comandini et al. (2009).
11. However, the growing electronic substitution of communication exchanges could modify this rule. Already, in Cazals et al. (2011), in the UK, the demand for First Class mail is more sensitive to price changes than Second Class and workshared mail.
12. Data provided by the observatory do not allow us to distinguish between those two types of customers whereas in contrast to households, a share of mail sent by SMEs is an intermediate consumption, as for businesses (all mail sent by households is a final consumption).
13. There are 25.7 million households and 2.5 million SMEs in France.
14. The authors show that the estimated markups are higher for professional services, real estate, renting and utilities, while they tended to be substantially lower for construction, computer services, retail and wholesale trade and catering. Markups in the telecommunications sector fall in-between these two ends of the spectrum. There is also large variation across countries in terms of the size of the estimated markups. Competitive pressures are large in the United Kingdom and most Scandinavian countries, and relatively small in Central European countries, Sweden and Italy. Spain, Germany and France lie in-between these two groups.

REFERENCES

ARCEP (2010), 'Observatoire annuel des activités postales en France – Année 2009', 28 October.

Barrantes, R. and H. Galperin (2008), 'Can the poor afford mobile telephony? Evidence from Latin America', *Telecommunications Policy*, **32**, 521–30.

Borsenberger, C., D. Joram and B. Roy (2011), 'How many outlets if the USP does not face any USO? A cross-country comparison', in M. Crew and P. Kleindorfer (eds), *Reinventing the Postal Sector in an Electronic Age*, Cheltenham, UK and Northampton, MA, USA: Edward Elgar, pp. 123–41.

Cazals, C., J.-P. Florens, L. Veruete-McKay, F. Rodriguez and S. Soteri (2011), 'UK letter mail demand: a content based time series analysis using overlapping market survey statistical techniques', in M. Crew and P. Kleindorfer (eds), *Reinventing the Postal Sector in an Electronic Age*, Cheltenham, UK and Northampton, MA, USA: Edward Elgar, pp. 91–108.

Copenhagen Economics (2010), 'Main Developments in the Postal Sector (2008–2010)', Final report for the European Commission, 29 November.

Deutsche Post (2010), *Letter Prices in Europe*, March.

Directive 97/67/CE of 15 December 1997 with regard to the full accomplishment of the internal market of Community postal services.

European Commission (2003), 'Green Paper on Services of General Interest', COM 2003-270 Final, 21 May.

Eurostat (2005), 'Household Budget Survey'.

Frontier Economics (2005), 'Front the envelope – Estimating the impacts on shift in postal charges', March.

Gan, Q. and R.J. Hill (2008), 'Measuring housing affordability: looking beyond the median', working paper, Australian School of Business, Sydney.

International Post Corporation (IPC) (2010), 'Role of Mail in 2020', Report from Copenhagen Economics.

Kleindorfer, P., H. Kunreuther, E. Michel-Kerjan and R. Zeckhauser (2009), 'Mitigating and financing catastrophic risks: principles and action framework', OECD working paper, Organization for Economic Cooperation and Development, Paris.

Molnar, M. and N. Bottini (2008), 'How large are competitive pressures in services markets?

Estimation of mark-ups for selected OECD countries', OECD Technical Workshop on Trade Barrier Assessment Methodology, Paris, 12 December.
Quigley, J. and S. Raphael (2003), 'Is housing unaffordable? Why is it not more affordable?', Working Paper series, Institute of Business and Economic Research, University of California, Berkeley, CA.
Robinson, A. (2007), 'A review of price elasticity models for postal products', Background Paper no. 2007-01, Direct Communications Group, Pitney Bowes Research Project.
Royal Bank of Canada (2010), 'Housing Trends and Affordability', Economics Research, November.
Smets, H. (2008), 'De l'eau potable à prix abordable – La pratique des États', Rapport de l'Académie de l'Eau, Paris.
Visco Comandini, V., M. Lintell, S. Gori, M.R. Pierleoni and B. Tisdahl (2009), 'Postal price elasticities and intermedia competition – a multisided market approach', in M. Crew and P. Kleindorfer (eds), *Progress in the Competitive Agenda in the Postal and Delivery Sector*, Cheltenham, UK and Northampton, MA, USA: Edward Elgar, pp. 163–83.
Yang, H., H. Dib, M. Zhu, G. Qi and X. Zhang (2010), 'Prices, availability and affordability of essential medicines in rural areas of Hubei Province, China', *Health Policy and Planning*, no. 25, 219–29.

APPENDIX 9A

Table 9A.1 *Pass-through cost increases on final prices/household expenditure*

	Additional cost for businesses (million €) due to a bulk-mail price increase of			Estimated mark-up for France (Molnar and Bottini, 2008)*	Pass-through ratio (%)	Indirect increase in household expenditure (million €)		
	2%	5%	10%			2%	5%	10%
Wholesale and retail distribution	10.11	18.68	31.73	1.38; 1.28	50	5.06	9.34	15.86
Hotels, catering, pubs	2.16	3.99	6.78	1.78	100	2.16	3.99	6.78
Health and veterinary services	1.69	3.12	5.31	na	100	1.69	3.12	5.31
Motor vehicle distribution & repair, fuel	1.83	3.37	5.73	1.27	50	0.91	1.69	2.86
Postal and courier services	4.48	8.27	14.06	na	100	4.48	8.27	14.06
Telecommunications	1.72	3.17	5.39	1.84	50	0.86	1.59	2.69
Recreational services	1.51	2.79	4.73	na	100	1.51	2.79	4.73
Education	2.50	4.62	7.84	2.82	75	1.87	3.46	5.88
Insurance and pension funds	14.72	27.19	46.18	na	100	14.72	27.19	46.18
Financial services	22.60	41.74	70.89	2.24; 1.74	50	11.30	20.87	35.45
Other goods	35.27	65.14	110.65	na	100	35.27	65.14	110.65
Total	98.58	182.09	309.29			79.83	147.45	250.46

Note: *M. Molnar and N. Bottini, 'How large are competitive pressures in services markets? Estimation of mark-ups for selected OECD countries', OECD Technical Workshop on Trade Barrier Assessment Methodology, Paris, 12 December 2008.

10. Towards a 21st century postal service

John C. Panzar[†]

1 INTRODUCTION

The global financial crisis accelerated a secular decline in postal sector volumes and finances. It now seems unlikely that either will recover along with the wider economy. Therefore, it is an appropriate time to reassess the role of the postal sector in the US going forward and to analyze the guiding principles under which it should be organized. This is the purpose of this chapter.

It seems that the cyclical downturn in mail volumes caused by the global financial crisis may finally have triggered the secular decline in volumes that has long been predicted. While this may signal the beginning of a painful period of adjustment for the Postal Service and its employees, it does not mean that postal sector issues are no longer important. Even a declining postal sector remains a vital part of a nation's transportation and communications infrastructure. Public policy during the forthcoming transition period remains vitally important. Indeed, I would argue that the task is no less urgent because the postal sector may be a 'declining industry'. The same can be said of the railroad industry in the twentieth century. By the end of that century, railroads had clearly lost the dominant place in the US economy that they had enjoyed in 1900. Yet their role remained crucial, nevertheless. More importantly for the present discussion, their decline was managed very poorly from the perspective of public policy. It is important that this saga is not repeated with the postal sector, which also continues to be a vital part of our nation's infrastructure, even in its decline. The following policy issues will be addressed in this chapter: ownership structure, scope of the Postal Service, and regulatory policy. As we shall see, these issues interact with one another. Therefore, appropriate policy approaches must be developed that recognize this interdependence.

I want to make clear at the outset that I am not addressing the Postal Service's overfunding of the retirement health and pension costs of past and current employees. This accounts for the majority of the revenue shortfall of the Postal Service.[1] As a policy matter, I certainly urge Congress to 'do the right thing'. However, even if the billions in question are restored to the Postal Service (and mailers), it will still be necessary to address the structural problems facing the Postal Service, its regulators, the mailing community and, ultimately, the nation.

Economists tend to view private ownership as the 'gold standard' in terms of creating strong incentives and achieving economic efficiency. However, the privatization of a

† Professor of Economics, University of Auckland, New Zealand and Louis W. Menk Professor Emeritus, Northwestern University, USA.

money-losing operation is, itself, fraught with difficulties. In particular, significant rent dissipation may arise in the process of awarding the required subsidies. This leads me to come down on the side of recommending continued operation of the Postal Service as a state-owned enterprise (SOE) rather than privatization. However, as we shall see, this complicates the policy choices in other areas.

At the heart of the policy dilemma is the fact that the provision of postal and delivery services exhibits significant economies of scale and economies of scope. Fortunately, these economies are located predominantly at the heart of the Postal Service: that is, in the local collection and delivery functions. As a result, I shall end up arguing that this 'first and last mile' of operation should be the primary focus of public policy and the core business of the Postal Service. Of course, there are many other markets that are more or less closely related to the core collection and delivery functions of the Postal Service. These ancillary markets may be connected in various ways: for example, through cross-elasticities of demand or supply; for example, vertical or horizontal economies of scope. *If* the Postal Service were a privately owned profit-maximizing competitive firm, it might be possible to leave these 'boundary of the enterprise' issues to the marketplace.

However, I argue that the Postal Service of the future should be increasingly focused on its natural monopoly core functions. Therefore, it will likely require continued scrutiny by regulatory and antitrust authorities despite increasing liberalization in the postal sector. This is because the core services provided by the Postal Service will be the platform on which the much larger private sector mailing industry is based. Fair and efficient competition in this larger marketplace will require regulatory surveillance of the rates charged for access to the core delivery network of the Postal Service. Retail customers should be subject to price-cap regulation for transparency and predictability. Rates for commercial access to the Postal Service's delivery network should be cost based in order to foster cost efficiency in the postal sector as a whole – including both the Postal Service and its private sector worksharing partners.

The discussion in this chapter proceeds as follows. Section 2 argues that, although declining, the Postal Service remains an important part of the nation's transportation and communications infrastructure. Section 3 examines the issues of public versus private ownership and the extent of the Universal Service Obligation (USO). I argue that continued operation of the Postal Service as an SOE provides the best strategy for achieving its important policy objectives. Section 4 discusses the future scope of the Postal Service, both horizontal and vertical. I conclude that *both* should be limited to those activities directly related to its core competency: the delivery of letters and parcels. Finally, Section 5 discusses the appropriate guidelines for the regulatory environment in which the Postal Service of the future will operate.

2 THE FUTURE OF THE MAILING INDUSTRY AND THE POSTAL SERVICE OF THE FUTURE (PSF)

Declines in mail volumes in the United States have been dramatic. From a peak of 213 billion pieces in 2006, it fell to 177 billion pieces in 2009, with a further projected fall to around 150 billion pieces by 2020 (Boston Consulting Group, 2010). However, mail remains big business in the US, involving hundreds of billions of dollars of GDP and millions of workers. In addition, the scale, scope and relative efficiency of mail operations in the US provide a variety of options to ensure the health of the sector going forward. In the face of such negative growth, it is easy to forget that the US exhibits a much greater 'mail intensity' than other developed economies. Thus, the question is not whether the Postal Service can survive, but rather how well it adjusts to declining mail volumes and the changing market environment.

There has been no shortage of proposals for 'new business models' for the Postal Service.[2] However, the objective should not be limited to merely restoring the Postal Service to profitability under current regulatory and policy parameters. The Postal Service is an important part of the nation's productive infrastructure. My goal in this chapter is to present economic arguments that support my particular vision of how the entire postal sector should be structured to best serve the public interest in the future. This requires analysis of both the PSF as well as the regulatory environment in which it operates.

To preview my conclusions, the PSF should be built around its core competency: its (first and) last mile collection and delivery network. This core network would be owned and operated by an SOE and subject to regulatory and antitrust surveillance. Its ability to enter related markets would be subject to close scrutiny and highly limited. The PSF would fulfill a USO *explicitly* specified by Congress. It may or may not be protected by a monopoly franchise in its local delivery markets.

The remainder of this chapter presents my arguments in support of this PSF proposal. However, at this point I would like to suggest a certain chain of reasoning for the reader to keep in mind:

1. Economies of scale and a significant USO require government intervention in the postal marketplace.
2. Public provision of a nationwide collection and delivery network is the best way to accomplish the government's policy objectives and, at the same time, provide an important infrastructure platform for the private mail economy.
3. Both economic theory and experience in other liberalized network industries suggests that vertical and horizontal integration by incumbents should be carefully monitored.
4. Regulating an infrastructure monopolist is a challenging task for regulatory and antitrust authorities. The most workable approach seems to be price-cap regulation for final products combined with cost-based regulation for access (worksharing) products.

Clearly, all of the steps in the above argument are at least somewhat controversial. My proposals are based on my weighing of the theoretical and empirical evidence and my experience with the postal sector and other network industries.

3 PUBLIC OWNERSHIP AND UNIVERSAL SERVICE

For largely historical reasons, most postal operators escaped the wave of privatizations beginning in the 1980s. Of course, this history is no argument against privatization as a policy going forward. The potential incentive and efficiency advantages of postal privatization must be traded off against the documented difficulties involved in regulating a private firm to fulfill the mandate of the Postal Service. What is this mandate, and why does it require governmental intervention? First, and foremost, postal delivery services are a *natural monopoly*, with the local delivery function characterized by significant economies of scale. Even in the absence of legal entry restrictions, market forces result in the domination of a single firm. Regulation, to some degree, has been required to prevent monopoly exploitation. Second, the Postal Service has a long-standing requirement to provide universal service.[3]

Natural monopoly and USOs are by no means unique to the postal sector. Indeed, the US has had long experience of the use of regulated private sector firms to pursue these goals in both the railroad and telecommunications sectors. However, it is precisely this experience that argues for an alternative mechanism in the postal sector! A major factor in the financial dilemma of the late twentieth-century US railroad industry was the maintenance of obsolete service requirements by the International Chamber of Commerce (ICC).[4] The railroad experience teaches that regulator mandated cross-subsidization is *not* the way to ensure that politically desirable services are provided. In order to be successful, such a policy requires (among other things) that the overall enterprise be financially viable. *That* mistake was not repeated in the telecommunications sector, but another monster was created.

The Telecommunications Act of 1996 explicitly recognized the government's interest in providing subsidized service to high-cost areas and low-income users without unduly burdening the firms providing such services. The Act empowered the Federal Communications Commission (FCC) to set up mechanisms including a Universal Service Fund supported by contributions from all industry providers. While the basic idea was theoretically sound, over the past 15 years the program has mushroomed out of control, involving billions of dollars of annual expenditures. Robert Crandall (2005) includes a discussion of the experience of the first decade of this policy. For a taste of the current level of activity in this area, the interested reader is directed to the FCC's universal service web page: www.fcc.gov/wcb/tapd/universal_service/.[5] It would be unfortunate if such a process were to be repeated in the postal sector.

What, then, should form the basis of universal service policy in the US? First, I agree with Campbell (2010) that it is necessary for Congress to explicitly spell out precisely what is meant by the concept; for example, quality of service standards, uniformity of rates, and so on. Since it hardly seems reasonable to literally require 'an Act of Congress' to change the details of such requirements as circumstances change, Congress should delegate the continuing enforcement of universal service provisions to the Postal Regulatory Commission (PRC). Their primary concern should be to match the dictates of any USO with the current needs of the mailing public.

How should the required services be provided? Here a bit of 'political forecasting' is required. One could make a serious argument that postal service should be left entirely to the private sector marketplace. After all, the primary function of the mail these days is to provide 'hard-copy' transfers among businesses and between businesses and their customers. Thus, unlike telecommunications, subsidies to high-cost areas do not go directly to residents of high-cost areas, they go largely to business mailers who send advertisements to residents of high-cost areas. If such a 'hands-off' policy were the outcome of the political decision process regarding universal service, there would be no funding issues. Then, in spite of its economies of scale and market dominance, one could deregulate (and even privatize) the Postal Service, relying on competition from other firms and communication modes to promote efficiency.

At the other extreme, suppose Congress decided that the formal USO provided by the Postal Service should resemble the prevailing operations of today's Postal Service, complete with thousands of excess post offices, a six days per week delivery, and so on. In that case, it seems likely that only massive government subsidies and/or drastically higher postal rates could get the job done. However, I do not believe that things will get to that point. First, serious discussions of reasonable alternative USO standards are already well under way.[6] Second, despite recent revenue and profit declines, the Postal Service is actually quite well positioned among postal operators with respect to costs, volumes and rates (USPS OIG 2010c). Thus, it is my expectation that an explicit process of USO determination will result in a significant reduction in current service levels: for example, a 3–5-day delivery, franchise retail outlets, and so on. The associated 'excess costs' (relative to a hypothetical market benchmark) should be treated as part of Postal Service institutional costs.

As an economist, it is with considerable reluctance that I cede the privatization option. The profit motive, combined with an active equity market, is unparalleled in its ability to provide the high-powered incentives needed to promote static and dynamic efficiency. I am particularly concerned about the ability of the Postal Service to get its employment costs under control without the 'hard budget constraint' provided by the market. However, the 'postal wage premium' is far from universal among postal operators. SOEs have been successfully structured to both provide efficient postal service and limit excess employee compensation demands; for example, in Sweden and New Zealand.

Let me summarize my views on the ownership question. Given the likely outcome of the political decision on universal service, the public interest is, on balance, best served if the Postal Service remains a regulated, SOE. This does not mean that I am advocating a continuation of the status quo. The SOE organizational form provides many opportunities for efficiency improvements that have not yet been exploited by the Postal Service.[7] I also fully support reforms in the collective bargaining process that would bring employee compensation costs in line with those in the private sector.

4 SCALE AND SCOPE OF THE POSTAL SERVICE OF THE FUTURE

The Postal Service consists of a vast network of facilities and operations. It can be considered to produce a very large number of distinct, but interrelated products. It is part of a larger postal and delivery sector that includes many private sector firms as well. Some are competitors, providing services to end users that compete with those offered by the Postal Service. Some are partners in the sense that they utilize the network of the Postal Service to provide services to their customers and, increasingly, some are both.[8] Together, all serve the vastly larger *mailing sector*: that portion of economy which uses the mail to make transactions, advertise its products, and generally conduct its business. This section addresses the question: in which businesses should the publicly owned and operated PSF participate, and, as importantly, who should decide?

In a perfectly competitive or contestable market, the answer would be quite simple. The profit-constrained enterprise should be allowed to diversify into any market in which it could obtain a profit contribution: for example, one that is related to its core offerings via economies of scope. When it enters such a market it has a cost advantage over a competitor without scope economies and efficiently replaces some of its quantity, and, in the process earning additional contributions towards covering its institutional costs. Such diversification benefits both the regulated firm and consumers. Displaced competitors are harmed, but by less than consumers gain. The policy message seems clear: the profit-constrained regulated firm should be encourage to diversify whenever it thinks it can earn a profit by doing so.

Not surprisingly, competitors have long claimed that incumbent posts 'compete unfairly'.[9] Sometimes these complaints have obvious merit; for example, the 'mailbox monopoly' of the USPS – which certainly has the effect of *raising rivals' costs*. More commonly, charges of cross-subsidization are thinly disguised attempts to influence the regulatory process to set higher rates for the incumbent's products that are close substitutes for those of the complaining rival.

However, it is here that the status of the incumbent as an SOE complicates matters. A profit-maximizing firm that has an opportunity to earn at least some profits will not price competitive products below their average incremental cost *except* as an attempt at predation. It would increase its profits by abandoning that product line altogether. In contrast, recent work by Sappington and Sidak (2003a,b) suggests that SOEs may have the incentive to engage in predatory behavior on a *continuing* basis. This may occur when the SOE's goal is *not* profit maximization, but the pursuit of some other, more bureaucratic, objective. Sappington and Sidak suggest 'revenue maximization' as a way to summarize, or proxy, the goals of SOE managers who pursue careerist considerations in the absence of access to the stock option incentive schemes available in privately owned companies. Profit considerations are reflected through a (typically binding) constraint that the firm achieves at least a 'satisfactory' level of profits.[10]

Mathematically, this does not require a major change in the formulation of the usual constrained optimization problem used to model the regulated firm. However, it leads to the possibility of profound changes in the nature of the choices of the firm. Now, it is entirely possible for the firm to wish to adopt prices below marginal costs on a long-term, continuing basis: that is, *not* as a predatory device with an eye toward raising rates as soon as the prey has exited the market. Unfortunately, regulatory cross-subsidy tests may be ill suited to deal with the situation. The SOE may also find it optimal to alter its strategic investment policies so as to distort the outcome of any incremental cost test to which its rates may be subject. There are many forms such distortion might take. As a very simple example, consider the following: an incumbent wishes to promote its 'X-Mail' service. However, instead of advertising that service explicitly, it decides upon an extensive 'corporate image' type advertising campaign. While not as cost effective as a targeted campaign, such an advertising strategy has one obvious advantage: its costs are truly 'joint and common costs'. If it had done an X-Mail ad campaign, its costs would be 'product-specific fixed costs', directly attributable to that product. As such, they would increase the average incremental cost floor pertaining to X-Mail rates.

Structural remedies may be required to deal with situations in which the incentives for anticompetitive behavior are ongoing and the regulatory safeguards in place to control it are subject to strategic manipulation. The most logical remedy is to prevent the incumbent from offering services outside its dominant market.

Structural separation remedies are frequently proposed in network industries such as telecommunications and electric power, even with privately owned incumbents. In those cases, as in the postal case, the tradeoff is the potential loss of the economies of scope enjoyed by the operator offering a wide range of products. The incumbent (and many regulators) see such economies of scope as an important factor in keeping basic service rates low, while competitors see them as the key source of the incumbent's (unfair) network advantage.

Theoretical arguments alone cannot resolve this debate. However, on balance, I am of the opinion that the risk of inefficient diversification is significant, a risk that is potentially increased by the SOE organizational form. The obvious safeguard is to continue the regulatory provisions that limit the Postal Service's ability to diversify outside its core delivery function.

The preceding discussion has dealt with what economists refer to as *horizontal* and/or *conglomerate* expansion by the Postal Service. That is, diversification into markets which are not part of the postal value chain. As we have seen, those diversification issues are intertwined with the status of the Postal Service as an SOE. Postal policy must also deal with the extent of the *vertical integration* of the Postal Service. Vertical relationships in liberalized network industries are fraught with both theoretical and practical problems.[11] Often vertical separation is imposed on the dominant firm. The downside of this policy is the potential sacrifice of economies of scope. On the other hand, anticompetitive behavior seems to proliferate when incumbents are allowed to compete with firms to whom they also sell access services. The remainder of this section (and much of the next) addresses this issue in the postal context.

I have described a PSF focused on its (first and) last mile core competency. But what happens in the middle? To the individual consumer ('Aunt Minnie'), the present 'face' of the Postal Service is (i) her carrier who delivers (and sometimes collects) her mail and (ii) the (often imposing) post office where she buys her stamps and mails her parcels. In contrast, large mailers have a variety of options for injecting their volumes into alternative points in the mail stream – either directly through the Postal Service or via third parties. I would not expect this situation to change much. I would expect that the USO mandated by Congress would continue to specify that a certain amount of retail presence must be maintained by the PSF.[12] Thus the face of the PSF would hardly change for Aunt Minnie. The question is, would large mailers be allowed to have the option of obtaining end-to-end from the PSF? (And, *could* Aunt Minnie's letter or parcel travel its entire journey through the PSF network, or *must* it be handed off for sorting and transport before being returned to the PSF for delivery?)

As noted above, the question of vertical separation always involves difficult tradeoffs. As will be discussed in some detail in the next section, the PRC's worksharing policies have been notably successful in enabling upstream activities to be efficiently shared between the Postal Service and competitors. However, as also discussed below, the recent change to price-cap regulation of workshared products may end this happy situation. In any event, as was the case in the telecommunications industry, operational details will undoubtedly have an important impact on any practical decision regarding vertical separation.

5 REGULATORY POLICY

I have argued for a publicly owned PSF that is tightly focused on its core function and competence. The policy questions that remain are: (i) How will its prices be regulated? (ii) Will the PSF continue to have a legal monopoly?

Let me begin by briefly addressing the second question. I am largely agnostic about the monopoly issue. While presently politically out of favor, franchise monopolies have been used for over a century to successfully procure services in markets characterized by significant economies of scale. In my view, it remains a perfectly acceptable and theoretically justified regulatory institution. The extent to which the legal prohibition has 'bite', depends largely on the extent to which the publicly mandated USO requires explicit cross-subsidization in terms of geographically uniform pricing, and so on. My expectation is that such uniform pricing constraints will apply to only a very small portion of mail volumes, for example, single-piece letters.[13] In that case, the Postal Service's overwhelming economies of scale will 'trump' mandated cross-subsidization, eventually rendering redundant any legal monopoly franchise.

The question of PRC rate regulation of the PSF is more complicated. First, there are two basic approaches to practical ratemaking: 'cost-plus', cost of service regulation and 'fixed-price', price-cap regulation. Second, there are two different *categories of prices* that must be controlled: (i) prices charged for final products sold to retail consumers; and (ii) worksharing (downstream access) prices charged to mailers and consolidators who inject their volumes at various points in the postal value chain.

The PRC is well acquainted with both of these aspects of rate regulation. First, from 1970 until 2006, the (then) Postal Rate Commission developed detailed costing methodologies to administer the cost of service regulation regime mandated by the Postal Reform Act (PRA). Since 2006, it has developed and implemented the price-cap regulatory framework specified in the Postal Accountability and Enhancement Act (PAEA). Second, the PRC pioneered access price regulation in practice through its introduction of worksharing discounts. Its pricing policies during the PRA period embodied a clear distinction between the pricing of retail products and wholesale/workshared products. In a nutshell, the former were priced to cover at least their average incremental (unit attributable) costs while making a positive contribution toward covering the overhead (institutional) costs of the Postal Service. The relative amounts of that contribution (markups over attributable costs) varied widely from service to service based on political and market demand considerations.

In contrast, the pricing of access evolved into a decidedly cost-based methodology. The guiding policy principle of the PRC toward worksharing was the efficient component pricing rule (ECPR). Considerable effort was made to equate worksharing discounts to the avoided costs of the Postal Service. The rationale was to give mailers the incentive to take over an operation (for example, sorting or transportation) previously performed by the Postal Service *if and only if* it could do so at a lower cost. This was an early application of the ECPR, long before the issue of access pricing had even begun to be addressed in most other network industries. ECPR decentralizes the minimization of postal sector end-to-end costs between the Postal Service and upstream competitive providers. Worksharing was the crowning achievement of postal policy under the PRA. Its use succeeded in 'liberalizing' a large share of postal sector value added and created a highly innovative competitive industry. The result was enhanced economic efficiency for both the postal sector and the Postal Service.

The passage of PAEA changed the system to one based upon price-cap regulation. Rather than requesting a rate case to adjust rates to cover increased costs of providing service, the Postal Service could adjust its rates at (more or less) any time as long as its *average* rate increased by no more than the Consumer Price Index (CPI). This framework lowers administrative costs and provides the Postal Service with the flexibility to respond to changes in market conditions. Price-cap regulation has two main theoretical advantages over PRA-style cost of service regulation. First, by breaking the link between revenues and costs, price-cap regulation gives a profit-seeking enterprise powerful incentives for cost reduction, for the simple reason that any cost savings achieved go directly to the bottom line. Second, and more abstractly, a quantity weighted price index constraint more directly aligns firm profits with consumers' surplus.[14] As has been discussed above, it is arguable how strong the cost incentive effect operates for the Postal Service. However, the ability to flexibly adjust rates for final products is a definite advantage – not only because of the greater ability of the Postal Service to respond to market conditions, but also because it replaced a highly politicized process in which the PRC determined relative markups rather than market forces.

On the other hand, the PAEA system of price caps threatens to unravel the painstakingly constructed system of cost-based worksharing discounts that the PRC had developed over decades. Discounts for workshared products have not yet been significantly reduced below avoided cost levels, but that is certainly a possibility if the Postal Service can freely adjust both workshared and non-workshared rates under a global price cap.[15] This is a serious problem with PAEA that should be rectified. Access prices (and workshared discounts) should be cost based in order to maximize the potential of the PSF platform for the mailing industry. This would comport with practice in other regulated network industries and international postal jurisdictions.[16]

This point is so important that it merits more detailed explanation. First, given its dominance in the delivery sector, the Postal Service will have monopsony power over the (largely competitive) providers of upstream services. It may well use this dominant position to extract additional rents from the firms supplying its upstream service components by reducing its worksharing discounts below its avoided costs. This should be avoided on the grounds that it would be *exclusionary*. That is, it would have the effect of excluding more efficient competitors from the markets for upstream service components such as acceptance, sorting and transportation. (Recall that the defining characteristic of avoided cost-based worksharing discounts is that they lead to the minimization of end-to-end postal sector costs.)

Second, in addition to this short-term efficiency effect, there is a long-term efficiency gain associated with ECPR-induced worksharing. That is, to the extent that productivity in the private sector grows more rapidly than that of the Postal Service, a larger and larger share of postal sector value added will move to the private sector. Thus, over time, less and less of the mailing industry is subject to the inherent inefficiencies of the SOE framework.

NOTES

1. See USPS OIG (2010a).
2. See, for example, USGAO (2010) USPS (2010), and presentations made available on the USPS website: www.usps.com/communications/newsroom/deliveringfuture/welcome.htm.
3. 'There is no doubt that USPS, and its, predecessor, the Post Office Department, were established by Congress to provide postal services to the Nation. In a general sense, USPS is "obliged" to provide a national postal service for that is its purpose'. (Campbell, 2010, p. 383).
4. See Levy and Field (2011) for an analysis of the parallels between the past problems of the railroads and the current problems of the Postal Service.
5. The European Union has also established elaborate policy guidelines for the establishment of USO and their funding. Procedures for auctioning the USO are discussed by Calzada et al. (2010).
6. See, for example, the discussion in USPS OIG (2010c).
7. See Crew and Kleindorfer (2008) for a discussion of opportunities for further efficiency gains obtainable under the current SOE structure.
8. See Smith and Vogel (2010) for a discussion of the partnership arrangements between the Postal Service and the USPS.
9. See, for example, Sidak and Spulber (1996).
10. Sappington and Sidak's formal model assumes that the SOE maximizes a weighted sum of revenue and profits.
11. Armstrong and Sappington (2007) provide a thorough discussion of the theoretical issues. Viscusi et al. (2005) discuss the US experience in various industries.
12. However, I would expect (and hope) that the PSF would be allowed to accomplish this ubiquity through kiosks, contracting with various retailers, and so on.
13. Campbell (2010) argues that very little uniform pricing is currently required. For a detailed discussion, see also (USPRC 2008).
14. Indeed, in a stationary setting, a profit-maximizing firm would gradually adjust its prices until the quantity demanded coincided with the constrained welfare-maximizing Ramsey optimum.
15. See the theoretical analyses in Panzar (2008, 2011) and the policy discussion in USPS OIG (2010b).
16. See Viscusi et al. (2005) for a general discussion of regulated network industries and Crandall (2005) for a detailed discussion of the US telecommunications sector.

REFERENCES

Armstrong, M. and D. Sappington (2007), 'Recent developments in the theory of regulation', in Robert H. Porter and Mark Armstrong (eds), *Handbook of Industrial Organization*, Vol. 3, Amsterdam: Elsevier–North-Holland, pp. 1560–687.

Boston Consulting Group (2010), 'Projecting US Mail Volumes to 2020', March 2.

Calzada, Joan, Christian Jagg and Urs Trinkner (2010), 'Universal service auctions in liberalized postal markets', in M.A. Crew and P.R. Kleindorfer (eds), *Heightening Competition in the Postal and Delivery Sector*, Cheltenham, UK and Northampton, MA, USA: Edward Elgar, pp. 263–77.

Campbell, James I. (2010), 'Historical development of a Universal Service Obligation in the United States', in M.A. Crew and P.R. Kleindorfer (eds), *Heightening Competition in the Postal and Delivery Sector*, Cheltenham, UK and Northampton, MA, USA: Edward Elgar, pp. 372–95.

Crandall, Robert W. (2005), *Competition and Chaos: U.S. Telecommunications since the 1996 Act*. Washington, DC: Brookings Institution.

Crew, Michael A. and Paul R. Kleindorfer (2008), 'Reform of the United States Postal Service: an unfinished task', in Crew, Kleindorfer and J. Campbell, Jr (eds), *Handbook of Worldwide Postal Reform*, Cheltenham, UK and Northampton, MA, USA: Edward Elgar.

Levy, David M. and Matthew D. Field (2011), 'The United States Postal Service business model: lessons from the American railroad industry?', in M.A. Crew and P.R. Kleindorfer (eds), *Reinventing the Postal Sector in an Electronic Age*, Cheltenham, UK and Northampton, MA, USA: Edward Elgar.

Panzar, John C. (2008), 'Interactions between regulatory and antitrust policies in a liberalized

postal sector', in M. Crew, P. Kleindorfer and J. Campbell Jr (eds), *Handbook of Worldwide Postal Reform*, Cheltenham, UK and Northampton, MA, USA: Edward Elgar.
Panzar, J.C. (2011), 'Postal service pricing policies after the transition to price cap regulation', *Review of Network Economics*, forthcoming.
Sappington, D. and J. Sidak (2003a), 'Incentives for anticompetitive behavior by public enterprises', *Review of Industrial Organization*, **22**, 183–206.
Sappington, D. and J. Sidak (2003b), 'Competition law for state-owned enterprises', *Antitrust Law Journal*, **71**(2) 479–523.
Sidak, J. and D. Spulber (1996), *Protecting Competition from the U.S. Postal Monopoly*, Washington, DC: AEI.
Smith, Paul C. and Paul E. Vogel (2010), 'A team of rivals: collaboration between USPS and UPS', in M.A. Crew and P.R. Kleindorfer (eds), *Heightening Competition in the Postal and Delivery Sector*, Cheltenham, UK and Northampton, MA, USA: Edward Elgar.
US Government Accountability Office (GAO) (2010), 'Strategies and Options to Facilitate Progress Toward Financial Viability', Report No. GAO-l0455, Washington, DC.
US Postal Regulatory Commission (PRC) (2008), 'Report on Universal Postal Service and the Postal Monopoly', December.
US Postal Service (USPS) (2010), 'Ensuring a Viable Postal Service for America: An Action Plan for the Future', March 3, available at www.usps.com/communications/newsroom/delivering future/welcome.htm (accessed 15 June 2011).
US Postal Service, Office of Inspector General (OIG) (2010a), 'The Postal Service's Share of CRSR Pension Responsibility', Report Number: RARCWP-10-001, January 20.
US Postal Service, Office of Inspector General (OIG) (2010b), 'Assessment of Worksharing', Report Number: RARCWP-10-005, July 12.
US Postal Service, Office of Inspector General (OIG) (2010c), 'Implications of Declining Mail Volumes for the Financial Sustainability of the Postal Service', Report Number: RARCWP-10-006, September 29.
Viscusi, W., J. Harrington and J. Vernon (2005), *Economics of Regulation and Antitrust*, 4th edn, Boston, MA, MIT Press.

11. Privatization: could the benefits seen in other network industries be realized in postal industries?

Stuart Holder[†] **and Helen Smith**[‡]

1 INTRODUCTION

At a time when national postal operators are facing many challenges, including falling demand and markets being opened up to competition, privatization is being actively considered as a policy option. Given the apparent success of privatization in other network industries, and the strong reactions to suggested privatization of postal services, it is an appropriate time to review the potential benefits of privatization, the extent to which they could be realized in the postal industry, and where any benefits may fall. In particular, it is important to consider whether privatization can help postal operators respond to the threat of e-substitution and an increasingly competitive market.

The term 'privatization' is used in a variety of contexts. These range from an increase in private sector involvement in an industry, through subcontracting or worksharing agreements, to full sale of a publicly owned business. In this chapter, we focus on the impacts of private ownership of the firm.

There have been several postal privatizations, including in Germany, Austria and the Netherlands. These privatizations have all been flotations but have varied in scale, with the government retaining a majority share in Austria, in contrast to the fuller privatizations in Germany and the Netherlands. Privatized European posts have benefited from the flexibility to adapt to changes in the market. In the case of Germany, privatization of Deutsche Post allowed the firm to adjust to changing market conditions and in the Netherlands, private ownership of PostNL has made it easier for the firm to completely restructure its operations.

In the UK, legislation has been passed that allows the sale of up to 90 percent of Royal Mail.[1] The basis for the possible privatization is a government-commissioned independent review of the postal sector, led by Richard Hooper, which was carried out in 2008 and updated in 2010. Hooper (2010) suggested opening Royal Mail to private sector capital to address problems including poor financial health, threats to the universal service and the need for modernization.

In addition, the option of privatization has been raised for a number of other countries including France, Canada and the US. For example, Cote and Takis (1997), Crew and

† Associate Director, NERA Economic Consulting.
‡ Analyst, NERA Economic Consulting.

Kleindorfer (2000, 2003, 2008) and Robinson (2009) have reviewed the theoretical and empirical arguments for US postal privatization. As described in Hickey (2008), although the US Postal Service (USPS) is publicly owned, there has been privatization in the industry in the form of worksharing and contracting-out. Similar discussions have taken place in relation to Canada (Iacobucci et al., 2007; Vannahme, 2009).

This chapter discusses a number of differences between public and private sector firms, summarizes the empirical evidence about the impact of these differences, and considers specific features of postal markets that could mean that privatization is more or less likely to succeed compared with other industries. Section 2 provides a qualitative overview of the differences between publicly and privately owned firms that may mean that publicly owned firms operate less efficiently. Section 3 summarizes the empirical evidence on the relative performance of publicly and privately owned firms and considers where the impacts of privatization may fall. Section 4 discusses how this evidence may apply to postal markets. Section 5 presents conclusions.

2 DIFFERENCES BETWEEN PUBLICLY AND PRIVATELY OWNED FIRMS

There are several broad areas of difference between publicly and privately owned firms that may mean that publicly owned firms operate less efficiently. These differences may vary depending on the circumstances or industry context of the firm in question. They may depend on the form of public and private ownership. Publicly owned firms may be run directly within a government department, as a non-departmental agency or a state-owned corporation. Privately owned firms may be traditional shareholder-owned companies, or have other forms such as companies limited by guarantee. Furthermore, the objectives, expertise and behavior of government affect the degree of difference. Governments may be self-interested or aim to maximize social welfare, or they may oversee state-owned enterprises on a purely commercial basis, and both public and private firms can be managed well or badly (Shirley and Walsh, 2001).

A country's markets and institutions, and the design of the privatization process, can have an impact on how successful it is and whether it achieves the same results as if the firm had always been in private ownership (ibid.). And even if a government does not supervise publicly owned firms as effectively as a private shareholder, there may be other pressures (such as competition or economic regulation) which help to remedy these shortcomings and therefore reduce the size of the additional benefits that could be obtained from privatization. However, the impact of regulation may be affected by whether the firm is publicly or privately owned, for example a system of fines imposed by the regulator may work less well under public ownership. Indeed, such fines may represent a transfer with government.

Profit Motive

The profit motive of privately owned firms is often cited as a reason why they may achieve greater efficiency than publicly owned firms. Private owners have clear objectives (to maximize profits) which may lead to improved cost and revenue efficiency. Furthermore, shareholders motivated by profit may be more active or effective than government shareholders. Conversely, the objectives of publicly owned firms may be less clear and there may be less pressure on the firm from its owners to improve performance. Implicitly or explicitly, government oversight of public sector firms may reflect political objectives, distributional considerations, employment effects and regional and macroeconomic policy.

Despite having clearer objectives, it is not necessarily straightforward for owners to ensure that privately owned firms are run effectively. Principal–agent theory suggests that both public and private sector owners may have difficulty getting managers (agents) to act in shareholders' (principals') interests.[2] However, private sector firms may be better equipped to deal with this problem. In the private sector, firms can offer managers incentives such as share options that provide potentially substantial rewards if they increase the value of the company. These options are not available to public sector firms, partly because shares are not publicly traded, and also because large rewards for managers would be very visible and possibly unpopular with taxpayers.

Capital Market Discipline

Private ownership brings capital market discipline which may reinforce the profit motive pressures outlined above. Private firms are subject to incentives such as maintaining a healthy share price, and capital markets provide information about managers' performance, both through share prices and analysts' reports. Both of these roles are likely to drive greater efficiency. Furthermore, private firms face the threat of takeover, and takeover bids may indicate that another party believes it can run the firm better than the current shareholders and managers. Takeover may lead to concentration of ownership and the ability to drive through changes in the management of the firm. This threat would be likely to motivate managers to run the firm efficiently.

In contrast, publicly owned firms may not be subject to the same degree of shareholder supervision, do not have publicly traded shares and are not subject to the threat of takeover. The difference in capital market discipline between public and private firms may be less if the government appoints a supervisor to fulfill the role of shareholder, or takes other measures to strengthen shareholder supervision of the public firm.

Further pressure to improve efficiency may be placed on private sector managers, especially those facing challenges (such as falling demand or rising costs), by the threat of bankruptcy. Managers of public sector firms, in contrast, are likely to perceive a soft budget constraint and therefore will not be concerned by the threat of bankruptcy. In theory, the government could commit to a hard budget constraint for the publicly owned firm, though it is questionable whether this could be made sufficiently credible. However, in the case of both private and public postal operators, the impact of the threat of bankruptcy may be diluted by arrangements (such as the appointment of a special administrator to keep the company running, with government support available at least in the short term) to ensure the continued provision of the universal postal service.[3]

Ability to Finance Investments and Reorganize

Private and public firms may differ in their ability to finance investments. Private firms are likely to have the flexibility and the means to finance profitable investments, allowing them to modernize and adapt to changes in the market. In the postal industry, this is a key issue given liberalization in some markets and falling demand as a result of e-substitution. Private firms are able to adapt their strategies and make investments to respond to market challenges.

Conversely, public firms may find it much more difficult to finance investments as a result of public sector financial controls. First, capital may be rationed due to constraints on public sector funds as a result of overall fiscal policy. Second, the process for applying for public funds may be restrictive and inflexible (for example, an annual process for investment approval). Without a reliable source of funding for investments, this may inhibit long-term planning and public firms' ability to adapt to changes in the market.

The act of privatization, and the resulting change of ownership and possibly management, may act as a catalyst for firms to undertake restructuring or reorganization in order to improve efficiency. If a privatization is achieved by a sale to one or more companies already active in relevant markets (overseas, or in related industries), this may also provide the privatized firm with access to a wider pool of knowledge and experience, and there may be economies of scope with the new owners' existing businesses. And a privatized firm will have more freedom to diversify in future in order to exploit similar opportunities.

Industrial Relations

Public and private sector firms may well take different approaches to industrial relations issues. Private sector firms will approach industrial relations issues from a mainly commercial perspective. This may mean that they choose to incur short-term losses by confronting unions in an attempt to weaken the union's position in the longer term. Or firms may take a long-term collaborative approach with unions. Whatever the chosen approach, private sector firms are free to adopt what they believe will be a profit-maximizing approach.

In the public sector, the approach to industrial relations is more complex. Governments may wish to avoid conflicts in some areas, for example discouraging management from taking efficiency-improving measures if the threat of job losses would lead to bad publicity. Furthermore, in the event of a dispute, governments may wish to settle quickly to keep services running. In relation to wages, in contrast, governments may adopt a tough approach in the hope that this will set a benchmark for other public sector (and possibly private sector) workers.

Public sector industrial relations are likely to be influenced by a variety of factors. Governments are concerned about public opinion, which may in turn be affected by how opposition parties are likely to respond. They may also be influenced by direct or indirect links between government and unions, for example if political parties are funded or supported in other ways by trade unions. In addition, unions may take a different approach to dealing with public sector firms than in the private sector.

Overall Impact

The extent of the benefits from private ownership that can be achieved depends on the counterfactual – how well national governments run publicly owned firms. Well-run government firms will have much less potential for efficiency improvements if privatized than those that are badly run. This can be split into several considerations.

The first consideration is whether the public company has clearly defined commercial objectives and the freedom to pursue these objectives without interference from government. If this is not the case, the firm may be under pressure to pursue other objectives, including for example being subject to pressure from government to accommodate union demands. A corporatized public firm is more likely to be able to define and pursue commercial objectives.

A further consideration is whether the government acts in a similar way to a commercial shareholder. This includes performing a variety of roles such as monitoring the firm, putting pressure on and eventually replacing poorly performing management, and paying market rates for senior management. This role could be fulfilled by a specific department or semi-autonomous agency of government with the remit of acting as a shareholder for public firms.[4]

Finally, even if the government runs the company well, there may be barriers in the public sector that are still difficult to overcome. For example, budgetary constraints and processes may restrict the success of the public sector firm and governments may find it difficult to commit to a hard budget constraint. In addition, the lack of an observable share price and the inability to offer share options in the public sector may affect the performance of the government-run firm.

3 EVIDENCE

To determine the materiality of the arguments for why privately owned firms may be more efficient than publicly owned firms, we consider a range of empirical evidence from the economic literature. Evidence in the postal industry is limited by the small number of postal privatizations that have taken place. The majority of quantitative evidence on the impact of privatization relates to the utility industries, primarily telecoms, water and electricity, as well as others such as the rail and aviation industries.

A number of studies have examined various aspects of these privatizations, including their impact on firm performance. Megginson and Netter (2001) survey the research on privatization as an economic policy. They conclude: 'Almost all studies that examine post-privatization changes in output, efficiency, profitability, capital investment spending, and leverage document significant increases in the first four and significant declines in leverage' (p. 356).

This evidence must be interpreted with caution. In many cases, industries have been subject to simultaneous reforms including privatization, liberalization, industry restructuring and regulatory reform, and it is difficult to disentangle the separate effects of different reforms. Even where privatization was the single reform it may be difficult to determine what features of the privatization have brought about the impacts, which means that it is more difficult to generalize these impacts to other industries such as post.

While there is some evidence that privatization has improved firm performance, to apply this observation to the postal industry we need to understand the reasons for privatization impacts and how they have varied by industry.

Industry Evidence

Post

A handful of European posts have undergone full or part privatization in recent years, and achieved a number of benefits. Maschke (2002) finds that privatization enabled Deutsche Post to achieve strategic reorientation and productivity gains, with the full support of the trade unions. Koppe et al. (2009) suggest that the privatization of Austria Post achieved an improvement in the image of Austria Post and its perception by the public. While this is not a concrete indicator of efficiency, it does suggest an improvement in the performance of the company following privatization.

There is also some evidence that privatization has led to lower prices. Evidence in Crew and Kleindorfer (2008) suggests that postal prices have decreased in most posts that have been either privatized or commercialized over the past 15 to 20 years (including Germany, the Netherlands and New Zealand).

Telecoms

Full or part privatization of national telecommunications operators has occurred in all OECD countries including the break-up of AT&T in the US and privatization of BT in the UK. In most cases, privatization has been accompanied by other changes including deregulation and rapid technological change, making it difficult to identify the separate impacts of private ownership. Technological change encompasses both traditional fixed-line telecoms, and the introduction of alternative technologies, in particular mobile technologies but also the Internet.

Empirical evidence for a positive impact of telecoms privatization is mixed. Several studies find significant telecommunications improvements associated with the combination of deregulation and privatization.[5] For example, Li and Xu (2002) find that across a panel dataset, half of the output growth in the telecommunications sector between 1990 and 1998 was attributable to privatization and competition after controlling for input growth. However, there is little evidence of an impact of privatization alone. Kwoka (1993) finds an increase in total factor productivity following the privatization of BT, of which 4.9 percent could be attributed to privatization. However, other studies such as Foreman-Peck and Manning (1988), Boylaud and Nicoletti (2001), and Daßler et al. (2002) find no efficiency impact specifically associated with privatization.

Water

Evidence on the impacts of privatization in the water industry is also mixed. Some surveys of the empirical evidence on water industry privatization find no effect of privatization on efficiency or costs, for example Bel and Warner (2008) and Pérard (2009). However, other studies such as Gassner et al. (2009) find that privatization brings about improvements in operational performance and labor productivity, although this study is focused on developing and transition economics. The UK water regulator Ofwat finds that 20 years after privatization, the privatized and regulated water industry in England and Wales has prices 30 percent lower than they otherwise would have been (Ofwat, 2009). In addition, in 2005 the Water Industry Commission for Scotland (WICS) found that publicly owned Scottish Water was less efficient than private sector companies in

England and Wales, although it now considers Scottish Water to have made significant improvements under price-cap regulation (WICS, 2005, 2011).

Privatization of water companies has generally been accompanied by fewer structural changes (for example, vertical or horizontal separation, introduction of meaningful competition) than in some other privatized industries.

Electricity

Internationally, there are both publicly and privately owned companies in the electricity industry. Electricity industries have often undergone extensive restructuring, including the separation and liberalization of generation and sometimes also supply activities. There is evidence of an increase in labor productivity following privatization but no change in total factor productivity. For example, in the UK, O'Mahony and Vecchi (2001) found an increase in labor productivity growth to 7.4 percent following reform, compared to a period average of 5.4 percent, although it is difficult to attribute this effect to privatization as opposed to liberalization or incentive-based regulation. A positive impact for private ownership is also supported by Gassner et al. (2009), who find evidence that privatization brings about improvements in operational performance and labor productivity in developing and transition economies.

Rail

In the rail industry, evidence is more limited as privatization is not widespread and evidence is limited to a small number of countries such as the UK, Switzerland and Canada. In the UK, there is some evidence of increases in efficiency in the period after privatization but causality is unclear. Pollitt and Smith (2002) find a post-privatization fall in unit costs of 2.7 percent per year. Affuso et al. (2009) find a significant improvement in total factor productivity (TFP) associated with privatization.

Internationally, there are several papers that support the hypothesis that privatization has a positive impact on productivity. In Switzerland, where there are both publicly and privately owned vertically integrated railways, there is evidence that privately owned railways are more efficient (Cowie, 1999). Case studies in Canada and Argentina also support this conclusion. Laurin and Bozec (2000) examine two large Canadian rail carriers and find evidence for an 'anticipation effect' before privatization and a 'follow-through' effect afterwards, both leading to improved firm performance. In a study of the restructuring and privatization of the Argentine national freight and passenger railway system, Ramamurti (1990) finds improvements in labor productivity, lower costs and increased quality, and concludes these improvements could not have been achieved without privatization.

Airlines

Due to the variety of ownership internationally, airlines are useful for comparing a cross-section of public and private firms, and they operate in a fairly comparable environment. There is strong evidence that privately owned airlines are more efficient. For example, Ehrlich et al. (1994) find good evidence for productivity differences between privately and publicly owned airlines over the 1973–83 period, and argue that they are able to separate the ownership impacts on productivity from the impact of other factors. Using more recent data, Ng and Seabright (2001) find a relationship between private ownership and costs, such that a 10 percent increase in the proportion of privately owned shares would be expected to reduce costs by 6.4 percent (largely due to a reduction in rents earned by labor). Eckel et al. (1997) find evidence to suggest that stock traders anticipated a much more competitive BA post-privatization.

Airports

Many airports around the world have been privatized. Time-series studies of privatized airports do not show an effect of privatization on TFP, although there could be mitigating factors in these cases (for example, government maintaining a 'golden share' in UK airports) (Parker, 1998). Oum et al. (1998) find evidence in favor of private ownership of airports via the relationship between non-aviation revenue and variable factor productivity, but interpretation of these results are problematic. International cross-sectional comparisons provide some evidence that privatized firms are more efficient but in some cases the evidence is indirect or difficult to interpret.

Summary of Evidence

Reviewing the empirical evidence on privatization shows that there is strong evidence that privatization has an impact in conjunction with liberalization or deregulation of markets. However, in many cases it is difficult to identify the impact of privatization separately from other reforms. In some industries, the evidence suggests that there is a separate (and positive) 'privatization effect', but evidence is mixed in other industries, particularly water supply and telecommunications.

In the postal industry, there is some evidence of performance improvements resulting from privatizations in Germany, the Netherlands and Austria. Privatization in these countries has allowed the incumbent postal operator to react and adapt to changes in the market such as European-wide liberalization and falling mail volumes.

Distribution of Impacts of Privatization

Privatization of a company has the potential to affect a large number of stakeholders from workers, suppliers and competitors to consumers. Improvements in efficiency may lead to changes in pay and conditions or cause job losses, suppliers to the firm may have to renegotiate contracts, competitors may face stronger competition from the privatized entity and consumers may see service quality levels and prices change.

The distribution of gains is also likely to depend on the privatization process. The price paid for shares in the privatized company is significant. If governments set low share prices (for example, to ensure a full sale or to promote wider share ownership), then the privatization will transfer resources from taxpayers to investors. Employee share ownership plans transfer gains to employees if shares are sold at a preferential rate or distributed gratis. Employees may also be affected by changes in terms and conditions (including pay), and possible reductions in numbers employed as a result of modernization or efficiency improvements (though these might be offset in the longer term if privatization also leads to increased demand).[6]

Consumers are likely to be affected by changes in the level and structure of prices following privatization, as well as possible improvements in product or service quality. If privatization improves efficiency, and if competition or price-cap regulation (or similar) aligns prices with costs in the long term, then consumers will benefit eventually. The speed with which this occurs will depend on several things including the strength of competition, whether the regulator anticipates the efficiency gains, how frequently the price cap is reviewed, and whether there are any specific mechanisms in place (such as rolling incentive mechanisms) (Shuttleworth, 2007). This in turn determines how the benefits from efficiency gains are shared between shareholders and consumers.

There is little empirical evidence of the impact of privatization on consumers (Megginson and Netter, 2001). Newbery and Pollitt (1997) find evidence from the UK electricity industry that producers and their shareholders captured the gains from privatization, causing the government and consumers to lose out. However, this study was completed relatively soon after privatization, and so is not able to assess whether gains fed through to consumers in the medium to long term.

4 PRIVATIZATION IN THE POSTAL INDUSTRY

To apply the evidence from other industries to the postal industry, we examine the differences between post and other industries, and how these differences might affect privatization impacts.

The most directly relevant evidence for the impact of privatization in the postal industry is from previous privatizations in countries such as Germany, the Netherlands and Austria. While evidence from the postal industry indicates that the impact of privatization may be positive for postal firms, the limited nature of this evidence makes it important to consider sources from other industries.

One of the difficulties in applying evidence from other industries to the postal industry is the lack of research into the reasons why privatization causes improvements in efficiency or other aspects of firm performance. Evidence on the drivers of privatization impacts would make it easier to assess how well the impacts would translate across to the postal industry.

In a comprehensive review of the evidence available on privatization impacts, Megginson and Netter (2001) find only one study, D'Souza et al. (2000), documenting why improvements occur after privatization. D'Souza et al. find stronger efficiency gains for firms in developing countries, regulated industries, firms that restructure operations post-privatization and in countries with greater shareholder protection.

Given the lack of comprehensive research on the reasons for privatization impacts, it is necessary to evaluate the likely impacts on a case-by-case basis. This view is supported by Vickers and Yarrow (1988, p. 40), who state that: 'when market power is significant, and particularly when company behaviour is subject to detailed regulation, there is little empirical justification for a general presumption of either type of ownership, and case-by-case evaluation of the various tradeoffs is therefore in order'.

Table 11.1 summarizes the key differences between the postal industry and other industries that may affect the impacts of privatization. As set out in the Table, there are several key areas of difference that may mean that the impacts of privatization in the postal industry could differ from those experienced in other industries.

Postal networks tend to be more labor intensive than networks in other industries such as water or electricity. This could change to some extent, as modernization provides

Table 11.1 Industry features comparison

	Post	Telecoms	Water	Electricity	Rail
Cost structure	Fixed costs in delivery	Fixed costs in fixed lines, less in mobile	Large fixed costs	Large fixed costs, but some choices how to provide future capacity	Large fixed costs in infrastructure
Input mix	Labor intensive	Capital intensive	Capital intensive	Capital intensive	Capital intensive
Significant technical change or modernization possible?	Yes	Yes	No	Some	No
Industrial relations	Often highly unionized	Less reliant on labor	Less reliant on labor	Less reliant on labor	Often highly unionized
Demand	Falling demand (e-substitution)	Changing demand (fixed to mobile, Internet, etc.)	No substitutes	Limited substitutes	Affected by other modes of transport
Liberalized?	Yes	Yes	Partially – in theory only	Yes	Somewhat
Restructured	No	Accounting separation (or stronger) of fixed networks	No	Separation of generation and wholesale trading (sometimes also retail supply) from transmission and distribution	Vertical separation of infrastructure from train operators, sometimes horizontal separation of train operators
Competitive?	Varies by country, delivery less competitive	Limited competition at privatization, now widespread competition	No	Often competition in generation, wholesale trading and/or retail supply	Competition for franchises
Regulation	Yes	Now limited to selected services	Yes	Some (mainly network)	Yes
USO?	Yes	Yes	Some provisions	Yes	No

Source: NERA analysis.

opportunities for substitution between labor and capital inputs, though postal networks may still be easier to change than the physical networks used, for example, to distribute water, electricity and gas. And some parts of postal networks (for example, final delivery) will remain labor intensive. Postal firms might therefore have more flexibility than some other network industries to address the challenges of falling demand, both by adapting their operations and possibly diversifying into other areas (for example, logistics or financial services).

High labor intensity is also likely to allow a stronger role for trade unions. This may make the privatization process (or subsequent changes that the new owners might wish to implement) more difficult if there is opposition from unions. Improvements in operating efficiency (for example, as a result of modernization) may not lead to higher cost efficiency if management secures union cooperation by offering higher wages. Evidence from the UK rail industry, also highly unionized, indicates that while efficiency increased following privatization, wages have also increased (McNulty, 2011). However, the proposed privatization of Royal Mail includes 10 percent employee share ownership, which will give employees an interest in the success of the firm and may reduce the likelihood of union disputes.

Another key difference between the postal industries and others is the level of competition at privatization. Where competition occurs before privatization, this may lead to significant efficiency improvements and mean that a subsequent privatization is likely to have a smaller impact than those seen in the evidence discussed in Section 0. This depends on how long the market has been competitive and whether competition has reached all parts of the value chain. In the UK, for example, while there is extensive competition in the upstream part of the value chain, Royal Mail still undertakes almost all delivery of letter mail, and so there may be further efficiency gains to be achieved in delivery.[7]

A further consideration in the postal industry is falling demand caused by e-substitution. Competition from electronic communications such as email, online billing and mobile phones has increased in recent years and worldwide letter volumes are expected to decline by 25 to 40 percent between 2010 and 2015 (Hooper, 2010). This may mean that the potential improvements in efficiency, innovation and customer service from privatization are more important than in other industries, because they may help to mitigate the effects of e-substitution. In theory, the prospect of falling demand may mean that private sector managers will have strong incentives to improve efficiency in order to reduce the threat of bankruptcy, though in practice this will also depend on how the government would be likely to respond to such an event (for example, whether there are special provisions to ensure the continued provision of services provided by the privatized firm).

The need to modernize also sets apart the postal industry from others. In the UK, the Hooper reports (Hooper et al., 2008; Hooper, 2010) on the UK postal industry highlighted this need, and modernization followed postal privatization in both Germany and the Netherlands. This may mean that postal privatization has a greater impact than in other industries, as privatization may be an important factor in facilitating modernization. However, this depends crucially on the existing level of technology in use by postal operators, which is increasing from year to year (Copenhagen Economics, 2010).

One of the features of postal markets that needs to be considered carefully during privatization is its status as an essential service, defined by a Universal Service Obligation (USO). This feature is also present in other privatized regulated industries such as water and electricity. However, there are some important differences between the USOs in post and other industries.

In most other industries, the network and the services provided over the network can be separated. Competition in these industries has focused on service provision, and the USO costs are associated with the network, meaning that provision of the USO is not directly affected by market entry. In contrast, in postal industries there is not a clear separation between the network and the services provided, and competition could occur over services that are part of the USO. This leads to a greater risk of cherry-picking in posts than in other industries, threatening the viability of the USO. For these reasons there could be concerns about the sustainability of the universal service following privatization, particularly if this is not adequately written into law at privatization. On the other hand, if privatization leads to a more efficient universal service provider (USP), this will help to protect universal service as it will be provided at lower cost. Privatization might also encourage governments to undertake useful reviews of both the definition of the USO and the way it is funded.

In Europe, there is provision for the USP to be compensated for providing the universal service by other participants in the industry. Privatization may have the benefit of forcing governments to confront this compensation problem, as it is less easy to ignore when the USO is not provided by a publicly owned firm. These considerations, combined with the fact that competition in some markets has been restricted to certain types of product or customer, mean that there is likely to be a continuing need for effective economic regulation following privatization.

5 CONCLUSIONS

There are several theoretical arguments favoring private over public ownership, relating to capital market discipline, the profit motive, the absence of other objectives and industrial relations. Evidence from a range of industries strongly suggests that privatization can help to improve efficiency as part of a package of reforms, and in some cases in its own right, although there are some industries where the benefits have been less clear.

There are some important differences between post and some of the other industries covered by the evidence. One is that liberalization has occurred before potential privatization in many countries. This may have driven some efficiency gains by forcing governments to become better at running public postal operators, and so reduced the potential gains from privatization (though there may still be parts of the industry that have not been exposed to competition).

Another important difference is the role of the workforce in the postal industry, which is more labor intensive than other industries covered, and as a result, some of the available efficiency gains are likely to come from substituting capital for labor inputs (for example, through increased mechanization of the sorting process). If there are factors that make a publicly owned operator less likely to succeed at making this type of efficiency gain then privatization might bring the greater focus on commercial issues that is necessary to realize the gains.

The USO is another important issue that would need to be considered during the privatization process. The USO may be considered a constraint by private investors if there is likely to be cherry-picking by competitors without adequate compensation for the USP. However, privatization could enhance the sustainability of the USO, for example if it leads to improvements in efficiency. The privatization process may also force governments to address the issue of funding the USO, or to review the definition of the USO.

Despite these differences with other industries, the evidence suggests that privatization has a positive role to play in the postal industry. Many of the challenges faced by privatized posts, such as e-substitution and the need to maintain the universal service, would also be faced by the equivalent publicly owned operator. Privatization is an available policy lever to help firms to meet these challenges by improving efficiency, innovation and customer service, and allowing the postal industry to benefit fully from the introduction of competition. This may allow the universal service to be protected at a lower cost to society than if it were provided in the public sector. And effective economic regulation will play an important role in ensuring that the potential gains from privatization are realized.

NOTES

1. The Postal Services Bill, published 13 October 2010, received Royal Assent on 13 June 2011.
2. See Laffont and Martimort (2002) for an overview of the principal–agent literature and an exploration of principal–agent models.
3. Following the UK government's decision to place Railtrack (the rail infrastructure manager) in administration in 2001, the payments that shareholders eventually received were more generous than some analysts' valuation of the company shortly before it entered administration.
4. In the UK, the Shareholder Executive assists with this role.
5. See discussion in Megginson and Netter (2001, p. 351).
6. Studies have reported a range of impacts on numbers employed ranging from strong and significant increases in employment to significant employment declines (Megginson and Netter, 2001).
7. Efficiency gains may also have been realized through regulatory pressure.

REFERENCES

Affuso, Luisa, Alvaro Angeriz and Michael Pollitt (2009), 'The impact of privatization on the efficiency of train operation in Britain', CGR Working Paper 28, Centre for Globalization Research, School of Business and Management, Queen Mary, University of London.

Bel, Germà and Mildred Warner (2008), 'Does privatization of solid waste and water services reduce costs? A review of empirical studies', *Resources, Conservation and Recycling*, **52**, 1337–48.

Boylaud, Olivier and Giuseppe Nicoletti (2001), 'Regulation, market structure and performance in telecommunications', OECD Economic Studies No. 32, 2001/I.

Copenhagen Economics (2010), 'Main Developments in the Postal Sector (2008–2010)', report for DG Internal Market, European Commission.

Cote, Lorraine M. and William M. Takis (1997), 'The future of the U.S. Postal Service: an assessment of options', in M.A. Crew and P.R. Kleindorfer (eds), *Managing Change in the Postal and Delivery Industries*, Boston, MA: Kluwer Academic Publishers, pp. 342–55.

Cowie, Jonathan (1999), 'The technical efficiency of public ownership', *Journal of Transport Economics and Policy*, **33**, 241–52.

Crew, Michael A. and Paul R. Kleindorfer (2000), 'Privatizing the U.S. Postal Service', in E.L. Hudgins (ed.), *Mail @ the Millennium: Will the Postal Service Go Private?*, Washington DC: Cato Institute.

Crew, Michael A. and Paul R. Kleindorfer (2003), 'Postal privatization in the United States', in

D. Parker and D. Saal (eds), *International Handbook on Privatization*, Cheltenham, UK and Northampton, MA, USA: Edward Elgar, pp. 187–206.
Crew, Michael A. and Paul R. Kleindorfer (2008), 'Reform of the United States Postal Service: an unfinished task', in Crew, Kleindorfer and J.I. Campbell Jr (eds), *Handbook of Worldwide Postal Reform*, Cheltenham, UK and Northampton, MA, USA: Edward Elgar, pp. 123–42.
D'Souza, Juliet, Robert Nash and William L. Megginson (2000), 'Determinants of performance improvement in newly-privatized firms: does restructuring and corporate governance matter?', working paper, University of Oklahoma.
Daßler, Thoralf, David Parker and David S. Saal (2002), 'Economic performance in European telecommunications, 1978–1998: a comparative study', *European Business Review*, **14** (3), 194–209.
Eckel, Catherine, Doug Eckel and Vijay Singal (1997), 'Privatisation and efficiency: industry effects of the sale of British Airways', *Journal of Financial Economics*, **43** (2), 275–98.
Ehrlich, Isaac, Georges Gallais-Hamonno, Zhiqiang Liu and Randall Lutter (1994), 'Productivity growth and firm ownership: an analytical and empirical investigation', *Journal of Political Economy*, **102** (5), 1006–38.
Foreman-Peck, James. S. and Dorothy Manning (1988), 'How well is BT performing? An international comparison of telecommunications total factor productivity', *Fiscal Studies*, **9** (3), 54–67.
Gassner, Katharina, Alexander Popov and Nataliya Pushak (2009), 'Does private sector participation improve performance in electricity and water distribution?', Trends and Policy Options No. 6, World Bank, Washington, DC.
Hickey, Robert (2008), 'Postal privatization and the transformation of the global logistics industry', *Management International*, **12**, 39–49.
Hooper, Richard (2010), 'Saving the Royal Mail's universal postal service in the digital age', London: HMSO, September.
Hooper, Richard, Deirdre Hutton and Ian Smith (2008), 'Modernise or Decline: Policies to Maintain the Universal Postal Service in the United Kingdom' an independent review of the UK postal services sector, London, 16 December.
Iacobucci, Edward M., Michael J. Trebilcock and Tracey D. Epps (2007), 'Rerouting the mail: why Canada Post is due for reform', Commentary No. 243, C.D. Howe Institute, Toronto.
Koppe, Peter, Christian Bosch, Silke Hömstreit and Stefan Pohl (2009), 'The IPO as a driving force in the change process', in M.A. Crew and P.R. Kleindorfer (eds), *Progress in the Competitive Agenda in the Postal and Delivery Sector*, Cheltenham, UK and Northampton, MA, USA: Edward Elgar, pp. 322–38.
Kwoka, John E. (1993), 'The effects of divestiture, privatization, and competition on productivity in U.S. and U.K. telecommunications', *Review of Industrial Organization*, **8**, 49–61.
Laffont, Jean-Jacques and David Martimort (2002), *The Theory of Incentives: the Principal–Agent Model*, Princeton, NJ: Princeton University Press.
Laurin, Claude and Yves Bozec (2001), 'Privatization and productivity improvement: the case of Canadian National', *Transportation Research Part E: Logistics and Transportation Review*, **37** (5), 355–74.
Li, Wei and Lixin C. Xu (2002), 'The impact of privatization and competition in the telecommunications sector around the world', Darden Business School Working Paper No. 02-13, Charlottesville.
Maschke, Walter (2002), 'Transformation at Deutsche Post World Net using the example of socially compatible workforce adjustment', in M.A. Crew and P.R. Kleindorfer (eds), *Postal and Delivery Services: Delivering on Competition*, Boston, MA: Kluwer Academic Publishers, pp. 303–19.
McNulty, Roy (2011), 'Realising the potential of GB Rail: final independent report of the rail value for money study – detailed report', UK Department for Transport and Office of Rail Regulation, London: May.
Megginson, William L. and Jeffry M. Netter (2001), 'From state to market: a survey of empirical studies on privatization', *Journal of Economic Literature*, **39** (2), June, 321–89.
Newbery, David M. and Michael G. Pollitt (1997), 'The restructuring and privatisation of Britain's CEGB – was it worth it?', *Journal of Industrial Economics*, **45** (3), 269–303.
Ng, Charles K. and Paul Seabright (2001), 'Competition, privatisation and productive efficiency: evidence from the airline industry', *Economic Journal*, **111**, 591–619.

O'Mahony, Mary and Michela Vecchi (2001), 'The electricity supply industry: a study of an industry in transition', *National Institute Economic Review*, **177** (1), 85–99.
Ofwat (2009), 'Ofwat's response to the independent review of charging for household water and sewerage services', London: October.
Oum, Tae H., Jia Yan and Chunyan Yu (1998), 'Ownership forms matter for airport efficiency: a stochastic frontier investigation of worldwide airports', *Journal of Urban Economics*, **64** (2), September, 422–35.
Parker, David (1998), 'The Performance of BAA before and after privatisation', *Journal of Transport Economics and Policy*, **33** (2), 133–46.
Pérard, Edouard (2009), 'Water supply: public or private? An approach based on cost of funds, transaction costs, efficiency and political costs', *Policy and Society*, **27**, 193–219.
Pollitt, Michael G. and Andrew S.J. Smith (2002), 'The restructuring and privatisation of British Rail: was it really that bad?', *Fiscal Studies*, **23** (4), 463–502.
Ramamurti, Ravi (1990), 'The new frontier of privatization', in Ramamurti (ed.), *Privatizing Monopolies: Lessons from the Telecommunications and Transport Sectors in Latin America*, Baltimore, MD: Johns Hopkins University Press, pp. 1–45.
Robinson, Alan (2009), 'Examination of potential postal business models', report for the United States Postal Service by Direct Communications Group, October.
Shirley, Mary M. and Patrick Walsh (2001), 'Public versus private ownership: the current state of the debate', World Bank Policy Research Working Paper No. 2420, World Bank, Washington, DC.
Shuttleworth, Graham (2007), 'Practicalities of price cap regulation', in S. Potts Voll and M.J. King (eds), *The Line in the Sand: The Shifting Boundary Between Markets and Regulation in Network Industries*, National Economic Research Associates, White Plains, New York, pp. 59–93.
Vannahme, Adrian (2009), 'Efficient, competitive and better service: Germany's post office model and lessons for Canada', FCPP Policy Series No. 74, Frontier Centre for Public Policy, Manitoba.
Vickers, John and George Yarrow (1988), *Privatization: An Economic Analysis*, Cambridge, MA: MIT Press.
Water Industry Commission for Scotland (WICS) (2005), 'The Strategic Review of Charges 2006–2010, The final determination', Stirling, p. 103.
Water Industry Commission for Scotland (WICS) (2011), 'Performance Report 2010', Stirling.

12. The confluence of the postal sector with the Internet economy and regulation*

John Hearn[†]

1 OBJECTIVES OF THE CURRENT EUROPEAN REGULATORY FRAMEWORK

The objective of this chapter is to identify how sector-specific regulation in the European Union (EU) might need to evolve in response to the confluence of the postal sector with the Internet economy. This section sets out the objectives of the current (2011) European regulatory framework. Section 2 examines market trends and considers how European postal markets might evolve over the coming years. Section 3 considers how regulatory frameworks might need to evolve to reflect these changes. Conclusions are set out in Section 4.

Postal services are a service of general economic interest. As an essential instrument for communication and information exchange they fulfill a vital role which contributes to the objectives of social, economic and territorial cohesion in the EU. In addition, there are specific features of the traditional postal service offered by state-owned or -controlled enterprises, which necessitate special provisions in order to protect the public interest.

Specifically enterprises providing such postal services act as agents for both the sender and the addressee. In common law countries such as Britain and Ireland 'the post office becomes irrevocably the agent of the addressee' immediately upon the posting of a postal packet and the sender of a postal packet has no right to reclaim it after it has been posted. However, even in jurisdictions where ownership remains with the sender until delivery[1] or where it is permissible to withdraw a letter from the post or have its address altered or corrected[2] the principle that the letter should nevertheless be forwarded to its addressee is still observed.[3]

The emergence, during the 1970s and 1980s, of the Courier and Express industry in response to the globalization of the manufacture and distribution of goods and the evolution of internationally traded services did not impact on the 'public interest' role of the traditional postal services. The Courier and Express services were in practice offered under ordinary private law contracts drafted in such a way as to avoid conflict with the postal monopolies then existing in most countries.

This meant that in law as well as in fact there were two classes of services – 'postal services' which were generally provided by a state-controlled enterprise protected by a statutory monopoly, and 'courier' or 'express' services provided on the basis of negotiable private law contracts. Agreements under international law, such as the Universal Postal

† Manager Postal Liberalisation, ComReg (Commission for Communications Regulation, Ireland).

Union's Convention (UPU) and the World Trade Organization General Agreement on Trade in Services (WTO/GATS), recognize this distinction in their definitions of the relevant markets.

This distinction between the traditional 'public postal services' and the Courier and Express services was endorsed by the European Court of Justice (ECJ), in the *Corbeau* case,[4] and the ECJ went on to declare that any statutory monopoly or 'exclusive rights' could not be extended to services other than the postal services provided in the public interest.

In a Resolution (1994) the European Council of Ministers declared that the main objective of EU postal policy would be to reconcile the gradual, controlled opening to competition of the postal market with a sustainable guarantee of the provision of a universal service. The first Postal Directive (1997) which established a regulatory framework to implement this policy defined the postal market very broadly, but recognized in recital 18 that express and courier services were essentially different from universal postal services.

Subsequently the European Council of Ministers and the European Parliament set a deadline of 31 December 2010 for full market opening (FMO) and the removal of all exclusive or special rights for the establishment and provision of postal services. The provisions of the third Postal Directive (2008) which implements this decision are focused almost exclusively on securing the guaranteed provision of universal services at prices affordable to all users. Providers of postal services outside the scope of universal service are subject only to minimal requirements.[5] The deadline for transposition has now passed, and from 1 January 2011, 95 percent of the EU postal market has been fully liberalized.[6]

According to the Lisbon Treaty (2010)[7] it is the result to be achieved that is to be considered when transposing and enforcing EU directives. It follows therefore that the distinction between universal service and other postal services is central in determining which services will be subject to sector regulation.

The concept underlying universal service within the EU is not unique to postal services; rather it applies to all services of general economic interest (SGEI). According to the European Commission (2000) such services 'are different from ordinary services in that public authorities consider that they need to be provided even where the market may not have sufficient incentives to do so'.

The characteristics of such services are set out not just in sector-specific legislation such as the Postal directives, but in other European legislation and in relevant decisions of the European courts. Taking into account the wider EU *acquis*, the universal service may be observed as having the following characteristics. It should meet the essential needs of all users and be provided by a licensed enterprise.[8] The obligation is to offer certain services to every user requesting them[9] and to contract, on consistent conditions, without being able to reject the other contracting party[10], that is, there is an 'offer' to the customer rather than an 'invitation to treat'. The nature of the services is not prescribed.[11] The service does not have to be provided through the entire territory or be of use to the whole population[12] but there must be transparency as to tariffs and terms and conditions.[13] Rates, conditions and quality standards should be as similar as possible for all users.[14] Uniform tariffs are the norm (that is, prices are fixed and not subject to individual negotiation).[15] Finally there must be an obligation/duty of care to the addressee as well as to the sender.[16]

The current European regulatory framework specifically excludes new and value-added services from the scope of sector regulation, as well as services provided under individually negotiated contracts There is no definition of 'new" services, so features which the ECJ in 1990 considered 'new', and outside the scope of universal service, such as collection from the customers' premises, may in the future be considered by users to be essential features of the universal service. The Research Perspective (2010) demonstrated that many small businesses consider such a facility to be an essential requirement, while Postcomm (2011) is seeking stakeholders' views on a proposal to include business collections as part of Royal Mail's Universal Service Obligation (USO).

Regulators are focused on ensuring universal service, but from a practical perspective it is prudent to assume that all services are subject to regulation unless it is absolutely clear that the service falls outside the scope of universal service. Box 12.1 provides a basic methodology for doing this.

2 MARKET TRENDS

The rationale for the 13-year transitional period from the first Postal Directive until FMO at the end of 2010 was to give the public postal operators sufficient time to adapt their operations to meet the needs of users in a competitive, innovative and customer-focused postal market. The European Parliament[17] noted that these reform measures had brought about significant positive developments in the postal sector, in particular increased quality, more efficiency and better user orientation.

Some postal enterprises have always offered a high standard of service in terms of transit time in their domestic service, while others have used the prospect of FMO to make significant improvements. For example ITA/WiK(2009, p. 86) report that 'the modernisation of Austrian Post has substantially improved the quality of service: the transit time performance of next day delivery increased from less than 80 percent in 2001 to more than 96 percent in 2007'. According to Eurostat (2009), Latvian Post increased its D+1 performance from 70 percent in 2004 to 95.6 percent in 2007 and the Hungarian Post Office increased performance from 83.5 to 92.3 percent over the same period.

Comparisons between one country and another are very difficult because circumstances differ. For example in large countries such as Britain or France it is necessary to maintain a network of special air services in order to provide next-day D+1 service, while in geographically compact countries such as the Netherlands or Ireland it is possible to move mail from one end of the country to another in a matter of hours by road. Comparison of performance against the targets set by national regulatory authorities is therefore the most appropriate measure. Most enterprises meet or exceed their targets, but as Copenhagen Economics (2010, p. 47) notes: 'The three USPs with worst performance in relation to the target are Poland, Lithuania and Ireland respectively, who failed to meet the target by 10-15 percentage points. Greece and Cyprus also severely failed to meet target by deviating around 5 percentage points'.

Performance in relation to cross-border mail was always more problematic because of the number of different interests – the postal enterprises in the country of origin and destination, the transport companies involved and possibly an enterprise in a transit country. The European Commission (2008) reported that D+3 performance for EU15

BOX 12.1 IS A SERVICE WITHIN OR OUTSIDE THE SCOPE OF UNIVERSAL SERVICE?

If the answer to *any* of these questions is 'YES' then the service is outside the scope of universal service and therefore outside the scope of detailed sector-specific regulation.

Is it an Express or Courier service?[1]
Is it a Document Exchange service?[2]
Is it a New service (i.e. quite distinct from conventional services)?[3]
Has it value-added features such as:

- collection from the senders' address,
- greater speed or reliability of distribution; or
- the possibility of changing the destination in the course of transit?[4]

Is it provided under individually negotiated contracts?[5]
Is the service provided under 'private law' and not on non-negotiable terms and conditions (including a published tariff) which are binding on the service provider?[6]

Notes

1. COM(2007)695 final, 9.11.2007 states 'The Commission confirms that in accordance with Recital 18 of Directive 97/67/EC and the consistent case law of the European Court of Justice (e.g. Case C-320/91 [*Corbeau*]), express and courier services constitute specific services that are characterised by being essentially different from universal postal services'.
2. Directive 97/67/EC Recital 21 provides 'Whereas . . . document exchange do not form part of the universal service and consequently there is no justification for their being reserved to the universal service providers'.
3. Directive 97/67/EC Recital 21 provides 'Whereas new services (services quite distinct from conventional services) . . . do not form part of the universal service and consequently there is no justification for their being reserved to the universal service providers'.
4. The ECJ in Case C-320/91 *Corbeau* [1993] ECR I-2533 at point 19 observed that 'the exclusion of competition is not justified as regards specific services dissociable from the service of general interest which meet special needs of economic operators and which call for certain additional services not offered by the traditional postal service, such as collection from the senders' address, greater speed or reliability of distribution or the possibility of changing the destination in the course of transit'. Also Recital 18 to Directive 97/67/EC observes that 'the essential difference between express mail and universal postal services lies in the value added (whatever form it takes) provided by express services and perceived by customers'.
5. The ECJ in Case C-357/07 *TNT Post UK Ltd* 23 April 2009 – point 48 – observed that 'it is apparent [from recital 15 to Directive 97/67] that the option to negotiate contracts with customers individually does not correspond, in principle, with the concept of universal service provision'. According to the Unfair Terms in Consumer Contracts Directive 'A term shall always be regarded as having not been individually negotiated where it has been drafted in advance and the consumer has therefore not been able to influence its substance, particularly in the context of a pre-formulated standard contract'.
6. The Advocat General in his opinion on Case C-320/91 *Corbeau* [1993] ECR I-2533 at point 18 argued that 'It should also be stated that that service is performed by virtue of contractual relations under private law and is therefore subject to a legal system differing from that applied to the services provided by the postal administration', and at point 22 that 'the service gives rise to a direct fiduciary relationship between the defendant and his customers'.

plus Iceland, Norway and Switzerland went up from 69.1 percent in 1994 to 94.9 percent in 2007. D+5 performance increased from 84.3 percent to 97.9 percent.

Many of the improvements in transit time performance were the result of improved efficiency and investment in automated processing. For example bPost (2010) reports that 81 percent of the volume of normal format mail was route-sorted at the end of 2010. Furthermore, 12 percent was also being sequenced, compared with 1 percent at the end of 2009. Similarly Royal Mail (2010) reports significant progress on its World Class Mail program to ensure that its mail centers are not just using the most modern equipment, but are operating at world-class levels of efficiency. It reported that 368 new or upgraded machines were in operation compared with 34 two years previously, and that it intended to install over 500 walk-sequencing machines. Both bPost and Royal Mail are rationalizing their networks of mail centers.

It might be expected that improvements in efficiency would be reflected in lower prices for users of the post, but this does not appear to be the case. Although ITA/WiK (2009, p. XXI, section 4.1.7) reported that 'In more than half of the Member States the tariff for a 20g letter of the fastest standard category has not increased in real terms (notably in most Western and Southern Member States plus Bulgaria, Estonia and Slovakia)', Deutsche Post (2011) reports that the real price for a standard domestic letter in the 29 European countries surveyed increased by an average of 51 percent, comparing prices in 2010 with prices in the year 2000. In only five countries had the standard letter become cheaper in real terms.

Some enterprises have sought to improve the service they offer. For example, the possibility of paying for postage over the Internet and printing the stamp on a home/office computer such as the SMARTSTAMP product offered by Royal Mail, or hybrid mail solutions whereby addressees have the option to have their mail delivered electronically. In the parcel field, measures have been taken to make the delivery of parcels more convenient for addressees. Specific examples include the introduction of packetstations where the parcel can be collected at any time of the day or night, evening deliveries and delivery to an alternative addressee (for example, a workplace) or on an alternative day.

Given the statutory obligation for cost-oriented pricing, it is not surprising that most public postal operators are profitable. Copenhagen Economics (2010) identified five countries where the state-owned operator reported deficits – Lithuania, Greece, Poland, Bulgaria and Spain. In other countries the levels of profit were described as modest, and characteristic of a mature and stable industry.

Role of 'Universal Service'

For the most part the traditional postal service, or 'universal service' as the EU terms it, has formed the vast bulk of the public postal operators 'postal' activities. Services outside the scope of universal service still form a relatively small part of their offering (Table 12.1).

However, according to IPC (2011) a key issue for postal enterprises is their tendency to want to control their markets and the terms and conditions of service that their customers can expect. Customers, however, want bespoke services. Time Warner (2007) articulated this as a user need for 'PPOs that work with, rather than dictate to, users!'. The 'one size fits all' approach inherent in the concept of universal service simply will not meet

Table 12.1 Services outside the scope of universal service as % of public postal operators 'postal' activities

Country	Operator	Services outside the scope of universal service %
Belgium	De Post-La Poste	15
France	La Poste	20
Netherlands	PostNL (formerly TNT)	33
Britain	Royal Mail	53

Source: Annual Reports of Postal Operators.

the needs of those businesses and organizations that generate most postal items. For the future, therefore, it is likely that universal service as currently defined will cease to be a significant component of the letter post market.

First, European procurement law applies to public bodies and state agencies that make large-scale use of postal services (such as Social Welfare, Taxation, Passports, Driver and Vehicle Licensing, Electoral Registration). Irrespective of which postal enterprise is successful in the tendering process, the contract terms will be individually negotiated and therefore such services will fall outside the scope of universal service.

Second, many large-scale users of letter post services (such as energy and telecommunications companies and distance selling companies) are registered for value-added tax (VAT). Following FMO they will wish to negotiate prices and other service features that reflect their specific needs. As such users can reclaim the VAT paid for the service and the enterprise can reclaim VAT on inputs (vehicles, diesel, electricity and so on) costs for the end user will be reduced, and of course the underlying costs will be further reduced by competitive pressures.

Third, although at present many incumbents make insignificant sales of letter post products outside the scope of universal service they will need to offer products on this basis in order to compete with new entrants on a level playing field. In particular they will need to offer bespoke services to large-scale users of the post, to be unconstrained by regulation in terms of the prices charged and the terms and other conditions imposed, and to be liable to charge VAT (which many customers will be able to reclaim).

Finally, declining mail volumes, alternative delivery methods such as 'virtual' electronic delivery, and the use of value-added services rather than standard services, will all tend to reduce the significance of the universal service products. It is worth noting that even small and medium-sized enterprises (SMEs) now consider that mail should be collected from their premises (Research Perspective, 2010).

Overall it might be argued that up to half of the incumbents' current universal service business might fall outside the scope of universal service within a relatively short timeframe.

Continuing Decline in Volume of Letters Posted

There is also now clear evidence of a notable and continuing decline in the overall volume of letters being posted (Table 12.2).

Table 12.2 Trends in letter volumes of public postal operators

Country	Operator	
Belgium	De Post-La Poste	Domestic Mail which includes Transactional and Advertising Mail as well as Press grew by 1.4% compared to the previous year as the volume decline of slightly less than 0.5% was more than compensated by a 1.7% improvement in pricing and mix
Britain	Royal Mail	The decline in inland addressed mail volumes has continued to accelerate year on year and now stands at 7.3% (2009 5.5%)
Denmark	Post Danmark	In the past two years, Post Danmark saw the number of letters sent declining by, respectively, 10% in 2010 and 9% in 2009
France	La Poste	Letters were down by –4.7% against –6.9% in 2009, and Écopli is trending downwards (–3.7% against –2.7% in 2009)
Ireland	An Post	Traditional Mail volumes declined by approximately 7% in 2010
Netherlands	TNT	In Mail, the ongoing substitution of physical mail by electronic forms of communication and competition in the first full year of a liberalized market led to a letter mail volume decline in the Netherlands of 9.0%

Source: Annual Reports of Postal Operators.

Some 135 years after the telephone was patented in 1876[18] electronic communication services are finally eclipsing postal services in terms of speed and price as the 'normal' means of communications. Ambrosini et al. (2009) observed that growth in mail volumes for many decades was attributable notably to the growth in direct mail which compensated for the downward trend in single-piece items and transactional mail. Postal enterprises, particularly those that do not have a significant direct mail business, are therefore very vulnerable to the impact of e-substitution on their letters businesses.

Initial forecasts in this regard were often overstated,[19] but it is now clear that e-substitution will have a major impact on letter post volumes over the coming decade. In the case of An Post, the Irish universal service provider, 15 companies account for 30 percent of the letters posted[20] and all but two of these customers are actively pursuing an e-substitution strategy. When government usage of post for Transactional Mail,[21] and mail posted by other large businesses, is taken into account almost half of current letter volumes are potentially under threat. In the case of Royal Mail, which was one of the first European enterprises to recognize the potential of Direct Mail, the 50 companies which make the most extensive use of the postal service account for 40 percent of mail volumes (Hooper et al. 2008).

EU policies are driving these trends. Currently the levels of 'e-billing' are very low, partially because the EU's VAT Directive (2006/12/EC) leaves the decision about whether to accept or reject 'e-billing' to the recipient, and high standards of security are set for those enterprises that do want to move to the digital storage of invoices. The European Commission (2009) recognizes that there is at present no single business-friendly technology to support e-invoicing throughout the EU that satisfies both large and small businesses and has the full support of all the tax authorities. The EU is seeking solutions to these problems. It is becoming clear, also, that advances in printing technology and digital imaging make it increasingly difficult to discern an original paper invoice from a forged version or a copy. Whatever way one looks at it, the advantage of paper over digital media is being eroded. Future development in this respect will have a significant impact on the demand for postal services.

IPC (2011) warns that external communications experts offer a far more pessimistic outlook than industry experts, predicting that the market will decline to half its current size over the next decade. The report argues that if cost savings by large mailers or 'pay to play' (where customers have to pay to receive physical mailings) become dominant models among senders, mail volumes could decline much faster than anticipated. Already energy utilities offer discounts of around 2 percent to encourage customers to opt into e-billing; it is not just the cost savings in printing and postage that are driving e-substitution, but when combined with direct debiting there are also improvements in cash flow and reductions in disputed bills.

The logical conclusion is that letter post is likely to become a much smaller part of the overall postal market, and the business offering of today's universal service providers.

Distribution of Merchandize

According to the EU Consumer Policy strategy (2009), 58 percent of EU GDP is attributable to consumption by the 493 million consumers in the EU. It recognizes that e-commerce has great potential to improve consumer welfare, by making a greater range of products available, boosting price competition and developing new markets. Traders can increasingly sell to EU consumers via e-commerce from anywhere in the world. This vision reflects very significant social and environmental changes in factors such as household size; work–life balance; preference for delivery times and locations; and the evolution of electronic communications.

But to date the potential of e-commerce is not being fully realized, particularly cross-border within the EU; in 2006, 27 percent of all consumers made a purchase through e-commerce but only 6 percent did so across borders; 50 percent of consumers with an Internet connection at home made e-commerce purchases but only 12 percent made them across borders: 57 percent of EU retailers (mostly SMEs) sell through e-commerce and 49 percent of them would be prepared to sell cross-border in at least one EU country – but only 29 percent actually do so. The figures for financial services are even more striking: 26 percent of consumers have bought a financial service at a distance from a seller or provider based in their home country, but only 1 percent have done so cross-border.

The reasons behind the low take-up of cross-border e-commerce are varied, and affect both buyers and sellers. They range from cultural and linguistic barriers to competitive, regulatory and operational barriers. The European Commission has set targets to bring about a truly single market for e-commerce. However, the EU's actions to increase consumer protection and make cross-border payments easier will mean nothing unless postal enterprises develop and offer high-quality, efficient and affordable cross-border delivery services.

Table 12.3 Postal service as % of all activities

Country	Operator	Accenture (2010)	Mollet (2008)	Current paper based on 2010 Annual Reports
Belgium	De Post–La Poste	83	79.1	86
Denmark	Post Danmark	75	79.4	n/a
Britain	Royal Mail	70	75.7	69
Ireland	An Post	74	n/a	72
Sweden	Posten SE	53	68.1	54
France	La Poste	54	56.3	60
Switzerland	La Poste/Die Post	40	28.8	44
Netherlands	TNT[1]	38	40.3	41
Germany	Deutsche Post	13	19.9	27

Note: 1. TNT has since separated its mail and express operations into two separate businesses – Post NL and TNT Express. These activities now form part of TNT Express.

Realizing the future potential of e-commerce depends on being able to deliver the goods purchased in a manner and at a time that is convenient for the purchaser. The likelihood that the purchaser will be at home when the postman calls can no longer be taken as a given when postal enterprises are planning their deliveries. Technology therefore has an important part to play in meeting customer needs. Experiments include the development of automated packet stations, and sophisticated tracking systems that enable packets and parcels to be delivered to alternative addresses (including workplaces and convenience stores) and to plan delivery routes in an optimal manner taking into account the needs of the addressee.

Are existing enterprises up to the task or will new pan-European enterprises emerge? Time Warner (2007) illustrates many of the problems of providing cross-border services involving the interoperability of existing enterprises or by direct injection into national networks. These include difficulties with the positioning of the address, barcodes, (editorial) content and postage-paid indicia (including a requirement to include specific logos). And of course requirements are often only published in the local language.

Diversification

Finally it must be noted that in many countries public postal operators are diversifying into other activities such as financial services, logistics and printing. Different surveys produce different figures but the trends are clear (Table 12.3).

Responding to the Threats and Opportunities of the Digital World

At this time there seem to be three discernible strategies being pursued by postal undertakings.

The first is based on an acceptance that some postal business will be lost to electronic substitutes, but that targeted mailings complementing electronic media and the delivery of merchandise will sustain efficient postal service providers in the future.

The traditional attributes of postal services such as affordability, reliability, confidentiality and ubiquity are increasingly associated with competing media, but Research Perspective (2010) identified four factors which will ensure a continued place for postal services in the communications mix. These are its unique capability to deliver universally; the value associated with physical delivery of a communication which makes postal service a premium communications service; the legal and contractual issues perceived as barriers to using other communication services; and an adoption ceiling for online service delivery.

Visco Comandini et al. (2009) argue that direct mail acts as strategic complement to other advertising media and that increasingly, upstream (mail creation) and downstream (mail handling) postal players need to work more closely with other actors in the broader advertising and communications industry to enhance the impact of multimedia communication. Nader and Lintell (2008) point out that advanced technologies are adding value to mail through personalization, targeted messages and customized marketing.

Finally, ITA/WiK (2009) show that letter post accounts for about 56 percent and parcels/express account for 44 percent of sector revenues.[22] In principle, therefore, growth in one sector might offset losses in the other. Initiatives include developing e-commerce websites for traders who use the postal operator to distribute goods ordered.

The second strategy is based on the argument that as currently provided electronic services are not attractive to senders, particularly government agencies, who require ubiquitous and certified delivery and therefore there is scope for postal operators to provide more innovative electronic services to meet these needs. Hybrid mail has been around for some 30 years. Now some postal operators, notably Deutsche Post AG and Swiss Post, are developing secure electronic mailboxes which make electronic mail more feasible for this group of customers.

The UPU is also pioneering provision of a range of electronic products and services that meet customers' new communication needs, and has secured rights to a '.post' top-level domain name. The justification is that this will enable the UPU to reach the full potential of its original mission, to build a worldwide space without borders where personal and business communication is facilitated in a secure environment.

This strategy seems to carry a number of risks. First, it will copper fasten the supremacy of electronic communications. Second, the reputation of postal service providers for providing ubiquitous, affordable and confidential services will not necessarily be sufficient to persuade customers to use the 'post' instead of an alternative provider with extensive expertise in electronic communications.

The third strategy seems to be to 'sit on the fence' until future trends become clearer. Predicting the future is difficult but history suggests that postal operators have demonstrated over the centuries that they are well able to evolve in response to changes in user requirements. In the author's opinion, strategies that envisage a strong postal presence in the future are most likely to be successful.

3 HOW REGULATORY FRAMEWORKS MIGHT NEED TO EVOLVE

This section considers the implications of these scenarios for regulation.

Continuing Need for Sector Regulation

Both the IPC (2007) and Leskinen et al. (2009) argue that there is no need for sector-specific regulation and that competition law is sufficient to regulate the postal market. The reality is that in the letters sector most incumbent enterprises still enjoy a *de jure* or *de facto* monopoly over delivery. That position came to an end on 31 December 2010, but for some time these enterprises will retain a dominant market position.

For a transitional period, therefore, regulators will face two key challenges, to avoid increased price pressure on the captive customers, especially users of the universal services; and to ensure that attempts to stimulate the market do not lead to anti-competitive practices. The danger is that incumbents might foreclose on competition developing in the potentially competitive markets by below cost selling or allocating a disproportionate amount of the costs of the shared delivery network to the universal service.

If regulators can meet these challenges and the market for letter post services outside the scope of universal service becomes just as competitive as the market for CEP (courier, express and postal service operators) services, then the question of further deregulation will be relevant.

Reduced Scope of 'Universal Service'

Leskinen et al. (2009, p. 277) also argue that 'the scope of the universal service should be defined to a minimum level needed by consumers and small and medium-sized enterprises, to a level no broader than is necessary to ensure that messages are conveyed'. It warns that an extensive USO interpretation will, especially in the case of First Class letters, result in increasing unit costs. The Dutch government and the British regulator have already adopted the policy of a *de minimis* scope of universal service, but in other countries legislators have decided upon the policy of mandating universal service provision for extended periods of up to 20 years.

However, as discussed in Section 2, postal services are changing rapidly. It seems that there will be a greater orientation towards the delivery of things rather than letters; value-added features are becoming the norm; and there is convergence between postal delivery and other services.

Universal service, while still important to particular users, will no longer be the driver of postal operators' investments and policy decisions. The postal delivery networks, and related infrastructure, will be needed to enable operators to provide innovative customer-focused services, which often will be 'bundled' with related services including printing, data management and stockholding and a wide diversity of collection and delivery options.

To attempt to regulate such services would be to strangle the market at birth. Innovation comes from competitive pressures and the desire to make profits. Regulation cannot substitute for this fundamental economic principle.

Furthermore, because universal service will be provided over a network that exists to provide customer focused services on a commercial basis, policy makers will have many options to secure its provision in the event of market failure.

Evolution of Universal Service

As has happened in the electronic communications sector, some of the new and innovative services may, after a period of time, acquire the characteristics of universal service. A good example is the provision of 'broadband' Internet connections. This was not originally regarded as part of the universal service that EU states were obliged to guarantee to their citizens, but the lack of access to such services in some areas is now a political issue in many countries. Already Italy, and Spain and Switzerland have imposed a USO for broadband.

Article 5(1) of the Postal Directive specifically requires that the universal service 'shall evolve in response to the technical, economic and social environment and to the needs of users'. The challenge for postal regulators will be to intervene only when there is a demonstrable need for intervention to ensure that all users have access to necessary services on non-discriminatory terms and conditions.

Regulating Integrated Networks

As e-commerce develops and achieves its full potential it is increasingly likely that there will be alliances and partnerships with other communications and distribution networks. The key will be to offer a one-stop shop providing website/electronic advertising and order taking, physical distribution of advertising and sales material and physical distribution of purchased goods often on a pan-European or global basis.

This will have implications for regulation. The British government intends to merge its postal and electronic communications regulators, but this is already the case in 22 of the 27 EU members countries. Crystal-ball gazing the future is always dangerous, but the regulatory debate in the future might well focus on the need to merge not only postal and electronic communications regulators but perhaps the likes of data protection and consumer protection regulators as well.

Consumers in Portugal purchasing an item from a pan-European distributor based in Poland needs to be sure that they receive what they want in good condition, in a timely manner, that their personal information is held securely and that if something goes wrong they can secure quick and effective redress. A recent case involved an Italian woman who ordered electronic equipment over the Internet, paid significant sums of money to the 'supplier' who gave a fictitious address in Mullingar (Ireland) and the fictitious 'postal enterprise' based at a fictitious address in Northampton (UK). The criminals behind this scam could well be based in Germany, France or some Far Eastern country. Regulators need to develop effective remedies to ensure that consumers can rely on e-commerce cross-border just as much as traditional retail distribution nationally. And of course the need is to ensure that no single company can dominate these vast interrelated markets. What role will national regulators have – or will we need a super European regulator?

4 CONCLUSION

In conclusion, sector-specific regulation will be needed following FMO to ensure an effective transition to full and effective competition in the non-universal letters market, and at the same time ensuring the provision of universal service.

If regulators are successful in this, the universal service will decline in importance – possibly to around a third of postal markets overall. The focus of the regulator and policy maker will then be to ensure provision of universal service in the event of market failure. Policy makers will have many options to secure universal service provision in these circumstances.

Ongoing developments in e-commerce, logistics, and communications markets, driven by rapid technological change, will be the most evident signs of the digital revolution. They will also present the most significant challenge for the sectors' regulators in managing the transition to an efficient integration of these interdependent networks, while ensuring that both households and businesses begin to realize the full benefits that the digital revolution can bring.

NOTES

* This chapter represents the personal views of the author and should not necessarily be taken to represent the policy of any organization with which he is associated. Responsibility for the content of this chapter and the views expressed therein rests with the author alone.

1. See Article 5.1 UPU Convention.
2. See Article 5.2 UPU Convention.
3. In this context, see not only the UPU Letter Post Regulations Article RL 118 but also the judgment of the Indian Supreme Court in *The Commissioner of Income Tax v Messrs Ogale Glass Works Ltd* (1954) which observed that '*This very narrow and qualified right can hardly be regarded as bringing about a position so different from that prevailing*' under the common law.
4. ECJ Case C-320/91 *Paul Corbeau* 19 May 1993, [1993] ECR 1-2563.
5. Registration, provision of statistical information and a requirement to have out of court dispute resolution procedures.
6. Four countries, Britain, Ireland, Italy and Portugal had failed to transpose the Postal Directive by the 31 December 2010 deadline. However the principle of 'Direct Effect' ensured that the existing laws granting 'reserved areas' to specified operators could no longer be enforced. Some 11 countries have a derogation until 31 December 2012 to open postal markets to competition.
7. Article 288 TFEU.
8. See Case 107/84 *Commission v Germany* [1985] ECR 2655 – point 16.
9. See Case T-289/03 *BUPA Ireland Ltd.* ECR 2008 Page II-00081 – point 188.
10. See Case T-289/03 *BUPA Ireland Ltd.* ECR 2008 Page II-00081 – point 190.
11. See Case T-289/03 *BUPA Ireland Ltd.* ECR 2008 Page II-00081 – point 189.
12. See Case T-289/03 *BUPA Ireland Ltd.* ECR 2008 Page II-00081 – points 186 and 187.
13. See Communication from the Commission (2001/C 17/04) – point 11.
14. The Postal Directive Article 5(1) provides that the universal service 'shall offer an identical service to users under comparable conditions'.
15. See Case T-289/03 *BUPA Ireland Ltd.* ECR 2008 Page II-00081 – point 202
16. The Postal Directive Article 2(17) defines 'User' as 'any natural or legal person benefiting from postal service provision as a sender or an addressee'.
17. 2 February 2006.
18. Alexander Graham Bell was awarded a patent for the electric telephone by the United States Patent and Trademark Office in March 1876.
19. For example, WiK (2005) reported at pp. 110–11 that forecast reductions in volume were more pessimistic than actual experience because changes in customer preferences, price policy, and the development of innovative, more customer-tailored services had not been taken into account.
20. See http://www.anpost.ie/AnPost/AnPostDM/KNOWLEDGECentre/Research+and+Insights/irish+Direct+Mail+Trends/.
21. The Minister for Communications, Energy and Natural Resources told the Dail (Irish Parliament) on 21 June 2011 that 'winning Government contracts perhaps ought not be the first focus of An Post from here on out because increasingly more Government business is going online and that will have its own implications'.
22. About €94 billion in 2007 – 0.7 percent of the GDP of the 27 member states.

REFERENCES

Accenture (2010), 'Is Diversification the Answer to Mail Woes? The Experience of International Posts', report for USPS, February.

Ambrosini, Xavier, Sébastien Bréville, Joel Cornée and Olaf Klargaard (2009), 'Mail order business demand: a conceptual approach', in Michael A. Crew and Paul R. Kleindorfer (eds), *Progress in the Competitive Agenda in the Postal and Delivery Sector*, Cheltenham, UK and Northampton, MA, USA: Edward Elgar.

bPost (2010) , Annual Report of the Belgian Post Office – bPost, Brussels.

Copenhagen Economics (2010), 'Main Developments in the Postal Sector (2008-2010)', report for DC, Internal Market, European Commission.

Deutsche Post (2011), 'Letter prices in Europe. Up-to-date international letter price survey'.

EU Consumer Policy Strategy (2009), Communication from the Commission to the Council, the European Parliament and the European Economic and Social Committee, 'EU Consumer Policy strategy 2007–2013, Empowering consumers, enhancing their welfare, effectively protecting them', COM(2007) 99 final, 13.3.2007.

European Commission (2000), COM(2000) 580 final 20.9.2000.

European Commission (2007), COM(2007)695 final, 9.11.2007.

European Commission (2008), SEC(2008) 3076, 22.12.2008.

European Commission (2009), COM(2009) 20 final, 28.1.2009.

Eurostat (2009), 'Statistics explained', available at: http://epp.eurostat.ec.europa.eu/statistics_explained/index.php/Postal_statistics, (accessed 8 May 2011).

Hooper, Richard, Deirdre Hutton and Ian Smith (2008), 'Modernise or Decline: Policies to Maintain the Universal Postal Service in the United Kingdom', an independent review of the UK postal services sector, Cm 7529 ISBN:9780101752923, 16 December.

International Post Corporation (IPC) (2007), 'How to regulate the postal industry' an economic approach', study prepared by the IPC in cooperation with DIW Berlin (German Institute for Economic Research).

International Post Corporation (IPC) (2011), 'Role of Mail 2020', report prepared for IPC by the Copenhagen Institute for Future Studies.

ITA/WiK (2009), 'Evolution of the European Postal Market since 1997', a report by ITA Consulting GmbH and WIK-Consult GmbH for the European Commission.

Leskinen, Pekka, Peter Karlsson, Heikki Nikali and Piiivi Rokkanen (2009), 'How should regulation be adjusted when universal service substitution grows?', in Michael A. Crew and Paul R. Kleindorfer (eds), *Progress in the Competitive Agenda in the Postal and Delivery Sector*, Cheltenham, UK and Northampton, MA, USA: Edward Elgar.

Lisbon Treaty (2010), 'Treaty on the functioning of the European Union', *Official Journal of the European Union*, C 83/47, 30.3.2010.

Mollet, Patrick (2008), 'Logistics industry as a difficult area of diversification for incumbent postal operators', *Network Industries Quarterly*, **10**(4), 15–17.

Nader, Fouad H. and Michael Lintell (2008), 'Mail Trends Update', (Nader: Adrenale Corporation; Lintell: Pitney Bowes), The Future of Mail Background Paper No. 2008-1, Pitney Bowes Inc., February.

Postal Directive (1997), Directive 97/67/EC of the European Parliament and of the Council of 15 December 1997 on common rules for the development of the internal market of Community postal services and the improvement of quality of service.

Postal Directive (2008), Directive 2008/6/EC of the European Parliament and of the Council of 20 February 2008 amending Directive 97/67/EC with regard to the full accomplishment of the internal market of Community postal services.

Postcomm (2011), 'The building blocks for a sustainable postal service. Proposals to remove bulk products from the universal service and clarify the status of other universal service products – a consultation', Postcomm, February available at: http://www.psc.gov.uk/documents/1808.pdf, accessed 28 February 2011).

Research Perspective (2010), 'Findings from qualitative research into the national need for

communication and distribution services', prepared by the Research Perspective Ltd on behalf of the Commission for Communications Regulation, available at: http://www.comreg.ie/_fileupload/publications/ComReg_10102.pdf, (6 December 2010).
Resolution (1994), *Official Journal of the European Union*, C 48, 16.2.1994, p. 3.
Royal Mail (2010), 'Annual Report and Financial Statements Year ended 28 March 2010', Royal Mail Holdings plc.
Time Warner (2007), 'Practical problems for cross-border mail users', presentation by Simon Hampton, Director, Public Policy to CERP Plenary, May.
Visco Comandini, Vincenzo, Michael Lintell, Stefano Gori, Maria Rita Pierleoni and Bradley Tisdahl (2009), 'Competition: a multisided market approach', in Michael A. Crew and Paul R. Kleindorfer (eds), *Progress in the Competitive Agenda in the Postal and Delivery Sector*, Cheltenham, UK and Northampton, MA, USA: Edward Elgar.
WiK (2005), 'The Evolution of the Regulatory Model for European Postal Services' report for European Commission.

13. Allocating costs between universal services and services outside the scope of universal service*

Heikki Nikali[†], Kari Elkelä[‡], Pekka Leskinen[§], Päivi Rokkanen[¶] and Peter Karlsson[††]

1 INTRODUCTION

Allocation of costs between universal services and services outside the scope of universal services is not clear. Different practices exist for cost allocation among European Union member states. There is a need to set clear rules for cost allocation. The objective of this chapter is to analyze theory and practices for allocating costs between universal services and services outside the scope of universal service.

This chapter proceeds as follows. Section 2 describes some background to cost allocation in the postal sector by presenting what has been included in the Postal Directive, the guidelines of the Committee of European Postal Regulators (CERP) and the role of the European Regulators Group for Post (ERGP). In Section 3, cost allocation in Finland is presented, and the dispute between the Finnish Communications Regulation Authority (Ficora) and Itella along with the 'Deutsche Post' example are discussed. In Section 4, econometric models of the postal delivery function are presented and discussed in the context of allocation of fixed and volume-based costs to Universal Service Obligation (USO) and non-USO services. In addition, Section 5 discusses how USO costs vary according to different theoretical USO 'definitions'. Conclusions are presented in Section 6.

2 BACKGROUND TO COST ALLOCATION REGULATION

The Postal Directive[1] aims to achieve an internal market for postal services and at the same time to safeguard a common level of universal services for all users in all EU countries. Article 14 of the Postal Directive requires national regulators to regulate the accounts of universal service providers. However, instead of prescribing detailed and binding rules on cost accounting, the Postal Directive lays down general principles and leaves flexibility in this area. The Directive calls for cooperation between national regulatory authorities for

[†] Research Director, Itella Corporation.
[‡] Research Manager, Itella Corporation.
[§] Vice President, Legal, Itella Corporation.
[¶] Legal Counsel, Itella Corporation.
[††] Legal Counsel, Itella Corporation.

developing best practices and common approaches (for example, by CERP). In a study for the European Commission in 2009 (Dieke et al., 2009), it was found that national regulators have adopted substantially different approaches to implementing the cost allocation principles laid out in the Postal Directive.

The Postal Directive distinguishes between 'direct costs', costs, which can be directly assigned to a particular service or product (art. 14 §3a) and 'common costs', costs which cannot be directly assigned to a particular service or product (art. 14 §3b). Whenever possible, common costs must be allocated on the basis of a direct analysis of the origin of the costs themselves. If direct analysis is not possible, these costs must be allocated on the basis of an indirect linkage to another cost category or group of costs categories for which a direct assignment is possible (art. 14 §3b ii). When neither direct nor indirect measures of cost allocation can be found, the cost category must be allocated on the basis of a general allocator computed by using the ratio of all expenses directly or indirectly assigned or allocated, on the one hand, to each of the universal services and, on the other, to the other services (art. 14 §3b iii). Common costs, which are necessary for the provision of both universal and non-universal services, must be allocated appropriately; the same cost drivers being applied to both universal services and non-universal services (art. 14 §3b iv). This complex rule can be summarized to mean that the common costs are assigned to each particular service as far as it is possible by direct or indirect means. Those common costs that are unassignable should be allocated to each service based on the proportion of total assigned costs.

Allocations should be based on cost causality, objectivity, consistency and transparency. The principle of causality means that costs are allocated to those services, which 'cause' the costs to be incurred. The postal sector is relatively labor intensive and the level of capital investment is relatively low compared to other network industries such as telecommunications. Typically in the postal sector many services are jointly produced and therefore a high proportion of the costs are shared between different services, which makes cost allocation very important but also challenging.

CERP prepared a report in 2009[2] in order to identify best practices for cost accounting in relation to the particular circumstances of the postal services industry. According to the principle of subsidiarity it is up to each country to decide whether or not to apply the CERP recommendations. The CERP report addresses the question of allocation of common costs but fails to give clear answers on the matter.

ERGP was created by a Commission decision in 2010 to advise and bring assistance to the Commission in ensuring the consistent application in all member states of the Postal Directive. This group is composed of the national regulatory authorities. Regulatory accounting is one of the five issues in ERGP's work program for 2011–12. ERGP aims to develop best practices on common cost allocation methods in order to properly define cost-oriented tariffs and build a common approach on common costs taking into account differences in national regulators' competence and objectives.

3 USO AND COST ALLOCATION IN FINLAND

On June 1, 2011 a new Postal Act entered into force which implements the Postal Directive into Finnish legislation. According to the Postal Act, the USO is limited to addressed letter mail up to 2kg paid with commonly used forms of cash payment, that is, stamps (single-piece letters), and parcels up to 10kg paid with commonly used forms of cash payment and which a user may collect at a post office.

Itella and Ficora are in dispute on the application of cost allocation rules. Itella contends that the USO in itself is a source of costs. However, Ficora has not accepted this, as in its opinion the USO is not based on the actual use of resources under the principle of cost causation. Ficora is concerned that Itella allocates costs to universal service products, which should be allocated to non-regulated products. According to Ficora, the costs of the postal network should be allocated to all products forwarded within the network solely on the basis of delivered volumes.

Ficora has not taken into account the fact that Itella's expenses are, to a significant degree, the result of implementing the USO. Volume-independent fixed costs account for the majority of Itella's expenses, since Itella is required to maintain a production network necessitated by the five-day delivery obligation, as well as an office network and resources for the uninterrupted provision of the universal service. Production volumes do not explain the costs of Itella's postal network; instead, Itella maintains that the key factor explaining the costs is the USO stipulated by law.

Under Article 14(3) of the Postal Directive, it is apparent that the USO is to be taken into account under the principle of cost causation. Common (volume-independent) costs shall be primarily allocated on the basis of the origin of the costs principle. The USO causes costs which, in accordance with the cost causation principle expressed in the Postal Directive, should primarily be allocated to universal service products.

Itella's interpretation of cost allocation complies with the cost-allocation principles determined by the European Commission in the *Deutsche Post* decision. In this case,[3] the European Commission applied an incremental costs standard in the postal sector. According to the decision, where Deutsche Post AG (DPAG) maintains an infrastructure to fulfill its public service mission (USO), a distinction must be made between the cost of maintaining capacity and the specific incremental costs of producing individual services.

In the decision, USO is defined as the obligation to serve as the 'carrier of last resort', which requires a firm to hold capacity in reserve in order to meet demand at peak load. The costs that arise from a company's obligation to serve as the carrier of last resort are appropriately treated as common fixed costs for the firm.[4]

According to the *Deutsche Post* decision,

> When calculating the share of the common fixed costs it must be borne in mind that DPAG is required by law to maintain a reserve capacity large enough to cover any peak demands that may arise in over-the counter parcel services while meeting statutory service-quality standards for those services. Even if DPAG were no longer to offer mail-order parcel services, it would still be obliged *vis-à-vis* every mail-order customer to provide catalogues and parcels over the counter within a specified delivery target. This results from the USO.

The Commission considered that incremental costs do not include the common fixed costs. The Commission also concluded that the prices of DPAG's (non-universal) services have to cover only the incremental costs incurred as a result of providing those services. Therefore, in the light of Article 14 (3) of the EC Postal Directive, it follows that the common fixed costs (costs of maintaining universal service capacity) should not be allocated to other services than universal services.

4 COST ALLOCATION MODEL[5]

This study has been carried out in order to understand the consequences of alternative methods of allocating fixed and volume-based costs of delivery to postal products requiring delivery services. Estimated models will be utilized to evaluate differences of delivery costs according to population density and the scope of the USO definition. With the aid of models, the extent to which advance information on delivery volumes reduces costs can also be estimated, when the correct resource allocations are made.

Delivery Resource Models and Data from Finland

The four most essential process stages of the production of postal services are collection, sorting, transportation and delivery. This study concentrates on costs related to the final process stage, that is, delivery,[6] which account for approximately 45 percent of the postal service provider's total production costs. This means that they form the major single-cost item and the item which is most closely related to the regional fluctuation resulting from the circumstances in which delivery takes place.

The present basic delivery resource model in Finland involves two different econometric approaches: the *cost–benefit model* explains how delivery conditions and the volumes of product groups for delivery affect postal expenditure, and the *working-time model* explains basic delivery daily working time in relation to the volumes delivered. The models are used to illustrate the cost effectiveness of the USO and the various cost savings which can be achieved, if delivery volumes are known well in advance.

The structure of the econometric model is as follows:

$$y = a + bx_1 + cx_2 + \dots + nx_n,$$

where:

y = costs or working time, use of resources as a whole, and
x_1 = conditioning factors, for example, population density, number of delivery points (households and companies) or length of delivery routes;
$x_2 \dots x_n$ = delivery volumes for different product groups, for example, addressed letter mail, newspapers and magazines as well as unaddressed deliveries.

In the delivery-cost model, those delivery expenses incurred during 2008 are explained by (i) delivery conditions, such as the length of delivery routes, and (ii) volumes of delivery according to different product groups. By using data for the year as a whole, fluctuations due to seasonal variations are eliminated.

Finland is divided into 481 districts for the purpose of postal deliveries. Each district has its own delivery office, where the preliminary work is carried out, that is, sorting and arranging for route deliveries. The real costs for 2008 of all 481 delivery districts have been used as research material. Delivery expenditure and working time include both preparatory delivery work and the resources needed for work performed on the delivery routes. Work related to the preparation for the reception of items for delivery, such as transportation to delivery offices, is not included in the costs being studied.

In the working-time model the actual daily working time for the whole of Finland in

Table 13.1 Results of the delivery-cost model

Variable	Model coefficient	Standard error	t-value	PR > $|t|$
Constant	0.119	0.025	4.72	<0.0001
x_1 = route km/delivery point	0.979	0.021	47.37	<0.0001
x_2 = volume of addressed mail/ delivery point	0.069	0.030	2.29	0.0225
x_3 = volume of newspapers/delivery point	0.131	0.016	8.38	<0.0001
x_4 = volume of magazines/delivery point	0.188	0.058	3.24	0.0013
R-square = 0.92				

October 2009 including preparation for deliveries at the delivery offices and the deliveries themselves, has been analyzed. October was chosen as the target of the study because, viewed from the perspective of seasonal variation, it can be called an average month. The explanatory variables in the working-time model are the delivery volumes of addressed letter mail, periodicals, newspapers and unaddressed mail.

Estimation of Cost Functions and Cost Distributions

Several different alternatives in estimating the cost model were experimented with, all of which were well able to explain fluctuation in delivery costs and returned similar results. There are considerable differences in Finland in the sizes and structure of delivery districts. In areas with a scattered population (countryside) the distance between two delivery points is, on average, 12 times that of densely populated (urban) areas. The delivery point is the mailbox of a household or company. There are a total of 2.9 million such delivery points. Because of these demographic variations, the analysis was delivery point specific. Total expenditure on basic delivery was €307 million in 2008, whereby the average cost per delivery point per day amounted to €0.56. There is considerable variation between delivery point costs, from €0.16 to €1.80. For calculating the model, all variables were converted to represent the average daily situation of each delivery point, whereby the model was estimated (Table 13.1).

In calculating the model the preferred order of the explanatory variables according to their relevance was: (i) route kilometers, (ii) number of periodicals delivered, (iii) delivered newspapers and (iv) delivered addressed letters. This model is able to explain 92 percent of delivery point expenditure variance. The volume of unaddressed mail offers no explanation for delivery costs, because its coefficient is almost zero and its explanatory power is not statistically significant. The model is statistically extremely reliable and its explanatory ability very good. The delivery-cost model is presented in Figure 13.1.

The model coefficients describe how each independent variable affects delivery costs. By multiplying the coefficients by the existing averages of the corresponding variables, cost shares for different factors are determined. This describes average and daily delivery-point specific cost (€0.56) and also annual total expenditure (€305m) distribution. The results are presented in Table 13.2.

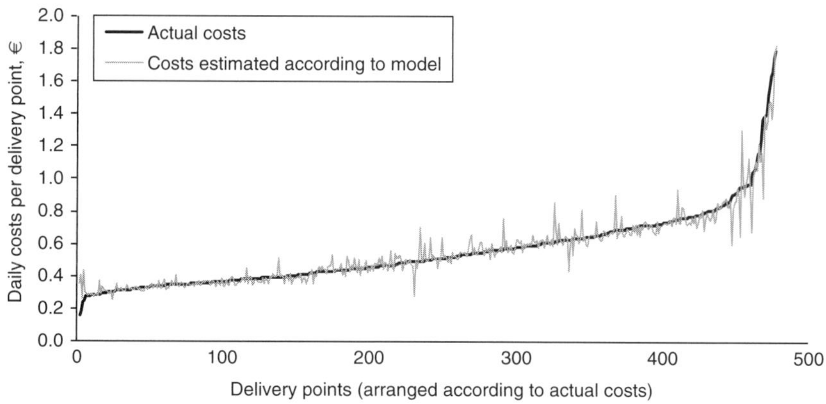

Figure 13.1 Delivery-cost model

Table 13.2 Interpretation of the delivery-cost model

Variable	(a) Model coefficient	(b) National mean	(a)*(b) Cost share, €	Cost share, %	Interpretation
Constant	0.119	1	0.12	21	Delivery infrastructure maintenance
x_1 = route km/delivery point	0.979	0.20 km	0.20	36	Daily delivery route covered
x_2 = volume of addressed mail/ delivery point	0.069	1.45 items	0.10	18	Delivery of addressed mail
x_3 = volume of newspapers/delivery point	0.131	0.36 items	0.05	9	Delivery of newspapers
x_4 = volume of magazines/ delivery point	0.188	0.48 items	0.09	16	Delivery of magazines
Total			0.56	100	

The constant term for the model can be interpreted as delivery infrastructure maintenance expenditure and route kilometer USO daily performance expenditure. These fixed costs total 57 percent of expenditure – constant plus x_1. When the 18 percent share of costs resulting from addressed mail deliveries is added to this, the cost of realizing the USO rises to a proportion of 75 percent. The share of the expenditure for periodicals remains at 16 percent and 9 percent for newspapers. The share of unaddressed deliveries has no meaningful effect on costs.

In the working-time model the explanatory variables represent the delivered volumes of the most important product groups. The estimated model explains 84 percent of daily delivery working-time fluctuation. It is evident from Figure 13.2 how well the model succeeds in describing each specific number of hours worked daily. On the basis of statistical

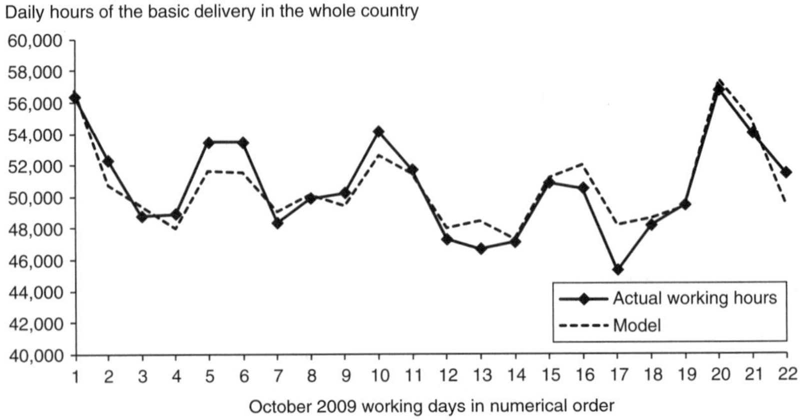

Figure 13.2 Distribution of daily delivery working time according to the working-time model

testing, the model is found to be quite reliable. Nevertheless, it does tend to flatten out the fluctuation in working hours, and is unable in all respects to explain the extremities in fluctuation. The fluctuation in the daily delivery volumes can be described using the term 'standard deviation per daily mean value'. The working-time model strives to explain just how flexible realized working time is in relation to the fluctuation of different types of daily deliveries. The results of the working-time model appear in Table 13.3.

The greatest fluctuation is in unaddressed deliveries and periodicals. These are the delivery items whose arrival in the delivery network is best known in advance. Compared to these there is considerably less daily fluctuation in letter mail, and there is no advance information on letter volumes, so that preparation has to be made using, in the main, standard resource allocation. Most of the newspapers in Finland arrive by early morning delivery, and are only delivered by basic postal delivery in certain parts of the country where the volumes are well known in advance.

It is apparent from the correlation coefficient that the delivery volumes of periodicals best explain the use of working hours. Newspaper and unaddressed letter deliveries also correlate rather strongly with working time. On the other hand, despite substantial correlation the coefficient of unaddressed deliveries is negligible, which means that working time devoted to these is quite small. Instead, the correlation between the volume of all addressed letters and performed working time is low. This then suggests that the arrival of addressed letters into the delivery network cannot be forecast in advance. The distribution of resources for different product groups according to the working-time model is presented in Figure 13.3.

The significance of the constant is decisive. This is understandable because the standard deviation of working time per daily mean value is only 6 percent, that is, significantly lower than the corresponding fluctuation for all types of delivery. This means that working time cannot be further adjusted to actual resource needs, because most of the consignment volumes intended for delivery are not known beforehand. It is particularly the unpredictability of the daily volume fluctuation of addressed letters, which enter the network more evenly, that leads to standard working-time resource allocation. The

Table 13.3 Results of the working-time model

Variable	Model coefficient	Standard error	t-value	PR > $\|t\|$	Mean daily number of items, (millions)	Volume standard deviation / mean, %	Correlation with the dependent variable (y)
Constant	42.711	2,446	17.46	<0.001			
1st and 2nd class letters	0.0000062	0.000635	0.01	0.9923	2.62	21	0.27
Addressed direct mail	0.0022	0.00076	2.94	0.0101	1.09	48	0.21
Magazines	0.0021	0.00047	4.48	0.0004	1.33	75	0.80
Newspapers	0.0019	0.00287	0.66	0.5222	0.64	52	0.59
Unaddressed advertising mail	0.0004	0.00014	3.02	0.0087	3.73	93	0.54
Daily working time (y), standard deviation/mean = 6 %							
R-square = 0.84							

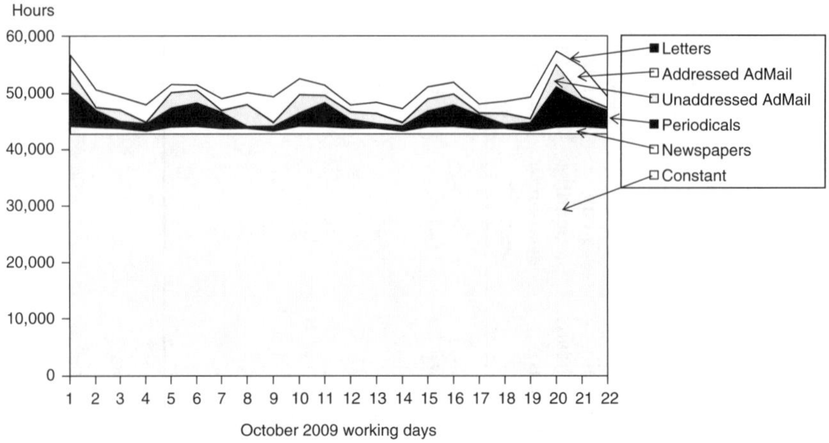

Figure 13.3 Distribution of daily delivery working time according to the working-time model

addressed mail share of all delivered items is 55 percent. On the basis of the daily fluctuation of 1st and 2nd class letters, this resource allocation is not visible in Figure 13.3, since it is so small.

Maintenance of USO Network Defines the Size of Delivery Costs

A comparison of the delivery-cost and working-time models reveals that these models present a fairly similar picture of basic delivery work and the resources required. It is only in the delivery-cost model that the route length is a variable, because this does not vary according to the working day in question, in which case its significance is transferred to the constant in the working-time model. The significance of the constant in both models is high, which means that delivery resources generally do not vary much with regard to the volumes delivered. Route length is a decisive influencing factor regarding costs. Apart from the route length, an essential resource that needs explanatory factor is the maintenance of the network. The share of these fixed costs of the total expenditure of delivery is about 60 percent.

From the point of view of the planning of work resources and efficient use, it is of primary importance to know in advance the size of the items to be delivered each day. The best advance information can be obtained for newspapers and periodicals as well as for volumes of unaddressed mail. It is most difficult to adjust the resources in advance to the volumes of 1st and 2nd class letters and bulk mail, because these are not generally known in advance. For this reason, in addressed letter delivery there must be preparation for standard allocation of resources, and this increases expenses. The letter share of volume-based expenditure is a scant 20 percent. Because the USO includes the maintenance of the postal delivery network and the five-day delivery obligation, the share of addressed letters of the total delivery expenditure rises in this case to about 75 percent.

5 HOW DO USO COSTS VARY ACCORDING TO DIFFERENT USO DEFINITIONS?

Population density greatly affects delivery costs. In Finland, one-third of the population live in areas that comprise only 2 percent of the total surface area. Correspondingly, one-fifth of the population live in areas that make up 80 percent of the country. The density of the population is shown in Table 13.4.

The difference between Finland and Central Europe is quite clear. For example, the average population density in Holland (430 persons/km^2) is much greater than in the densely populated areas of Finland. Correspondingly, the population density of Germany (230 persons/km^2) is not much less than that of Finland's densely populated areas. The implication of the USO becomes emphasized in countries such as Finland, the surface area of which is mostly sparsely populated and where a five-day weekly delivery is required. Because of the great diversity of population density, the cost model demonstrated in the previous section was estimated for different areas separately. The final results of those models are presented in Table 13.5.

In less populated areas the share of delivery infrastructure maintenance is halved and the daily delivery routes covered are 10 times those of densely populated areas. The shares of fixed costs – infrastructure maintenance plus length of daily delivery routes – in densely populated areas total 34 percent and in sparsely populated areas 60 percent. Respectively, volume-based costs fall to 66 and 40 percent. In densely populated areas the share of letter volume expenditure is critical (52 percent), whereas in sparsely populated

Table 13.4 Demographic data from Finland

Data	Share of the area (%)	Share of households (%)	Population density
Densely populated area	2	34	340 persons/km^2
Average populated area	18	44	39 persons/km^2
Sparsely populated area	80	22	4 persons/km^2
Total	100	100	16 persons/km^2

Table 13.5 Delivery cost shares based on cost models for different populated areas in Finland

Variable	Densely populated area	Average populated area	Sparsely populated area	The whole country
	Delivery cost share, %			
Delivery infrastructure maintenance	30	35	16	21
Daily delivery route covered	4	14	44	36
Delivery of addressed mail	52	31	9	18
Delivery of newspapers	4	9	8	9
Delivery of magazines	10	11	23	16
Total	100	100	100	100

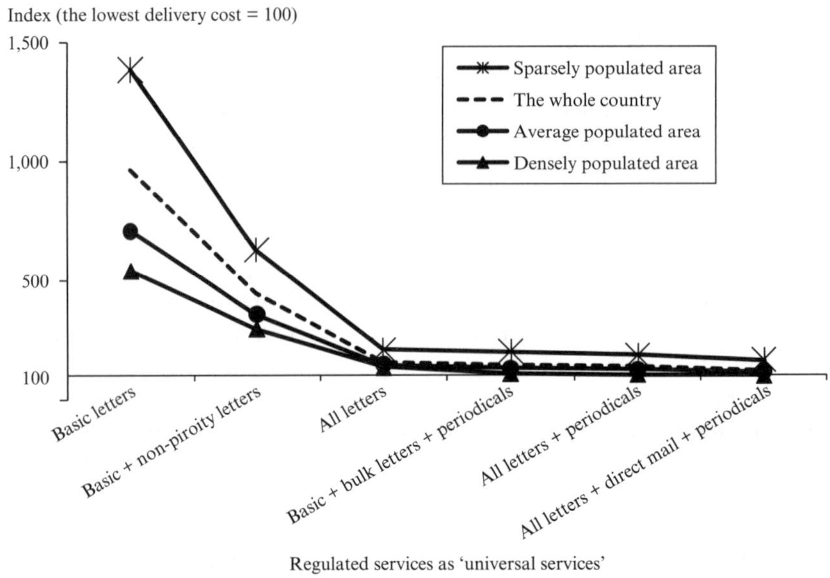

Figure 13.4 Delivery USO unit costs according to different theoretical USO 'definitions'

areas it is the distance covered (44 percent) that is critical. Delivery unit cost in sparsely populated areas is double that of the densely populated areas.

By utilizing the cost models presented in Table 13.5, a theoretical calculation can be made of how the unit cost of regulated deliveries changes with different USO 'definitions'. In this comparison, USO has been 'defined' most broadly to include all items for delivery and most narrowly to include only single-piece posted letters. The five-times-a-week delivery obligation stays the same regardless of the alternative chosen. In different theoretical USO 'definitions', two factors have been taken into consideration in unit cost calculation: the changing fixed and volume-based costs. The calculations were made in areas of varying population density and are presented in Figure 13.4.

The variation in fixed costs of different alternatives was controlled by using fixed-cost elasticity coefficients. Elasticity coefficients have been estimated by comparing existing delivery-point-specific costs for different areas in relation to the corresponding volumes. As delivery volumes and, accordingly, expenses diminish, the basic proportion based on volumes has first been separated from the change in costs with the help of the results of cost models, which means that the rest of the decrease in expenses is centered on fixed costs. Note that the elasticity of fixed costs describes the changes over a long period of time, because structural and permanent changes of resources cannot be implemented in the short term. The fixed-cost volume-based elasticity coefficients obtained for different density areas are shown in Table 13.6.

The elasticity coefficients describe the percentage change in long-term fixed costs when the volume of USO regulated postal deliveries changes by 1 percent as, for example, in sparely populated areas where a 10 percent drop in volume means a 4 percent fall in fixed costs. In sparsely populated areas, cost elasticity is significantly greater than in densely populated areas. It is possible to optimize delivery routes more easily when there are

Table 13.6 Fixed-cost volume-based elasticity coefficients

Densely populated area	Average populated area	Sparsely populated area	The whole country
0.1	0.3	0.4	0.25

fewer delivery points and the distances between them are long; further, the share of costs based on volume in sparsely populated areas is quite obviously smaller than in densely populated areas. The cost curves in Figure 13.4 include not only fixed-cost elasticity but also take into consideration the reduction in volume-based total costs when USO content decreases.

Figure 13.4 shows that the unit costs hardly change when the 'definition' of the USO is extended from all letters to bulk letters, periodicals or direct mail. On the other hand, when the USO definition is narrowed to include only non-priority or single-piece posted letters, unit costs immediately rise. If the USO covers only single-piece posted letters, the *whole country* unit cost per USO letter is eight-fold compared to when the USO covers all items for delivery.

The results for *sparsely populated* areas stand out from the cost curves according to population density. The unit cost will rise especially rapidly when the USO content is defined more narrowly. This is because in sparsely populated areas the daily delivery route covered dominates costs. Nevertheless, the unit cost caused by the USO is independent of population density, if the content of the universal service is more broadly defined.[7]

The cost curves in Figure 13.4 can also be interpreted as unit cost comparisons depending on which cost-allocation principle is applied. The principles discussed in Section 3 can be considered extreme cases: the significance of the USO could be taken into consideration in relation to the extent to which it generates real expenditure; and costs could be allocated to all products delivered according to their volume. The cost curve for densely populated areas in Figure 13.4 is close to this volume-based cost allocation. The volume-based approach rests on the concept that delivery route length costs in densely populated areas are marginal (4 percent), whereas in the sparsely populated areas delivery route length costs tend to be dominant (44 percent). Since only 2 percent of Finland's surface area is densely populated, concentration on volume-based cost allocation is inappropriate in the case of those postal service operators subject to the USO, for whom the USO also applies in the less densely populated areas.

6 CONCLUSIONS

Our chapter shows that the five-day-delivery obligation leads to a high fixed cost share of total delivery costs, irrespective of how broadly or narrowly the USO is defined. Nearly 60 percent of the delivery total costs are fixed and only 40 percent are volume variable. The fact that letters have to be delivered every working day and that the letter volumes are not well known beforehand results in standard working-time resource allocation and with it high fixed costs. According to the principle of causality, these fixed costs should properly be allocated to universal service products because the USO is the reason for these costs.

The five-day delivery obligation is itself unnecessarily strict as most users of letter services no longer require this level of service. One result of this is that letter senders are shifting their service use from overnight to the slower two- or three-day service on their own initiative. Consequently in Finland the volume of 1st class letters has fallen by one-third in 10 years. This is because the need for overnight service has diminished, since urgent messages are now transferred electronically. As late as 2001 about 70–80 percent of letter senders and recipients expected their letters to be delivered within one working day (Elkelä et al., 2001a and b). By the time the next study was published in 2010, the share of the overnight service requirement had dropped to 20 percent (Elkelä, 2010a and b).

In 2010, a digital delivery experiment was carried out in the country village of Anttila, 50km from Helsinki. Letter recipients were asked for permission to allow their letters to be digitized, so that they would receive them the following day through the Internet. During this time there were only two weekly paper letter deliveries. Consumer satisfaction with this service was very high. Twice weekly traditional deliveries fulfilled their expectations and many villagers could not even understand the need for the digitized versions of their letters (Kuusisto and Niemelä, 2010).

The second most important single factor in the cost structure of postal deliveries is the length of the delivery routes. Its effect is largely dependent on population density: the denser the population, the smaller the share of route length costs. Its significance in the delivery cost structure is so central, because the share of fixed costs decreases as population density grows. At the same time the significance of the volumes to be delivered in relation to expenditure increases.

From the point of view of unit cost, in defining the content of the USO the critical factor is the retention of bulk letter mail. When the content of the USO is narrower than bulk letters, unit cost increases significantly. However, when the USO includes bulk letters, broader definitions of the USO no longer lead to significant decreases in unit cost.

Population density is a central factor that affects the unit cost resulting from the USO. When population density is high, the effect of the route length on unit costs is only a few percentage points, and volume starts to dominate delivery costs. However, in sparsely populated areas the significance of route length on delivery costs is crucial.

USO cost-allocation practices seem to be developing in different directions and vary from one EU member state to another. Since cost-allocation practices have impacts on pricing and on delivery competition, there is a need to create a common European-level practice for cost allocation which properly takes into consideration the different conditions in different countries. Several stakeholders should be involved: regulators, operators, and legislative bodies.

In addition, the benefits of five-day versus six-day physical home delivery in the most sparsely populated areas need to be considered. It is not at all clear how long the citizens of densely populated areas would be willing to continue to subsidize the added expenditure that this would incur. This is now a topical issue when there are many electronic alternatives available as substitutes for paper communication. Paper mail could be delivered to the most sparsely populated areas only two or three times per week and on other days it could be retrieved, for example, from the municipal center, if desired. It is particularly important to define a reasonable 'light USO' for sparsely populated areas. The criteria could be, for example, the distance from a population center, the distance between delivery points or the distance of extra branches from the main delivery routes. Before the volumes of paper mail diminish to a third or half of the present amount, the possibility of a USO which would require only two deliveries per week should be seriously debated.

As was stated in Leskinen et al. (2009), restricting the pricing of a postal undertaking in the future is not a well-founded proposition in a situation in which letter messaging is, from the point of view of the customer, only one way of sending a message. It will be possible for a postal undertaking to adapt to changes in demand only if postal operations are guaranteed equal, innovative and, most of all, flexible conditions under competition. We have earlier argued that the scope of the USO should be defined to the minimum level needed by consumers and small and medium-sized enterprises. Now the present study has demonstrated that in order to restrain the costs of the USO, a narrow product definition of the USO will not be enough on its own, since the crucial element is delivery density! To cope with differences in delivery density in a country such as Finland will require a fundamental rethinking of the USO itself. An important element of this from the point of view of postal operators will be understanding the cost causation principles underlying the allocation of delivery costs to USO and non-USO services.

NOTES

* The views expressed in this chapter are those of the authors and do not necessarily reflect the views of Itella Corporation.

1. Directive 2008/6/EC of the European Parliament and of the Council amending Directive 97/67/EC with regard to the full accomplishment of the internal market of Community postal services, 'Postal Directive'.
2. CERP Recommendation on Best Practices for Cost Accounting Rules III, Draft 2009.
3. 2001/354/EC: Commission Decision of 20 March 2001 relating to a proceeding under Article 82 of the EC Treaty (Case COMP/35.141 – Deutsche Post AG).
4. Buigues (2006, Section 4.3).
5. This section is based on Nikali and Elkelä (2010).
6. 'Delivery' is defined here as daily delivery of letter mail and other postal deliveries, that is, basic delivery. Although Itella is also responsible for early morning delivery of newspapers in Finland, this process is totally separate from the basic delivery, and it does not belong to the sphere of the use of resources being considered here.
7. The various USO 'definitions' are based on the study Dieke et al. (2009): Basic letters = single-piece posted letters; Bulk letters = letters posted in large quantities; Non-priority letters = other than the above-mentioned letters; Periodicals = newspapers and magazines; Direct mail = addressed advertising mail.

REFERENCES

Buigues, P.-A. (2006), 'Competition policy versus sector-specific regulation in network industries – the EU experience', submitted to UNCTAD's Seventh Session of the Intergovernmental Group of Experts on Competition Law and Policy, Geneva, 30 October–2 November.

Dieke, A., J. Campbell Jr, N. Angenendt and G. Müller (2009), 'The role of regulators in a more competitive postal market', WIK-Consult, Bad Honnef, September.

Elkelä, K. (2010a), 'Kirjeen asiakasterve kuluttajilla', Helsinki: Finland Post Corp., Research Publications 5/2010.

Elkelä, K. (2010b), 'Kirjeen asiakasterve PK-yrityksissä', Helsinki: Finland Post Corp., Research Publications 11/2010.

Elkelä, K., K. Jakosuo and H. Nikali (2001a), 'Kotitalouksien viestinvälitystarpeet 2001', Helsinki: Finland Post Corp., Research Publications 19/2001.

Elkelä, K., K. Jakosuo and H. Nikali (2001b), 'Organisaatioiden viestinvälitystarpeet 2001', Helsinki: Finland Post Corp., Research Publications 20/2001.

Kuusisto, O. and M. Niemelä (2010), 'Jakelu 2.0 – postinjakelukokeilu Porvoon Anttilassa. Kokemukset ja palaute lomakekyselyn pohjalta', Espoo: Technical Research Centre of Finland (VTT), October.

Leskinen, P., P. Karlsson, H. Nikali and P. Rokkanen (2009), 'How should regulation be adjusted when universal service substitution grows?', in M.A. Crew and P.R. Kleindorfer (eds), *Progress in the Competitive Agenda in the Postal and Delivery Sector*, Cheltenham, UK and Northampton, MA, USA: Edward Elgar, pp. 263–79.

Nikali, H. and K. Elkelä (2010), 'Delivery resource models 2009: allocation of the postal basic delivery resources to the fixed one and volume-based costs with the help of econometric models', Helsinki: Finland Post Corp., Research Publications 52/2010.

14. Price-cap regulation in the postal sector: single versus multiple baskets*

Claire Borsenberger[†], Sébastien Bréville[‡], Helmuth Cremer[§], Philippe De Donder[¶] and Denis Joram[††]

1 INTRODUCTION

Starting in the mid-1980s, many incumbents have become subject to price caps. Roughly speaking, a price cap defines an average price level not to be exceeded by the operator. The operator is otherwise free to adjust the relative prices of its different products. Price-cap regulation is an extreme form of incentive regulation which provides powerful incentives for cost reduction. The system is also intended to reduce political interference in the setting of individual prices and the resulting price flexibility may also enable incumbent operators to become more business oriented. While their average price is capped by the regulator, they could adjust the prices of their different products to reflect costs, elasticity of demand, complementarities between segments, and competitive pressure.

In the postal sector, price-cap schemes are by now widely used. However, in reality their design differs, often significantly, from the idealized policy just described. In particular, regulators very often are tempted to add additional constraints limiting price variations of so-called 'sub-baskets'. This is justified by the need to offer special protection to some groups of customers who for a variety of reasons may receive an extra weight in the regulator's objective. For instance, the regulator may want to restrict the increase in single-piece rates. In addition, it is sometimes argued that sub-baskets may restrict the incumbent's ability to engage in anticompetitive behavior (for example, 'squeezing' competitors' markups).

In this chapter, we examine the design of price-cap schemes in the postal sector. In particular, we analyze whether or not it is appropriate to impose sub-baskets. First, we analyze a setting where some customers (or products) receive an extra weight in the regulator's objective and study to what extent this provides an argument for the imposition of extra constraints. The literature has shown that a global price cap can be used to decentralize Ramsey prices (which maximize unweighted surplus). We show that this result can be generalized in a variety of directions including welfare weights and the

[†] Economist, European and National Regulation Division, La Poste.
[‡] Economist, European and National Regulation Division, La Poste.
[§] Professor of Economics, IDEI, Toulouse School of Economics.
[¶] Professor of Economics, IDEI, Toulouse School of Economics.
[††] Chief Economist, European and National Regulation Division, La Poste.

presence of competition. Second, we examine the role of demand uncertainty, which is a major feature in today's postal markets. Sub-baskets introduce *ex ante* constraints on the pricing structure, which can prevent the operator from abusing market power in some states of nature. On the other hand, they reduce the possibility *ex post* to adapt relative prices to the realized structure of demand. We show that while the overall effect appears to be ambiguous, a number of arguments argue against the imposition of sub-baskets. In particular, we show that *ex ante* constraints tend to increase the overall price level.

The analysis thus leads to similar conclusions and argues in favor of a price cap with a single basket. In other words, the constraint caps the (appropriately weighted) *average* price of all the regulated products. In either case, we restrict ourselves to a simple model to represent the main effects and tradeoffs involved. In particular, we assume for notational convenience that the operator sells only two products and we ignore dynamic issues (multi-period tradeoffs). The generality of our results will be discussed in detail below.

The remainder of this chapter is organized as follows. Section 2 studies the impact of welfare weights on Ramsey prices and on their decentralization through a price cap. Section 3 examines the effect of demand uncertainty. Finally, Section 4 concludes.

2 REDISTRIBUTION AND WELFARE WEIGHTS

In regulation models (and more generally in the industrial economics literature), welfare is often measured by total surplus. This approach relies on a number of implicit or explicit assumptions (such as the quasi-linearity of preferences). Most significantly, it also assumes that the regulator is concerned with efficiency only. This simple setting is most useful to address many of the relevant issues. However, in reality, issues of redistribution, fairness or equity are omnipresent in the regulatory debate. In this section, we study how such a concern for redistribution affects the design of price-cap regulation. To do so, we assume that the regulator maximizes a weighted sum of individual utilities (surpluses). Specifically, the consumers of some type of product receive a larger weight. This relies on a very stylized view of the postal sector. There are two postal products (say, single piece and bulk mail) and two types of customers (say, households and firms). Households consume single-piece mail while firms send bulk mail. For some reason, the welfare function puts a larger weight on households than on firms so that the regulator will be particularly concerned about the single-piece rate. We examine whether this concerns requires a specific regulation of each price or whether a price-cap specifying the average price level is sufficient.

The Regulator's Problem

There are two postal products, single-piece mail x, consumed by individuals of type h, and z, bulk mail, consumed by type f customers. Let $V_h(x)$ and $V_f(z)$ denote the consumers' utilities, while the demand functions are denoted $x(p_x)$ and $z(p_z)$. Marginal costs of both products are constant and given by c_x and c_z. In addition, the single operator has a fixed cost F. Assume that the regulator maximizes a weighted sum of the customers' utilities (putting a higher weight on type h individuals) subject to the operator breaking even:

$$\max_{p_x, p_z, \lambda} (1 + \beta) V_h[x(p_x)] + V_f[z(p_z)] + (1 + \lambda)[(p_x - c_x)x(p_x) + (p_z - c_z)z(p_z) - F], \tag{14.1}$$

where $\beta \geq 0$ represents the extra weight attached to type h individuals and λ the Lagrange multiplier of the operator's break-even constraint.

Differentiating (14.1) with respect to p_x and p_z and rearranging the first-order conditions, we obtain the following expressions for the optimal prices p_x^* and p_z^*:

$$\frac{p_x^* - c_x}{p_x^*} = \frac{(\lambda^* - \beta)}{(1 + \lambda^*)} \frac{1}{\varepsilon_x}, \tag{14.2}$$

$$\frac{p_z^* - c_z}{p_z^*} = \frac{\lambda^*}{(1 + \lambda^*)} \frac{1}{\varepsilon_z}, \tag{14.3}$$

where ε_x and ε_z denote the absolute values of the demand elasticities.

These expressions reflect both efficiency and equity considerations. Like in the pure efficiency Ramsey pricing problem, we obtain inverse elasticity rules.[1] Equations (14.2) and (14.3) show how the prices are affected by the welfare weights. Not surprisingly, a higher level of β tends to reduce the price of the product consumed by households. Observe that when β is sufficiently large, it may be optimal to set p_x below marginal cost.

Pricing of the Operator under Price-cap Regulation

In the previous subsection, we have assumed that the regulator has full control and directly sets all the operator's prices. We now show that this solution can be *decentralized* through a price-cap regulation that restricts solely the 'average' level of *all* prices. In other words, a profit-maximizing operator submitted to the appropriate price-cap constraint 'spontaneously' sets the socially optimal levels of all prices. There is no need to use multiple baskets for which separate constraints are imposed. This property is well known for the standard Ramsey case where the regulator is concerned with efficiency only and does not use any welfare weights.[2] The appropriate price-cap constraint states that the *weighted* average of all the prices does not exceed a certain threshold. Observe that the weights are *exogenous* from the operator's perspective. Specifically, the Ramsey solution is achieved when the weight attached to the price of a given commodity in the price-cap formula corresponds to the socially *optimal* quantity of the commodity (that is, the quantity that solves the regulator's problem).[3] We shall now show that this result continues to apply in the case considered in the previous subsection where welfare weights are used. The argument we present is inspired by Billette de Villemeur et al. (2002) who obtain similar results in a different context.

Assume that the postal operator is subject to the following price-cap constraint,

$$\alpha_x p_x + \alpha_z p_z \leq \bar{p}, \tag{14.4}$$

where α_x and α_y are exogenous weights while $\bar{p}$ is a constant. A profit-maximizing operator then solves the following problem:

$$\max_{p_x, p_z, \mu} (p_x - c_x)x(p_x) + (p_z - c_z)z(p_z) - F - \mu(\alpha_x p_x + \alpha_z p_z - \bar{p}). \tag{14.5}$$

Differentiating (14.5) with respect to p_x and p_z and rearranging the first-order conditions yields the following expressions for the optimal prices $\tilde{p}_x$ and $\tilde{p}_z$:

$$\frac{\tilde{p}_x - c_x}{\tilde{p}_x} = \left(1 - \frac{\alpha_x \tilde{\mu}}{x}\right)\frac{1}{\varepsilon_x} \tag{14.6}$$

$$\frac{\tilde{p}_z - c_z}{\tilde{p}_x} = \left(1 - \frac{\alpha_z \tilde{\mu}}{z}\right)\frac{1}{\varepsilon_z}. \tag{14.7}$$

Recall that these prices are optimal from the operator's perspective (solution to (14.5)). One can expect these prices $\tilde{p}_x$ and $\tilde{p}_z$ to differ in general from the socially optimal prices p^*_x and p^*_z determined by (14.2) and (14.3). However, $\tilde{p}_x$ and $\tilde{p}_z$ depend on the weights α_x and α_z of the commodities in the price-cap formula. When these weights are set in an appropriate way, one can have $\tilde{p}_x = p^*_x$ and $\tilde{p}_z = p^*_z$. In other words, a profit-maximizing monopolistic operator will spontaneously choose the socially optimal prices provided of course that the weights are set at their appropriate levels.

To establish this result formally, define:

$$\alpha_x = (1 + \beta)x^*, \tag{14.8}$$

$$\alpha_z = z^*, \tag{14.9}$$

$$\bar{p} = \alpha_x p^*_x + \alpha_z p^*_z. \tag{14.10}$$

It is then sufficient to compare (14.2)–(14.3) and (14.6)–(14.7) to show that $\tilde{p}_x = p^*_x$, $\tilde{p}_z = p^*_z$, while $\tilde{\mu} = 1/(1 + \lambda^*)$.[4]

When $\beta = 0$ we have a standard (pure efficiency) Ramsey pricing problem, which is decentralized by using the optimal quantities as weights in the price-cap formula. When good x receives a larger weight in the welfare function, the weight in the price-cap formula has to be multiplied by the same factor (namely, $1 + \beta$).

To implement this outcome directly the regulator has to know that optimal quantities. However, this solution can also be achieved in a more indirect way through an iterative procedure *à la* Vogelsang and Finsinger (1979).[5] The idea is to set the weight of the goods in period t respectively equal to $\alpha^t_x = (1 + \beta)x^{t-1}$ and $\alpha^t_z = z^{t-1}$. In words, the weight in period t is equal to the quantity produced in the previous period times the welfare weight ($1 + \beta$ for x and 1 for z).[6] This algorithm works provided that the managers of the operator take the weights in any given period as given. In other words, they are myopic in the sense that they do not take into account the impact of their choice and the future design of regulation.[7]

While we have established this result in this simple setting, it reflects effectively a very general property. It depends neither on the separability of demand nor on the assumption that each individual only consumes a single product. The result also generalizes to the situation where the regulated firm is not a monopoly but competes with other operators. In either case, the appropriate weight of a product is given by the (partial) derivative of welfare with respect to its price (evaluated at the optimum solution).[8] In the Ramsey case, the derivative of welfare with respect to p_x is equal to x^*.[9] With the welfare function defined in (14.1), the derivative is $(1 + \beta)x^*$. With more general preferences and/or under competition, the expressions will be more complicated, but the basic rule determining the optimal weight remains the same. In all cases, the single price-cap constraint is sufficient to decentralize the (socially) optimal pricing policy.

3 UNCERTAIN DEMAND

We now turn to the second aspect that may affect the design of price-cap regulation, namely demand uncertainty. The notion of pricing flexibility becomes most relevant when future demand is uncertain at the moment when the price-cap formula is determined. This argues for a single price-cap formula with no sub-baskets, which allows the operator to adapt the pricing structure to the realized demand conditions. However, there might also be the danger that this flexibility allows too much market power to the operator, allowing it to extract excess profits in some states of nature. Consequently, one can expect there to be a tradeoff between costs and benefits of flexibility.

We represent this tradeoff in a simple model. Consequently, we cannot expect general results (such as a property that one solution *always* dominates the other one). However, the simple model brings out the different effects that are at work and illustrates the factors which are relevant to determine the appropriate degree of flexibility.

Model of Price Caps under Uncertainty

Consider an operator who sells two products, indexed by $k = 1, 2$, whose demands, x_k, are given by:

$$x_k = \theta_k - p_k, \tag{14.11}$$

where θ_k is a random variable, while p_k denotes the price. Suppose that $\theta_k \in \{\theta_L, \theta_H\}$, where $\theta_L < \theta_H$, and where both realizations have the same probability of 1/2.[10] In words, demand can be low or high in each of the markets (which yields a total of four possible combinations). Observe that demand shocks affect only the intercept of the demand function and not its slope. Let $\bar{\theta} = E(\theta) = (\theta_L + \theta_H)/2$ denote the expected level of θ. Assume that θ_ks are distributed independently. Marginal production costs are constant and normalized to zero. There is a (joint) fixed cost, F, which is independent of demand uncertainty. Using the demand functions (14.11), one easily derives the following expression for consumer surplus, CS, total surplus, TS, and profits, π:

$$CS = \sum_k \frac{(\theta_k - p_k)^2}{2}, \tag{14.12}$$

$$TS = \sum_k \frac{(\theta_k - p_k)^2}{2} + \pi, \tag{14.13}$$

$$\pi = \sum_k p_k(\theta_k - p_k) - F. \tag{14.14}$$

Maximizing (14.14) with respect to p_k yields the (profit-maximizing) monopoly price $p_k^M = \theta_k/2$. The corresponding level of total profits is given by:

$$\pi^M = (\theta_1/2)^2 + (\theta_2/2)^2 - F. \tag{14.15}$$

Observe for future reference that the monopoly profit is positive in the worst state of nature ($\theta_1 = \theta_2 = \theta_L$) if and only if $2(\theta_L/2)^2 > F$.

We consider two methods of regulatory pricing. The first procedure, referred to as 'administered prices', is to set both prices *ex ante*, while the second one is to impose a price cap specifying the average price *ex ante*, while letting the operator choose the price structure *ex post*. In other words, the operator sets both prices once demand is known, but has to respect the price-cap constraint (imposed *ex ante*). We can think about the first procedure as a price cap with sub-baskets, while the second one corresponds to a price cap with a single basket.

We shall now successively examine these two solutions. In both cases, the regulatory policy is chosen *ex ante* and subject to the constraint that the operator's expected profits are zero, that is $E(\pi) = 0$. Consequently, (14.12)–(14.14) imply $E(TS) = E(CS)$ so that (expected) total surplus is measured by (expected) consumer surplus.

Administered Prices

The regulator maximizes expected surplus and sets both prices *ex ante* subject to the operator's (expected) break-even constraint $E(\pi) = 0$. With our symmetry assumptions, the solution to this problem is very simple. Demand and costs conditions for both products are identical *ex ante*. Consequently, it is plain that their prices should be equal and we have $p_1 = p_2 = p^*$. This price level is obtained by setting the expected value of (14.14) equal to zero and by taking the smallest root of this quadratic equation:

$$2p^*(\bar{\theta} - p^*) = F. \tag{14.16}$$

Using equations (14.12)–(14.14) one can determine the corresponding levels of welfare $E(ST) = E(SC)$ which is given by:[11]

$$W^{ap} = (\bar{\theta} - p^*)^2 + \frac{(\theta_2 - \theta_1)^2}{4}. \tag{14.17}$$

Price Cap

Suppose now that the regulator imposes a price cap defined by:

$$\frac{p_1 + p_2}{2} \leq \bar{p}, \tag{14.18}$$

where $\bar{p}$ is determined to ensure $E(\pi) = 0$. In this formula both products obtain the same weight, which is the optimal policy given the symmetry of the problem. The operator sets p_1 and p_2 *ex post* to maximize profits subject to (14.18). Depending on the realizations of demand, four different configurations can arise (two of which being equivalent). To determine the expected welfare achieved under the price-cap regime, we have to determine the price set by the operator in the following three situations:

- *Case 1*: $\theta_1 = \theta_L$ and $\theta_2 = \theta_L$ This is the most unfavorable state of nature, in which demand is low in both markets. It occurs with a probability of 1/4. The operator then chooses:

$$p_1 = p_2 = \min\left(\frac{\theta_L}{2}, \bar{p}\right). \tag{14.19}$$

  Given the symmetry of the demand realizations, the operator sets the same price in both markets. This price can either be equal to the monopoly price (under low demand), namely $\theta_L/2$, or set at the price ceiling $\bar{p}$ (whichever of these two prices is lower). In other words, it is possible that the price cap set *ex ante* by the regulator is effectively larger than the monopoly price under low demand. This will happen when the revenue under low demand $(2(\theta_L/2)^2)$ is significantly lower than the fixed cost, so that large losses are incurred in this case.[12]
- *Case 2*: $\theta_1 = \theta_H$ and $\theta_2 = \theta_H$ This is the most favorable case, for which demand is high in both markets (and occurs with probability 1/4). Once again, it follows from the symmetry of the problem that the operator sets the same price in both markets. It follows immediately that this price is equal to the price-cap level:

$$p_1 = p_2 = \bar{p}, \tag{14.20}$$

  as long as $\bar{p} < \theta_H/2$, which necessarily holds when $\bar{p}$ is set to ensure $E(\pi) = 0$.[13]
- *Case 3*: $\theta_1 = \theta_L$ and $\theta_2 = \theta_H$ or $\theta_1 = \theta_H$ and $\theta_2 = \theta_L$ In words, demand is low for one good and high for the other. Given the symmetry of our problem, these two cases are equivalent and this configuration thus occurs with a probability of 1/2. The operator now chooses different prices for the two products. Maximizing the operator's profit (14.14) subject to the price cap (14.18) yields:

$$p_k = \bar{p} + \frac{\theta_k - \bar{\theta}}{2}. \tag{14.21}$$

  Not surprisingly, the price is an increasing function of θ_k so that it will be larger in the market with high demand than in the market with low demand. Welfare in this case is given by

$$W^{LH} = (\bar{\theta} - \bar{p})^2 + \frac{9(\theta_2 - \theta_1)^2}{64}. \tag{14.22}$$

  Using (14.22) along with the welfare levels implied by the prices defined by (14.19) and (14.20) and weighting with the respective probabilities, one can then determine the level of expected welfare associated with the price-cap policy, W^{pc}. As illustrated in the next section, this welfare level can then be compared with the level of welfare achieved in the administered prices regime, namely W^{ap} given by equation (14.17).

While these welfare comparisons are complex, expression (14.21) suggests that the increased flexibility the operator enjoys in the price-cap regime may in fact also benefit the customers. Indeed, it shows that prices better reflect demand conditions than under the other policy; they are higher when demand is high and lower when demand is low, and this is what an efficient pricing policy calls for. Furthermore, one obtains an unambiguous analytical result comparing the expected price level under the two policies. A simple argument shows that $\bar{p} \leq p^*$.[14] In other words, the larger flexibility allows break-even (coverage of fixed costs) with a smaller expected price level.

We now turn to the numerical illustration which shows that the (single-basket) price-cap policy can effectively yield a higher welfare while pointing out more clearly than the analytical expression how this result comes about.

Numerical Example

Let $\theta_L = 5, \theta_H = 15$ and $F = 50$. Solving the break-even constraint (14.16) yields $p^* = 5$ (as unique root). With this price, one easily calculates consumer surplus in the different states of nature: 0 for *LL*, 100 for *HH* and 50 for *LH* or *HL*. Consequently, expected surplus is given by $(0 + 100 + 2*50)/4 = 50$; this value can also be directly obtained from (14.17).

Computations are more involved for the case of a price cap. Using the various expressions derived in previous subsection, one can determine first that $\bar{p} = 3.2$ yields $E(\pi) = 0$. This confirms the result that $\bar{p} < p^*$. With all prices above marginal cost, a lower expected price opens the door to the possibility of having a larger surplus under a price cap. Observe that we have $\bar{p} > \theta_L/2 = 2.5$ (monopoly price with low demand *LL*). In words, when the demand is low in both markets, the operator will want to set both prices below the price cap (so that the constraint is effectively not binding).

With simple numerical calculations, one can then determine the level of consumer surplus in the different states of nature: 6.25 for *LL*, 139.3 for *HH* and 52.5 for *LH* and *HL*. Consequently, the expected surplus is given by $(6.25 + 139.3 + 2*52.5)/4 = 62.67$ which is effectively higher than the expected surplus achieved when prices are set *ex ante* (namely 50). The results of this numerical illustration are summarized in Table 14.1.

This finding confirms the conjecture suggested by the analytical results presented in the previous subsection, namely that the expected welfare (consumer surplus) may be higher under a price cap with a single basket than when sub-baskets are imposed *ex ante.* Indeed, in the case presented in Table 14.1, the price-cap regime gives a higher welfare (total surplus) in *all* states of nature. Furthermore, the example helps us understand why this result emerges. The single price cap has two advantages. First, the average price is smaller (recall that this is a general property). Second, the price can be adapted to reflect demand conditions. While this is always true, this may or may not be welfare enhancing in all possible states of nature. In our example, it turns out that the enhanced flexibility effectively benefits consumers in all states of nature; see Table 14.1. Observe that because $\bar{p} = 3.2 > \theta_L/2 = 2.5$, the expected price under the price-cap regime (namely 3) is effectively below $\bar{p}$. This property will occur whenever the monopoly price in the least favorable state of nature for the operator is below the price cap.

Table 14.1 Allocations in the different states of nature under the price cap (with $\bar{p} = 3.2$) and administered prices regime

Price cap								
Scenario	p_1	p_2	x_1	x_2	CS_1	CS_2	π	TS
LL	2.5	2.5	2.5	2.5	3.1	3.1	–37.5	–31.3
HH	3.2	3.2	11.8	11.8	69.7	69.7	25.5	164.8
LH	0.7	5.7	4.3	9.3	9.3	43.3	6.0	58.5
Expected	3.0	3.0	7.0	7.0	31.3	31.3	0.0	62.6

Administered prices							
Scenario	$p^*=p_1=p_2$	x_1	x_2	CS_1	CS_2	π	TS
LL	5.0	0.0	0.0	0.0	0.0	–50.0	–50.0
HH	5.0	10.0	10.0	50.0	50.0	50.0	150.0
LH	5.0	0.0	10.0	0.0	50.0	0.0	50.0
Expected	5.0	5.0	5.0	25.0	25.0	0.0	50.0

4 CONCLUSION

We have examined the design of price-cap schemes in the postal sector and have analyzed whether or not it is appropriate to impose 'sub-baskets'. The imposition of such sub-baskets is sometimes justified by considerations of redistribution and the concern to 'protect' certain groups of customers. Accordingly, we have first looked at a setting where some customers (or products) receive an extra weight in the regulator's objective. We have shown that the socially optimal price structure can be *decentralized* through a price-cap regulation that restricts solely the 'average' level of *all* prices. The appropriate price-cap constraint states that the *weighted* average of all the prices does not exceed a certain threshold. While we have obtained this result in a simple setting, we have argued that the decentralization result, as well as the basic rule determining the optimal weight, remains the same with more general preferences and/or under competition. In all cases, the single price-cap constraint is sufficient to decentralize the (socially) optimal pricing policy. Formally, achieving this result requires that the regulator know the socially optimal quantities, but we also showed that the Vogelsang–Finsinger iterative approach can be used to converge to these optimal quantities, subject to the usual assumption of non-strategic behavior on the part of the regulated firm.

Second, we have examined the role of demand uncertainty. In this context, sub-baskets introduce *ex ante* constraints on the pricing structure which can prevent the operator from abusing market power in some states of nature. However, they reduce the possibility *ex post* to adapt relative prices to the realized structure of demand. We have shown that while the overall effect appears to be ambiguous, a number of arguments plead against the imposition of sub-baskets. In particular, we have shown that *ex ante* constraints tend to increase the overall price level. Furthermore, they may prevent the price from being adapted to demand conditions.

The two settings thus lead to similar conclusions and argue in favor of a price cap with a single basket. In other words, the constraint should cap the (appropriately weighted) *average* price of all regulated products.

NOTES

* We thank our discussants Michael MacClancy and John Panzar and for their constructive and helpful comments. We are also grateful to Michael Crew and Paul Kleindorfer for their insightful remarks and suggestions.

1. The elasticity determines the 'deadweight loss' of the implicit tax (markup over marginal cost) imposed on the good.
2. See Laffont and Tirole (2000, p. 67).
3. When the optimal quantity is not known, the same result can be achieved through an iterative procedure under which the price in period t is weighted by the quantity sold in period t–1; see Vogelsang and Finsinger (1979).
4. The weights defined by (14.8) and (14.9) generally do not add up to one. However, this is just a matter of normalization. To ensure that the sum of the weights equals one, it is sufficient to divide both sides of (14.4) by $(\alpha_x + \alpha_z)$.
5. We thank John Panzar for bringing this property to our attention.
6. The price cap $\bar{p}$ is set so that $\bar{p}^t = \alpha_x^t p_x^{t-1} + \alpha_z^t p_z^{t-1}$.
7. The proof of this property follows directly from the proof of Proposition 1 in Vogelsang and Finsinger (1979). To accommodate the welfare weights one simply has to realize that the gradient of welfare (denoted grad $W(p)$ in their proof) is now equal to the vector of quantities multiplied by the respective welfare weights. This follows from Roy's identity and the property that with quasi-linear preferences the marginal utility of income is equal to one.
8. It is plain that the result remains valid when there is a competitive fringe. Under imperfect competition the Ramsey problem is more complex because the other operator's equilibrium prices are affected by the regulated operator's prices. This problem is studied, for instance, by Ware and Winter (1986) under various assumptions regarding the strategic interaction between operators (Stackelberg or Nash). One can easily show that their expressions can be decentralized by a price-cap regulation with suitably designed weights. However, it is an open question at this point whether one can design an iterative procedure that converges to these weights.
9. To see this, recall the discussion in note 7.
10. This specification is inspired by Laffont and Tirole (2000, pp. 93–4). They introduce the demand functions (14.11) to study the impact of asymmetric information pertaining to the demand level. In their setting, θ_L applies to one product and θ_H to the other. That is, demand levels are observed by the operator but not by the regulator.
11. Since we provide numerical illustrations below, we shall refrain from reporting a full set of analytical expressions. Some of them are quite lengthy and their inspection is not very insightful.
12. When the maximum profit with low demand in both markets is positive $(2(\theta_L/2)^2 > F)$, we necessarily have $\bar{p} < \theta_L/2$. However, in the opposite case $(2(\theta_L/2)^2 < F)$, we can have $\bar{p} > \theta_L/2$.
13. A price cap exceeding the monopoly price in the most favorable demand condition $(\bar{p} > \theta_H/2)$ would be a completely empty constraint that is never binding.
14. By definition, p^* implies $E(\pi) = 0$. When $\bar{p} = p^*$, the operator has the option to set the price $\bar{p}$ in all states of nature (and realize a profit of zero). As our various pricing expressions show, this is of course not the optimal policy. By adopting this optimal policy, the operator can then realize a strictly positive profit. Consequently, to achieve $E(\pi) = 0$, $\bar{p}$ can be set below p^*.

REFERENCES

Billette de Villemeur, É., H. Cremer, B. Roy and J. Toledano (2002), 'Pricing and worksharing discounts in the postal sector', in M.A. Crew and P.R. Kleindorfer (eds), *Postal and Delivery Services: Delivering on Competition*, Boston, MA: Kluwer Academic Publishers, pp. 33–48.

Laffont, J.-J. and J. Tirole (2000), *Competition in Telecommunications*, Cambridge, MA: MIT Press.

Vogelsang, I. and J. Finsinger (1979), 'Regulatory adjustment process for optimal pricing of multiproduct firm', *Bell Journal of Economics*, **10**, 157–71.
Ware, R. and R. Winter (1986), 'Public pricing under imperfect competition', *International Journal of Industrial Organization*, **4**, 87–97.

15. Optimal pricing of mail in the transactional market and welfare for the wider communications market*

Philippe De Donder[†], Helmuth Cremer[‡], Paul Dudley[§] and Frank Rodriguez[¶]

1 INTRODUCTION

The traditional bulk-mail market can be thought of as serving business communication needs with other businesses and customers, and includes transactional and advertising mail, as distinct from single-piece mail. Through transactional mail the sender is able to meet its obligation of providing information to the recipient (examples including bank statements and utility invoices). However, transactional mail can also be seen as one of several alternative media for financial institutions to communicate to their customers. Within this wider communications market, the financial institutions can and have started to develop internal profit centers in Europe to charge for their transactional activities. Such centers may form only one part of financial institutions' overall profits and are investigated alongside the need for the universal service provider (USP) to break even and therefore within a wider communications market than just the mail market (but not within an even wider context of the financial institutions' overall profits).

In recent years mail volumes have declined within single-piece (SP) mail and bulk mail (BM) and while this is in part a consequence of the economic downturn, it is also due to the substitution of mail by other communication media. SP mail has been replaced by texting and email; advertising or direct mail (DM) has been replaced by alternative electronic communication; and transactional or non-direct mail (NDM) has been replaced by statements and invoices conveyed by email or over the Internet. Our particular focus is on the senders of NDM-transactional items from financial institutions (which we subsequently refer to as 'banks') sending statements.

Following on from previous literature relating to optimal pricing within a global price cap and pricing (Billette de Villemeur et al., 2002, 2003; De Donder et al., 2006, 2008), in De Donder et al. (2011a) we developed a model to look at how a monopoly USP can enhance welfare and break even if it can differentiate between the prices it charges for DM and NDM, where the demand functions for the two segments differ as represented

[†] Professor of Economics, Toulouse School of Economics (IDEI & GREMAQ-CNRS).
[‡] Professor of Economics, Toulouse School of Economics (IDEI & GREMAQ).
[§] Head of Regulatory Economics, Royal Mail Group.
[¶] Associate, Oxera.

by distinct price elasticities, but the marginal costs of the mailings are the same. We then introduced competition from another medium within the DM advertising segment, and from postal entrants accessing the USP's network downstream and calibrated the model to derive illustrative results in terms of welfare and pricing where the DM and NDM price elasticities are assumed to differ, in line with empirical evidence. In De Donder et al. (2011b) we extended this analysis by looking at the optimal pricing and welfare implications, under alternative pricing conditions introduced by business strategies or regulatory constraints, for the USP and entrants. In these papers, and calibrated illustrations reflective of the postal sector, the NDM contributed significantly to the recovery of the fixed costs of meeting the Universal Service Obligation, through differential pricing between NDM and DM by the USP.

In this chapter we look at the effects on welfare and pricing of introducing an electronic alternative to the USP's NDM service. We proceed with the economic model developed in De Donder et al. (2011a and 2011b), with independent mail segments for SP, DM and NDM and alternative media competing with DM and NDM. We focus attention on representative senders of NDM, or banks, who are charged an input price by suppliers for the provision of transactional services and charge a final price to their customers, for mail and the alternative medium. Our focus throughout is on the impact of an alternative medium to NDM on pricing and economic welfare and so, for ease of exposition and unlike De Donder et al. (2011a and 2011b), we do not introduce the possibility of entrants into the postal market. While such an extension would be quite feasible, we consider that it would complicate our results without adding much to the insights gained from the development of our earlier model.

In our initial analysis we assume that a social planner sets the input (producer) and final (consumer) prices to maximize welfare. Subsequently we analyze the results assuming that the banks profit maximize within their profit centers for statements in setting their consumer prices in the NDM transactional segment. We assume that bank customers switch on price not only between paper and electronic statements but also between banks – with the social planner then setting other prices for postal products to maximize welfare. Finally, we consider the consequences of a binding price cap on the USP's SP price within the main calibrations and some sensitivity analysis.

In Section 2 we summarize the model. In Section 3 we describe the model calibration used. We show the results of our analysis when the social planner sets all prices in Section 4 and then in Section 5 when the social planner sets only the USP prices and the banks set their prices to maximize profit within their profit centers for statements. In Section 6 we conclude.

2 THE MODEL

The USP provides both SP mail and BM. We consider two types of the latter: DM and NDM. The demands for the three types of mail (SP, DM and NDM) are assumed to be independent from one another.

The USP has a de facto monopoly on SP mail and faces the demand function $x(p^x)$, where x stands for SP mail quantity and p^x for its unit price. Both types of BM face competition from alternative media. We start by describing the market for DM. We denote by z^I the quantity of DM sold by the USP, and by p^z_I its unit price. DM faces the competition of an alternative medium whose unit price is p^z_A and total quantity z_A. Both types of goods are imperfect substitutes, so that the demand for the USP's DM is given by $z_I(p^z_I, p^z_A)$ while the demand for the alternative medium is $z_A(p^z_I, p^z_A)$.

NDM is transactional mail, and is sold by the USP to intermediaries or banks. These banks make use of this product to send information to their final clients. They also use alternative electronic media. Banks buy NDM from the USP at a unit price of p^y_I, and alternative medium at a unit price of p^y_A (which may be nil). Banks then sell both forms of transactional media to their own final customers, at consumer prices equal to q^y_I for mail, and q^y_A for the electronic form. Final customers decide how much of these two imperfect substitutes they want to buy. The demand for the USP's NDM is given by $y_I(q^z_I, q^z_A)$ while the demand for the electronic alternative to NDM is $y_A(q^z_I, q^z_A)$.[1]

The USP faces a fixed cost of F, and constant marginal upstream (collection, sorting) and downstream (delivery) costs of, respectively, c_x and d_x for SP and c_I and d_I for (the two types of) BM. The unit cost of the alternative medium to DM is denoted by c^z, and for the electronic alternative to NDM by c^y.

To sum up, the profit function of the USP is given by:

$$\Pi_I = (p_x - c_x - d_x)x(p_x) + (p^z_I - c_I - d_I)z_I(p^z_I, p^z_A) + (p^y_I - c_I - d_I)y_I(q^y_I, q^y_A) - F,$$

while the profit function for the transactional services of a bank (as a representative sender of NDM) is given by:

$$\Pi_B = (q^y_I - p^y_I)y_I(q^y_I, q^y_A) + (q^y_A - p^y_A)y_A(q^y_I, q^y_A).$$

In Section 4, the social planner sets all producer and consumer prices to maximize welfare. In Section 5, banks choose their profit-maximizing consumer prices (q^y_I, q^y_A) as a function of (p^y_I, p^y_A), and the planner anticipates this move when setting its prices. Moreover, we make explicit that the extent to which banks are able to charge a markup over these input costs when pricing transactional media depends on the degree of competition in the banking sector, measured by the number of banks. We attain this objective by modeling the market for transactional media as a Cournot game between n banks (see Appendix 15A). Since the modeling of the whole banking sector is beyond the scope of this chapter, we take a partial equilibrium approach, assuming that all (price and non-price) determinants of the demand for transactional media used by banks are exogenously set and constant, so that we concentrate on how (q^y_I, q^y_A) affects this demand. In all cases, we impose the condition that the USP breaks even.

3 CALIBRATION

Both our model and initial calibrations are the same as those of De Donder et al. (2011a and 2011b), which applied linear demand functions and commenced from a monopoly USP. The assumptions are not from a particular postal operator, but are reflective, in our view, of the general nature of postal markets and cost structures found in published empirical studies.

As in our previous studies in De Donder et al. (2011a and 2011b) we commence from the hypothetical situation where the USP faces no competition. The USP sets a price p^x of €0.50 for the SP product and a price of €0.40 for DM (p_I^z) and NDM (p_I^y). Total quantities sold at those prices are $x = 2$ billion, $z_I = 2$ billion and $y_I = 6$ billion items, respectively. The direct own-price elasticities are –0.2 for SP, –1.0 for DM and –0.2 for NDM.[2] We calibrate linear demands based on these quantities, prices and elasticities.

We need further information to calibrate the demand functions for DM and NDM products when one alternative medium competes with DM and another alternative medium competes with NDM. We use two types of information: the extent of entry for different price configurations and the substitutability between the products within the DM advertising segment and the NDM transactional segment (which ultimately includes the products of the USP and an alternative medium in both market segments). For DM, we define the measurement unit for the alternative medium such that one 'item' of alternative medium refers to the quantity of this medium that is necessary to have the same response rate as one item of DM.[3] We then assume that the alternative medium's market share is 25 percent if 50 percent cheaper than the USP and 35 percent if 75 percent cheaper than the USP. For NDM, we assume that one item of the alternative medium corresponds to one item of mail. We do not have data to calibrate the switching between the USP and alternative medium and so illustrate by reference to the prices to final customers, q_I^y and q_A^y, such that the alternative medium's market share is 20 percent if q_I^y and q_A^y are both zero (for example, if the banks do not charge for the mail or Internet item) and 40 percent when q_I^y = €0.40 and q_A^y is zero (for example, if the banks charge the initial calibrated price of the USP for each mail item and zero for each item of the alternative electronic medium). On substitution, we assume the displacement ratio of mail transferring to the alternative medium in NDM or DM is 0.9.[4] Thereby, the USP products and alternative medium are assumed to be imperfect substitutes.

The USP unit upstream cost is equal to €0.18 for SP (c^x) and €0.12 (c^I) for the mail items in DM and NDM.[5] The USP delivery cost is €0.12 for all mail items ($d^x = d^I$). Hence the end-to-end unit costs are the same for the USP's mail products in DM and NDM. The value of the fixed costs, F, equals €1.680 billion so that the USP breaks even in the hypothetical monopoly situation (without any alternative media). We assume the cost of the alternative medium for DM, c^z, is €0.20 per item and, for simplicity, zero for NDM (c^y).

These assumptions determine the linear demand functions and costs for the calibrated model consistent with the analytical presentation in this chapter.

4 RESULTS WHEN THE SOCIAL PLANNER SETS ALL OF THE PRICES

We set out below the results of the calibrated model, starting with the case developed in De Donder et al. (2011b) with an alternative medium introduced for DM but without an NDM alternative medium. In Table 15.1 we show the results where the social planner is assumed to set all of the producer and consumer prices to maximize welfare subject to the USP breaking even and discuss this further below.

Table 15.1 Calibrated results for the USP without and then with an NDM alternative medium

			With NDM medium alternative		
		Differentiated NDM/DM prices, without NDM medium alternative	Second-best outcome, with additional constraint of $p_I^y = q_I^y$	Second-best outcome, with a bank's non-negative profit constraint	Second-best outcome, with a bank's zero profit constraint, with greater market share held by alternative medium
Prices (€)					
SP	p^x	0.539	0.670	0.558	0.656
NDM – Mail – USP	p_I^y	0.431	0.455	0.498	0.596
NDM – Mail – Banks	q_I^y	–	0.455	0.405	0.321
NDM – Medium – Alternative	p_A^y	–	0.000	0.000	0.000
NDM – Medium – Banks	q_A^y	–	0.230	0.219	0.181
DM – Mail – USP	p_I^z	0.274	0.274	0.272	0.272
DM – Medium – Alternative	p_A^z	0.200	0.200	0.200	0.200
Quantities (bn)					
SP	x	1.969	1.864	1.953	1.875
NDM – Mail – USP	y_I	5.907	4.051	4.255	2.631
DM – Mail – USP	z_I	2.383	2.255	2.398	2.400
Sub-total		10.259	8.170	8.606	6.906
NDM – Medium	y_A	–	1.983	1.917	4.008
DM – Medium	z_A	0.272	0.309	0.268	0.268
Total		10.531	10.462	10.791	11.182
Contribution to fixed cost – USP (€bn)					
SP		0.470	0.690	0.504	0.667
NDM		1.128	0.870	1.099	0.936
DM		0.082	0.120	0.077	0.076
Total USP profit (€bn)		0.000	0.000	0.000	0.000
Medium – Alternative		–	–	–	–
Bank		–	0.456	0.000	0.000
Sum of profits (€bn)		0.000	0.456	0.000	0.000
Consumer surplus (€bn)					
SP		2.423	2.171	2.385	2.198
NDM		5.816	6.364	6.616	10.463
DM		0.708	0.664	0.713	0.714
Total		8.947	9.199	9.714	13.376
Welfare (€bn)		8.947	9.654	9.714	13.376
Lagrange multiplier		0.107	0.189	0.099	0.098

USP with Different Prices in DM and NDM and Competition to DM from an Alternative Medium

The first column of figures in Table 15.1 reflects the results shown in De Donder et al. (2011b) for the second-best (Ramsey) solution[6] with differentiated prices p_I^y and p_I^z and competition in DM from an alternative medium. The USP charges €0.539 for SP, €0.431 for NDM and €0.274 for DM with the price of the DM alternative medium assumed to be €0.200. The USP breaks even reasonably easily with a value for the Lagrange multiplier of the USP profit constraint of 0.107 and with the profit contributions of €0.470 billion for SP, €1.128 billion for NDM and €0.082 billion for DM offset by the fixed cost of €1.68 billion. The NDM product makes the largest single contribution to break even for the USP, and this is also reflected in it providing the most significant contribution to net consumer surplus. Consequently, NDM features prominently in the welfare analysis and financial position of the USP.

Competition to NDM from an Alternative Medium with Producer and Consumer Prices Equal for Mail

The second column of figures shows the second-best prices when there are alternative media to both DM and NDM, and the banks' consumer price (q_I^y) and the producer price (p_I^y) are the same in the mail segment of NDM (such that $q_I^y = p_I^y$). This is akin to a form of regulation on the banks that limits the resale price for mail to be the same as that charged to it by the USP. The SP price (p^x) and NDM prices (q_I^y, p_I^y) are higher (and DM prices are the same). The Lagrange multiplier of the USP break-even constraint is also higher at 0.189 as the introduction of the NDM alternative medium makes it more difficult for the USP to break even. Nevertheless the USP breaks even, the banks make a total profit of €0.456 billion, and both consumer surplus and welfare increase in the presence of the NDM alternative medium for our calibration.[7]

We also observe that, within the NDM segment, the consumer price, q_A^y (at €0.230), is more than the producer price, p_A^y (equal to the marginal cost at zero)[8], even though the selling of the NDM medium alternative does not bring revenue to the USP. The positive price of q_A^y is related to efficiency (since q_I^y is pushed above marginal cost in order to recover fixed costs, the planner also increases q_A^y in order not to distort too much the choice between goods y_I and y_A), so that the social planner marks up the marginal costs when setting consumer prices for both NDM and the NDM alternative medium.

In addition to the results shown in Table 15.1, we also considered the effect of an additional constraint where not only the banks' consumer price (q_I^y) and the producer price (p_I^y) are the same for NDM, but also the banks' consumer price (q_A^y) and the producer price (p_A^y) are the same for the NDM alternative medium. In this instance, the outcome is the same (as the second column of figures in Table 15.1) other than $p_A^y = q_A^y$ so that the banks make zero profit and the previous profit of €0.456 billion transfers to the provider of the NDM alternative medium.

Competition to NDM from an Alternative Medium with Break-even Constraint for the Representative Bank

The third column of figures shows the second-best prices when there are alternative media to both DM and NDM and where we lift the constraint that $p_I^y = q_I^y$ while ensuring that the banks' profits (as well as the USP's profit) are non-negative. For the banks to break even, the social planner sets prices so that the banks subsidize NDM (with q_I^y less than p_I^y) at the expense of the NDM alternative medium (with q_A^y more than p_A^y). Recall that p_I^y does not affect allocative efficiency, only the USP's financial position, and that p_A^y is not set by the USP but equals zero. In the first-best scenario, consumer prices equate to marginal cost, and p_I^y may be set at its marginal cost of €0.24. When the USP is required to break even, but the banks are not, p_I^y increases above q_I^y, with the latter remaining set at marginal cost.[9] When the banks and the USP are both required to break even, the banks profit from $q_A^y > p_A^y = 0$ and the social planner looks to reduce q_I^y to increase mail volumes and increase p_I^y to contribute to the USP's break-even with the banks' profit in the NDM alternative medium being offset by the banks' loss in NDM. The fact that $q_I^y < p_I^y$ while $q_A^y > p_A^y$ comes from the asymmetry between the two goods in terms of the USP break-even constraint – the USP is not involved in the selling of y_A so that it does not affect its break-even, while for y_I the social planner has an incentive to both lower the consumer price (q_I^y, to stimulate demand) and to increase the producer price (p_I^y) to increase the USP's per item revenue.

When compared to the second column of figures, the additional degree of freedom given to the USP allows it to increase the contribution of NDM towards recovering its fixed cost while decreasing both the prices for DM and SP; the constraint that p^x is not less than p_I^y + €0.06 is binding. The Lagrange multiplier is also lower at 0.099 as it is easier for the USP to break even. The banks can charge less for both their services in the NDM transactional segment and still break even, and the USP can charge more for its NDM service without reducing demand as this is determined by the banks' consumer price. Total volumes, consumer surplus and welfare all increase with the NDM medium alternative for our calibration.[10]

The fourth column of figures shows the second-best prices under the same assumptions other than that there is a greater preference and market share for the NDM alternative medium. We assume that the alternative medium's market share is 50 percent if q_I^y and q_A^y are both zero (for example, if the banks do not charge for the mail or Internet item) and 70 percent when q_I^y = €0.40 and q_A^y is zero (for example, if the banks charge the initial calibrated price of the USP for each mail item and zero for each item over the Internet). Comparing the fourth column with the third column of figures in Table 15.1, the USP's share of the NDM market segment falls from 69 percent to 40 percent as demand transfers to the alternative medium. The social planner increases USP prices p^x and p_I^y, and reduces q_I^y such that the banks make a greater loss in NDM. However, this loss is offset by a lower price and greater volume in the NDM alternative medium. While the SP consumer surplus reduces with the rise in SP price, the consumer surplus for the NDM transactional segment increases with the reductions in consumer prices and the change in calibration. There are relatively small changes in DM advertising such that its consumer surplus remains largely unaffected. Overall, the USP continues to break even and its ease in doing so remains similar to that with a lower market share for the alternative medium (with a Lagrange multiplier of 0.098). Hence, when the social planner sets the second-best prices within our calibrations and there is a greater preference and market share for the NDM alternative medium, it benefits customers in the NDM transactional segment at the expense of SP customers, with negligible effect on the USP's ability to reach break-even.

Implications When the Social Planner Sets All of the Prices

In each second-best case when the social planner sets all of the prices, the producer price for NDM exceeds that for DM, as was the case in De Donder et al. (2011b). Indeed, the presence of competition from an alternative medium increases the price differential between NDM and DM for the USP.

The consumer price for NDM (q_I^y) is also greater than its marginal cost, and the consumer price for the NDM alternative medium (q_A^y) also increases above its (zero) marginal costs. The market distortion in one good (from the markup over marginal costs for q_I^y due to the fixed cost associated with meeting the USO in the mail market) causes a market distortion in the price of substitute good q_A^y. Hence, for efficiency reasons, a value of q_I^y above marginal cost is accompanied by a value of q_A^y also above marginal cost in second-best settings – a result that is common to all the second-best cases considered in this chapter.

When the social planner sets the second-best prices to maximize welfare subject to the USP breaking even and the consumer and producer prices to be equal in NDM (in the second set of figures in Table 15.1), we observe that the banks make a profit and the USP has greater financial difficulties in the presence of the NDM medium alternative. However, when the social planner sets the second-best prices to maximize welfare (without constraining producer prices to equate to consumer prices) subject to the USP and banks breaking even (in the third and fourth set of figures in Table 15.1), the banks use their charge for the NDM alternative medium to subsidize their mail activity and enhance welfare – when the marginal cost of the alternative medium is sufficiently low (or, as we assume it to be zero) – and the USP finds it easier to break even because the lower consumer price increases volumes.

The second-best optimal prices without a constraint that consumer prices for NDM be equal to producer prices appear preferable to a resale price constraint in NDM (that is, $q_I^y = p_I^y$) not only in terms of welfare but also for the USP in terms of financial ease in break-even, within the calibrations used. Nevertheless it may not be feasible for a social planner to set all of these prices on behalf of the banks and the USP. Consequently in the next section we consider cases when the banks are able to set the consumer prices in order to profit maximize within their profit centers for statements.

5 RESULTS WHEN THE SOCIAL PLANNER SETS ONLY MAIL PRODUCT PRICES AND BANKS PROFIT MAXIMIZE

In our second set of results, in Table 15.2, we assume that the banks maximize profits within their profit centers for statements by setting of the consumer prices while the social planner anticipates this reaction when setting the prices for the postal products

Table 15.2 Calibrated results for the USP with an NDM alternative medium and profit maximizing of transactional statements by the banks

		Number of banks with original assumption of the market share held by alternative medium		Number of banks, with greater market share held by alternative medium	
		$n = 10$	$n =$ infinity	$n = 10$	$n =$ infinity
Prices (€)					
SP	p^x	0.884	0.818	1.082	1.047
NDM – Mail – USP	p_I^y	0.390	0.406	0.391	0.400
NDM – Mail – Banks	q_I^y	0.573	0.406	0.574	0.400
NDM – Medium – Alternative	p_A^y	0.000	0.000	0.000	0.000
NDM – Medium – Banks	q_A^y	0.243	0.000	0.367	0.000
DM – Mail – USP	p_I^z	0.324	0.315	0.353	0.348
DM – Medium – Alternative	p_A^z	0.200	0.200	0.200	0.200
Quantities (bn)					
SP	x	1.693	1.745	1.535	1.562
NDM – Mail – USP*	y_I	3.456	3.718	1.798	1.936
DM – Mail – USP	z_I	2.250	2.516	1.857	1.891
Sub-total		7.399	7.979	5.190	5.389
NDM – Medium	y_A	2.250	2.516	4.091	4.516
DM – Medium	z_A	0.368	0.350	0.422	0.413
Total		9.684	10.440	9.703	10.318
Contribution to fixed cost – USP (€bn)					
SP		0.989	0.905	1.200	1.167
NDM		0.519	0.617	0.271	0.309
DM		0.172	0.158	0.209	0.203
Total USP profit (€bn)		0.000	0.000	0.000	0.000
Medium – Alternative		–	–	–	–
Bank		1.178	0.000	1.830	0.000
Sum of profit (€bn)		1.178	0.000	1.830	0.000
Consumer surplus (€bn)					
SP		1.791	1.904	1.472	1.526
NDM		5.891	7.069	9.149	11.053
DM		0.598	0.618	0.542	0.552
Total		8.280	9.590	11.163	13.130
Welfare (€bn)		9.459	9.590	12.993	13.130
Lagrange multiplier		0.381	0.312	0.688	0.619

Note: * We report total quantities across the n banks, hence the uppercase symbols Y_I and Y_A (see Appendix 15A).

to maximize welfare. As discussed in Sections 2 and 3, we analyze banks as profit maximizers competing for the transactional services in a Cournot game and we assume that there are a number of n banks (of 10 or infinity) that set the consumer prices (q_I^y, q_A^y). We then consider the same model but with the addition of a price cap on the SP price.

Competition to NDM from an Alternative Medium with Cournot Pricing by the Banks

In the first two columns of Table 15.2 we show the results consistent with the original assumption of the market share held by an alternative medium. When the number of banks increases, the banks reduce their consumer prices (q_I^y, q_A^y) relative to their corresponding producer prices (p_I^y, p_A^y), and profit levels decrease to zero when the industry moves to a competitive fringe (n = infinity). Meanwhile, the social planner seeks to minimize the adverse effect on welfare of the banks' ability to charge a higher consumer price in mail (q_I^y) for lower n by reducing the producer price (p_I^y). The lower producer price (p_I^y) makes it more difficult for the USP to break even, and the value of the Lagrange multiplier of the USP break-even constraint and prices in SP and DM (p^x and p_I^z, respectively) increase.

We again observe, as in Section 4, that the consumer price for the NDM alternative medium (q_A^y) in each case is less than the consumer price for mail (q_I^y) and each is above their respective marginal costs. This is a feature of second-best outcomes when the revenue from selling one good (NDM) contributes towards recovering the USP fixed cost while the other (NDM alternative medium) does not.

The consumer prices (q_I^y and q_A^y) decrease as the banks' market power decreases with higher n and they apply a lower markup over marginal costs. For the alternative medium to NDM, the marginal cost is zero so that q_A^y decreases with higher n. For NDM, the banks' marginal cost (which equals producer price) p_I^y is controlled by the social planner. Anticipating a lower markup on q_I^y, the social planner sets a higher p_I^y (since there is less need to keep p_I^y low in order to prevent the banks from setting q_I^y too high). We then have a smaller markup on p_I^y and lower q_I^y as n increases. Hence the direct effect of a larger n (a smaller markup on the banks' marginal cost p_I^y) is greater than the indirect effect (the social planner reacts by increasing p_I^y), resulting in lower consumer prices q_I^y and q_A^y and enhanced welfare.

In fact, the social planner faces a conflict as it tries both to induce consumer prices q_I^y and q_A^y which do not distort too much the relative market shares between the two goods (for productive efficiency) and to drive the producer prices down towards marginal costs (for allocative efficiency). The consumer prices (q_I^y and q_A^y) diverge as the markups decline. When n is infinite (a competitive fringe), the banks have no market power, such that $q_I^y = p_I^y$ and $q_A^y = p_A^y$. The social planner controls p_I^y but not p_A^y, which is set exogenously (by banks' providers of electronic services) to zero (and p_A^z is set to €0.20). In this limit case, $q_A^y = 0$, while $q_I^y > 0$. The social planner would like to increase p_A^y from zero, increase p_I^y and decrease p^x. The large gap between q_A^y and q_I^y with a large n is then caused by q_A^y being constrained to be zero.

Hence, greater competition in the banking sector for transactional statements reduces the financial pressure on the USP and increases welfare in the presence of a NDM medium alternative. Conversely, markups and profit for the banks from transactional statements increase with lower n, and cause the USP greater financial pressures. While the USP charges lower prices for NDM, its prices for SP and DM increase and overall consumer surplus and welfare decrease.

In the final two columns of Table 15.2 (and as in Table 15.1), we show the impact of a greater preference by consumers and thus market share for the alternative medium.[11] The USP increases all its prices to recover its costs with the banks charging a similar price for mail (q_I^y), but a higher price for the alternative medium (q_A^y). While the USP breaks even, it has significantly greater difficulty in doing so. Meanwhile the banks raise greater profits at a lower n. Hence, when there is a greater preference and market share for the NDM alternative medium, this benefits the banks and NDM transactional customers at the expense of SP and DM advertising customers, and makes it more difficult for the USP to break even.

When compared to the results in Table 15.1, the profit-maximizing behavior of the banks causes the USP greater financial difficulty and the SP price rises. Consequently we consider the case where the USP's SP price p^x is capped at €0.75, and binding within our calibrations.

Competition to NDM from an Alternative Medium, with Cournot Pricing by the Banks and a Price Cap on SP Mail

When we introduce a price cap of €0.75 on p^x, the USP prices (p_I^y, p_I^z) and consumer price for NDM (q_I^y) increase, while the other prices (p_A^y, q_A^y and p_A^z) are unaffected. In fact, the cap on SP causes the consumer prices in both DM advertising and NDM transactional to increase, with the exception of q_A^y (which is a function of n and of p_A^y (= 0) only).

With the price cap on SP, the consumer prices q_A^y and q_I^y remain decreasing in n, but p_I^y decreases in n (whereas, as reported in Table 15.2, p_I^y increased in n without the cap on p^x). The price cap causes the USP greater financial difficulty in breaking even, as reflected in higher values of the Lagrange multiplier, and higher price p_I^y relative to those in Table 15.2. The social planner would still like to charge a lower p_I^y to offset higher consumer prices for lower n, but the need for the USP to break even overrides this and leads to increases in p_I^y relative to those in Table 15.2. We also observe that p_I^y rises more than p_I^z, because of the difference in price elasticity, thereby increasing the price differential between NDM and DM.

The increase in q_I^y leads to lower consumer surplus and welfare with the introduction of the cap on p^x. The price cap leads to an increase in consumer surplus for SP and reduction in consumer surplus for the NDM transactional and DM advertising segments. The net effect is a reduction in welfare which is greater where the cap acts as a more significant constraint; that is, when n is low.

When we extend this further and assume a greater preference and market share for the alternative medium,[12] the USP looks to increase all its prices but fails to break even for each n. The banks set higher consumer prices (q_I^y and q_A^y) to maintain a constant share for NDM on the NDM transactional segment and the scale of the banks profit exceeds the USP's loss for n in excess of 10, but less then infinity – raising the possibility of part of the banks' profit being used to help fund the USP's loss.

6 CONCLUSIONS

Financial institutions might look to make statement information profit centers for their businesses. While there are some social obstacles to implementing such an approach, with customers used to accessing information without any charge, the charging of statements is beginning and may continue. In this chapter we have looked at the implications of such institutions paying USPs and an alternative medium for the provision of such services, and recharging them to the customer.

Our focus has been on the NDM/transactional segment where there is imperfect competition between paper statements delivered by the USP and electronic statements provided by an electronic alternative. We have looked at this through an extension to the economic model of De Donder et al. (2011a and 2011b) by focusing on the welfare and pricing implications of imperfect competition between the USP and alternative media in NDM/transactional and DM advertising. In each case, the USP continues to differentiate the prices of its NDM and DM services to reflect different price elasticities assumed for the two markets.

In Section 4, we considered the case where a social planner sets the producer and consumer prices (other than those assumed to be constant) to maximize welfare. When only the USP is assumed to break even, the banks' activities might not be profitable. If the banks charge a resale price for paper statements equal to the producer price from the USP, then the banks might be profitable provided that the sale of their electronic statements is priced above its marginal cost. However, within our calibrations, it is welfare enhancing for the social planner to set consumer prices differing from producer prices and such that both the USP and banks break even. In this case the profits to the banks from the electronic statements subsidize a lower consumer price (stimulating growth) and a loss to the banks for paper statements.

Subsequently, in Section 5, we considered the case where the banks profit maximize in setting their consumer prices in the NDM/transactional market – using markups of producer prices (p_I^y, p_A^y) to consumer prices (q_I^y, q_A^y) determined by the degree of competition assumed for the n banks' transactional services – with the social planner then setting other prices for postal products to maximize welfare. In the absence of any price cap on SP, the USP is able to break even, within our calibrations, but with lower consumer surplus and welfare than before. In the presence of a price cap on SP, the USP is under greater financial pressure and not able to break even when the calibrations are amended to reflect a greater preference and market share for the electronic medium, while the banks make substantial profits from charging their customers for transactional services. In such circumstances, where banks charge their customers for transactional services and rely on the USP's network for provision of their mail services and there is a public policy objective to limit the price of SP, part of the banks' profit from transactional statements might be used to help fund the deficit to the USP.

We conclude that the introduction of an alternative medium for NDM, in addition to DM, has the potential to enhance welfare, if the USP and banks' profit centers relating to statements could be regulated to break even. Alternatively, if the banks profit maximize their profit centers for statements, then it might lead to increased financial pressure on the USP, and particularly so if there is either a binding price-cap regulation on the USP or significant changes in customer behavior in switching to an electronic medium.

This could result in the USP being unable to break even, at which point some means of funding the universal service provision would need to be considered. Within our model, there is no scope to raise funds through charging postal entrants, but there could be scope to raise funds through general taxation, taxation on the banks' relevant profit centers from transactional statements or through charges for the alternative electronic medium – though not currently envisaged within the current (Third) European Postal Services Directive. This brings to the fore the consideration of public policy and the balance of choices between the consumer demand for the universal service and associated fixed costs of the USP, the incentives and profit-maximizing behavior of the banks and the consumer demand for and development of the alternative electronic medium.

NOTES

* The analysis contained in this chapter reflects the view of the authors and may not necessarily be those of Royal Mail Group.

1. The demand for transactional media is actually a derived demand, since transactional media are used as inputs by banks. As explained below in the text, we assume that all determinants of this demand other than transactional media prices are held constant, so that we can concentrate on how the demand for transactional media is affected by the price of NDM and its electronic substitutes.
2. These values are broadly in line, as approximations, with the empirical literature in this area (see, for example, Cazals et al., 2011).
3. So, if the alternative medium is email, and if the response rate of prospective customers to email is, say, 20 times less than for DM, then one item of alternative medium corresponds to 20 emails.
4. This means that nine out of ten items of the alternative medium are displaced BM mail (either DM or NDM as relevant) from the USP, while one in ten are additional volumes created in the sector.
5. We add a price constraint that p^x is not less than p_I^y + €0.06.
6. This corresponds to the prices which maximize total welfare in the economy (measured as the sum of consumer surpluses and firms' profits) under the constraint that the USP breaks even. See De Donder et al. (2011b) for the formal statement.
7. Alternative pricing constraints relating to y could be applied such that $q_I^y = q_A^y$ or $q_A^y = p_A^y$, where the banks make negative profit, or $p_I^y = p_A^y (= 0)$ where y_I is close to zero within the calibrations. Hence these alternatives are not pursued further.
8. An increase in the producer price, p_A^y, transfers the profit of the banks to the provider of the NDM medium alternative when in the range $(0, q_A^y)$. Hence the level of the producer price of the alternative medium in NDM only has a distributional effect in allocating the total profit between the banks and provider of the alternative medium.
9. If the only constraint were rather for the banks to break even, we would get $p_I^y < q_I^y$.
10. We also considered the effect of an increase in the marginal cost of the alternative medium in NDM above zero. This makes it more difficult for the banks to break even. Consequently, the banks increase their consumer prices. The USP also increases its prices as the total volumes fall and it finds it more difficult to break even.
11. The alternative medium's market share is 50 percent if q_I^y and q_A^y are both zero (for example, if the banks do not charge for the mail or Internet item) and 70 percent when q_I^y = €0.40 and q_A^y is zero.
12. See note 11.

REFERENCES

Billette de Villemeur, É., H. Cremer, B. Roy and J. Toledano (2002), 'Access and (non)-uniform pricing in the postal sector', in M.A. Crew and P.R. Kleindorfer (eds), *Competition Transformation of the Postal and Delivery Sector*, Boston, MA: Kluwer Academic Publishers, pp. 43–68.

Billette de Villemeur, É., H. Cremer, B. Roy and J. Toledano (2003), 'Pricing and worksharing discounts in the postal sector', in M.A. Crew and P.R. Kleindorfer (eds), *Postal and Delivery Services: Delivering on Competition*, Boston, MA: Kluwer Academic Publishers, pp. 43–68.

Cazals, C., J. Florens, L. Veruete-McKay, F. Rodriguez and S. Soteri (2011), 'UK letter mail demand: a content-based time series analysis using overlapping market survey statistical techniques', in M.A. Crew and P.R. Kleindorfer (eds), *Reinventing the Postal Sector in the Electronic Age*, Cheltenham, UK and Northampton, MA, USA: Edward Elgar, pp. 91–108.

De Donder, Ph., H. Cremer, P. Dudley and F. Rodriguez (2006), 'A welfare analysis of price controls with end-to-end mail and access services', in M.A. Crew and P.R. Kleindorfer (eds), *Liberalization of the Postal and Delivery Sector*, Cheltenham, UK and Northampton, MA, USA: Edward Elgar, pp. 307–26.

De Donder, Ph., H. Cremer, P. Dudley and F. Rodriguez (2008), 'Pricing, welfare and organizational constraints for postal operators', in M.A. Crew and P.R. Kleindorfer (eds), *Competition and Regulation in the Postal and Delivery Sector*, Cheltenham, UK and Northampton, MA, USA: Edward Elgar, pp. 150–66.

De Donder, Ph., H. Cremer, P. Dudley and F. Rodriguez (2011a), 'Welfare and pricing of mail in a communications market', *Review of Network Economics*, **10** (3).

De Donder, Ph., H. Cremer, P. Dudley and F. Rodriguez (2011b), 'Optimal pricing for mail and welfare implications in a communications market', in M.A. Crew and P.R. Kleindorfer (eds), *Reinventing the Postal Sector in the Electronic Age*, Cheltenham, UK and Northampton, MA, USA: Edward Elgar, pp. 73–90.

APPENDIX 15A COURNOT COMPETITION BETWEEN BANKS

In Section 5, we consider the following two-stage procedure. In the first stage, the USP chooses optimally the producer prices p^x, p_I^y, p_I^z. In the second stage, n banks compete *à la* Cournot – that is, each bank simultaneously sets its quantity (of both NDM mail and its alternative medium) in order to maximize its profit, given the quantities chosen by the other $n - 1$ firms. Observe that this implies that some final consumers switch from one bank to another when transactional media prices vary between banks. As usual, we solve the game by backward induction – that is, we assume that the USP perfectly anticipates the Cournot game result when setting its optimal prices.

To model this situation, we proceed to the following change of notation: there are n identical banks, and each bank is represented by the index $i = 1, 2, \ldots, n$. We denote by y_I^i (resp., y_A^i) the quantity of NDM (resp., of alternative medium) sold by bank i. We denote by Y_I (resp., Y_A) the total quantity of NDM (resp., of alternative medium) sold by the n banks, that is:

$$Y_I = \sum_{i=1}^{n} y_I^i \text{ and } Y_A = \sum_{i=1}^{n} y_A^i .$$

The inverse demand function for these two goods is then given by:

$$q_I^y(Y_I, Y_A) \text{ and } q_A^y(Y_I, Y_A).$$

The profit of bank i is given by:

$$\pi_B^i = [q_I^y(Y_I, Y_A) - p_I^y]y_I^i + [q_A^y(Y_I, Y_A) - p_A^y]y_A^i,$$

with total banks' profit given by $\Pi_B = \Sigma_{i=1}^{n}\pi_B^i$ and the equilibrium of the Cournot game solving:

$$\max_{y_I^i, y_A^i} \pi_B^i \text{ for all } i = 1, 2, \ldots, n.$$

Finally, note that, since we have assumed identical banks, we have that $Y_I = ny_I^i$ and $Y_A = ny_A^i$ (that is, each bank sells the same amount of NDM and of its alternative medium).

16. A market study of packets and parcels services*

Stephen Gibson[†] and Nancy Race[‡]

1 INTRODUCTION

Market studies are widely used by UK economic regulators[1] to assess the need for regulatory intervention and to support their regulatory proposals. Conducting a market study of the postal sector was one of the key recommendations of the independent review of the UK postal services sector (the Hooper Review).[2] Postcomm has undertaken a series of market studies[3] of the different markets in which Royal Mail is active as part of its work to establish the new regulatory framework to be in place from April 2012. This is (to the authors' best knowledge) the first market study to be undertaken of any postal market and was a major two-year exercise utilizing a significant body of internal and external evidence and analysis. The packets and parcels services[4] (PPS) market study is part of this wider study which includes wholesale and retail Letter and Large Letter markets and international mail markets. The overall objective is to inform the setting of appropriate regulation by: (a) formally defining a set of relevant markets and (b) determining the extent of Royal Mail's market power in these markets.

This chapter is organized as follows. Section 2 sets out the analytical framework and evidence base used in the market study. Section 3 sets out the analysis of market definition in the PPS market. Section 4 sets out the market power analysis. Section 5 sets out the regulatory consequences of the market definition and market power findings. Section 6 sets out the conclusions.

2 ANALYTICAL FRAMEWORK AND EVIDENCE BASE

Analytical Framework

The market definition analysis is based on the hypothetical monopolist framework or SSNIP test (Small but Significant Non-transitory Increase in Price). A market is defined as the smallest set of products for which a hypothetical monopolist could profitably raise its prices by 5–10 percent above the competitive level on a permanent basis. This methodology is well established and used by regulators and competition authorities in anticompetitive investigations and merger references and considers both demand- and

[†] Chief Economist, Postcomm.
[‡] Principal, Economic Policy, Postcomm.

supply-side substitution effects.[5] Markets are also defined on a geographic basis using the same framework of whether demand- or supply-side substitution from a wider geographic area would constrain prices in the narrower area. It is, however, likely to be more difficult to define markets where they have been subject to regulation, in particular price-control remedies.

Demand-side substitution refers to the extent to which customers would change their consumption following an increase in the price of one product either switching to alternative products or ceasing buying the product. Supply-side substitution refers to the extent to which suppliers would switch production in response to a change in relative prices. For example, if in response to a 5–10 percent price increase of Product A, providers of Product B quickly began providing Product A to an extent that made the price increase in Product A unprofitable, then Product A and Product B should be included in the same market. An additional consideration is whether there is a common pricing constraint across customers, services or areas such that they should be included within the same relevant market even if other indications of demand- and supply-side substitution are not present.

However, market definition is not an end in itself – it is an intermediate step in an assessment of whether a firm, in this case Royal Mail, has market power. The analysis therefore focuses on the competitive constraints imposed on the relevant services rather than whether a service lies just 'inside' or 'outside' a market. When assessing whether and to what extent market power exists, the market factors that prevent Royal Mail from profitably sustaining prices above competitive levels or restricting output or quality below competitive levels are considered, as well as Royal Mail's ability and incentive to harm the process of competition, for example, by weakening existing competitors, raising entry barriers or slowing innovation. This includes consideration of existing competition, the potential for competition, countervailing buyer power and the effects of regulation.

In order to avoid circular reasoning when assessing market power, the analysis seeks to consider as far as possible the situation without the elements of the regulatory regime which were put in place to address market power concerns. Stated another way, market power cannot be said to be absent from a market, if its absence is the result of regulation in place to protect against the exercise of market power.

Evidence Base

Postcomm collected a large amount of evidence for the PPS market study. This included structured interviews with 19 operators and over 90 customers providing qualitative and quantitative information. Frontier Economics undertook research on the wider market for parcels including non-postal alternatives[6] and used information from Postcomm's Business Customer Survey (an annual survey of over 800 business customers). Postcomm published a discussion document[7] and a detailed consultation[8] on the provisional conclusions, held workshops with interested parties and received substantial responses from 21 stakeholders. Royal Mail also provided a position paper on the fulfillment market[9] and a detailed market survey by Accent Marketing Research. Postcomm also considered reports from: Oxera, Triangle, Verdict, Freshminds, Datamonitor, Continental Research and IMRG.

3 MARKET DEFINITION

To define separate economic markets within the PPS sector, the main characteristics[10] which influence the price of the services were identified and these were used as the basis for determining whether to segment the sector into separate markets. These characteristics were: identity of the sending customer and method of collection, speed of delivery, average weight and total contract value.

Customer Segmentation

The market was segmented on the basis of the identity of the sending customer and method of collection: businesses – where operators collect directly from the business premises[11] (B2X); consumers – where operators collect directly from residential consumers[12] (C2X); and items sent by either businesses or consumers from a collection point, for example, a Post Office or pillar box (Y2X). Postcomm found that the distinction between receiving customers B2B (business to business) and B2C (business to consumer) is becoming blurred and many operators have the ability to serve both parts of the market delivering to business and residential addresses, therefore the market was not segmented further by receiving customers.

B2X and C2X were found to be in separate markets because on the demand side it would be unlikely for a customer to switch between these services on the basis of SSNIP price changes as these were volume dependent. On the supply side, an operator offering B2X services could not easily switch to C2X services and vice versa as this requires a separate and very different fleet and collection network serving customers with very different volumes and collection requirements. B2X and Y2X services were also considered separate as it would also require significant investment to set up a national collection network.

Customers of C2X services are likely to compare the price with the Y2X service and see them as reasonable substitutes before purchasing the C2X service. While the price of the Y2X service is generally available and the service is well known, this is not the case of C2X services which exhibit very low customer awareness. Moreover, the demand for these services is presently too small to have an impact on the price setting of Y2X services. There is therefore an asymmetric price restraint[13] from Y2X on C2X, but not vice versa.

Postcomm concluded that there are two market segments: Y2X/C2X and B2X. The Y2X/C2X market was not segmented further since this would not substantially affect the market power analysis. The B2X segment was analysed further to consider differences in competitive conditions across this segment.

Speed of Delivery

The European Commission[14] identified the express postal market as a separate market. This market is described as being different to the basic postal service owing to the 'value added' consisting of faster and more reliable collection, transportation and delivery of postal items than in the basic postal service and containing supplementary services for which customers are in principle prepared to pay a higher price.[15] Express delivery is typically same-day or overnight, time-certain[16] and includes a number of the following value-added services: proof of delivery, track and trace, possibility of changing destination or address in transit, desk-to-desk delivery, flexible billing and pricing, insurance and money-back guarantee. The Commission has noted a 'growing trend towards product segregation on the basis of time-frame concepts',[17] that is, a distinction between express and expedited parcel services in terms of time-certain as opposed to day-certain delivery.

Deferred (non-time-guaranteed) services are operationally sufficiently different to be in a separate market from Express services. Speed of delivery and quality of service requirements are driven by consumer preferences and are relatively insensitive to price. Postcomm therefore segmented the B2X market into Deferred and Express services based on whether they are time guaranteed or not. The question of whether further segmentation of the Express markets into Same Day and Next Day services is necessary was left open as it would not substantially affect the market power analysis.

The Deferred B2X market segment was analysed further to consider differences in the competitive conditions across this segment by item weight and customers' contract volumes.

Item Weight and Contract Volume

The key drivers affecting whether an alternative company can compete with Royal Mail are its own costs and Royal Mail's costs. Other end-to-end operators' pricing structures differ considerably from that of Royal Mail and are not in the main weight driven, but dependent on contract volume and volumetrics.[18] Royal Mail's and other operators' costs vary with both item weight and contract volume – heavier items are more likely to be delivered by van (which is more expensive) than by foot and there are economies of scale (particularly in collection) for higher volumes. Royal Mail's pricing structure is weight based and many customers purchasing decisions are driven by weight. Many customers multi-source their parcel service providers using Royal Mail and alternative operators generally separating their items by weight (sending lighter items by Royal Mail and heavier items by other operators).

PPS are largely a volume-driven business. High-volume contracts are more attractive to operators providing a significant proportion of the volume required to make networks viable. The level of competition and therefore the competitive pressure increases as volume increases (see Figure 16.1). There are also economies of scale involved with larger contracts, in particular in collection and administrative costs, as well as benefits to delivery drop density. Customers with higher-volume requirements also felt that they had more choice of operators although this also depended on the weight of their items with choice increasing with average packet weight. Evidence from alternative end-to-end operators also suggested that within the deferred PPS segment, they tended to carry traffic from mostly high-volume clients. Postcomm therefore concluded that both item weight and contract volume were important indicators determining the ability of other operators to compete with Royal Mail and the competitive conditions in the market.

Weight and Volume Break Point

For contracts above 2kg there are many operators who are able to compete, and Royal Mail only has a small market share (approximately 6 percent). Above 2kg, end-to-end

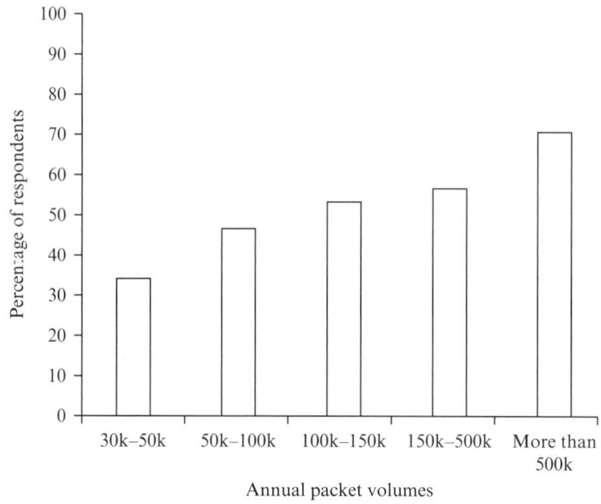

Source: Accent Survey.

Figure 16.1 Proportion of respondents that use another carrier as well as Royal Mail

operators and Royal Mail have similar costs as they both use a van-based distribution network and are able to compete head to head for contracts. For these reasons, Postcomm defined a separate economic market for deferred B2X PPS above 2kg (heavy market). Postcomm concluded that this market was competitive.

Below 500g there is little competition as other operators were unable to offer a competitive price for these items which were generally delivered by Royal Mail using a foot-based network. For contracts between 500g and 2kg, a number of different factors influence the extent to which operators are able to compete with Royal Mail. The analysis examined whether there was a break point in this weight range. From the demand side, consumer behavior including evidence of customer switching and multi-sourcing is consistent with competition and choice increasing at higher weights and volumes within this weight range. However, the evidence is not sufficiently robust to draw clear inferences about whether there is a break point in competitive conditions or where that break point might be. On the supply side, the relative cost economics of different business models is important because competition is more likely to be effective where Royal Mail and its end-to-end competitors have similar costs. The evidence from consumer behavior and Postcomm's analysis of operators' costs, suggests that there are greater levels of competition at higher weights and volumes. The evidence does not, however, indicate that there is a unique volume or weight break point at which the conditions of competition change significantly. Postcomm therefore concluded that it is appropriate to define a single market for all deferred B2X PPS up to 2kg (light market), while considering the different levels of competition in different segments of this market in the market power assessment and in setting appropriate regulatory safeguards.

Geographic Market Definition

Postcomm considered the differences in the geographic reach between different services and examined the delivery areas of 272 services offered by 16 operators. The vast majority (270) of these services offered delivery to the UK mainland of which 44 required a surcharge for remote locations and 71 did not offer a service to remote locations such as the Scottish Islands. Most of Royal Mail's packets and parcels services are part of the Universal Service Obligation (USO) and are delivered to every address in the UK for the same uniform price. This forms a common pricing constraint across geographic areas. Where common pricing constraints exist, the geographic areas in which they apply could be included within the same relevant market even if demand- and supply-side substitutes are not present. The other main operators also generally price on a national basis despite the absence of a regulatory obligation to do so. They have national delivery networks, and their sales and marketing advertises their services on a national rather than a local or regional basis. While some smaller operators only offer services on a local basis and some same-day operators restrict their delivery to specified urban areas, there was no evidence to suggest that the level of competitive constraint was sufficiently different to warrant defining local markets. Postcomm therefore concluded that all packets and parcels markets should be defined on a national (UK)-wide basis.

Summary of Market Definition

Postcomm therefore defined the following economic markets in the packets and parcels sector: Y2X/C2X – where items are collected either from a residence or dropped off at a collection point, such as a post office; B2X Express – where items are collected from a business address for a same-day or next-day guaranteed delivery; B2X Deferred Light – where items are collected from a business address for a non-guaranteed next-day or later delivery, where the items weigh up to 2kg; and B2X Deferred Heavy – where items are collected from a business address for a non-guaranteed next-day or later delivery, where the items weigh more than 2kg. All markets are national (UK)-wide, and are illustrated in Figure 16.2.

4 MARKET POWER

Postcomm's assessment of market power within the markets defined above was based on a number of indicators including: Royal Mail's market share (taking account of changes over time); barriers to entry, exit and expansion; customer characteristics; non-postal alternatives and the effects of the regulatory regime.

The C2X/Y2X Market

The C2X market is very small and customers have low awareness about the services offered and that they are alternatives to using a Y2X service. It is therefore unlikely to provide a significant constraint on Royal Mail's Y2X (pillar box and post office) services. While there are other operators offering Y2X services using, for example, newsagents and other

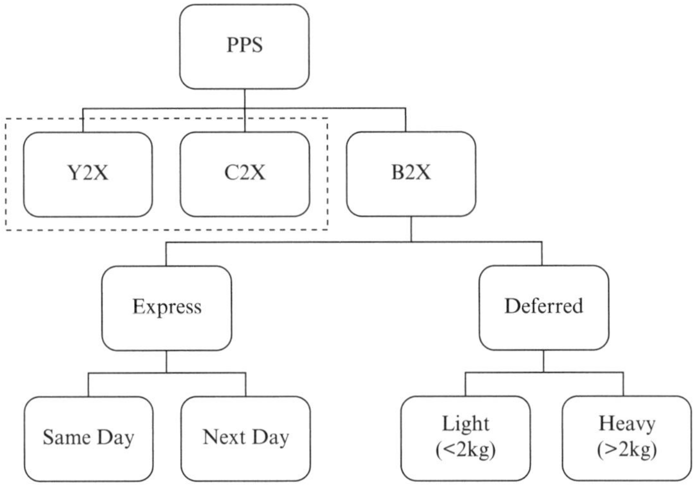

Notes:
B2X: Business to other (where the item is collected from the sender's premises).
C2X: Consumers to other (where the item is collected from the sender's residence).
Y2X: Business or consumer to other (where the item is sent from an access point, e.g., post office).
[dotted box] One market.

Figure 16.2 Summary of Postcomm's decision on PPS market definition

retailers as collection points, the small scale of their networks and low customer awareness of their services compared to Royal Mail's network of 11,820 post offices and over 115,000 pillar boxes led Postcomm to conclude that Royal Mail has market power in this market.

The Same-day and Next-day Express Market

Analysis by Datamonitor[19] of the Express market points to the market being competitive with no one company controlling over 15 percent of the market. Barriers to entry were seen as low at the local level but higher nationally, although entrants could reduce entry costs by leasing assets such as vehicles rather than purchasing them. Barriers to expansion were low as once a network is in place it would be relatively easy to expand through leasing additional assets or franchising. There was no indication of strategic barriers to entry, expansion or exit. Evidence of general customer awareness on the B2C sector suggests that business customers are aware of a range of different suppliers (see Figure 16.3) and regularly tender to obtain the best deals with low switching costs. Postcomm therefore concluded that the next-day and same-day Express markets were effectively competitive and that Royal Mail did not have market power.

The Deferred B2X Markets

Market-share estimates in the deferred B2X markets are based upon responses to regulatory information requests, data from operators' public accounts and information provided by individual operators during the market study and are set out in Table 16.1.

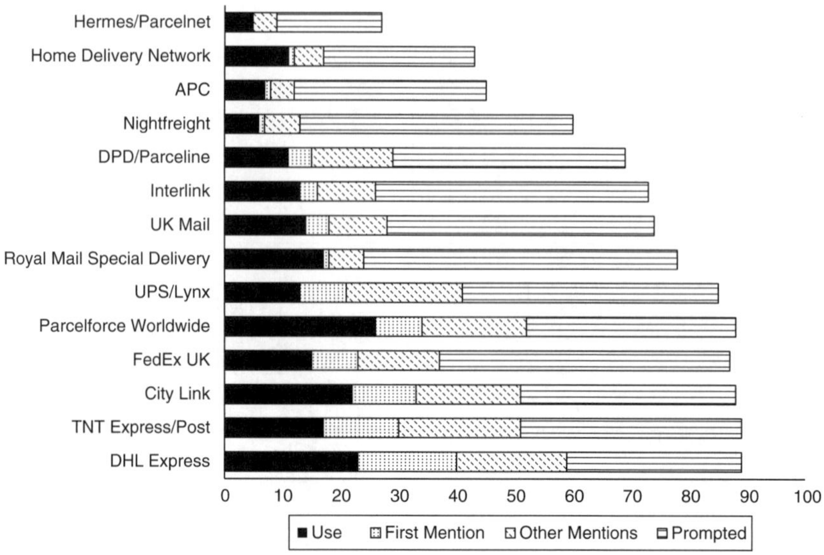

Source: Triangle (2009).

Figure 16.3 Business customer awareness of alternative suppliers

Table 16.1 Postcomm estimates of Royal Mail market shares in the deferred B2X market (2008–09)*

Deferred B2X market	Estimated total market revenue (£m)	Estimated Royal Mail market share (%)
Light (up to 2kg)	730	70
Heavy (above 2kg)	1,300	6

Note: * Excluding Parcelforce.

Source: Postcomm estimates based on Royal Mail data and public account information.

The Accent Survey[20] showed that 69 percent of customers, who typically send items above 2kg believe that they have a choice of operator, and 77 percent indicated that it is easy to switch between operators. In the Heavy market, other operators generally use a similar van-based business model to Royal Mail which does not rely on economies of density or drop in collection. While Royal Mail might enjoy some cost advantage in remote areas by virtue of its USO, Postcomm concluded that it does not have market power in the Heavy market.

Royal Mail is the largest operator in the Light market with an estimated market share of 70 percent. Royal Mail's principal competition comes from end-to-end operators. In the Light market, Royal Mail has an incumbency advantage in that it is the only PPS operator that has a nationwide foot-based delivery network. This allows it to obtain significant cost advantages over its end-to-end rivals, particularly for low-weight and

Table 16.2 Decision on market definition and market power in retail PPS markets

Segment	Market	Market power conclusions
C2X	C2X/Y2X	Market power
Y2X	C2X/Y2X	Market power
B2X Express	B2X Express Same Day	Competitive market
	B2X Express Next Day	Competitive market
B2X Deferred	B2X Deferred Light (<2Kg)	Market power, but increasingly competitive for higher weights
	B2X Deferred Heavy (>2Kg)	Competitive market

low-volume contracts, which enable it to offer more competitive prices. For example, the price of a 500g packet using Royal Mail's Second Class packet post service is £1.38, compared to £2.66 for Royal Mail's tracked product (which is a similar product to those provided by end-to-end competitors). While the cost advantage diminishes as weight and volume increase, this nevertheless provides an obstacle to end-to-end competitors providing effective competition in the Light market. The standard offering by end-to-end operators does not appear to be price competitive against Royal Mail up to 2kg, and many operators only contest very large volume contracts.

While there are only limited barriers to entry for an end-to-end operator using a van-based delivery network, there are very substantial sunk costs associated with attempting to replicate Royal Mail's foot-based delivery network. It is the latter that provides Royal Mail with its cost advantage over its rivals at lower weights and lower volumes. Entry barriers are therefore unlikely to be sufficiently low for the threat of entry to fully constrain the prices set by Royal Mail.

Postcomm's conclusions on market definition and market power in the packets and parcels markets defined above are summarized in Table 16.2.

Effectiveness of Competition within the Light Market

Within the Light market the analysis suggests that Royal Mail faces greater competition as weights and volumes increase. In particular, Royal Mail's unique foot-based delivery network provides it with a cost advantage over its end-to-end competitors at lower weights, but as weight and volumes increase, Royal Mail's competitive advantage progressively diminishes as shown in Figure 16.4.[21]

At weights above 2kg, it is generally economic for Royal Mail to switch from its foot-based to its van-based network. Royal Mail and end-to-end operators therefore have similar costs above 2kg. Between 1 and 2kg, the evidence suggests that van-based networks are likely to be less cost effective for low-volume contracts, and that end-to-end operators find it difficult to compete. However, for very high volumes (above 300,000 units per annum) the cost disadvantage is lower and end-to-end operators have won some market share.

Nevertheless, this developing competition is not fully effective in constraining Royal Mail's prices. The cost disadvantage faced by end-to-end competitors means that they have generally only been able to win market share though deep discounting or bundling

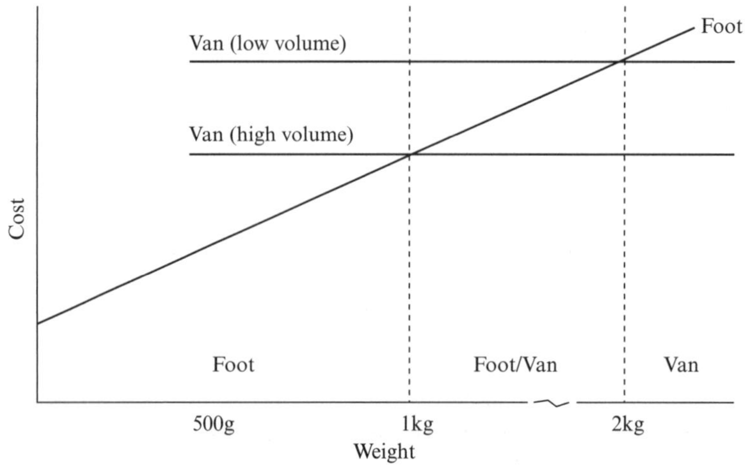

Figure 16.4 Indicative costs of foot-based and van-based networks

low-weight with high-weight items. Many customers multi-source, using Royal Mail's network for their lower-weight items (where Royal Mail's prices are lower for non-premium products).[22] As a consequence, Royal Mail retains a number of competitive advantages over its end-to-end rivals in the 1–2kg weight range. There is some evidence of end-to-end competitors competing for contracts down to as low as 150,000 units per annum in the 1–2kg weight range, however, they appear to have had very limited success in winning contracts at this level of volume, and the level of competition could be characterized as fragile.

In the 500g–1kg segment, Royal Mail's foot-based network is more efficient than those of its end-to-end competitors, with the possible exception of contracts with volumes in excess of 500,000 items per annum where competition is developing. Major end-to-end operators are winning limited amounts of business down to as low as 500g, despite an apparent cost disadvantage. This success has come mostly in the 300,000 to 500,000 volume range. This may be because customers are prepared to pay a premium for a 'one-stop shop' or, more generally have a preference for the quality of service provided by the end-to-end competitor. Alternatively, it may be that end-to-end competitors are prepared to price at, or even below, incremental cost in order to win contracts for higher-weight services or to engender customer loyalty. In either event, the evidence suggests strongly that such competition is both limited and fragile.

Below 500g the only competition Royal Mail faces is from access operators. To date, access operators have tended to focus on the Letters and Large Letters market with limited presence (less than 1 percent) in the PPS market.

Postcomm's analysis of the effectiveness of competition in different parts of the Light market is summarized in Figure 16.5. While Royal Mail has market power throughout the Light market, there is evidence of developing competition in the 1–2kg segment for contracts above 300,000 units per annum, and in the 500g–1kg segment above 500,000 units per annum. There is also some limited, fragile competition developing in the 1–2kg weight range for contracts between 150,000 to 300,000 units per annum, and in the 500g–1kg segment for contracts between 300,000 and 500,000 units per annum.

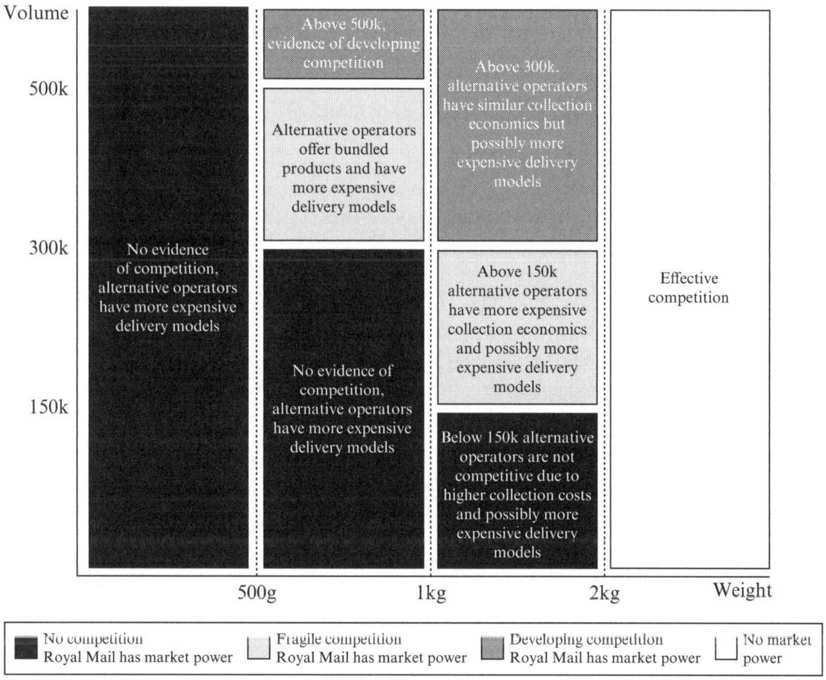

Figure 16.5 Summary of deferred PPS B2X market power assessment

5 REGULATORY CONSEQUENCES

Markets Where There Is No Market Power

Ex ante regulation (such as price-control constraints and obligations to notify and publish prices) are put in place to address concerns about the exercise of market power and to ensure the USO. Where Postcomm have determined that Royal Mail does not have market power (in the B2X Express and B2X Heavy Deferred markets), Postcomm proposed the removal of price and headroom controls and that notification and publication requirements be removed subject to a transition period while accounting separation was piloted as shown in Table 16.3.

Markets Where Competition Is Developing

Although Postcomm concluded that Royal Mail had market power for B2X Deferred services below 2kg, it recognized that the level of competitive constraint was higher for higher weights and volumes. It therefore sought to reflect the different levels of competitive constraint across this market in its regulatory proposals, while at the same time recognizing the practical consideration that imposing regulatory constraints that were based on size could be very complicated and difficult to implement in practice. Postcomm also considered that the regulatory concerns that might arise across this market varied: for higher

Table 16.3 Regulatory safeguards for Royal Mail products: no market power

Market	Product	Price control	Headroom control	Notification and publication requirements
B2X Express	Same day	No	No	No
	Special Delivery Next Day	No	No	Yes
	Special Delivery by 9am	No	No	Yes
B2X Deferred > 2kg	Packetpost 1st Class	Yes	No	Yes
	Packetsort 1st Class	Yes	No	Yes
	Royal Mail Tracked	No	No	Yes
	Royal Mail Heavyweight	No	No	Yes

weights and volumes Postcomm was concerned to prevent predation and undue cross-subsidy; while for lower-weight or lower-volume contracts Postcomm was concerned to prevent price increases above the competitive level that might lead to excessive pricing.

Given the concern that for higher volumes and weights Royal Mail could use its market power to offer contracts at prices below incremental cost, cross-subsidizing with revenue generated from more captive customers, Postcomm proposed that limited notification and publication in advance by Royal Mail of its prices together with the power to investigate anticompetitive behavior would provide targeted and proportionate regulatory protection. For lower volumes, more detailed publication requirements were proposed given the more fragile nature of the competitive constraints.

Markets Where There Is No Competition

For lower weights below 500g where there was no evidence of alternative operators competing in the market, Postcomm proposed price controls to protect against the risk of Royal Mail increasing its prices above the competitive level.

Summary of Regulatory Safeguards

The proposed regulatory safeguards in the B2X Deferred market reflect the level of competitive constraint in the market and are summarized in Table 16.4.

6 CONCLUSIONS

This analysis shows how Postcomm has used the analytical framework developed in other areas of competition policy and utility regulation (particularly telecoms) to carry out a structured analysis of a postal market. It outlines the work to define the relevant markets and assess market power in the packets and parcels markets to provide the basis on which to design appropriate proposals for regulatory safeguards. These safeguards can then be structured to protect consumers where the company retains market power and to relax regulation and deregulate where there is effective competition

Table 16.4 Regulatory safeguards in the B2X Deferred market

Segment	Royal Mail's market power	Price control	Advanced notification and publication of tariff	*Ex post* anticompetitive measures
0–500g	Market power	✓	✓	✓
500g–2kg and <150k	Market power	✗	✓	✓
500g–1kg and 150k–300k	Market power	✗	Limited publication	✓
1kg–2kg and 150k–300k	Market power but fragile competition	✗	Limited publication	✓
500g–2kg and >300k	Market power but fragile or developing competition	✗	Limited publication	✓
Above 2kg	Effective competition	✗	Limited publication for transition period	✗

or where the competitive constraints on the incumbent provide adequate protection without the need for regulatory measures. This approach underpinned the decisions made by Postcomm on the regulatory regime for Royal Mail from April 2011 to March 2012.[23] A similar approach based on market studies of the Letters and Large Letters markets, wholesale markets and outbound international postal markets is likely to inform the decisions on the medium-term regulatory framework for Royal Mail from April 2012 onwards.

The Postal Services Act 2011 transfers responsibility for regulation of the postal sector in the UK from Postcomm to Ofcom. Going forward, the postal market is undergoing significant structural change which may change both the scope of the markets currently defined and the competitive constraints within these markets. The analytical framework set out above will allow Ofcom to consider the impact of such changes on the requirement for and scope of future *ex ante* regulation in the postal sector. The Postal Services Act 2011 also gives Ofcom concurrent powers with the OFT under the Competition Act 1998, allowing it to take forward complaints about potential abuses by Royal Mail of its dominant position. While such investigations would require case-specific considerations of market definition and market power dependent on the focal product of the particular case, the evidence base and approach would be likely to rest on a similar analytical approach to that set out above.

The analytical approach in this chapter could also be applied to the regulation of postal markets elsewhere. Although there will be important national differences between different postal markets, it is likely that the characteristics which are important to UK consumers will also be relevant to analysis of PPS and other postal markets in the EU, the US or other countries.

NOTES

* The views expressed are those of the authors and do not necessarily reflect the opinion of Postcomm. Postcomm is the UK's independent regulator for postal services.
1. See for Ofcom http://stakeholders.ofcom.org.uk/market-data-research/; for OFT http://www.oft.gov.uk/OFTwork/markets-work/;jsessionid=B7758C5EC3140198010CE0AEFA5E7E6A; and for ORR http://www.rail-reg.gov.uk/server/show/nav.2117.
2. Hooper et al. (2008).
3. For the full market study, see Postcomm (2010a and 2010b).
4. We define PPS services as: all packets and parcels weighing up to 32kg and all Letters and Large Letters which are not subject to the licensing requirements but excluding those Letters and Large Letters conveyed using vanilla services. A licence is not required to convey letters which cost £1 or more to send or which weigh 350g or more. Vanilla services are services without any added value such as tracking or signed for.
5. See, for example, OFT (2004).
6. Frontier Economics (2010).
7. A discussion document setting out Postcomm's thoughts on the competitive environment for packets, Postcomm (2009b).
8. Postcomm (2010a).
9. Royal Mail (2010).
10. See, for example, OFT (2004): 'Evidence on product characteristics may provide useful information where customer substitution patterns are likely to be influenced significantly by those characteristics'.
11. Operators will pick up varying numbers of PPS items from each customer primarily depending on customer location and whether other items are collected nearby. Operators tend to operate on an accounts system in which higher volumes may attract discounts due to economies of scale in collection. They will also collect low volumes from customers, but the additional cost of the collection would generally be reflected in the price of the service. Royal Mail, for example, will collect low volumes, but if the customer spends less than £15,000 a year on account this involves an extra charge (although this spend is not restricted to PPS services). For businesses that spend less than this, Royal Mail offers two options: either £12.50 (plus VAT) for single collections or regular collections starting at £650 (plus VAT) per annum.
12. This market is currently very small and customer awareness about the services offered is low.
13. This refers to a case where there are two relevant markets (A and B) where there is a competitive constraint from market A on market B, but the reverse is not the case
14. European Commission (1998, at para. 2.4).
15. This description is not specific to the PPS market – it relates to the postal market in general. However, in previous decisions relating specifically to the PPS market (and the differences between Express and Standard delivery) the Commission has separated the parcel and document delivery market into an Express and a Standard (also referred to as Deferred), parcel and document delivery services market, see European Commission (1991, 2003, 2005, para. 21).
16. The Commission sets out characteristics usually associated with a day or time-certain delivery service, see European Commission (2000, at footnote 1 to para. 17).
17. See European Commission (1999, para. 26). This point was also confirmed in European Commission (2000, paras 16 to 21). Hybrid electronic mail is an example of recent technical innovation enabling postal market segmentation on, *inter alia*, time grounds.
18. The physical dimensions of the parcel or packet.
19. Datamonitor (2009b).
20. Accent Marketing Research (2010).
21. In practice the costs of Royal Mail's foot-based network will vary by both weight and volume, however, weight is the primary driver of their costs. End-to-end competitors' costs may also vary by weight, although volumetrics is a more important factor.
22. Accent Marketing Research (2010).
23. See Annex 3 of Postcomm (2010b).

REFERENCES

Accent Marketing Research (2010), 'Packet and Parcel Switching research', August.
Continental Research (2009), Survey of 1,000 packets and parcels customers commissioned by Royal Mail to gather key fulfillment spend metrics.

Datamonitor (2009a), 'Express Market Profile United Kingdom 2009', Autumn.
Datamonitor (2009b), 'Express Benchmarking – United Kingdom', Autumn.
European Commission (1991), Decision of 2/12/1991, COMP/M.102, *TNT/Canada Post, DBP Postdienst, La Poste, PTT Post & Sweden Post.*
European Commission (1998), 'Notice on the application of the competition rules to the postal sector and on the assessment of certain State measures relating to postal services', OJ 1998 C39/02.
European Commission (1999), Decision of 23/02/1999, Case IV/M.1347, *Deutsche Post/Securicor.*
European Commission (2000), Decision of 21/12/2000, Case COMP/37.721, *Consorzio Risposta & Consorzio Recapitali/Italy.*
European Commission (2003), Decision of 19/06/2003, Case COMP/M.3155, *Deutsche Post/ Securicor.*
European Commission (2005), Decision of 24/11/2005, COMP/M.3971, *Deutsche Post/Exel.*
Freshminds (2009), Desk-based market research on market offerings on behalf of Royal Mail.
Frontier Economics (2010), 'Research on the Wider Market for Packets/Parcels Services', report prepared for Postcomm.
Hooper R., D. Hutton and I. Smith (2008), 'Modernise or decline: policies to maintain the universal postal service in the United Kingdom', Cm7592 Crown Copyright, available at: http://www.bis.gov.uk/files/file49389.pdf, (accessed 30 August 2011).
Interactive Media in Retail Group (IMRG) (2008), 'Valuing home delivery 2008: e-retailing industry review', July.
Office of Fair Trading (OFT) (2004), 'Market Definition – understanding competition law', OFT 403, available at: http://www.oft.gov.uk/OFTwork/publications/publication-categories/guidance/competition-act/, (accessed 30 August 2011).
Oxera (2008), 'Business Customer Interviews: Summary of qualitative findings', prepared for Royal Mail, 12 September.
Postcomm (2009a), 'Business Customer Survey', available at: http://www.psc.gov.uk/regulating/surveys (accessed 30 August 2011).
Postcomm (2009b), 'The competitive environment for packets – a discussion document'.
Postcomm (2010a), May Consultation Document, 'Laying the foundations for a sustainable postal service MCD 2010, Annex 2 Analysis of Markets', available at: http://www.psc.gov.uk/consultations, (accessed 30 August 2011).
Postcomm (2010b), November Decision Document, 'Laying the foundations for a sustainable postal service, Annex 1 Analysis of Markets – Decision Document', available at: http://www.psc.gov.uk/consultations (accessed 30 August 2011).
Royal Mail (2010), 'A position Paper by Royal Mail on the Fulfilment Market', March, non-confidential version available at http://www.psc.gov.uk/documents/157.pdf (accessed 30 August 2011).
Triangle (2009), 'UK B2C Parcels Distribution Survey', Triangle, Bourne End, Bucks, UK.
Verdict Research Limited (2008), 'UK Home delivery and Fulfilment', London.

17. Defending mail markets against new entrants: an application of the defender model

Christian Jaag†, Helmut Dietl‡, Urs Trinkner§ and Oliver Fürst¶

1 INTRODUCTION

Market positioning has long been an intensely discussed topic in the economics and marketing literature. Until the early 1980s, the literature mainly tackled the issue of optimal new brand positioning. Existing brands thus had an idea of how a new brand might attack. The reverse question of how to optimally defend its market share and profit against an attack remained unanswered until the paper by Hauser and Shugan (1983), in which they introduced a model that goes beyond the traditional analysis of offensive new-brand positioning by focusing on the defending rather than the attacking brand ('defender model').

One basic observation of the authors was that in most markets incumbents react to competition by lowering prices. In some industries, however, established firms defend their profits against market entrants by increasing product prices. These differences are explained by heterogeneous consumer preferences. Hauser and Shugan modeled this heterogeneity with a continuous distribution of consumer tastes. Another key assumption of their model is the 'per-dollar' measure of product utility. Instead of integrating price as a separate dimension in a traditional perceptual map (such as Urban and Hauser, 1980; Hauser and Gaskin, 1984), the authors plotted each quality dimension in relation to the product's price as proposed by Hauser and Simmie (1981).

From the model, qualitative normative implications on how established firms should defend their profits when facing an attack by a new competitive product can be derived. Hauser and Shugan did not limit the scope of strategic instruments to the dimension of price. They allowed for incumbents to react by adjusting distribution and awareness advertising expenditures, budgets for repositioning advertising, and product quality improvements. The main recommendations were that prices are to be decreased in non-segmented markets and potentially increased in highly segmented markets; distribution and awareness advertising expenditures should be lowered while budgets for

† Managing Partner, Swiss Economics & Lecturer, University of St. Gallen.
‡ Professor, University of Zurich.
§ Managing Partner, Swiss Economics & Senior Research Associate and Lecturer, University of Zurich.
¶ Consultant, Swiss Economics.

repositioning advertising and product improvement 'away' from the strengths of the new products should be increased.

The model and its results have since been verified empirically for several industries, such as food, software and pharmaceuticals (see Hauser and Gaskin, 1984; Kuester et al., 2001). While the defender model predicts the optimal direction of response, later empirical studies in the field of defensive strategies examined further aspects of defensive actions, such as the reaction speed and the intensity of reactions. MacMillan et al. (1985) find that reaction speed increases in the threat posed by the attacker and decreases in the size of the defending brand.[1] A high reaction speed has been examined in markets with high growth rates and low switching costs (for example, by Bowman and Gatignon, 1995).

Other studies focus on the intensity of the defending brands' reactions. These studies find that the intensity of reactions increases in the threat posed by the attacker and in market size and growth (see Heil and Walters, 1993; Shankar, 1999). The incumbent's market dominance and the extent of the attacker's investments have been identified as being negatively correlated to reaction intensity (for example by Shankar, 1999). Kuester et al. (2001) summarize the most-relevant studies in the field of defensive strategies: reaction speed and intensity are highest in highly concentrated and growing markets, while size and innovation capabilities of the attacking firm have negative effects on the defending firm's reaction intensity. The empirical significance of the model is demonstrated by Hauser and Gaskin (1984) and Shugan (1987) who apply the defender model to different markets. Shugan concludes that '[their] model fits well and provides potentially useful information' (p. 14) and Hauser and Gaskin posit that 'the defender model is an adequate representation of aggregate consumer response' (p. 347). Nevertheless, the success of each application highly depends on the choice of attributes (see Hauser and Shugan, 2008).

The objective of this contribution is to apply the defender model to the postal market, which is increasingly opened up to competition in many countries. There is a limited literature on competitive entry strategies in postal markets. Based on a game-theoretic model and interviews with market participants, Dietl and Waller (2002) argue that competition in letter markets will mean new services and lower, but differentiated prices. While businesses and customers in urban areas will benefit from price decreases, households and rural areas will face higher prices. New business models such as mass mail providers, networked mail services, and consolidators with differentiated service propositions will emerge, targeting selected segments of the market. Incumbents will have to change their behavior significantly, become more efficient, and tailor their services to individual needs.

Cohen et al. (2007) discuss the impact of competitive entry into the Swedish postal market. They find that almost immediately after CityMail, the first competitor in the Swedish market for mail, entered the market, Sweden Post began to adjust its pricing structure by introducing discounts for bulk and presorted mail. Sweden Post's bulk-mail price has decreased (unlike single piece), reflecting the intense competition from CityMail.

The interaction between competition and (universal service) regulation has been studied before, cf. Crew and Kleindorfer (2001, 2007) for a general discussion. Dietl et al. (2005) and Jaag (2007) provide applications to the mail market in Switzerland. Kleindorfer and Szirmay (2009) review pricing practices of incumbent postal operators in Europe in the context of liberalization, but they also note the rudimentary state of marketing practices and capabilities in many of these operators.

While the studies mentioned above focus on the need for incumbents to adjust prices as a result of competitive entry (and still being restricted by the Universal Service Obligation: USO), our contribution assesses the possibility of reacting by a universal service provider (USP) by adjusting its overall value proposition accordingly, including non-price product attributes. The remainder of this chapter is organized as follows. Section 2 describes the basic model and its assumptions. In Section 3, we deduce revenue-optimal pricing and product differentiation strategies by simulating different attacks. Section 4 concludes.

2 THE MODEL

Customer Preferences

Our model of customer preferences follows the main assumptions of the original model.[2] Every customer in the market maximizes his or her utility, u. Let u_j be the utility which a randomly selected customer places on the purchase of one unit of brand j. Each brand j's position is defined by the amount of attribute 1 obtainable from one unit of brand j, Q_{1j}, and the amount of attribute 2 obtainable from one unit of brand j, Q_{2j}. The utility a customer places on one unit of brand j is noted as $\tilde{u}_j$, which is a random variable to reflect customer heterogeneity. We define

$$\tilde{u}_j \equiv \frac{\tilde{w}_1 Q_{1j} + \tilde{w}_2 Q_{2j}}{P_j}, \tag{17.1}$$

where we follow the original defender model by using $\tilde{w}_k$ as the weight a customer places on attribute k and P_j denoting the price of brand j. In a market where the customer finds more than one brand available he or she decides to purchase the brand closest to his or her preferences. The probability that a randomly chosen customer chooses brand j is denoted as m_j. It is defined as:

$$m_j \equiv \text{Prob}[\tilde{u}_j > \tilde{u}_i \text{ for all } i \neq j] \tag{17.2}$$

where Prob[·] is a probability function. From (17.1) and (17.2) it follows that:

$$m_j = \text{Prob}\left[\frac{\tilde{w}_1 Q_{1j} + \tilde{w}_2 Q_{2j}}{P_j} > \frac{\tilde{w}_1 Q_{1i} + \tilde{w}_2 Q_{2i}}{P_i}\right] \tag{17.3}$$

or, after some algebraic manipulation,

$$m_j = \text{Prob}\left[\left(\frac{Q_{1j}}{P_j} - \frac{Q_{1i}}{P_i}\right) > \frac{\tilde{w}_2}{\tilde{w}_1}\left(\frac{Q_{2i}}{P_i} - \frac{Q_{2j}}{P_j}\right)\right]. \tag{17.4}$$

Hence, in a two-attribute space, the preferences of each customer can be represented by $\tilde{w}_2/\tilde{w}_1$ which is a sufficient parameter for computing choice probabilities. We define

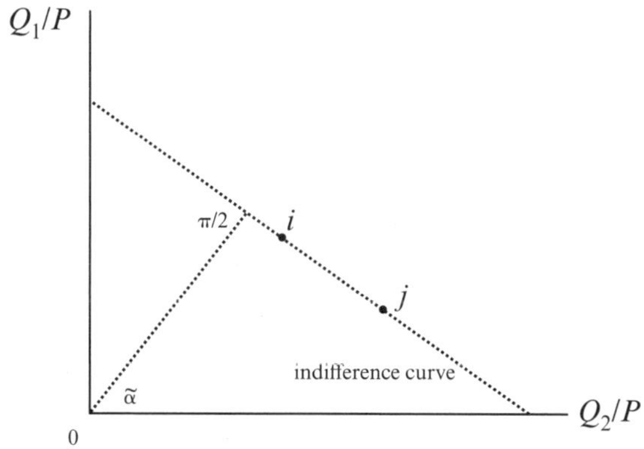

Figure 17.1 Geometric illustration of a randomly chosen customer's preferences

$\tilde{\alpha} \equiv \tan^{-1}(\tilde{w}_2/\tilde{w}_1)$ which represents a measure of consumer preference that varies between 0 and $\pi/2$. Figure 17.1 illustrates a randomly chosen customer's preferences who is indifferent between brand *i* and brand *j*. $\tilde{\alpha}$ is the angle shown in Figure 17.1. Any customer will naturally favor the brand that maximizes his or her utility. In the figure, customers whose indifference curve is steeper would prefer *j* to *i* while customers whose indifference curve is flatter would prefer *i* to *j*.

For the sake of simplicity, we assume customer preferences to be uniformly distributed, that is,

$$\tilde{\alpha} \sim U\left(0, \frac{\pi}{2}\right). \tag{17.5}$$

Brand Positioning and Market Share

We start with the initial market equilibrium with only one firm being active in the market, offering brand *I*. The brand's position in the two-attribute space is defined by its perceived attribute levels (Q_{1I}, Q_{2I}) and its unit price (P_I). In the initial situation, the monopolist serves the entire market. Consider a second firm *A* deciding on its position in the two-attribute space and entering the market. Intuitively, in order to be positioned profitably, it will set quality levels and price such that its brand is positioned within the shaded areas in Figure 17.2 on the upper left or lower right of the monopolist's brand.[3] Hence, there is a restriction on the second brand's positioning,

$$\left(\frac{Q_{1I}}{P_I} - \frac{Q_{1A}}{P_A}\right)\left(\frac{Q_{2I}}{P_I} - \frac{Q_{2A}}{P_A}\right) \leq 0, \tag{17.6}$$

which implies that each of the two firms' products has a 'strong' and a 'weak' quality dimension. Product characteristics are substitutive, that is, both characteristics cannot be at their maximum at the same time. Qualities are normalized such that:

$$\max(Q_1) = \max(Q_2) = 1. \tag{17.7}$$

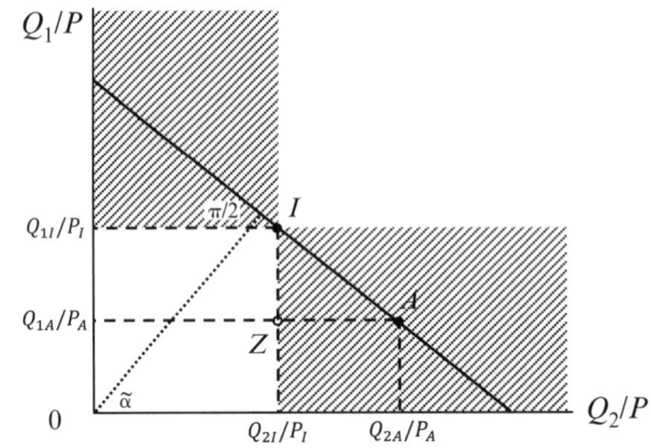

Figure 17.2 Positioning and market shares

Figure 17.2 illustrates an attack by brand A which is represented by point A. The straight line with slope

$$r \equiv \frac{Q_{1A}/P_A - Q_{1I}/P_I}{Q_{2A}/P_A - Q_{2I}/P_I} \tag{17.8}$$

represents the indifference curve of the customer that is precisely indifferent between brands I and A. All customers with a steeper indifference curve than the one shown will choose brand A; those with a flatter indifference curve will opt for brand I. As we assume customer preferences to be uniformly distributed, the ray from the origin that intersects this indifference curve orthogonally now segregates the market in the shares attained by brands I and A. The incumbent's market share is thus given as:

$$m_I = \begin{cases} \frac{2}{\pi}\arctan(-r) \text{ if } \frac{Q_{1I}}{P_I} - \frac{Q_{1A}}{P_A} > 0; \\ 1 - \frac{2}{\pi}\arctan(-r) \text{ if } \frac{Q_{1I}}{P_I} - \frac{Q_{1A}}{P_A} \leq 0. \end{cases} \tag{17.9}$$

Market share m_A can be computed and $1 - m_I = m_A$. Total market size is assumed constant and equal to N. Hence, a brand J's total sales volume is Nm_j.

Attributes

A feasible application of the defender model to any market requires a meaningful selection of quality attributes. Three conditions have to be met. First, the attributes have to affect the buying decision of customers, that is, have to be relevant. Second, they are substitutive in nature.[4] This ensures that (a) no brand can have high characteristics in all attributes at the same time and (b) each brand has to be positioned efficiently (as no customer will choose a brand that is inferior to another in all attributes shaded area in Figure 17.2). Third, the attributes have to be measurable. Many qualitative attributes can possibly be deployed in the model, depending on the research objectives. In order to analyze the impact of market entry in regulated postal markets, it is useful to choose attributes that allow regulatory measures to be integrated into the model. This should grant additional insights into post-liberalization market dynamics. In this application, we employ the attributes *area coverage of delivery* (Q_1) and *end-to-end transit time* (Q_2). The normalization (17.7) of Q_1 and Q_2 means that ($Q_1/100$)% of all households have to be served daily to the doorstep and that delivery speed reaches a score of ($Q_2/100$)% with 100% meaning same day (express) delivery of all items.

Operators' Profit

The production of a certain level of quality entails cost. We assume costs to be convex in quality. Functional forms are stylized to represent the costs incurred when providing wide area coverage and high delivery speed. For simplicity, we assume that $C(Q_1)$ is fixed (volume independent) cost due to fixed delivery routes. $C(Q_2)$ is variable cost. Total cost and profit for the two operators are defined as follows:

$$\mathit{Total\ Cost} = TC = C(Q_1) + C(Q_2) = fQ_1^b + NmgQ_2^d - Nmc - F \quad (17.10)$$

$$\mathit{Profit} = \pi = NmP - (fQ_1^b + NmgQ_2^d) = Nm(P - c - gQ_2^d) - fQ_1^b - F, \quad (17.11)$$

where $0 \leq Q_1, Q_2 \leq 1$. Parameters *f*, *g* govern the absolute cost level associated with the choices of Q_1 and Q_2, while $b, d > 1$ determine the convexity of the cost functions. Parameter *c* is general marginal cost while *F* is fixed cost.

3. OPTIMAL PRICING AND POSITIONING REACTION

The contribution proceeds with a two-step game describing an incumbent's optimal marketing response to market entry. The sequence of decisions is shown in Figure 17.3.

In the initial situation, the incumbent serves the entire market. As a monopolist, its positioning strategy has to account for regulatory limitations. One limitation a USP is bound to is the offering of a wide-area coverage with doorstep delivery – this means it cannot choose the level of accessibility freely. Then, another service provider will enter the market by choosing its quality characteristics Q_1 and Q_2. Naturally, the attacking brand is positioned such that it attacks the defending brand's weaker attribute. With this product differentiation strategy, the new brand serves a significant share of the market leading to a decrease in profits for the incumbent. Strategically, the defending firm has two main options to defend its profits: adjusting price or differentiation by altering its product attributes.

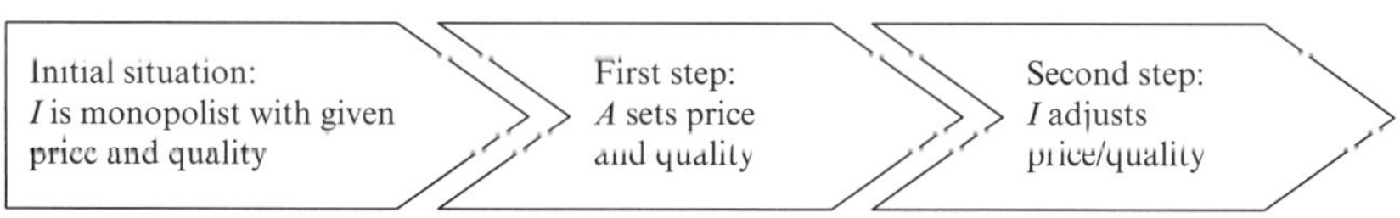

Figure 17.3 Sequence of decisions

Table 17.1 Incumbent's optimum reaction in quality dimension 1 (strong dimension)

	Attack			Defense			Market outcome			
	Q_{1A}	Q_{2A}	P_A	Q_{1I}	Q_{2I}	P_I	m_I (%)	π_I	$\Delta\pi_I$ (monop.) (%)	$\Delta\pi_I$ (no reaction) (%)
Monoply	–	–	–	0.80	0.40	2.00	100	155.20	0.00	0.00
Competition	0.50	0.50	1.80	0.90	0.40	2.00	73	95.53	–38.44	6.18
Competition	0.40	0.60	1.80	0.88	0.40	2.00	65	83.49	–46.20	2.91
Competition	0.20	0.80	1.80	0.81	0.40	2.00	56	74.38	–52.08	0.01
Competition	0.60	0.40	1.80	0.87	0.40	2.00	87	123.11	–20.67	4.19

From (17.11) it follows that the incumbent maximizes its profit function:

$$\pi_I = Nm_I(P_I - c - gQ_{2I}^d) - fQ_{1I}^b - F. \tag{17.12}$$

There is no closed-form solution to the incumbent's optimal reaction to the entrant's attack. We therefore deduce its optimal reaction with numerical simulations. To do so, we proceed by comparing the competitive outcome to the incumbent's monopolistic profit before entry. In monopolistic mail markets, prices are assumed to be regulated by a price cap. It is plausible to assume regulated quality, too. Especially, coverage is regulated by a USO. We assume that both quality dimensions are regulated under the USO. With respect to quality Q_1, the USO prescribes ubiquitous delivery. Items may be delivered to PO boxes or postboxes near major routes, not necessarily to the receiver's doorstep. Hence, the USP is able to increase performance on this attribute in excess to what is prescribed in the USO. The USO in quality Q_2 prescribes a service with a minimum quality of D+3.

We use stylized data and set a regulated price of $P_I = 2.00$ and quality levels of $Q_{1I} = 0.8$ and $Q_{2I} = 0.4$, respectively. This implies that area coverage Q_1 is the incumbent's strong quality characteristic. This is also the quality attribute causing fixed costs. The other variables are set as follows: $c = F = 0$, $N = 100$, $f = 50$, $g = 3$, $b = 3.0$ and $d = 3.0$. In this setting, the simulation predicts that the incumbent would optimally position itself by providing minimum quality and charging maximum price. Hence, all regulatory restrictions are binding. The incumbent's profit before entry amounts to 155.20.

Defense by Adjusting Product Attributes

We assume first that the incumbent is allowed to react to the entrant's attack by adjusting its attribute Q_1 only, that is, the strong-quality dimension. With an optimal response, the incumbent can minimize losses compared to the initial situation. Simulating several possible attacks (P_A, Q_{1A}, Q_{2A}) given the incumbent's regulated price P_I and regulated quality Q_{2I} yields the results as in Table 17.1. We simplify the analysis by assuming an attacker's price which is constant at a value of 1.8, that is, 10 percent below the incumbent's price.

Table 17.2 Incumbent's optimum reaction in quality dimension 2 (weak dimension)

	Attack			Defense			Market outcome			
	Q_{1A}	Q_{2A}	P_A	Q_{1I}	Q_{2I}	P_I	m_I (%)	π_I	$\Delta\pi_I$ (monop.) (%)	$\Delta\pi_I$ (no reaction) (%)
Monopoly	–	–	–	0.80	0.40	2.00	100	155.20	0.00	0.00
Competition	0.50	0.50	1.80	0.80	0.56	2.00	100	122.96	–20.77	36.67
Competition	0.40	0.60	1.80	0.80	0.57	2.00	83	94.43	–39.15	16.39
Competition	0.20	0.80	1.80	0.80	0.47	2.00	60	75.83	–51.14	1.96
Competition	0.60	0.40	1.80	0.80	0.44	2.00	100	148.06	–4.60	25.30

Table 17.1 shows that if the incumbent is assumed to react with product attribute adjustments in its strong dimension only, it will always minimize its profit loss by increasing its own strength. For an incumbent USP bound by price and quality regulation it can therefore be optimal to increase area coverage in our example. The more intensely the entrant attacks (by choosing high quality), the more intense will also be the incumbent's reaction.

Table 17.2 displays the incumbent's reaction to attacks by adjusting its weak-quality dimension Q_{2A} (transit time). A comparison to the results in Table 17.1 shows that the incumbent now has more room to react (starting from a low-quality level) which results in a lower loss in market share compared to the monopoly situation. In some scenarios, the incumbent is even able to retain 100 percent market share. However, in order to fight off competition, it has to increase quality, which is costly, and sacrifice part of its monopoly profit.

Defense by Price Adjustment

In a third set of scenarios, we assume that the incumbent is allowed to defend its profits by adjusting price instead of quality attributes. Table 17.3 shows that it is optimal for the incumbent to decrease its price in order to defend its market share. This result is not surprising; it can be observed in most markets where competition increases (see, for example, Ambrosini et al., 2011).

Table 17.3 Incumbent's optimum price reaction

	Attack			Defense			Market outcome			
	Q_{1A}	Q_{2A}	P_A	Q_{1I}	Q_{2I}	P_I	m_I (%)	π_I	$\Delta\pi_I$ (monop.) (%)	$\Delta\pi_I$ (no reaction) (%)
Monopoly	–	–	–	0.80	0.40	2.00	100	155.20	0.00	0.00
Competition	0.50	0.50	1.80	0.80	0.40	1.66	88	104.53	–32.65	16.18
Competition	0.40	0.60	1.80	0.80	0.40	1.65	79	89.27	–42.48	10.03
Competition	0.20	0.80	1.80	0.80	0.40	1.83	62	75.02	–51.66	0.88
Competition	0.60	0.40	1.80	0.80	0.40	1.80	100	135.20	–12.89	14.42

Comparing the scenarios with quality repositioning and price adjustment indicates that the possibility to react on the weak quality dimension is most valuable to the incumbent. Hence, quality adjustment in this dimension dominates a reaction in price. From the comparison of the three tables it can also be concluded that with our assumptions of a fixed and a variable cost attribute, a low-price attack on the variable cost attribute – as often seen in liberalized network markets – harms the incumbent the most. However, it can be dampened both by lowering prices and by strengthening own product quality.

If the incumbent is only able to adjust its strong-quality attribute, competing at the price margin is more profitable. If the incumbent is able to react on its weak-quality dimension, however, it should rather do so instead of entering a price war. Of course, this result depends on the possibility of the incumbent to actually react on the quality margin. This may not be an option in all quality dimensions with binding USO in place which sets some attributes extremely high.

Concluding from the competitive situation in the Swedish postal market with selective market entry in the low-quality mail segment, Cohen et al. (2007) find that 'the primary response of incumbents when confronted with significant competition will be to embark on a stringent cost reduction program, establish cost and volume based prices, and compete vigorously for large customers through aggressive negotiated prices'. This is also what airlines and banks did when competition first arose. More creative competitors then showed them that there are other quality attributes that were not being paid attention. In the postal sector, these may include improved billing procedures, and customer account management, increased flexibility and hours of operation, date certain delivery and many more.

4 SUMMARY AND CONCLUSION

Mail markets have recently been opened up to competition in most European countries. Market entry will force incumbent postal operators to (re-)position themselves strategically. In this chapter we analyzed the strategic competition between incumbent postal operators and market entrants in liberalized letter markets based on the 'defender consumer model' pioneered by Hauser and Shugan (1983) and derived qualitative normative implications on how an established firm should defend its profits when facing an attack by a new competitive product.

Our results extend the literature on competition in liberalized mail markets by combining pricing and positioning strategies from a marketing perspective. Our analysis based on the defender model highlights that incumbent postal operators can defend their market shares by differentiating their services along one or more quality dimensions. Postal services are not necessarily homogeneous. If postal operators focus solely on pricing strategies they will run into the more serious problems than if they compete on quality too.

Examples from other industries such as the airline industry have shown that differentiation is essential for the success of individual firms and the industry as a whole. Postal operators can also segment the market and escape the vicious circle of price competition. So far, incumbent postal operators have little experience in developing differentiation strategies. Moreover, as Kleindorfer and Szirmay (2009) have highlighted, many incumbent operators do not have strategy and marketing departments with the necessary knowledge to analyze consumer preferences and optimal brand positioning in the digital age and with increasing competition.

Our analysis highlights the importance of these strategies and explains the basics of important analytical tools in this field. The model is potentially quite general and able to represent several forms of competition in the market for mail. In principle, even intermodal competition can be modeled. However, to this end, additional quality dimensions would have to be introduced because email is superior to letter mail in both quality dimensions modeled.

Similarly, the effect of various USO specifications can be taken into account. This would allow for a calculation of the net cost of the USO according to the established profitability approach in an entirely different model environment than the ones applied before (see, for example, Jaag and Trinkner, 2011). We leave these extensions to our analysis to future research.

NOTES

1. In some industries, a delayed reaction could as well be explained by signaling reasons (see Kalra et al., 1998).
2. These are: representation by a product position, utility maximization and linearity (see Hauser and Shugan, 1983, pp. 322–5).
3. A position in the upper right of the incumbent would result in the entire market being served by the entrant while if positioned in the lower left, the entrant would attract zero market share.
4. In the original paper, the authors chose for liquid dish-washing detergents the attributes efficacy and mildness. They are relevant to the customers and they meet the condition of substitutability.

REFERENCES

Ambrosini, X., S. Bréville, J. Cornée and O. Klargaard (2011), 'Pricing strategies in regulated markets – innovative pricing in the postal sector', *Competition and Regulation in Network Industries*, **12**, 57–82.

Bowman, D. and H. Gatignon (1995), 'Determinants of competitor response time to a new product introduction', *Journal of Marketing Research*, **32**(1), 42–53.

Cohen, R., P. Jonsson, M. Robinson, S. Selander, J. Waller, S. Xenakis (2007), 'The impact of competitive entry into the Swedish postal market', paper presented at the WIK 10th Königswinter Seminar on 'Postal Markets between Monopoly and Competition', 12–14 February.

Crew, M.A. and P.R. Kleindorfer (2001), 'Whither the USO under competitive entry: a microstructure approach', in Crew and Kleindorfer (eds), *Future Directions in Postal Reform*, Boston, MA: Kluwer Academic Publishers.

Crew, M.A. and P.R. Kleindorfer (2007), 'Approaches to the USO under entry', in Crew and Kleindorfer (eds), *Liberalization of the Postal and Delivery Sector*, Cheltenham, UK and Northampton, MA, USA: Edward Elgar.

Dietl, H., U. Trinkner and R. Bleisch (2005), 'Liberalization and regulation of the Swiss letter market', in M.A. Crew and P.R. Kleindorfer (eds), *Regulatory and Economic Challenges in the Postal and Delivery Sector*, Boston, MA: Kluwer Academic Publishers.

Dietl, H. and P. Waller (2002), 'Competing with Mr Postman: business strategies, industry structure, and competitive prices in liberalized letter markets', *Schmalenbach Business Review*, **54**, 148–70.

Hauser, J. and S. Gaskin (1984), 'Application of the "defender" consumer model', *Marketing Science*, **3**(4), 327–51.

Hauser, J. and S. Shugan (1983), 'Defensive marketing strategies', *Marketing Science*, **2**(4), 319–60.
Hauser, J. and S. Shugan (2008), 'Commentary. Defensive marketing strategies', *Marketing Science*, **27**(1), 85–7.
Hauser, J. and P. Simmie (1981), 'Profit maximizing perceptual positions: an integrated theory for the selection of product features and price', *Management Science*, **27**(1), 33–56.
Heil, O. and R. Walters (1993), 'Explaining competitive reactions to new products: an empirical signaling study', *Journal of Product Innovation Management*, **10**(1), 53–65.
Jaag, C. (2007), 'Liberalization of the Swiss letter market and the viability of Universal Service Obligations', *Swiss Journal of Economics and Statistics*, **143**(3), 261–82.
Jaag, C. and U. Trinkner (2011), 'The interaction between universal service costing and financing in the postal sector: a calibrated approach', *Journal of Regulatory Economics*, **39**(1), 89–110.
Kalra, A., S. Rajiv and K. Srinivasan (1998), 'Response to competitive entry: a rationale for delayed defensive reaction', *Marketing Science*, **17**(4), 380–405.
Kleindorfer, P.R. and Z. Szirmay (2009), 'Pricing practice in the postal industry: current approaches and challenges under liberalization', Research paper, INSEAD & Roland Berger.
Kuester, S., C. Homburg, T. Robertson and H. Schaefer (2001), 'Verteidigungsstrategien gegen neue Wettbewerber. Bestandsaufnahme und empirische Untersuchung', *Zeitschrift für Betriebswirtschaft*, **71**(10), 1191–215.
MacMillan, I., M. McCaffery and G. Van Wijk (1985), 'Competitors' responses to easily imitated new products – exploring commercial banking product introductions', *Strategic Management Journal*, **6**(1), 75–86.
Shankar, V. (1999), 'New product introduction and incumbent response strategies: their interrelationship and the role of multimarket contact', *Journal of Marketing Research*, **36**(3), 327–44.
Shugan, S. (1987), 'Estimating brand positioning maps using supermarket scanning', *Journal of Marketing Research*, **24**(1), 1–18.
Urban, G. and J. Hauser (1980), *Design and Marketing of New Products*, Englewood Cliffs, NJ: Prentice-Hall.

18. Liberalization and postal workers*

Henrik B. Okholm[†] and Anna Möller[‡]

1 INTRODUCTION

Since January 2011, most postal markets in the EU are fully liberalized and the national postal operators (NPOs) are exposed to competition in all market segments. This has created a concern among Europe's 1.8 million postal workers about the effect of full market opening (FMO) on wages and employment conditions.

The fear of deteriorating wages and employment conditions is strongly linked to the high labor intensity of postal services. On average, labor costs represent 60 percent of European NPOs' total costs, varying from 40 percent in Sweden and the Netherlands to over 70 percent in Ireland, Spain and Greece (see Copenhagen Economics, 2010). Consequently, an effective cost-reduction measure is changes in wages and employment conditions. New postal operators often employ younger or less educated workers, more part-time workers, or use self-employed deliverers. The fact that these operators can enter more market segments after FMO has increased social tensions in the sector.

This chapter examines whether the anticipated fear among postal workers is justified or not. Will wages and other employment conditions deteriorate unconditionally at FMO and what are the consequences for postal workers? Section 2 reviews the methodology of the study. Sections 3–7 provide the individual country studies, divided into 'before' and 'after' FMO. Section 8 summarizes the main findings and discusses their implications.

2 METHODOLOGY

Although the effect of liberalization on postal workers is of great interest for many stakeholders there has been very little empirical research in this area. The discussion so far has focused on the general relationship between deregulation and wages, for instance analyzed by Card (1986) and Peoples (1998). The common conclusion is that monopolies often pay their employees a wage premium which is eliminated at FMO.

These theories have never been empirically tested in the context of the European postal sector. A recent paper that touches on this subject, assessing postal operators' future adaptation to changing market conditions through operational and social optimization, is provided by Bailly and Meidinger (2010).

[†] Partner, Copenhagen Economics A/S.
[‡] Economist, Copenhagen Economics A/S.

Wage premiums in the postal sector have been studied before. By comparing wages in the postal sector with wages in comparable sectors in the late 1980s, Wachter and Perloff (1990) concluded that a significant wage premium existed in the US postal sector. A small postal sector wage premium was also found for some regions in the UK. When controlling for other non-wage benefits, such as high job security, the estimated wage premiums were found to be even higher than first estimated. Later research by Wachter et al. (1999) also suggests that, almost 10 years after the previous study, significant wage premiums remained in the non-liberalized US postal market.

Although these previous studies never addressed the context of liberalized versus non-liberalized postal markets, they provide substantial insight into how to analyze postal sector wage premiums. For example, Wachter et al. explicitly address the question about comparability of sectors as regards skill requirements and working conditions, and they also discuss the inclusion of fringe benefits in the computation of the total compensation premium.

This chapter complements these earlier contributions. It tests the theoretical predictions made by Card (1986) and Peoples (1998) and analyzes how wages and non-wage employment conditions have been affected in five countries with fully liberalized postal sectors: Sweden, Germany, the Netherlands, New Zealand and the UK. In July and August 2010, telephone interviews with NPOs, new postal operators, and trade unions in these countries were conducted. This primary source of information was thereafter supplemented with input from previous studies and official statistics. The subsequent analysis consisted of two steps, conducted on a country-by-country basis.

First, the existence of wage premiums in the postal sector prior to liberalization was investigated. This was done by analyzing pre-liberalization wage differences between the postal sector and comparable sectors hiring workers with similar skill levels.[1] A higher wage at the NPO compared to the other sectors was interpreted as a postal sector wage premium.

Second, the development in wage differences after market opening was examined. This exercise reveals whether the introduction of competition has affected wages in the postal sector and, if that is the case, to what extent.

Since the available data do not allow for the calculation of the monetary value of fringe benefits for postal and non-postal workers, an explicit valuation of fringe benefits was not included in the computation of the wage premium. However, to control for possibly large fringe benefits in the postal sector, a brief assessment of non-wage employment conditions, such as social security payments and pension benefits, was conducted. This is similar to the approach used by Wachter et al. (1999), who also took into account the high degree of job security in the postal sector by assessing the risk of job loss.

3 SWEDEN

Situation before FMO

In the late 1980s and early 1990s, before FMO, postal sector wages in Sweden were regulated by a central public sector collective agreement. As observed by Regelutredningen

(2005), although there was no competition in the market, postal sector wages at that time were on average only 2 percentage points lower than private sector wages.

This observation indicates that there was no wage premium in the Swedish postal sector prior to market opening, something that can be explained by a strong tradition of industrial relations, for instance discussed by Brandt and Schulten (2007).

Developments after FMO

In January 1993, the postal market was fully liberalized. However, in 1991 CityMail[2] had already started to distribute industrial mail in Stockholm. Despite entry of competition, there was no significant change in wage levels from 1991 to 1993. Regelutredningen (2005) observed an increase in the difference between postal and private sector wages in the years after FMO with wages in the postal sector falling by 9 percentage points relative to wages in the private sector in general between 1993 and 2002.

This development could indicate that FMO as such has led to deteriorating wages at Posten. However, this does not seem to be the case. When looking at education and age structure among postal sector employees and all private sector employees in general in the years from 1993 to 2002, increased differences which might explain this development are observed.

For instance, between 1993 and 2002 the share of employees with only primary education increased by 19 percentage points in the postal sector relative to the private sector. Simultaneously, the share of employees under the age of 25 increased by 10 percentage points in the postal sector relative to the private sector. These changes in workforce structure and the resulting lower average wage in the postal sector are most likely caused by two factors: increased automation (reducing the required skill level of employees in sorting and logistics) and CityMail's business model (distribution by bike every third weekday in larger cities, performed mainly by younger people).

To assess whether wages at CityMail have been disproportionately low compared with wages at Posten, a comparison of the two operators' minimum wages is made. Although there has been no common labor agreement guaranteeing equal conditions in the examined time period, wage levels have been very similar. In fact, minimum wages have been almost identical as far back as data are available (Table 18.1).

This supports the statements made by the stakeholders – that there was no attempt by new operators to compete on the basis of low wages in the postal market.

The findings also indicate that wages in the postal sector are market based[3] and have not been affected by FMO. To verify this, recent postal sector wage levels are compared with wages in comparable sectors hiring workers of similar skill level. If collective bargaining has forced CityMail to above market wages, one would expect wages in the postal sector to be higher than in comparable sectors. If FMO has created a downward pressure on wages at Posten, one would expect postal wages to be lower than wages in comparable sectors.

However, the comparison reveals that wages in the postal sector over a period of 10 years correspond to those applied in comparable sectors. Although the difference in minimum wages between CityMail and Posten has increased in this time, no indication of deteriorating wages at Posten or wage premiums at CityMail can be found (Figure 18.1). This confirms the earlier conclusion.

Table 18.1 Lowest monthly wage for new employees, Posten and CityMail, 1997–2009

Year	Posten (€ per month)	CityMail (€ per month)	% deviation*
1997	1,116	1,154	3
1998	1,148	1,181	3
1999	1,180	1,220	3
2000	1,213	1,254	3
2001	1,249	1,291	3
2002	1,280	1,330	4
2003	1,318	1,370	4
2004	1,457	1,403	4
2005	1,494	1,436	4
2006	1,530	1,472	4
2007	1,666	1,522	9
2008	1,749	1,575	10
2009	1,822	1,628	11

Note: * The deviation in wage development in 2004 was triggered by the fact that Posten at this point hired new employees at the minimum wage level. The postal sector trade union 'Facket för service och kommunikation' (SEKO) realized this and considered it crucial to negotiate a higher initial wage level at Posten. The deviation starting in 2007 is explained by fact that SEKO's negotiations with CityMail that year mainly focused on working-time conditions, providing less room for wage increases. Transformation from SEK to € has been done using a constant exchange rate.

Sources: Copenhagen Economics (2010), based on Almega Tjänsteförbunden and SEKO (2007) and SEKO (2007).

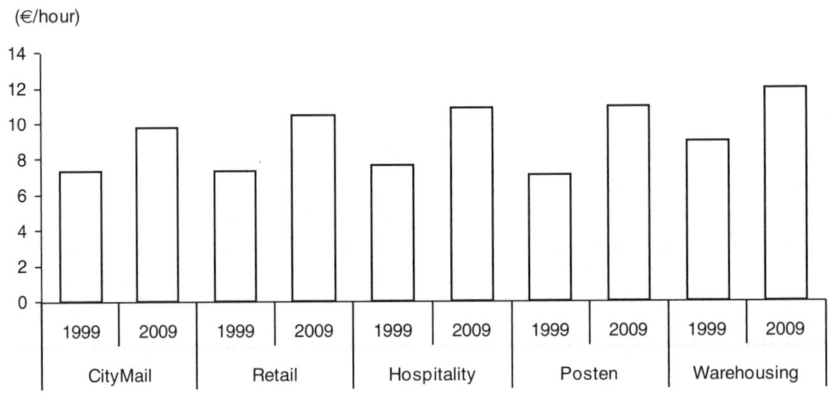

Note: * The wage comparison is made for employees who are at least 18 years old.

Sources: Copenhagen Economics (2010), based on Handelsanställdas förbund (2009), Hotell och restaurangfacket (2009), Almega Tjänsteförbunden and SEKO (2007) and SEKO (2007).

Figure 18.1 Hourly minimum wage in various sectors, 1999 and 2009*

To control for fringe benefits that might provide postal workers at Posten with a compensation premium in relation to postal workers at CityMail or workers in comparable sectors, a brief assessment of non-wage employment conditions is made. The assessment reveals that large work-time flexibility at CityMail in the past might have had an impact on the overall value of employment conditions. Whereas all employees at Posten since 1993 work eight hours per day,[4] employees at CityMail were until 2007 subject to a more flexible work-time arrangement.[5] If this kind of flexibility had a negative value for employees this might indicate a larger difference in compensation between the two operators than indicated by the wage differences.

However, over time we observe a convergence in work-time flexibility and other non-wage employment conditions between the two operators. We also observe that the convergence has always been to the benefit of employees (irrespective of which operator originally provided the higher level). That is, non-wage employment conditions have not deteriorated over time and are today similar at both operators.

Based on this, we conclude that wages and other employment conditions have not been significantly affected by the liberalization of the Swedish postal market and that FMO has led to neither below-market wage, nor an entry-deterring wage level in the postal sector.

4 GERMANY

Situation before FMO

The liberalization of the German postal market began in 1998 with a new postal law introducing a gradual reduction of the reserved area. In 1999, the first challenger PIN AG[6] was founded and in 2001 the Dutch operator TNT Post entered the German postal market. These operators applied alternative, low-cost, business models including, for instance, delivery less than six days per week, lower wages, and a higher share of part-time or 'mini job' contracts in delivery.[7]

At the same time as competition started to emerge, DPAG decided in 2000 to revise its employment conditions. The result was a two-tier structure where employees hired before 2000 were guaranteed their existing wages and employment conditions and new employees became subject to new conditions, oriented toward those in the logistics sector. As well as a wage reduction of approximately 30 percent, the new conditions also included a change in bonus schemes and other non-wage benefits.

Despite this development, employment conditions at DPAG in 2007 (one year prior to FMO) were still observed to be significantly above its competitors. For instance, the lowest pay level was approximately 70 percent higher at DPAG, and there were large differences in other non-wage benefits as well (Table 18.2).

To assess whether the wage difference indicates wage dumping by new operators or a wage premium paid by DPAG, postal sector wages are compared with wages in comparable sectors. The comparison reveals that wages at the new operators appear to be in line with those in comparable industries (Figure 18.2).

Based on this, we can conclude that postal workers at DPAG probably enjoyed a pre-liberalization wage premium. As acknowledged by, for instance, Wachter and Perloff

Table 18.2 Employment conditions at DPAG and competitors, 2007

Employment condition	DPAG	Competitors
Lowest wage applied	11.4€/hour*	6.54 €/hour
Weekly working hours	38.5	38.8
Annual vacation days	28	22.9
Share of mini jobs	5%	53%
Pension benefits, holiday and Christmas allowance	Yes	No

Note: * Inclusive of holiday and vacation pay.

Sources: Copenhagen Economics (2010) based on Dieke and Zauner (2007), Brandt and Schulten (2007), Dieke and Wojtek (2008), Bundesnetzagentur (2009), Verdi (2010) and Wey and Heitzler (2010).

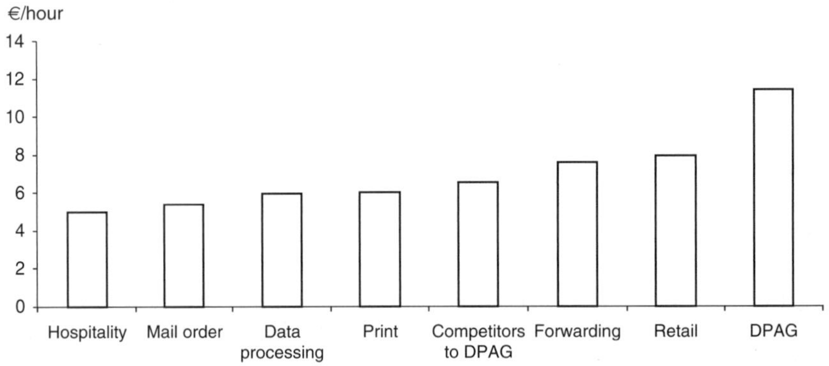

Sources: Copenhagen Economics (2010), based on Brandt and Schulten (2007) and Dieke and Zauner (2007).

Figure 18.2 Hourly minimum wages in various sectors, Germany 2007

(1990) and Wachter et al. (1999) in earlier studies of postal sector wage premiums, difference in non-wage conditions, such as pension benefits, and holiday and Christmas allowances, increases the size of the total compensation premium further.

Developments after FMO

An assessment of the development of wages and employment conditions at DPAG over time does not reveal any significant changes after 2000 when the two-tier structure was introduced. However, to compete with low-cost competitors DPAG has set up its own subsidiary, First Mail. Wages at First Mail are slightly above those at other new operators but close to those found in retail and warehousing. In 2010, the minimum wage paid at the mother company was approximately 11 percent above the wage level at First Mail, and 40 percent above the level at other new operators (Figure 18.3).

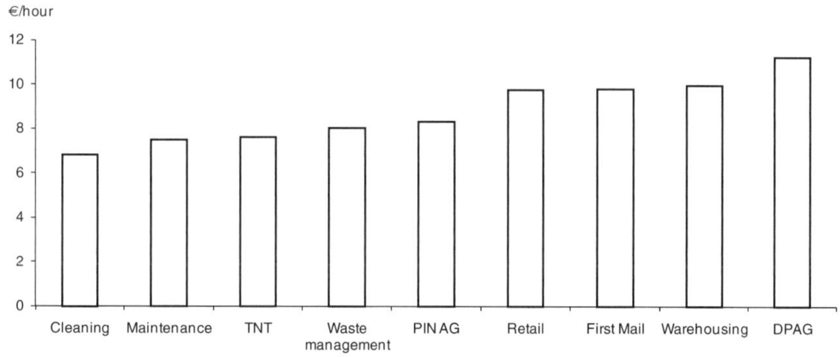

Note: * The minimum wage paid to postmen at DPAG does not include holiday allowance and productivity benefits, meaning that the actual pay difference might be larger than in the figure.

Sources: Copenhagen Economics (2010), based on ver.di (2010) and interview with representatives from ver.di.

Figure 18.3 Hourly minimum wages in postal and comparable sectors, 2010*

The decrease in wage differences between DPAG and the new operators or comparable sectors in the years following FMO can be interpreted as a movement towards more market-based wages in the German postal sector. This view is also confirmed by representatives from DPAG, who stated that the observed decrease in wages in 2000 and the subsequent convergence to the level in comparable sectors were not driven by the entry or threat of competition but by existing above-market conditions. However, workers at DPAG still seem to enjoy a wage premium although the difference in non-wage conditions compared with other operators seems to have decreased over time.

Pension benefits, holiday and Christmas allowances are now common among all operators.

It can be concluded that FMO has not led to deteriorating wages and employment conditions in the German postal sector, but to a reduction in the wage premium and more market-based employment conditions.

5 NETHERLANDS

Situation before FMO

The full liberalization of the Dutch postal market took place in April 2009. However, the process started in the late 1990s, followed by the entry of two new postal operators into the market, Sandd and Selekt Mail.[8] These operators remain the main competitors to the NPO, PostNL (TNT Post before 2011). PostNL has also established an own subsidiary, Netwerk VSP, competing directly with Sandd and Selekt Mail in the market for non-time critical mail.

The new postal operators' business models are based on delivery 1–2 days a week,

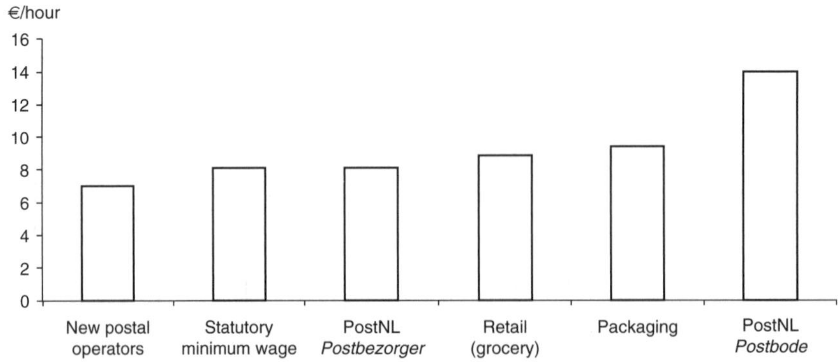

Note: * That per piece payments paid to self-employed workers (recalculated to correspond to hourly payments) were below the statutory minimum wage level was discovered in a governmental investigation of the employment conditions in the postal sector in 2007. Thereafter, the new operators promised to revise the per piece rates paid to ensure that they comply with the statutory minimum.

Sources: Copenhagen Economics (2010), based on Schulten and Watt (2007), TNT Post (2009), *Salarisinformatie.nl* (2010).

Figure 18.4 Minimum wage level at PostNL and in comparable sectors, 2007*

often performed by self-employed part-time deliverers without ordinary labor contracts and with payments and employment conditions below those applied at the NPO. Self-employed deliverers are paid on a per piece basis and do not enjoy social protection, pension benefits, holiday or illness allowances. Self-employed deliverers are also not covered by the statutory minimum wage regulation. According to the new operators, this business model is necessary in order to build up a delivery network based on initially small and fluctuating mail volumes.

Due to declining mail volumes, technological development and the low-cost pressure from new operators, PostNL started an internal restructuring process in 2003. The goal is to transform PostNL from a full-time-dominated organization into a part-time-dominated organization with focus on three peak-delivery days per week (however, delivery will still be conducted six days a week). As a part of this process, a new type of employee – the mail deliverer (*postbezorger*) – has been introduced.[9]

Wages and other employment conditions of *postbezorgers* are inferior to those of the traditional postal workers. Due to the evolution of electronic communication and new payment measures, mail delivery no longer includes tasks such as delivery of pension payments or special items. This has reduced the skill level required and consequently also the applicable wage level.

When comparing the wages paid by the Dutch postal operators with wages in comparable sectors, we observe that other low-skill sectors often apply a minimum wage close to, or slightly above, the statutory one. Whereas wages paid to traditional postal workers at PostNL were considerably above this level in 2007, wages paid to the *postbezorgers* at the same time were very close to the statutory minimum wage. Payments at the new operators[10] were slightly lower (Figure 18.4).

This observation indicates that the payments at new operators might be below the level

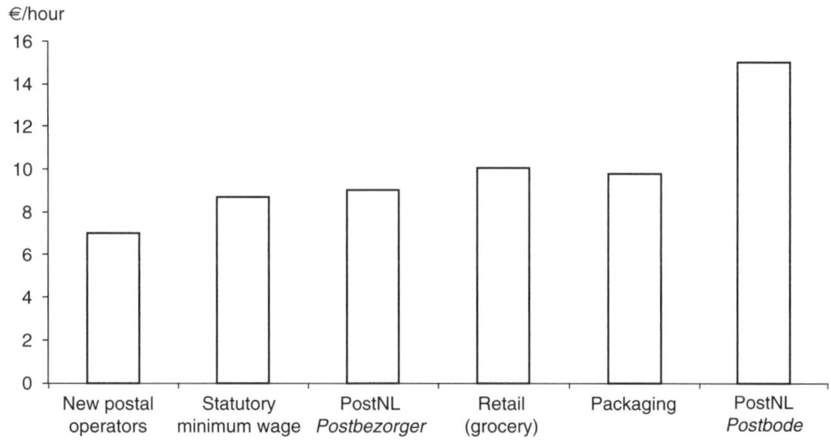

Sources: Copenhagen Economics (2010), based on interviews with representatives from TNT Post (Hans Blikman, Public Affairs, TNT Post Netherlands, 4 August 2010) and AbvaKabo (Peter Wiechmann, National Officer Postal Sector, AbvaKabo, 19 July 2010) and *Salarisinformatie.nl* (2010).

Figure 18.5 Minimum wage level at PostNL and in comparable sectors, 2010

paid in comparable sectors and possibly also below the level of the statutory minimum wage. This is most likely due to the fact that most postal workers at the new operators are self-employed to which the statutory minimum wage regulation do not apply. The observation also indicates that postal workers at PostNL enjoyed a pre-liberalization wage premium.

Developments after FMO

A comparison of wages one year after FMO reveals that wages paid to the *postbezorgers* still seems to be the most market oriented. It also reveals that a wage premium still seems to exist for the traditional postal workers (Figure 18.5).

Taking into account the fact that traditional postal workers also enjoy more generous provision of, for instance, pension and vacation benefits than both *postbezorgers* and self-employed deliverers (Table 18.3), suggests that the total compensation premium accruing to the traditional postal workers are higher than estimated by the monetary wage premium.

Interviews with the largest trade union for postal workers in the Netherlands reveal that both wage and non-wage employment conditions for *postbezorgers* are similar to the conditions in comparable sectors. Hence, an increased share of *postbezorgers* at PostNL would indicate a movement towards more market-based conditions in the Dutch postal sector, created by liberalization of the postal market, entry of low-cost competition and structural changes stemming from declining mail volumes and increased automation.

Table 18.3 Non-wage employment conditions at PostNL and competitors, 2010

Employment condition	PostNL *Postbodes*	PostNL *Postbezorgers*	Self-employed deliverers
Contract type	Full-time	Part-time	Part-time
Weekly working hours	37	38*	40
Annual vacation days	26	20	20
Pension benefits	Good	Modest	None
Holiday allowance, social benefits, protection against dismissal	Yes	Yes	No

Note: * According to interviews with the trade union AbvaKabo, PostNL *Postbezorgers* work 38 hours per week, although they do not have the status of full-time employees.

Sources: Copenhagen Economics (2010), based on interviews with representatives from PostNL and AbvaKabo.

6 NEW ZEALAND

Situation before FMO

The New Zealand postal market was fully liberalized in 1998. However, as early as 1987, the NPO was restructured, creating NZ Post Ltd, a state-owned enterprise operating with a revenue target.

Despite significant restructuring measures,[11] the wage received by workers at NZ Post in 1997 (after 10 years of NZ Post being run as a commercial company and just before FMO) was between 15 and 38 percent higher than wages in metal industry occupations with a similar skill level, and approximately 70 percent above the statutory minimum wage (Figure 18.6).

These differences most likely indicate a pre-liberalization wage premium enjoyed by the workers at NZ Post. Moreover, non-wage conditions from the time when all postal workers were civil servants still ensured generous provision of parental leave and training for employees at NZ Post. This observation indicates that the total compensation premium provided to postal workers at NZ Post is larger than the estimated wage premium.

Development after FMO

Since FMO a number of postal operators have come and gone or merged. By 2006 there were 27 operators competing with NZ Post in various segments of the market. This number has remained fairly stable. In 2010 there were 25 alternative operators, holding some 20 percent of the total market.

Most alternative operators do not have their own processing and delivery networks, but use NZ Post's delivery network to compete on customer service, marketing, retail distribution and postage production costs. Only one operator provides a nationwide

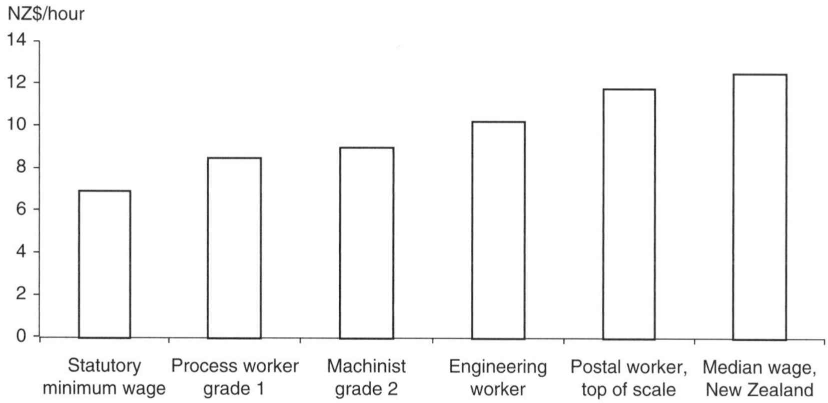

Note: * Engineering personnel, machinists and process workers all working in the metals industry. Postal workers, top of scale – maximum wage rate for a postal worker, usually achieved after 3–4 years of experience.

Source: Copenhagen Economics (2010), based on Kenny (2006).

Figure 18.6 Wage rates per hour at NZ Post and in comparable occupations, 1997*

alternative (for business mail) to NZ Post: DX Mail.[12] The workforce of DX Mail has a diverse age structure and contains a mix of people, from secondary income earners to mothers and students.

According to the trade union EPMU, DX Mail pays its deliverers the statutory minimum wage (or a lower youth rate where applicable). However, there is no overtime compensation, shift or night rate. Furthermore, pension benefits and other non-wage conditions are below the level applied at NZ Post and there is no collective labor agreement covering the workers.

In 2005, seven years after FMO, wages at NZ Post were significantly above the statutory minimum wage paid by its competitors and similar to or slightly above those in comparable sectors (Figure 18.7).

However, low-cost competition from new operators seems to have initiated a slight deterioration of wages at NZ Post. In the first years after FMO (1997–2005), we observe a decline in the wage difference between postal workers and comparable occupations. In this time period, the wage for a worker at NZ Post increased by 18.9 percent whereas the increase in the NZ median wage was 28.3 percent and the increase for a machinist in the metal industry was 26 percent. The non-wage benefits at NZ Post have also been reduced. The old privileges granted to civil servants are about to, or have already, disappeared and no improvements in pension benefits, working time or annual holidays except for statutory ones have been made.

Based on this, we conclude that liberalization of the postal market has led to some reduction of a pre-liberalization wage premium and some convergence towards more market-based non-wage employment conditions in the New Zealand postal sector.

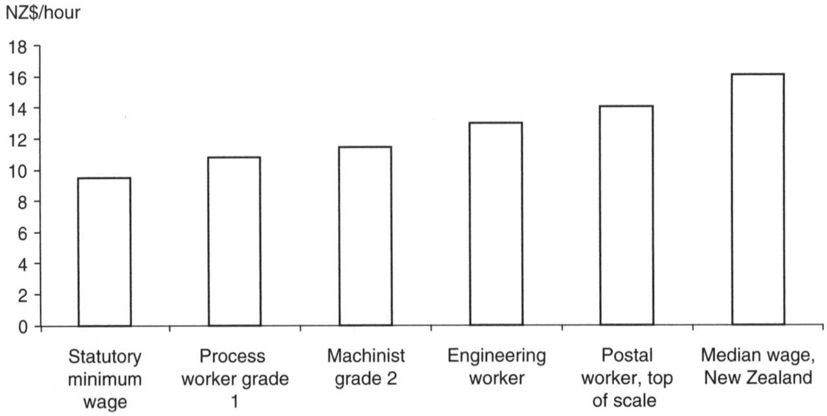

Note: * Engineering personnel, machinists and process workers all working in the metals industry. Postal workers, top of scale – maximum wage rate for a postal worker, usually achieved after 3–4 years of experience. Due to high seniority of staff at NZ Post, this represents the average actual wage.

Source: Copenhagen Economics (2010), based on Kenny (2006).

Figure 18.7 Actual wage rates per hour at NZ Post and in comparable sectors, 2005*

7 UNITED KINGDOM

Situation before FMO

The UK postal market was fully liberalized in 2006. However, the restructuring of the NPO, Royal Mail, started in 1981 and the tasks of postal workers have changed and been simplified over time. For instance, postal workers no longer handle pension payments or perform other demanding tasks.

A comparison of wage levels in the postal sector with other similar sectors before FMO reveals that wages at Royal Mail were rather similar to or slightly above those in other low-skill sectors such as retail and repairs and slightly below the wages in the transport, storage and communications industries (Figure 18.8).

This observation indicates that postal workers in the UK most likely did not enjoy a large wage premium created by the monopoly position of Royal Mail prior to liberalization. This conclusion was also made by Wachter and Perloff (1990), who observed the lack of a wage premium paid to the postal workers of Royal Mail in almost all regions of the UK (excluding London and the southeast region of the country) in the late 1980s. However, the authors also concluded that a high level of job security and the existence of other fringe benefits at Royal Mail might indicate a total positive compensation premium paid to postal workers at Royal Mail, irrespective of region.

An assessment of non-wage benefits prior to FMO reveals that postal workers at Royal Mail enjoyed pension and vacation benefits above the statutory minimum. This was most likely a heritage from the time prior to the privatization of Royal Mail in 2001 when all postal workers enjoyed civil servant status. This observation implies that there still might

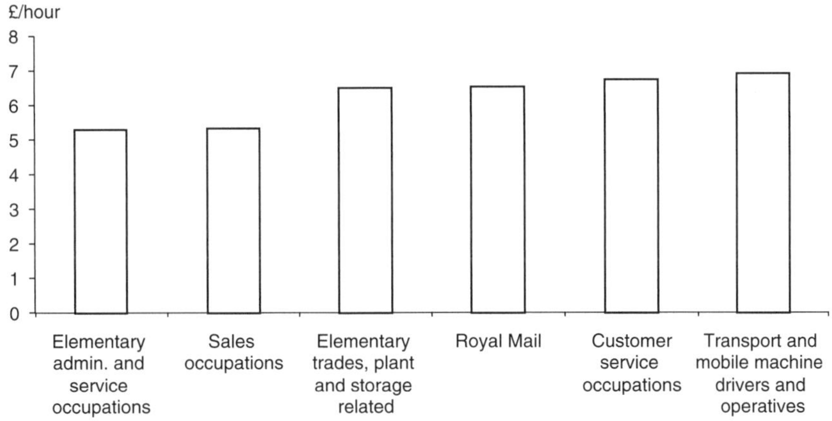

Note: * Hourly median wages, excluding overtime. Royal Mail wage (October 2002 to October 2003) calculated from weekly earnings, working 40 hours per week.

Source: Copenhagen Economics (2010), based on interviews and data from UK National Statistics (2010).

Figure 18.8 Hourly median wages Royal Mail and comparable sectors, 2003*

have been a positive overall compensation premium paid to the postal workers at Royal Mail at that time.

Developments after FMO

Five years after FMO, Royal Mail still delivers almost all mail in the UK. The main element of competition takes place in collection and presorting of mail. For instance, in 2009, more than one-third of all bulk-mail items were posted with alternative providers (although delivered by Royal Mail). In total, less than 1 percent of letters were delivered by alternative operators.

The only alternative operator with its own delivery network is TNT Post, which entered the market in 2004 and since 2008 provides final delivery in the area of Liverpool. TNT provides delivery two days per week by part-time, low-skilled workers with no previous experience, typically men between 20 and 40 years old. The wage level at TNT is slightly below that at Royal Mail but similar to that applied in other low-skill sectors such as retail and repairs (Figure 18.9).

The difference in wage level between TNT and Royal Mail can most likely be explained by the difference in workforce composition at the two operators. Based on these observations, the lower wage applied by TNT Post cannot be interpreted as a sign of wage dumping in the sector, but might instead be an indication of a market-based wage level applied by the new operator.

Over the past seven years, the wage development at Royal Mail has been similar to or slightly better than in other low-skill sectors. From 2003 to 2010, the minimum as well as the median wage at Royal Mail increased by approximately 38 percent. This can be compared with comparable sectors, where wages increased by 20–30 percent between 2003

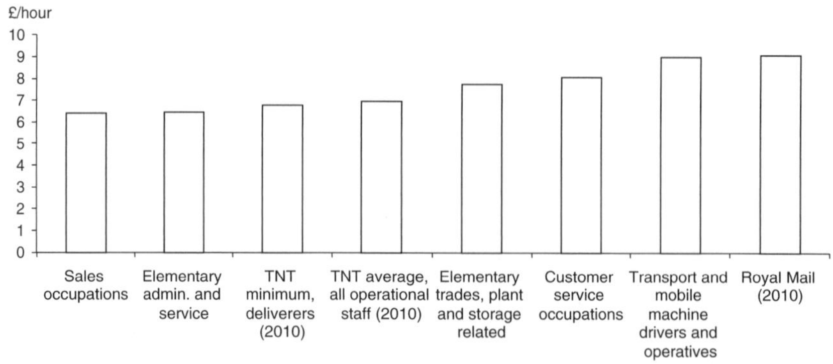

Note: * Hourly median wages, excluding overtime. Royal Mail wage (October 2009 to October 2010) calculated from weekly earnings, working 39 hours per week. Royal Mail and TNT wages are from 2010, comparable sectors from 2009. Comparable sectors are most likely somewhat higher in 2010.

Source: Copenhagen Economics (2010), based on interviews and data from UK National Statistics (2010).

Figure 18.9 Hourly median wages Royal Mail and comparable sectors, 2009*

and 2009, and the statutory minimum wage which increased by approximately 36 percent in the same period.

This development is likely a result of strong industrial relations at Royal Mail, in combination with limited competitive pressure and a low degree of automation compared with many other European NPOs.[13]

Regarding non-wage conditions such as pension benefits, working hours and annual vacation, the conditions at Royal Mail are observed to be superior to those applied by its competitors. This might be explained by a conservation of privileges from the time when workers at Royal Mail still enjoyed civil servant status. However, this has changed slightly in the past few years. For example, from April 2008, Royal Mail's defined-benefit pension scheme was closed to new members. Based on this, it is concluded that liberalization of the postal market in the UK has not had any significant effect on wages and employment conditions in the sector. FMO has not caused wages and employment conditions at Royal Mail to deteriorate and there is no indication of below-market wages applied by new operators.

8 MAIN FINDINGS

This study finds that liberalization affects postal workers' wages and employment conditions in two ways depending on the situation before FMO.

On the one hand, if wages in the postal sector prior to liberalization are similar to those in comparable private sectors with similar skill levels, there is no room for new operators to offer lower wages and still attract qualified labor.[14] Developments in Sweden and in the UK provide examples of this situation.

On the other hand, if wages in the postal sector are above those in private sectors with similar skill levels (in which case the NPO employees enjoy a pre-liberalization wage

Table 18.4 The effect on FMO on postal sector employment conditions

	Sweden	UK	New Zealand	Germany	Netherlands
Year of FMO	1993	2006	1998	2008	2009
Pre-liberalization wage premium*	No	No	Yes	Yes	Yes
Wage level at new entrants vs. NPO	Similar	Similar	Lower	Lower	Lower
Wage development at NPO vs. comparable sectors	Similar	Better than similar sectors, similar to statutory minimum wage	Slower wage development than in comparable sectors	Lower entry wage for new employees introduced in 2000	Lower wages for deliverers introduced in 2003
Changes in other employment conditions	Reduction in privileges connected to civil servant status	Reduction in privileges connected to civil servant status	Reduction in privileges connected to civil servant status	Lower at new entrants, unchanged at NPO	Lower at new entrants, two-tier structure at NPO
Explanation	Strong industrial relations + corpora-tization of NPO	Strong industrial relations + corpora-tization of NPO	Pre-liberali-zation wage premium, corpora-tization of NPO	Pre-liberali-zation wage-premium + changing market structure	Pre-liberali-zation wage premium + changing market structure

Note: * Wage premium is defined as the difference in wages applied by the NPO and wages applied in comparable sectors. The pure wage premium does not take into consideration fringe benefits and other non-wage employment conditions. Thus, in the absence of a wage premium there might still be an overall compensation premium paid to postal workers at the NPO.

Source: Copenhagen Economics (2010).

premium), new operators will most likely create a downward pressure on wages towards a more market-based level. Developments in Germany, New Zealand and the Netherlands illustrate this context.

There is also a possibility that payments below the market based level in comparable industries may arise in certain market segments. However, this development is most likely connected to a broad use of self-employed deliverers (often with the postal service as a secondary source of income and to whom the statutory minimum wage regulation does not apply) who are prepared to work for below-market payments.

Our findings are summarized in Table 18.4.

Another important finding from the case studies is that postal sector wages (in parallel with market liberalization) have been affected by other factors. Two examples are technological development and declining mail volumes, which have reduced the need for full-time employees as less time is needed in sorting and delivery. In addition, technological development has led to a simplification of the manual tasks performed. This has provoked a change in the structure and skill composition of postal sector employment and a subsequent reduction in wages. Consequently, the conclusion is that overall changes in wages and employment conditions are driven by a combination of several factors, such as pre-liberalization wage premiums in the postal sector, increased automation, lower mail volume and increased competition from new operators.

NOTES

* This chapter is based on the results of research undertaken by Copenhagen Economics in connection with the study 'Wages and employment conditions in liberalised postal markets', completed for the Norwegian Ministry for Transport and Communications in August 2010, and the study 'Main Developments in the Postal Sector, 2008–2010' completed for the European Commission in December 2010.

1. Comparable sectors were chosen on the basis of interviews with trade unions and postal operators as the most common sectors from which the inflow of workers to the postal sector comes, and to which the outflow of workers from the postal sector goes.
2. CityMail is still the main competitor of Posten, active in the distribution of industrial mail.
3. By market-based wages we mean the wage level paid to workers with a similar skill level as postal workers, employed in comparable sectors.
4. The introduction of the eight-hour working day had also been considered necessary prior to FMO, but due to strong industrial relations, Posten's monopoly position and the lack of a revenue target, it had been difficult to bring about the change. FMO in 1993 and a forthcoming corporatization of Posten in 1994 with a predefined revenue target changed this situation.
5. The system implied that employees at CityMail could work more than eight hours one day, and less than eight hours the next. The hours of 'overtime' were set off against the hours of 'undertime' without extra compensation.
6. Briefdienstleistungsunternehmen PIN intelligente Dienstleistungen AG.
7. A 'mini job' is a contract type common for part-time jobs. The earnings (which cannot exceed €400 per month) are tax free and the employer pays a lump sum of 30 percent (covering health insurance, pension fund and wage tax) to the insurance association. On the one hand, it can be argued that mini jobs are inferior to full-time or other part-time jobs due to the few hours worked. Alternatively, mini jobs provide opportunities for people who are not able, or do not want, to work more than only a few hours per week. Thus, mini jobs provided by the new postal operators do not necessarily decrease the quality of employment in the sector since there are people who prefer these jobs to ordinary full-time contracts. For instance, whereas DPAG hired 0.8 percent of its workforce on mini-job contracts in 2001, the corresponding figure at the alternative operators was approximately 60 percent.
8. In 2011, Sandd bought SelektMail.
9. In contrast to traditional postal workers (*postbodes*), the *postbezorgers* are hired on a part-time basis and *only* perform delivery tasks. That is, they never enter the premises of PostNL but collect the presorted mail batches from depots along the delivery route.
10. The hourly payment for deliverers for the new postal operators is calculated through a conversion of the average payment per piece to an average hourly payment rate based on the average number of items delivered per hour.
11. In the years following corporatization of NZ Post, several post offices and agencies were closed and significant staff reductions were made. From 1987 until the liberalization of the postal market in 1998, the number of full-time equivalents fell by 43 percent Kenny, 2006.
12. DX Mail has a nationwide delivery network for business-to-business mail. Reachmedia has an urban delivery network for unaddressed mail. Rural delivery utilizes the services of NZ Post Ltd.
13. According to Hooper (2008 et al.), in 2008 only 70 percent of letters were mechanically sorted at Royal Mail and sequencing was performed entirely by hand. The corresponding rates at leading European NPOs at the same time were 95 percent mechanical sorting and 85 percent automatic sequencing.
14. Given that new operators do not apply non-wage employment conditions significantly above those applied by the NPO.

REFERENCES

Almega Tjänsteförbunden and SEKO (2007), 'Allmänna anställningsvillkor 2007–2010', Postdistribution, Beställningsnummer: 60110712.

Bailly, Dominique and Margaux Meidinger (2010), 'The dual trend towards operational efficiencies and social regulation in European postal service', Chapter 24 in Michael A. Crew, Paul R. Kleindorfer and James I. Campbell Jr (eds), *Reinventing the Postal Sector in an Electronic Age: Advances in Regulatory Economics*, Cheltenham, UK and Northampton, MA, USA: Edward Elgar, pp. 336–50.

Brandt, Torsten and Thorsten Schulten (2007), 'Liberalisation and privatisation of public services and the impact on labour relations: a comparative view from six countries in the postal, hospital, local public transport and electricity sectors', Düsseldorf, December, available at: http://www.pique.at/reports/pubs/PIQUE_028478_Del8.pdf (accessed 14 July 2011).

Bundesnetzagentur (2009), 'Zwölfte Marktuntersuchung für den Bereich der lizenspflichtigen Postdienstleistungen', available at: http://www.bundesnetzagentur.de/SharedDocs/Downloads/DE/BNetzA/Sachgebiete/Post/Marktbeobachtung/Marktuntersuchung12ID18118.pdf?__blob=publicationFile (accessed 14 July 2011).

Card, David (1986), 'The impact of deregulation on the employment and wages of airline mechanics', *Industrial and Labour Relations Review*, **39,** 527–38.

Copenhagen Economics (2010), 'Main developments in the postal sector (2008–2010)', available at: http://ec.europa.eu/internal_market/post/doc/studies/2010-main-developments_en.pdf (accessed 30 August 2011).

Dieke, Alex K. and Ralf Wojtek (2008), 'Competition, wages and politics in the delivery sector: the case of postal minimum wages in Germany', Chapter 16 in Michael A. Crew, Paul R. Kleindorfer and James I. Campbell Jr (eds), *Handbook of Worldwide Postal Reform: Advances in Regulatory Economics*, Cheltenham, UK and Northampton, MA, USA: Edward Elgar, pp. 282–97.

Dieke, Alex K. and Martin Zauner (2007), 'Arbeitsbedingungen im Briefmarkt', No. 295, WIK, May, available at: http://www.post-und-telekommunikation.de/PuT/1Fundus/Dokumente/BNetzA_WIK-Studie_Arbeitsbedingungen_BDL_10235.pdf (accessed 14 July 2011).

Handelsanställdas förbund (2009), 'Får du rätt lön i sommar?', June 3, available at: http://www.avd17.handels.se/home/handels2/home.nsf/unidView/601060809C8D7F15C12575CA003975A5 (accessed 23 July 2010).

Hooper, Richard, Dame Deirdre Hutton and Ian R. Smith (2008), 'Modernise or Decline: Policies to Maintain the Universal Postal Service in the United Kingdom. An Independent Review of the UK Postal Service Sector', 16 December, available at: http://www.bis.gov.uk/files/file49389.pdf (accessed 14 July 2011).

Hotell och restaurangfacket (2009), 'Minimilön för kvalificerat yrkesarbete 2008–2009', available at: http://www.hrf.net/index.php?p=391 (accessed 23 July 2010).

Kenny, Anna (2006), 'Beyond the propaganda, postal deregulation in New Zealand', available at: http://www.uniglobalunion.org/apps/UNINEWS.nsf/New%20zealand%20EPMU.pdf (accessed 14 July 2011).

Peoples, James (1998), 'Deregulation and the labour market', *Journal of Economic Perspectives*, **12**(3), 111–30.

Regelutredningen (2005), 'Liberalisering, regler och marknader', SOU 2005:4, available at: http://www.regeringen.se/sb/d/5142/a/37042 (accessed 14 July 2011).

Salarisinformatie.nl (2010), 'Collective labour agreements for retail and packaging', available at: www.salaris-informatie.nl (accessed 18 August 2010).

Schulten, Thorsten and Andrew Watt (2007), 'European minimum wage policy – a concrete project for a social Europe', European Economic and Employment Policy Brief No. 2, available at: http://www.boeckler.de/pdf/p_etui_2007_minimum%20wage.pdf (accessed 14 July 2011).

SEKO (2007), 'Postens villkorsavtal 2007–2010', available at: http://www.sekoposten.org/avtal/Postens%20Villkorsavtal%202007-2010.pdf (accessed 14 July 2011).

TNT Post (2009), 'Economic and social model for the postal sector: the TNT experience', presentation by Herna Verhagen at the final conference on Evolution of the Postal Sector, Brussels,

22 October 2009, available at: http://www.postsocialdialog.org/images/stories/TNT_presentation,_final_conference_social_observatory_22102009.pdf (accessed 14 July 2011).

UK National Statistics (2010), 'Average Weekly Earnings – Supplementary Tables', available at: http://www.statistics.gov.uk/downloads/theme_labour/AWE_Supplementary_tables.xls (accessed 18 August 2010).

Vereint Dienstieistungsgewerkschaft (Ver.di) (2010), 'Working conditions in the mail service sector in Germany', presentation by Stephan Teuscher, Brussels, 30 May 2010.

Wachter, Michael L., Barry T. Hirsch and James W. Gillula (1999), 'Postal service compensation and the comparability standard', *Research in Labor Economics*, **18**, 243–79.

Wachter, Michael L. and Jeffrey M. Perloff (1990), 'A comparative analysis of wage premiums and industrial relations in the British Post Office and the United States Postal Service', Chapter 6 in Michael A. Crew and Paul R. Kleindorfer (eds), *Competition and Innovation in Postal Services*, Dordrecht, NL and Norwell, MA: Kluwer Academic Publishers, pp. 115–34.

Wey, Christian and Sven Heitzler (2010), 'Raising rivals', fixed (labor) costs: the *Deutsche Post* case', Discussion Paper 1008, Deutsches Institut für Wirtschaftsforschung, Berlin, May, available at: http://www.diw.de/documents/publikationen/73/diw_01.c.357066.de/dp1008.pdf (accessed 14 July 2011).

19. Government use of the postal system: an ignored USO component*

Michael J. Ravnitzky[†] and J.P. Klingenberg[‡]

1 INTRODUCTION

As the number and variety of available communication channels proliferates, postal services continue to play a vital role as a fundamental method for government/constituent communications. The government is a significant customer of the mail and a major postal stakeholder. Governments rely upon their ability to administer operations and reach all their citizenry and constituents via the mail.

The purpose of this chapter is to review the government use of mail in the United States and its implications for the Universal Service Obligation (USO). The United States Postal Service (USPS) comprises a communications backbone for all levels of government in the United States, ensuring reliable and timely delivery of messages essential to governmental functions. Though some government mail is vulnerable to electronic substitution, a comparison of United States First-Class mail revenue to the US government's expenditures on First-Class mail indicates that government usage of postal services is comparatively resistant to substitution.

US federal government agencies, in total, spent at least US$1 billion on mailing and shipping services each year between 1997 and 2010.[1] State and local government spent at least as much, and the mail volume from state agencies does not appear to be declining.[2] This chapter identifies three ways in which governments could mail more efficiently, significantly reduce postal expenditures and also promote mail-handling efficiency.

Section 2 discusses why governments use the mail, and reasons why communicating by mail is important to the government. Section 3 describes the size and scope of the US federal government use of the mail, and potential savings due to available changes in mailing operations. Section 4 addresses how substitution lag impacts the government mailer. Section 5 discusses why government mail is an important aspect of the USO, and how the attributes of government mail could influence government policy regarding postal liberalization or changes to the USO. Finally, Section 6 concludes.

† Chief Counsel to the Chairman, US Postal Regulatory Commission.
‡ Economist, US Postal Regulatory Commission.

2 GOVERNMENT USAGE OF MAIL

The earliest postal networks were established for the purpose of official communications.[3] Today, governments need to communicate with their citizens, and vice versa. Governments also must communicate with other levels of government. In many countries, postal communications play a unique, invaluable role associated with the delivery of mail to a mailbox or some other physical location associated with a person or household.[4] Electronic communications do not typically contain such an embedded personalized or geographic link. Linking a person to a postal address allows postal communication to retain its value for many users of the mail – this is especially true for governments. While advertising mail may or may not target a specific recipient, or a specific set of addresses, government entities generally send private, recipient-specific communications.[5]

In the United States, all levels of government send mail tailored to their duties and objectives. Purposes of mail include categories such as notices, invoices, permits/licensing, benefits, voting, warning letters, education, surveys, military service, account statements, employment and tax information, legal correspondence, regulatory compliance, immigration documents, product recalls, voting materials, and aspects of law enforcement. Agencies use mail for recruiting, hiring, training, credentialing and security clearances, and retirement materials.

Many government communications are triggered by legal mandates requiring the use of the mail for transmission and delivery. The purpose is to provide assurance that the recipient (and only the recipient) receives and views their communication. The government is still dependent on the Postal Service, because the Postal Service is the only ubiquitous and affordable delivery service with addresses legally attached to recipient identity.

In countries with federal forms of government, mail is used to reinforce and cement the connections between citizens and their government at each level (local, state and federal). Thus, a national postal system helps preserve a vigorous federal system consisting of a federal government, state governments and subordinate governmental bodies.[6] Furthermore, a federal system has more layers of government, and thus requires more communications, and more mail volume.

Vote by Mail

Vote by mail represents a particularly important facet of government mail. In most locations in the US, voters can cast an absentee ballot by mail. In the United States, certain counties and one state[7] (Oregon) have switched entirely to vote by mail.[8] In those jurisdictions, switching to vote by mail has increased voter turnout and reduced the costs of administering an election[9] by reducing the need for polling places, during a time when it is becoming increasingly difficult to staff those polling places with volunteers. The rising cost of holding traditional elections and opening polling places may be a major factor that encourages the use of vote by mail. In other jurisdictions, an increasing proportion of votes are cast by mail, particularly in jurisdictions that allow voters to receive an absentee ballot without requiring the voter to provide a reason.

Mail can be used in many aspects of elections. These uses include sending registration materials, informational materials, address verifications, sample ballots, actual ballots, and the return of the completed ballot. Most locations have primary elections and general elections, as well as local ballots or referenda. Vote by mail, if it continues to be adopted by states and counties, could generate increasingly large volumes of First-Class mail, both outbound and inbound.

Outgoing and Incoming Government Mail Distinguished

Incoming and outgoing government mail have different characteristics and implications. Incoming mail is largely single-piece First-Class mail and requires manual handling and other special accommodation by the governmental recipient. The need for staff and the handling costs makes it desirable to reduce the quantity of this type of mail. Outgoing mail, however, contains a larger proportion of bulk First-Class letter mail. It obligates capital expenditures rather than tying up labor resources. Government relies primarily on outgoing mail to reach individuals, households and businesses in a way that gains the attention of the recipient. As a result, some outgoing government mail is unlikely to be subject to substitution in the near future.

The Impact of Government Written Communications

A letter from the government is perceived as more important by the recipient than other forms of government communication for several reasons. First, the government sender paid money to send it and to identify the proper location to which to send it, and the recipient generally feels obliged to open and read it. Electronic transmission does not involve the same administrative investment, lacks the guarantee of personalized delivery, and is more likely to be regarded with suspicion by the recipient.[10]

Second, email is not tied to a geographic location and thus does not carry the same implicit jurisdictional message. An email sent to an incorrect address will not find the intended recipient, while a First-Class mail piece will be forwarded. Letters say unequivocally: 'We know where you live'.

Third, 'the medium is the message'.[11] The tangible nature of hard-copy communication makes its receipt more salient and harder to ignore. For example, warning letters from the Food and Drug Administration notifying companies of a regulatory problem convey a sense of gravity and importance that would not be found in an email or a fax. While the conversational nature of email has in many cases supplanted ordinary letter correspondence, the goal of most government communications is not conversation.

3 SIZE AND SCOPE OF US GOVERNMENT MAIL

The US government has grown as a user of the mail. Based on the government's own measures of postal usage, it appears that in the United States, the federal government is the largest user of the mail. The federal government alone spends more than 2 percent of First-Class mail revenue. Counting state and other governmental users, at least 5 percent

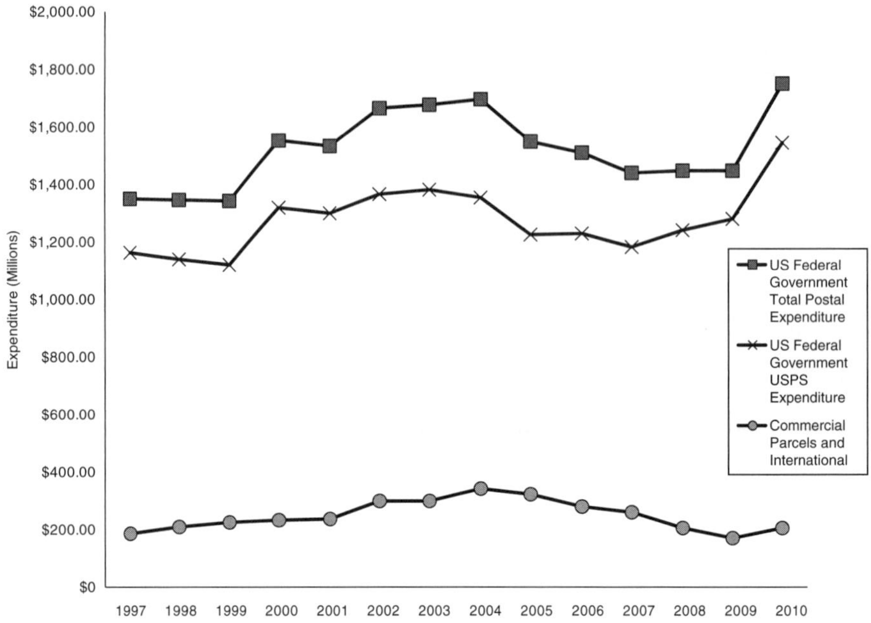

Figure 19.1 US federal government postal expenditure, 1997 to 2010

of First-Class revenue is due to government mailers. Figure 19.1 provides historical details as to the amount of mail sent via the USPS and private carriers by federal agencies.

From 1997 to 2010, the federal government averaged US$1.2 billion annually in USPS expenditures.[12] This ranks the federal government as one of USPS's largest customers. The federal government is also a major customer of FedEx and UPS, spending between $200 and $250 million on private carriers (for example, FedEx Express Mail, UPS Ground) each year between 1997 and 2010.[13] The federal government's market power with respect to private carriers is highlighted by the negotiated rate of US$5.16 for a FedEx Priority overnight 1 lb parcel.[14] The government purchases a large amount of Express services. While the need for quick communication is clearly vital, this is an area where more judicious use could result in cost savings.

Long-term Dependency of the Government on the Postal Service

Electronic substitution is a fundamental phenomenon impacting postal volumes and postal operators. Figure 19.2 contains a comparison of US federal government postal expenditure with overall USPS First-Class revenue. The temporary peaks in 2000 and 2010 are attributable to the impact of the US decennial census.

USPS revenue from First-Class mail has entered a period of accelerating decline. In contrast, the federal government expenditure on First-Class mail has increased 12 percent from 1997 to 2009. This analysis excludes the volume-inflating effects of the Census in 2010. Thus, federal government mail expenditures has run countertrend, increasing First-Class mail spending in a decade in which that class of mail experienced a 2.8 percent annual decline in volume.

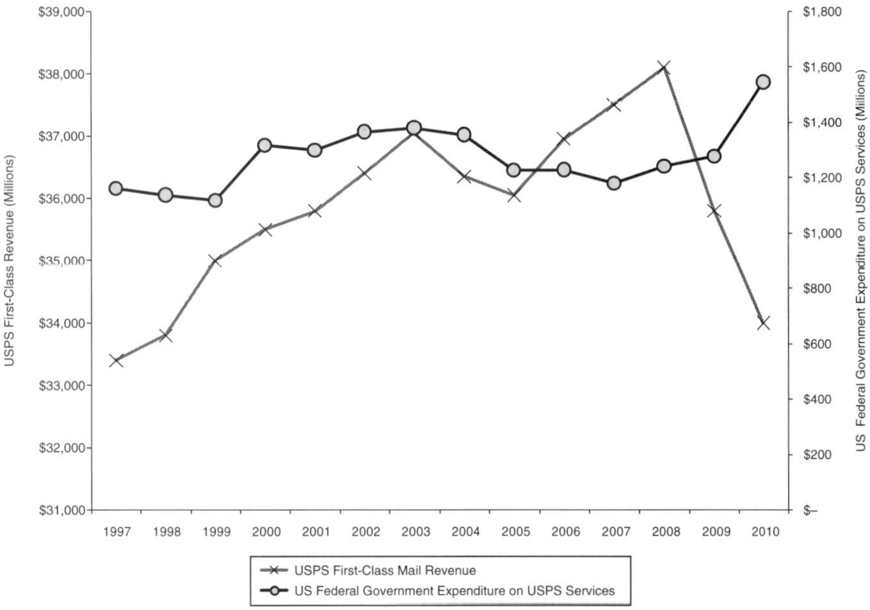

Figure 19.2 *Comparison of total USPS First-Class revenue and US federal government expenditure on USPS services*

Table 19.1 *USPS expenditures for the top eight federal agencies, by 2010 expenditure ($)*

	1999	2000	2009	2010
Social Security Administration	126,705,684	158,803,802	242,992,445	237,748,139
Department of Commerce	16,792,676	185,088,783	19,654,258	223,925,175
Department of Veterans Affairs	82,390,608	99,438,957	164,684,744	223,511,335
Department of Treasury	220,084,969	220,511,897	237,511,498	210,812,059
Department of State	7,093,690	6,876,636	73,669,019	77,664,551
Department of Health and Human Services	33,522,205	27,325,244	7,004,983	55,194,882
Department of Homeland Security	27,424,876	27,964,461	54,571,834	54,411,185
Department of Defense	110,328,505	108,460,646	57,792,798	52,762,032

Most Active Federal Government Mailers

The largest government mailers are listed in Table 19.1. In 1999, these agencies accounted for 57 percent of federal government expenditures with the USPS. By 2010, these mailers accounted for 90 percent of USPS federal expenditures. Certain agencies not listed, such as the Department of Justice, spend more on privately carried commercial parcels than USPS parcel products. Federal agencies are composed of many sub-agencies, and getting all sub-agencies to report timely, accurate and complete information often proves difficult.[15]

The change in spending by each agency is due to agency-specific factors, but connected by the government's mandate at large. Social Security and Veterans Affairs send large amounts of benefit-related mail, and the change in their spending is likely due to an increasingly retirement-age population. The increase in spending by the Departments of Homeland Security, State, and Health and Human Services is likely due to changes in security and health-related legislation.

Savings from Federal Government Presorting of Mail

Many postal operators provide discounts to mailers that send presorted mail. This arrangement in the United States is referred to as 'worksharing'. The volume of mail sent by government agencies makes it amenable to presort operations and discounts.[16] Mail passing through presort channels achieves better address quality, and thus requires less forwarding and fewer returns, resulting in better overall service. A small number of federal agencies (such as the US Navy Anacostia and the Department of Homeland Security) have established successful presort mail facilities. These agency-operated presort mail facilities accept mail from other nearby (different) agencies, prepare the mail to permit access to postal worksharing discounts, and split the cost savings with the originating agencies. This interagency mailing process produces cleaner, better-prepared and finely sorted mail that is more efficiently handled by the Postal Service at reduced cost.[17]

Federal government agencies should follow the lead of components of the Department of Homeland Security and the Department of Defense by consolidating their mail preparation and mailing activities, and significantly expand interagency presort mail operations. By consolidating and presorting in key locations,[18] the federal government could save at least US$100 million per year.[19]

Savings from States Establishing Centralized Mail Operations

In addition to the federal government's use of the mail, states, counties, municipalities, and other public institutions rely on the mail for communication purposes. Based on data from a small sample of four states, it appears that state governments send up to US$1 billion in mail every year.

A number of state governments use outside presort mail businesses to handle some of their outgoing mail. In approximately 10 of the 50 states, however, state government mail operations have been centralized, either by an executive order of the Governor (for example, South Dakota) or else by statute (for example, Tennessee). Such centralization reduces waste, redundancy, and excess metering equipment; reduces the possibility of financial leakage, and builds mailing expertise in one location. It encourages the use of presorted discount rates for state agency mailers who are currently paying more expensive single-piece postage. It also improves the coordination with the postal operator, reduces the opportunities for mail failure, and coordinates mail piece design and production to achieve mailing efficiency. States adopting centralized mail services have recorded savings amounting to millions of dollars each year, up to 50 percent of both postage and mailing operations costs.[20] These states provide a source of institutional experience for presorting the mail that can be assist other government entities that participate in efforts to centralize mail operations. If all state governments centralized their mailing operations, they would save up to US$250 million per year in the aggregate.[21]

Possible Savings from Governmental Negotiated Service Agreements

The federal government, via procurement channels at GSA, has negotiated discounted pricing available on government procurement schedules for services from private Express carriers such as FedEx and UPS. Inclusion on these procurement schedules makes it simpler and cheaper for agencies to use those private carriers. The federal government makes substantial use of FedEx and UPS services, according to GSA statistics. Recently, the USPS has been added to these procurement schedules, but without significant discounting as compared to publicly available commercial rates.

4 SUBSTITUTION LAG AND GOVERNMENT MAIL

Substitution lag associated with government mail use appears to play an important role in this countertrend. Two drivers for volume reduction are electronic substitution and price elasticity. The government, as a customer, has very low price elasticity; the government has few readily available substitution options (alternatives based on price or non-price factors) and may not be inclined to exercise such options.

The Social Security Administration and the Department of Veterans Affairs send a variety of benefits-related materials through the post. Those agencies have taken widely publicized phased steps to halt the mailing of periodic benefit payments, citing yearly savings of over $100 million, including costs such as postage, mailing operations, and overhead. While agencies that provide benefits can shift to offering direct deposit only, the success of these agencies of reducing their costs by sending fewer benefit checks has not changed their status as major mailers. Currently, over 85 percent of Social Security beneficiaries are enrolled in direct deposit, and do not receive checks through the mail.[22] Yet there has been an increase of over $100 million in postal expenditures by the Social Security Administration in the past 10 years. This may be because most recipients already received direct deposit. The increases are due to other mail communications, potentially related to an increase in the number of citizens that require communications with the agency.[23] Government mail is not immune from electronic substitution (or price effects), but the effects of electronic substitution may be deferred for some time by certain unique attributes of government mail.[24]

Government use of mail differs appreciably from the use of mail by companies and other organizations because non-government mailers have greater flexibility to move to alternative electronic communications for some or all of their customers. Non-government mailers can offer a variety of incentives and penalties to convert customers from the mail channel to electronic channels. They can differentiate communication methods with their constituents by market segment or by geography. They can even accept the loss of some customers reluctant to alter communication methods. In contrast, a government entity must serve everyone, and thus does not possess the same type of operational flexibility. It appears that most outgoing government mailings do not differentiate communication channel options (that is, electronic and hard-copy) between citizens, in contrast to private mailers. Laws that both obligate and specify the use of the mail channel mandate much government use of mail. For example, the government mandates that federal agencies notify affected citizens following electronic data breaches.

Citizens largely expect their communications with the government to be by mail. Citizens may want the flexibility to contact government agencies through various means, but the link from government to household, resident and business relies on the mail. This may be affected by demographics, as studies have shown that older people prefer to receive communications through the mail. These citizens, as recipients of benefits, may require more frequent communication with the government. Individuals and households with lower income are also less likely to have regular, secure and convenient access to broadband Internet services. Despite initiatives designed to bridge the 'digital divide', many Americans still lack affordable broadband access.

While companies can provide incentives and penalties to encourage electronic substitution, the government–citizen relationship tends to be mandatory. Private companies can choose not to communicate with potential clients if the costs of communicating via the mail outweigh the benefits. The government usually cannot act in that manner. From another perspective, government electronic substitution occurs by fiat or dictate. Government agencies are often obliged by law to conduct official business through the mail. There is an interlaced web of federal, state, and local laws, regulatory directives and court rules that necessitate notification by mail or personal delivery; there is not yet the flexibility in the laws to substitute electronic methods without an explicit arrangement. It also appears that government communications that are not legally obliged to use the mail (such as informational newsletters) have in large part already migrated to other communication channels. Rarely have agencies seized the authority to alter the operant law to permit substitution; the Internal Revenue Service is an example.

Government agencies may not perceive electronic substitutes as sufficiently robust, reliable or ubiquitous to conduct necessary official business.[25] The mailbox links the physical address with the identity of the recipient, and no widely accepted mechanism exists to tie email addresses with physical addresses. There are companies offering various forms of address-based email, but no accepted standards. Email is oriented toward individuals rather than households, yet much government mail relates to the household as well as the individual. The mail system provides sophisticated forwarding and return services at a reasonable price. The postal provider owns the mail-handling channel from start to finish, providing security and integrity assurances that are missing in most electronic communications where data are handed off through a series of unrelated parties.

The government does not face competitive pressure, as do commercial mailers.[26] In the commercial market for mail, the aggregate demand curve is a function of many firms who individually determine how to use the mail in a competitive market. The same constraints do not apply to the government, which generally does not compete for citizens. As such, the government demand curve will more closely resemble a step function, where individual agencies decide to use substitution. A handful of agencies produce the majority of all federal government mail. Thus, the individual decisions of the largest government agencies have a disproportionate effect on postal expenditures by the government. Agencies are not competing against other government agencies for the most cost-effective medium for communicating. The government acts more like a single-source buyer. An innovation in communication methods by one agency does not force another agency to change its approach to interacting with citizens or risk losing those constituents.

In contrast, commercial firms compete within a single market, impelling each other to create new efficiencies. These firms are constantly developing new methods to interact with consumers, including novel uses of the mail. Effective innovation by one firm can force other firms engaged in the competitive marketplace to alter their communications tactics.

Electronic substitution of government mail is slowed by these factors. Other factors can accelerate electronic substitution in the government environment. In the fall of 2001, an anthrax agent was mailed to certain legislative offices. This action, which caused fatalities, altered the way in which citizens communicate with federal officials. Screening and irradiation practices were instituted that caused delays and damaged mail, and has induced some senders to use alternative means.

5 THE GOVERNMENT MAILER AND THE USO

The Importance of the USO to the Government

The interests of the government, an important mailstream participant, should be taken into consideration in defining and executing the USO. It is possible that the interests of the government mailers are taken into consideration through political oversight and involvement. In a 2008 report, the Postal Regulatory Commission defined the USO using seven principal attributes: geographic scope, product range, access, delivery, pricing, service quality, and enforcement mechanism.[27]

Many of the attributes of the USO are important to the government as a mailer. These attributes include an accurate central mail address system with a timely address correction mechanism;[28] the ability to mail everywhere in the nation; geographically uniform rates throughout the nation; predictable and consistent delivery performance (and for state and local government mailers, rapid delivery within a geographic area); security and sanctity of the mail, legal protections for the mail and an enforcement apparatus such as the Postal Inspection Service; security screening of inbound mail but avoiding excessive delays in receipt; and the contingency value of continuing to operate a communication channel of last resort, even if at a reduced level, in the event of natural disaster or other disruption in normal electronic communications. For the government agencies that send mail, a mail provider must effectively offer these USO attributes.

The manner in which the government currently uses the mail highlights why these attributes are of particular concern. Predictable delivery performance and service performance measurement is evidenced by over US$200 million spent by the government each year on Express mail when First-Class service is fast enough or traceable enough. The security of the mail is vital for incoming mail service due to the threat of mail-related terrorism and the importance of protecting government agencies from this threat. The government has a vested interest in ensuring that citizens are not 'spoofed' by counterfeit mail that appears official. Law enforcement ensures that both of these USO security goals are achieved.

Delivery frequency may be more important to government users than to other mailers because of a lack of electronic alternatives due to legal and operational constraints. For similar reasons, geographically uniform rates affect a government mailer more than other postal users. Government mailing lists contain the name and address of every citizen, rural or urban. Since the government mails due to legal mandate or obligation rather than a profit motive, the government cannot adjust its mailing list to selectively send only to profitable customers.

Effects of Liberalization or Reduction in the USO on the Government Mailer

Given the size and importance of the government as a mailer, the impact of a change on postal provider is very important to the government. When a post is liberalized or privatized, the effect on mailers is uncertain. Much research has been done on what occurs when a post's monopoly is reduced, but these effects have not focused on the government mailer. Historical analysis has shown that bulk-mail prices are generally reduced. Single-piece prices have risen in some instances, remained stable in some countries (reduced in inflation-adjusted terms), and been reduced as postal liberalization takes effect.[29] As such, the price effect of reduced postal monopoly varies for single-piece mailers, but is favorable for bulk mailers.

Collectively, the government, including all federal agencies, states, and localities, is the largest mailer in the United States. Yet, paradoxically, it can be most appropriately characterized as a single-piece mailer. Many government agencies presort some of their mail, but most government agencies send mail primarily at single-piece rates. This is of significant concern for the government mailer in a liberalized environment. In the United States, the USPS monopoly includes many restrictions, such as price regulation and the USO. The government (as a mailer) benefits financially from these obligations and restrictions. Reduction of the monopoly and changes to the USO can impair the government mailer.

Because the government uses the mail as its primary communication channel and sends much of it at single-piece rates, liberalization could have a negative impact. The mail generally considered most likely to be attractive to postal competitors is bulk mail, often Standard bulk mail. The government sends relatively little of this mail. Governments find the following important: speed of communication (Express mail), geographically equal rates (much government mail is sent to rural citizens) and frequency. The government could exercise market power, but a decentralized infrastructure for entering government mail may not provide negotiation flexibility that the overall scope of the government mailing operation might imply.

6 CONCLUSIONS

In the US, the federal structure of the government, as well as the trends of mail-based government communication, has led to the government being a major user of postal services. All levels of government could realize significant savings by working together to presort their mail. Federal agencies could save at least US$100 million per year by expanding worksharing and establishing cooperative presort operations in cities with a significant federal presence. States could generate aggregate savings of US$250 million per year by instituting centralized mail operations in geographic proximity to the state capital. Government mailers may benefit from entering into negotiated service agreements, individually or collectively.[30] To date, electronic substitution for the mail has occurred less in government-related communications than it has in other sectors; agencies rely on the secure, reliable and ubiquitous communication services provided by postal networks. The duration of substitution lag for government mailers remains to be quantified.

Government agencies value the unique link between address and identity more than other types of postal consumers. In the United States, this is exhibited by the fact that government use of First-Class mail has increased at a greater rate than the industry at large. Changes in USO and ownership affect all users of the mail, but government may be affected by these changes more than other users.

In the United States, the government currently reaps significant financial and operational benefit from the current structure of the mailstream, and this benefit may cause resistance to systemic change. Specifically, the heavy dependency of government on the mails and the USO function of government mail may influence (and constrain) the degree to which postal 'liberalization' or privatization can be encouraged and endorsed by the government. Because the federal government ultimately decides the degree to which postal liberalization takes place, its reliance on the mail is likely to be a significant factor in that decision making.

NOTES

* The views in this chapter are those of the authors and do not necessarily reflect those of the Postal Regulatory Commission.

1. US federal government agency postal expenditure data was provided by the US General Services Agency (GSA), which instructs all federal agencies to report their mail expenditures yearly. The data for 2010 can be found at http://www.gsa.gov/portal/category/101091. The authors are grateful for the assistance and insights provided by the GSA mail management staff and the mail managers at several federal agencies and states.
2. The survey conducted was incomplete, consisting of data from the centralized mail operations of four states and discussions with other state mailing offices.
3. The Persians, Chinese, Greeks, Romans, the Maurya Dynasty in India, the Mongol Empire and the European monarchs, among others, had well-organized postal networks, but those networks were largely limited to official purposes such as intelligence gathering, tax collection, and civil administration. This changed when, on July 31, 1635, Charles I of England opened the Royal Mail to public use.
4. For a survey of how many governments use the mail, see Kogler and Jakovljevic (2011), available at: http://www.executive-magazine.com/getarticle.php?article=14324.
5. Describing postal system in terms of electronic communication networks can help explain its attractiveness to governments. In electronic network terms, postal mail is a two-way synchronous communication channel with dynamic expansive capacity, high packet reliability, very low loss/error rates, multi-layer error correction capability, and low delay jitter. Postal mail permits the sender to select a delivery priority and to specify reduced latency by paying a premium. Postal mail incorporates the capability of message acknowledgement, auto-forwarding, and auto-return in the event of non-delivery, and provides the capability for address feedback in the event of forwarding or return. It is particularly resistant to spoofing, piggybacking malware and other illicit behavior. From a network analysis perspective, this particular grouping of characteristics makes the mail highly desirable as a governmental channel.
6. Several nations have federal governments, including, for example, Switzerland, Canada, India, Germany, Australia, and Austria. Although data are not yet available, it is reasonable to speculate that a country with a federalist structure may produce more mail and may place greater reliance on the postal system than countries with a unitary structure (such as France). Similarly, localities with extensive local home rule provisions or an extensive array of local governmental units may produce more mail.

7. See, generally, Brown (2010), available at: http://www.prc.gov/Docs/69/69484/Brown2.pdf (accessed on July 7, 2011).
8. In California, nearly 50 percent of all the votes cast in the 2008 election were mail ballots. In Washington State, 38 of the 39 counties vote exclusively by mail. Colorado approved a plan letting counties decide to hold primary elections exclusively by mail (Brown Testimony).
9. See Southwell (2004, pp. 2, 7–10). There is an extensive body of literature on the impact of vote by mail on elections.
10. Hard-copy communications are intrinsically less vulnerable to forgery or impersonation, both because they require a transactional cost for printing and postage, and because the recipient can open them without danger of electronic malware.
11. See McLuhan (1964).
12. GSA (2011).
13. Ibid.
14. The GSA contracts for Express small package delivery service with all eligible suppliers can be found at: http://www.gsaelibrary.gsar.gov/ElibMain/SinDetails?executeQuery=YES&schedule Number=48&flag=&filter=&specialItemNumber=451+1 (accessed July 7, 2011). In comparison, the GSA rate for a 1 lb USPS Express mail piece is US$12.74.
15. The data provided in Table 19.1 should be considered a lower-bound estimate. Information regarding the 2009 and 2010 Postal Service expenditures for the Treasury Department sub-agency FMS (over $100 million in 2008) is not currently available.
16. Mail volume sent by individual agencies can vary significantly from day to day, and each individual agency may not have the critical mass of volume required to be eligible for presorting discounts. By combining agencies, critical mass can easily be reached on a daily basis.
17. Data provided by US federal agencies states that the return rate (undeliverable mail) ranges from 1–5 percent depending on the agency, suggesting that some agencies can improve service, as well as reduce the postage cost of mailings, by participating in a presorting program.
18. The federal executive boards are existing governmental structures well-suited to establishing such federal presort mail operations. Some 28 federal executive boards exist in key locations throughout the nation where a significant federal agency presence exists. See http://www.feb.gov.
19. Government mailing at the lowest possible presort rate would improve the Postal Service's finances and the overall contribution to institutional costs, even though it would collect less revenue. There are also operational advantages to cleaner, better prepared mail for the Postal Service. At least US$500 million in mail was sent as First-Class OMAS metered mail in 2010. If this mail is sent at single-piece rates, entering this mail as 5-digit presorted (the furthest downstream access price) would yield over 20 percent savings, or at least US$100 million.
20. Within-state mailings often have a one-day processing standard. Presorting helps ensure that the operator can provide this high level of service.
21. Of the four states sampled, the states averaged 25 percent postage savings by centralizing mail operations to reduce redundancy and maximize presorting discounts. Notably, the centralization of postal operations also led to improved service performance. The estimation of potential savings can be refined through additional data transparency by each state regarding current mailing operations and expenditures.
22. Available at: http://newsfeedresearcher.com/data/articles_b19/security-social-checks.html (accessed July 7, 2011).
23. As the United States population ages, it is possible that the Social Security Administration is sending fewer pieces to more people, on balance leading to an increase.
24. It remains to be assessed how much lag or deferral exists.
25. Moreover, in large parts of the United States, broadband Internet service is simply not available. See, for example, http://www.broadbandmap.gov; OECD broadband portal available at: http://www.oecd.org/document/54/0,3746,en_2649_33703_38690102_1_1_1_1,00.html (accessed July 7, 2011). See also Severson (2011).
26. Until postal reorganization legislation was enacted in 1970, federal agencies sent much official mail franked (that is, at no charge).
27. US Postal Regulatory Commission (2008), at 16.
28. The United States has a mobile population; a large percentage of the US population changes its address each year.
29. See generally, Groebel (2010).
30. Crew and Kleindorfer (2006).

REFERENCES

Brown, Kate (2010), Testimony of Oregon Secretary of State, Docket No. N2010-1, Filed August 3, Postal Regulatory Commission.
Crew, Michael A. and Paul R. Kleindorfer (eds) (2006), *Progress toward Liberalization of the Postal and Delivery Sector*, New York: Springer Science + Business Media, Inc.
General Services Administration (GSA) (1997–2010), Data on federal agency mail usage, extracted from the annual Mail Management and Security Plans provided to GSA by federal agencies.
Groebel, Annegret (2010), 'Regulatory challenges in the German postal market', paper presented at the WIK, 12th Königswinter Seminar, 24 February, available at: http://www.wik.org/filead-min/Konferenzbeitraege/2010/12th_Koenigswinter_Seminar/S3_5_Groebel.pdf (accessed July 7, 2011).
Kogler, Ulrich and Ivan Jakovljevic (2011), 'Proving there's still a place for snail mail in the digital age', *Executive Magazine*, June 2.
McLuhan, Marshall (1964), *The Media Extensions of Man*, New York: McGraw Hill.
Severson, Kim (2011), 'For much of rural America, broadband is a dividing line', *New York Times*, February 18, at A1, A18.
Southwell, Priscilla L. (2004), 'Five years later: a re-assessment of Oregon's vote by mail electoral process', *PS: Politics and Political Science*, **98**(1), 1–10.
US Postal Regulatory Commission (2008), 'Report on Universal Postal Service and the Postal Monopoly', available at: http://www.prc.gov/Docs/61/61628/USO%20Report.pdf (accessed July 7, 2011).

20. UPU terminal dues: winners and losers*

James I. Campbell Jr,[†] Alex Kalevi Dieke[‡] and Martin Zauner[§]

1 INTRODUCTION

Modern industrialized countries have long accepted the principle that postage rates should be based on the costs of production. Yet what is taken for granted in regulating postage rates at the national level is almost wholly ignored when it comes to international postage rates. Post offices do not charge each other the same for delivery of inbound international mail as they charge their own citizens for delivery of similar mail. For example, the US Postal Service charges substantially less for delivery of German and Japanese letters than for delivery of identical American letters.

Why have international postage rates resisted the otherwise universally accepted principle that postage rates should be based on costs? For more than 40 years, the Universal Postal Union (UPU), the intergovernmental organization which establishes rules for exchanging international documents and parcels, has labored to develop a fair and efficient approach towards 'terminal dues' – fees that a destination post office collects for delivery of inbound international mail. For at least 20 years, officials in the US government, the European Union, and the UPU itself have recognized that the only reasonable solution is to align terminal dues with already cost-based domestic postage rates. Yet little progress has been made.

A primary obstacle to reform has been the system's impenetrable complexity. A system of non-cost-based terminal dues results in winners and losers. Some post offices are underpaid for delivery of inbound international mail forcing up prices of domestic mailers. Other post offices benefit from overpayments and are effectively subsidized by mailers in other countries. Yet policy makers are wholly in the dark as to who wins and who loses and by how much. Without such basic information it is impossible to propose solutions.

This chapter seeks to clarify how the UPU terminal dues system produces winners and losers. It is divided as follows. Section 2 briefly describes the historical development of terminal dues. Section 3 explains the mathematical model used to estimate bilateral payments for delivery of inbound international mail under different compensation schemes. Section 4 analyzes the distortions created, that is, the discrepancies between UPU terminal dues and delivery charges aligned with domestic postage. Section 5 summarizes our conclusions.

† Attorney, Washington, DC.

‡ Head of Postal and Logistics Studies, Wissenschaftliches Institut für Instruktur und Kommunikationsdienste (WIK), Bad Honnef, Germany.

§ Senior Economist, WIK.

2 UPU TERMINAL DUES IN 2008

Until 1969, each UPU member country delivered inbound international mail without charge. This system benefited post offices that exported more mail than they imported (usually in industrialized countries) and penalized those that imported more than they exported (usually in developing countries). In 1969 a UPU Congress recognized the problem but was unable to agree on a simple, economically sound principle for compensating post offices for inbound imbalances. Instead, the 1969 Congress adopted an arbitrary 'terminal dues' charge of 0.50 gold francs per kilogram (about 0.16 SDR: special drawing rights). Henceforth, if post office A sent post office B more kilograms of letter post mail than B sent A, then B could demand terminal dues for the excess.

Terminal dues introduced a divisive factor into UPU congresses. Countries benefitting from higher terminal dues far outnumbered net payers. The terminal dues rate was tripled in 1974 to 1.5 gold francs (about 0.49 SDR) and more than tripled in 1979 to 5.5 gold francs (fixed at 1.90 SDR). In the 1984 Congress, major post offices joined forces to prevent a similar increase. Delegates compromised on a 45 percent increase, to 2.641 SDR per kg.

In holding down terminal dues, however, industrialized countries inadvertently created incentives for bypassing regular international mail channels. Typically, a post office would charge outbound international mailers much more than justified by the cost of terminal dues paid to destination post offices. In the 1980s, outbound mailers began to work with private transport companies to circumvent the UPU system. Private carriers would collect international mail from mailers in country A and convey it to country B, where post office B would forward the mail to other post offices (C, D, E, and so on) for rates that were more closely aligned to terminal dues charges. Why? Post office B offered this 'remail' service for a small markup because remail allowed post office B to profit from international distribution of mail that would otherwise never pass through post office B – that is, it would go directly from post office A to post office C. Remail offered international mailers lower rates – and often better service – for mail sent to industrialized countries where domestic postage rates exceeded UPU terminal dues.

Growth of remail required the UPU to reconsider the principles of terminal dues. Ten years later, in 1999, the UPU officially accepted the principle that terminal dues should reflect the costs of services rendered. In practice, this implied that terminal dues should be equal to domestic postage rates for comparable mail. In reality, however, the UPU has done little to make it so. Instead, starting in 1989, the UPU adopted a two-tiered approach to terminal dues designed to protect industrialized countries against remail while satisfying demands of developing countries for continuation of artificially low terminal dues rates for their mail. Evolution of the terminal dues system for industrialized countries since 1989 has been convoluted. For our purposes, it is sufficient to summarize the terminal dues system as it existed in 2008, the date of key data in the terminal dues model presented below.

In the Universal Postal Convention of 2004, in effect in 2008, the terminal dues system for industrialized countries was called the 'target system', and the one for developing countries the 'transitional system'. These labels implied that the 'transitional' countries (that is, the developing countries) would one day adopt the terminal dues system of the 'target' countries (that is, the industrialized countries). Omitting territories not

UPU members in their own right (for example, Gibraltar, Norfolk Island), the 28 target system countries were Australia, Austria, Belgium, Canada, Denmark, Finland, France, Germany, Greece, Iceland, Ireland, Israel, Italy, Japan, Liechtenstein, Luxembourg, Monaco, the Netherlands, New Zealand, Norway, Portugal, San Marino, Spain, Sweden, Switzerland, the United Kingdom, the United States, and the Vatican.

The target terminal dues system of 2004 applied only to mail that both originated in and was destined for a target system country. For 'letter post' items – regular letters, large flat envelopes, and small packets weighing up to 2kg – target system post offices charged each other terminal dues calculated by applying a charge per item and a charge per kilogram. In 2008, the charges were supposed to be related to 66 percent of the domestic postage rate for a 20 gram letter sent by priority or first class domestic postal service. In fact, terminal dues charges were constrained within tight cap and floor provisions. Charges could not exceed 0.237 SDR per item and 1.858 SDR per kg, or fall below 0.158 per item and 1.598 per kg. Terminal dues for almost all industrialized countries were established by this rate band, not the link to domestic postage rates. Hence, the target system was not truly cost based. For letter post items sent to, from, or between 'transitional' countries, the terminal dues rate in 2008 was 3.727 SDR per kg regardless of the number of postal items per kilogram.

3 TERMINAL DUES MODEL

As neutral observers have recognized, the straightforward way to eliminate distortions in payments for delivery of international letter post items is for each post office to charge other post offices the domestic postage that would be due for delivery of similar items. Domestic postage is the proper standard for two reasons. First, while it is impossible to obtain definitive cost data for inbound delivery services of most national post offices, one may reasonably rely on domestic postage rates as a proxy for costs. Indeed, in most industrialized countries, national law requires domestic postage rates to be based on costs. Second, domestic postage is the proper standard because in the modern world it is unjustifiable to discriminate against foreign mailers in the pricing of universal postal services. Put simply, it is no more acceptable for the French post office (for example) to charge the British post office a rate for delivery of inbound international letters that differs from comparable domestic postage than it would be for a Parisian postal clerk to charge English tourists a higher or lower postage rate than paid by local French citizens.

Therefore, in order to estimate the economic distortions caused by UPU or other terminal dues arrangements, the authors have developed a mathematical model that estimates differences between delivery charges for inbound international mail calculated according to (i) domestic postage rates and (ii) the terminal dues scheme under study. Our model focuses on the exchange of letter post mail among the 34 member countries of the Organization for Economic Cooperation and Development (OECD) and mail exchanges between OECD and non-OECD countries collectively. To simplify the exposition, we shall refer to OECD countries as industrialized countries (ICs) and non-OECD countries as developing countries (DCs) even though not all OECD member countries are included in the UPU's target system for terminal dues purposes. Similarly, rather than using the UPU's confusing 'target' and 'transitional' labels for its two terminal dues regimes, we shall refer to the IC and DC terminal dues systems. In the model itself, however, calculations conform to the rules for the target and transitional systems in effect in 2008.

What, precisely, is the domestic postage that would be due for delivery of inbound international letter post items? The appropriate rate is not the full retail rate but something closer to the discounted rates charged bulk domestic mailers. Typically, a bulk mailer receives a discount of about 15 to 25 percent from the retail rate because the post office does not have to collect bulk mail and bulk mail is already sorted by the mailer. For non-priority mail, often advertisements, post offices usually offer additional discounts that can be as high as 50 or 60 percent off the priority retail rate. Calculating the domestic bulk-mail postage that post office A should pay to post office B requires several bits of information: (i) the volume of mail dispatched by post office A; (ii) the postage rates of post office B; and (iii) the distribution of post office A's mail according the rate categories of post office B. Most of this information is not publicly available so our model necessarily relies on proxies and reasonable assumptions. This section describes the premises of the model.

Estimating Bilateral Mail Flows

Figures for bilateral volumes of mail are derived from the total outbound letter post volumes of each post office for 2007 (available from the UPU) and from OECD statistics for bilateral trade in goods and services. These calculations require several steps.

According to UPU statistics, in 2007 the world's post offices dispatched about 5.85 billion outbound letter post items and received about 7.52 billion inbound items. Obviously, there is a statistical mismatch. For the world as a whole, total outbound volume must equal total inbound volume. If inbound figures are correct, then the origin post office is unknown for 30 percent of all outbound international mail (1.7 billion items). In developing a terminal dues model, the first question that must be asked is whether the total volume of mail received by post offices is 5.85 or 7.52 billion items? As noted above, in the last 15 years large mailers have begun to tender significant amounts of international mail to foreign post offices, that is, to a post office other than the national post office where the mailer resides. This 'extra-territorial' mail might be physically transported to a foreign post office ('remail,' in UPU parlance), tendered to the local office of a foreign post office (an 'extra-territorial office of exchange' or 'ETOE'), or electronically transmitted to a foreign country where it is printed and tendered to the post office ('non-physical remail'). Indeed, some post offices appear to be using such practices to save costs on outbound mail. Since competition among post offices is considered unseemly at the UPU, it may be that post offices that handle large amounts of extra-territorial mail are omitting this mail from their reported outbound volumes. Whether the large discrepancy between the reported outbound and inbound mail volumes can be explained by extra-territorial mail of unknown origin or by systemic accounting errors is unknown. The model therefore considers both possibilities. The 'known origin' and 'unknown origin' calculations may be considered as, roughly, lower and upper boundaries for the estimated distortions caused by non-cost-based terminal dues.

The next step is to allocate 'known origin' *outbound* mail volumes sent from IC post offices. UPU studies and our analyses suggest that the amount of outbound international mail sent to a given country is closely correlated to revenues earned from the export of commodities and services to that country. For the OECD as a whole, trade data imply that between 75 percent (commodities) and 83 percent (services) of outbound IC international mail is destined for another IC. The model adopts a figure of 80 percent. Intra-OECD mail is then allocated to bilateral pairs of ICs based on bilateral trade statistics.[1] For example, if 15.1 percent of French exports go to Germany, then the model assumes that 15.1 percent of the outbound international mail reported by La Poste also goes to Germany. For each IC post office, the letter post volume sent to DCs – that is, to the rest of the world – is the mail not allocated to another IC country. As with trade generally, the result is that ICs differ significantly in the proportion of mail sent to DCs.

The volume of known origin *inbound* mail for each IC post office is determined as follows. The volume of inbound mail received from other ICs is given by the outbound analysis. The volume of mail received from DCs is unknown, but an approximation is suggested by UPU studies. It appears that DCs receive from ICs about twice as much mail as they send to ICs. The model assumes that this is the case for the OECD as a whole and then allocates the inbound mail to individual ICs in proportion to their shares of the outbound mail from ICs collectively. For example, if France accounted for 9.7 percent of all IC to DC letter post items, then the model assumes that 9.7 percent of DC to IC letter post was destined for France. In a few countries, these calculations imply a total inbound volume that exceeds what the IC post office reports. In such cases, all bilateral flows have been adjusted proportionally to avoid this contradiction.

At this point, the model addresses the mail of *unknown origin* described above. The foregoing calculations imply that IC post offices received 4.25 billion items whereas they reported a total inbound volume of 5.20 billion items. This is 953 million of the global 1.67 billion discrepancy between inbound and outbound volumes reported by the world's post offices. The model assumes, as an upper limit possibility, that all of these 953 million letter post items of unknown origin actually originated from mailers in other ICs and were tendered to foreign post offices using remail, ETOEs, or distant printing but not reported as outbound mail by those post offices. Half of the mail is assumed to have been presented to IC post offices and half to DC post offices.

In sum, the model begins with a plausible pattern of bilateral mail flows among ICs (the OECD countries) and between ICs and DCs (the non-OECD countries) that fits known facts. According to the model, the IC to IC letter post consisted of about 3.77 billion items (65 percent of the world total) or 4.73 billion items if inbound items of unknown origin are included (63 percent of the world total that includes all mail of unknown origin). The ICs exported 943 million letter post items to DCs and received 472 million items in return.

Domestic Postage Rates

The second requirement for the model is domestic postage rates. An almost complete set of 2008 retail priority postage rates for each country is available from the UPU. In the model the appropriate domestic postage for delivery of inbound international priority letter post items is assumed to be 80 percent of the retail rate for delivery in ICs and 100 percent in DCs. Since UPU data are limited to priority or first class services, it is also necessary to make an assumption about the extent of non-priority mail in international mail flows and the discount from priority rates given to non-priority mail. The model assumes that 40 percent of letter post items sent by ICs are non-priority and 10 percent of letter post items sent by DCs. The discount from delivery of non-priority inbound mail is assumed to be 40 percent for mail delivered in ICs and 20 percent in DCs.

Profiles of Outbound International Mail

The third piece of information needed in our model is the distribution or 'profile' of letter post items across the shape- and weight-based categories of domestic postage rates in the destination country. UPU studies indicate that the average weight of cross-border items has increased since 1998. A recent survey provides a breakdown by shape and weight of letter post items dispatched by 12 countries and less detailed information about a larger number of countries. While it is unclear how representative these figures are, it appears that the increase in average weight per item is due primarily to a decrease in the proportion of small letters and a corresponding increase in the proportion of large envelopes and small packets and, to a lesser extent, to a decrease in the lighter items within each shape. In our model, we use the 12-country profile as a starting point and adjust these proportions to modify the average weight per letter post item to 80.0 grams (12.50 items per kg) for mail dispatched by IC countries and 75.5 grams (13.25 items per kg) for mail dispatched by DCs.

Domestic Postage for a Typical Letter Post Item

Using these assumptions, it is straightforward to calculate the domestic bulk-mail rate that would be charged for delivery of a typical letter post item. The amount varies according to the postage in each destination country and the profile of mail dispatched by the origin post office. For example, the model posits that a shipment of letter post mail from an IC post office includes 69.8 percent letter envelopes, 19.1 percent large envelopes, and 11.1 percent packets. Forty percent of these items are assumed to qualify for a non-priority discount. In 2008, the average bulk domestic postage per item for a shipment of such mail was (in SDRs) 1.14 in Italy, 0.71 in Germany, 0.47 in the United States, and 0.47 in Spain.

Table 20.1 shows, for each of the ICs, the estimated domestic postage charges in SDR that would be assessed for delivery of a typical inbound international letter post item (using the profile of an IC post office). The table also shows the UPU terminal dues charge assessed on the same mail if received from a DC (second column) or an IC (third column). The model can also calculate the delivery charge under alternative terminal dues schemes. The fourth column shows the delivery charge that would result from the UPU IC terminal dues without the floor and cap provisions.

As shown in Table 20.1, UPU IC terminal dues are substantially below comparable domestic postage rates in almost all ICs. Because of tight cap and floor constraints, UPU IC terminal dues rates poorly reflect variations in national postage rates. On average, UPU terminal dues payments are 31 percent below domestic postage charges for comparable mail. Even if the cap and floor constraints are removed, terminal dues remain about 27 percent too low.

Table 20.1 Domestic bulk rates versus UPU terminal dues systems for a typical IC origin letter post item (SDR)

		Estimated domestic postage	UPU DC terminal dues	UPU IC terminal dues	UPU IC w/o floor or cap
AT	Austria	0.544	0.298	0.386	0.436
AU	Australia	0.429	0.298	0.286	0.261
BE	Belgium	0.588	0.298	0.386	0.430
CA	Canada	0.718	0.298	0.332	0.323
CH	Switzerland	0.736	0.298	0.386	0.486
CL	Chile	0.319	0.298	0.298	0.281
CZ	Czech Republic	0.362	0.298	0.298	0.281
DE	Germany	0.706	0.298	0.386	0.436
DK	Denmark	0.826	0.298	0.386	0.550
EE	Estonia	0.295	0.298	0.298	0.281
EL	Greece	0.584	0.298	0.386	0.430
ES	Spain	0.468	0.298	0.286	0.277
FI	Finland	0.899	0.298	0.386	0.497
FR	France	0.659	0.298	0.386	0.424
HU	Hungary	0.420	0.298	0.298	0.281
IE	Ireland	0.684	0.298	0.386	0.436
IL	Israel	0.423	0.298	0.386	0.442
IS	Iceland	0.382	0.298	0.368	0.359
IT	Italy	1.136	0.298	0.386	0.467
JP	Japan	0.582	0.298	0.386	0.420
KR	Korea	0.238	0.298	0.298	0.281
LU	Luxembourg	0.543	0.298	0.386	0.406
MX	Mexico	0.348	0.298	0.298	0.281
NL	Netherlands	0.888	0.298	0.378	0.370
NO	Norway	1.303	0.298	0.386	0.615
NZ	New Zealand	0.423	0.298	0.368	0.360
PL	Poland	0.455	0.298	0.298	0.281
PT	Portugal	0.521	0.298	0.384	0.376
SE	Sweden	0.840	0.298	0.386	0.446
SI	Slovenia	0.328	0.298	0.298	0.281
SK	Slovak Republic	0.383	0.298	0.298	0.281
TR	Turkey	0.370	0.298	0.298	0.281
UK	United Kingdom	0.499	0.298	0.355	0.347
US	United States	0.473	0.298	0.286	0.261

4 WHO WINS, WHO LOSES?

Whether or not a post office wins or loses using the understated charges of the UPU terminal dues system rather than comparable domestic postage depends on two major factors. First, low, relatively uniform rates favor exporters over importers for the simple reason that they are buying more of an underpriced service, inward mail delivery. Second,

Table 20.2 Gain or loss from UPU terminal dues compared to domestic postage

		ICs to ICs				ICs to/from DCs	
		Gain (loss) known origin mail (mil SDR)	Per outbound item (SDR)	Gain (loss) all inbound mail (mil SDR)	Per outbound item (SDR)	Gain (loss) inbound mail (mil SDR)	Per outbound item (SDR)
AT	Austria	7.3	0.110	0.9	0.014	–1.7	–0.180
AU	Australia	11.7	0.105	5.9	0.053	–6.2	–0.114
BE	Belgium	12.9	0.080	11.5	0.071	–6.5	–0.201
CA	Canada	–32.7	–0.160	–106.8	–0.521	–17.0	–0.262
CH	Switzerland	2.2	0.012	–26.2	–0.146	–3.9	–0.278
CL	Chile	0.2	0.177	0.2	0.171	0.0	–0.018
CZ	Czech Republic	13.7	0.328	12.5	0.299	–0.2	–0.042
DE	Germany	1.5	0.003	–150.8	–0.262	–29.4	–0.262
DK	Denmark	–15.1	–0.298	–22.8	–0.450	–4.4	–0.326
EE	Estonia	1.2	0.546	1.2	0.546	0.0	–0.004
EL	Greece	4.4	0.114	3.6	0.094	–2.3	–0.200
ES	Spain	41.6	0.183	41.4	0.182	–3.4	–0.135
FI	Finland	–11.9	–0.558	–11.9	–0.558	–4.7	–0.359
FR	France	–5.7	–0.020	–16.8	–0.059	–21.8	–0.238
HU	Hungary	2.5	0.190	2.5	0.190	–0.2	–0.070
IE	Ireland	–10.1	–0.151	–10.1	–0.151	–4.1	–0.249
IL	Israel	0.4	0.090	0.2	0.040	–1.3	–0.118
IS	Iceland	0.4	0.295	0.4	0.271	0.0	–0.094
IT	Italy	–135.9	–1.836	–135.9	–1.836	–9.7	–0.481
JP	Japan	–27.9	–0.583	–35.4	–0.739	–7.2	–0.198
KR	Korea	4.3	0.649	4.3	0.649	0.2	0.028
LU	Luxembourg	6.3	0.194	6.3	0.194	–0.4	–0.178
MX	Mexico	2.0	0.068	2.0	0.068	–0.3	–0.033
NL	Netherlands	–8.1	–0.042	–8.1	–0.042	–12.9	–0.350
NO	Norway	–47.3	–1.556	–86.1	–2.831	–2.8	–0.570
NZ	New Zealand	1.4	0.100	0.5	0.035	–1.3	–0.114
PL	Poland	9.3	0.236	9.3	0.235	–0.6	–0.091
PT	Portugal	5.6	0.137	5.2	0.127	–0.7	–0.166
SE	Sweden	–4.1	–0.045	–6.7	–0.075	–6.7	–0.331
SI	Slovenia	2.8	0.435	2.8	0.432	0.0	–0.018
SK	Slovak Republic	3.2	0.219	3.0	0.205	–0.1	–0.053
TR	Turkey	6.4	0.317	4.3	0.211	–0.5	–0.044
UK	United Kingdom	68.6	0.172	68.6	0.172	–21.2	–0.152
US	United States	88.8	0.131	88.8	0.131	–21.1	–0.137

the UPU system favors low-cost post offices over high-cost post offices, because they are, in effect, trading their own low-cost delivery services for the more costly delivery services of other post offices. Thus, a low-cost exporter such as the UK's Royal Mail wins, and a high-cost importer such as Italy's Poste Italiane loses.

Table 20.2 shows the estimated net gains or losses on the exchange of international mail between IC countries if UPU terminal dues were charged consistently by all post offices instead of bulk domestic postage charges. Since some post offices participated in alternative non-UPU terminal dues arrangements in 2008 (REIMS or bilateral agreements), this table shows the effects of the UPU terminal dues scheme *in principle*, not actual net payments among IC post offices. Net gain or loss per country is derived by comparing the balance that remains after paying UPU terminal dues for outbound mail and receiving UPU terminal dues for inbound mail and comparing that figure to the balance that would result if the same country had paid and received charges based on domestic postage rates. For each IC, the net gain or loss is calculated by disregarding inbound mail of unknown origin and again by including inbound mail of unknown origin.

The overall effect of the UPU terminal dues system is to transfer a substantial sum of money from losers to winners. Taking into account only the outbound mail reported by origin post offices ('known origin' mail), it appears that winners gain about 299 million SDR. The big winners are the Royal Mail (UK), the US Postal Service, and the Spanish Post Office. The major losers are Poste Italiane, Norway Post, Japan Post, Canada Post, Irish An Post, Finland Post, and Post Denmark. If mail of unknown origin is also taken into account – that is, if post offices actually received all of the inbound mail they reported – then losses are exacerbated significantly, especially for Deutsche Post, which reports much more inbound mail than our trade-based model predicts. Counting unknown origin mail also implies major losses for Swiss Post and La Poste (France), and the transfer from losers to winners jumps to 618 million SDR. Assuming that half of the intra-OECD mail of unknown origin is posted via IC post offices and half via DC post offices, post offices dispatching this unreported extra-territorial mail collectively gain 133 million SDR on mail dispatched via IC post offices and 187 million SDR on mail dispatched via DC post offices. These economic distortions result primarily from underpayment for inward delivery services. According to the model, IC post offices collectively undercharge each other by about 1.1 billion SDR, 1.4 billion SDR if unknown origin mail is included.

Table 20.2 also presents gains or losses per outbound letter post item. Typically, an IC post office is required by law to set domestic postage rates to cover costs. This implies that outbound international postage rates must also be adjusted so that total international mail revenues cover the costs of international services. If a post office gains in the exchange of international mail, then outbound mailers are, in effect, subsidized by foreign mailers. If a post loses, then the loss is reflected in higher outbound postage rates. For example, Italian outbound mailers would need to pay about 1.84 SDR more per typical outbound letter post item to offset net losses incurred in the exchange of mail among ICs. In Norway, outbound mailers would need to contribute between 1.56 to 2.83 SDR per typical outbound item depending on how much unknown origin mail is received. For Japanese mailers, the comparable figures are 0.58 to 0.74 SDR. On the other hand, mailers in the United Kingdom could benefit by 0.17 SDR per outbound item while Spanish and American mailers could receive a subsidy of 0.18 and 0.13 SDR, respectively.

The last two columns in Table 20.2 show the effects of the UPU system on exchanges of mail between ICs and DCs. For outbound letter post items, the model calculates that in 2008 ICs paid DCs about 281 million SDR for delivery under the UPU terminal dues system. If they had paid domestic postage rates instead, the bill would have been about 253 million SDR, essentially the same. Thus, ICs collectively paid DCs collectively about the right amount for delivery of international mail. The story is much different for inbound letter post items. Assuming that ICs received half as much mail from DCs as they sent to DCs, the model indicates that the ICs charged DCs about 133 million SDR in UPU terminal dues whereas they would have received 297 million SDR in domestic postage. The effect is a subsidy of 164 million SDR for DCs in the form of low postage charges. The burden of this subsidy falls unevenly on IC post offices. For an average letter post item received from DCs, UPU terminal dues come to only 0.28 SDR. High-cost post offices are more adversely affected than low-cost post offices because the UPU terminal dues cover a smaller percentage of costs incurred. For example, Norway Post loses about 1.08 SDR per average letter post item received from a DC, and Poste Italiane loses 0.90 SDR, whereas the Spanish Post Office and the US Postal Service lose about 0.21 SDR.

Peering deeper into the model yields additional insights. It is clear, for example, that net gains and losses do not capture fully the distortions caused by the UPU terminal dues system. Consider the case of Sweden Post. Sweden Post's net loss under the UPU system is a composite of positive and negative distortions in bilateral relations with other IC post offices. For example, Sweden Post would pay the UK's Royal Mail 3.00 million SDR for delivery of 8.44 million inbound letter post items, an underpayment of 1.21 million SDR compared to the domestic postage charge. On the other hand, Sweden Post would charge Royal Mail 3.88 million SDR for delivery of 10.05 million items, 4.57 million SDR less than comparable domestic postage. In this bilateral exchange Sweden Post suffers a net loss of 3.36 million SDR. If the absolute values of the bilateral losses and gains are added up, the *total bilateral distortions* (as we shall term it) in Sweden Post's postal relations with other ICs is almost 34.2 million SDR, including 2.7 million SDR in underpayment for delivery of inbound international mail of unknown origin. Indeed, if all of the individual underpayments and overpayments are added together – instead of offset against one another in each bilateral exchange – the sum would come to 76 million SDR.

Table 20.3 shows the sum of net gains and losses in bilateral relations for IC post offices. Predictably, net winners tend to have more net gains than losses while net losers exhibit an opposite balance. For the IC to IC international mail market as a whole, the total value of the delivery of known origin letter post – measured by the domestic postage that should have been paid – is about 2.4 billion SDR. The total distortions implied by UPU terminal dues – both gains and losses experienced in bilateral exchanges – is about 0.92 billion SDR. Taking into account unknown origin mail would add another 0.34 billion SDR in distortions.

The terminal dues model also allows analysis of alternative terminal dues scheme. One often proposed variation of the UPU terminal dues system is to eliminate floor and cap restraints. The last four columns of Table 20.3 give the net gains and losses by country if the UPU terminal dues system were applied without cap and floor limits.[2] Elimination of the cap provides some relief to high-cost post offices but fails to change significantly the pattern of distortions. The essential problem is that the UPU terminal dues formula is too simplistic and fails to reflect accurately variations in domestic postage. Without floor and cap constraints, the total economic transfer from losers to winners is reduced from a range of 299 to 618 million SDR to a range of 258 to 545 million SDR (the higher figures assume that unknown origin mail is included). Total distortions decline correspondingly.

Table 20.3 Total bilateral distortions from UPU terminal dues and net gains or loss from UPU terminal dues without cap

		ICs to ICs UPU TDs		ICs to ICs UPU TD uncapped			
		Bilateral losses (mil SDR)	Bilateral gains (mil SDR)	Gain (loss) known origin mail (mil SDR)	Per outbound item (SDR)	Gain (loss) all inbound mail (mil SDR)	Per outbound item (SDR)
AT	Austria	–1.8	9.1	8.0	0.122	2.5	0.038
AU	Australia	–0.8	12.5	8.3	0.074	2.0	0.018
BE	Belgium	–5.6	18.5	15.5	0.096	14.2	0.088
CA	Canada	–35.5	2.7	–32.1	–0.157	–107.0	–0.521
CH	Switzerland	–15.8	18.0	10.6	0.059	–14.2	–0.079
CL	Chile	–0.1	0.3	0.2	0.177	0.2	0.171
CZ	Czech Republic	0.0	13.7	13.7	0.328	12.5	0.299
DE	Germany	–50.9	52.3	3.7	0.006	–137.9	–0.240
DK	Denmark	–20.0	4.9	–5.8	–0.115	–12.2	–0.241
EE	Estonia	0.0	1.2	1.2	0.546	1.2	0.546
EL	Greece	–0.7	5.1	4.8	0.123	4.0	0.105
ES	Spain	–0.8	42.5	32.6	0.143	32.3	0.142
FI	Finland	–13.1	1.2	–9.0	–0.421	–9.0	–0.421
FR	France	–28.3	22.7	–2.7	–0.009	–13.1	–0.046
HU	Hungary	–0.3	2.7	2.5	0.190	2.5	0.190
IE	Ireland	–17.7	7.5	–7.1	–0.105	–7.1	–0.105
IL	Israel	–0.2	0.6	1.3	0.263	1.1	0.230
IS	Iceland	0.0	0.5	0.3	0.225	0.3	0.199
IT	Italy	–135.9	0.0	–122.4	–1.654	–122.4	–1.654
JP	Japan	–28.7	0.8	–21.6	–0.450	–28.5	–0.595
KR	Korea	0.0	4.3	4.3	0.649	4.3	0.649
LU	Luxembourg	–0.3	6.6	5.4	0.164	5.4	0.164
MX	Mexico	–0.2	2.2	2.0	0.068	2.0	0.068
NL	Netherlands	–22.6	14.5	–16.9	–0.087	–16.9	–0.087
NO	Norway	–47.4	0.1	–34.7	–1.143	–68.9	–2.266
NZ	New Zealand	0.0	1.4	1.2	0.087	0.2	0.018
PL	Poland	–0.5	9.8	9.3	0.236	9.3	0.235
PT	Portugal	–0.7	6.3	4.2	0.101	3.7	0.091
SE	Sweden	–17.8	13.7	–5.6	–0.062	–8.1	–0.090
SI	Slovenia	0.0	2.8	2.8	0.435	2.8	0.432
SK	Slovak Republic	–0.3	3.4	3.2	0.219	3.0	0.205
TR	Turkey	–0.1	6.6	6.4	0.317	4.3	0.211
UK	United Kingdom	–4.5	73.0	53.2	0.133	53.2	0.133
US	United States	–8.2	97.0	63.1	0.093	63.1	0.093

5 CONCLUSIONS

Because details of international exchanges of mail among post offices are, for the most part, hidden from public view, this terminal dues model can only demonstrate the basic effects of the UPU terminal dues regime. It does not attempt to calculate financial effects with precision. Moreover, post offices have, to some extent, ameliorated the effects of the UPU terminal dues system through bilateral or multilateral, non-UPU terminal dues agreements, although the extent is unknown.

These caveats notwithstanding, divergences between delivery costs and terminal dues charges are still very much part of the international postal system. It is hoped that the model presented in this chapter will help policy makers to understand better what players in the game of international postal politics have long known: that the UPU terminal dues regime produces significant distortions in the flow of international mail. These distortions are not random or peripheral to the terminal dues system. Countries with low domestic postage and/or net exports benefit, while countries with high domestic postage and/or net imports are disadvantaged. Distortions have been perpetuated by the winners to gain at the expense of the losers. More fundamentally, the system creates a pervasive pattern of distortions that affects international postal relations generally. Overall, in postal relations among OECD countries, the sum of the distortions – net gains and losses in bilateral relations taken together – would equal about 40 percent of the value of the market if appropriate domestic postage were charged for delivery of inbound international mail.

NOTES

* This chapter presents the personal views of the authors only.

1. The model uses revenues from service exports plus 25 percent of revenue from commodity exports. In a few cases, revenues from service exports are reported as negative, for example, when insurance pays out more in claims than collected in insurance premiums. In such cases, the model uses the absolute value of the export revenues since mail is likely generated regardless of the direction of the revenue flow.
2. UPU IC terminal dues are calculated in two steps. Step 1 calculates a per kg rate and applies per kg floor/cap constraints. Step 2 calculates a per item rate from the – possibly constrained – per kg rate and applies per item rate floor/cap constraints. Step 1 reflects the weight and item relationships in the UPU's floor constraints. An 'uncapped' version of the UPU terminal dues system could be constructed by either of two methods. The first would calculate both steps without reference to floor/cap constraints. The second method would be to calculate the per kg rate with floor/cap constraints and then calculate the per item rate without floor/cap constraints. The second method results in somewhat higher terminal dues for high-cost post offices, and this is the method used in the model.

BIBLIOGRAPHY

Adrenale Corporation (2010), *Market Research on International Letters and Lightweight Parcels and Express Mail Service Items*, Bern: Universal Postal Union.

Bruun, Christian (1993), 'Nordic measurements 1991: service performance and terminal dues payments', in Michael A. Crew and Paul R. Kleindorfer (eds), *Regulation and the Nature of Postal and Delivery Services*, Boston, MA: Kluwer Academic Publishers.

WIK-Consult and J. Campbell (2010), 'External Dimension of the EU Postal *Acquis*', Study for the European Commission, Bad Honnef.

21. On the use of reverse auctions to designate universal postal service providers*

Carlos Costa†

1 INTRODUCTION

There has been an intense debate on the conditions regarding the permanent provision of a minimum set of postal services for the whole of each nation's territory and across borders, with adequate quality of service (QoS) levels and at affordable prices and, in particular, regarding the necessity to continue imposing the Universal Service Obligation (USO) upon operators to ensure that goal, within a full market opening (FMO) environment.

However, the literature regarding the use of reverse auctions specifically to designate the postal universal service provider (USP), is fairly limited – Borrmann (2004) and Calzada et al. (2010) seem to be the most interesting exceptions – and, in the case of the particular conditions of the Portuguese market, nonexistent.

After a very brief sketch of the Portuguese experience on USO policy, Section 2 provides the context of the discussion of reverse auctions for USPs. Section 3 draws attention to conceptual and design issues associated with reverse auctions. Sections 4 and 5 discuss, respectively, the advantages and the disadvantages of reverse auctions in the postal USO. Finally, Section 6 provides a brief summary, the main conclusions and some ideas that seem to need additional research if the use of reverse auctions is to be considered an appropriate measure in the Portuguese market.

2 THE FUTURE: REVERSE AUCTIONS TO DESIGNATE POSTAL USPS?

The enforcement of a USO in Portugal ensured the reliable provision of postal services for the whole of the country, with an appropriate QoS[1] and at an affordable price,[2] notwithstanding significant differences between urban and rural areas.[3] However, the question arises of how to ensure the USO in an FMO environment, contributing to social inclusion and avoiding market distortions.

Among the issues discussed concerning the safeguarding of consumer interests and the promotion of sustained competition, should be the efficiency of different USP designation methods, its geographical scope and the optimal range of services ascribed to the USPs.

† Principal Consultant, ICP-ANACOM.

The objective of the different USP designation procedures is essentially the same, that is, to select an entity which guarantees the provision of postal services, with a defined QoS and coverage target, in a certain geographical area, at a given affordable price and during a fixed period.[4]

Directive 2008/6/EC of the European Parliament and of the Council of 20 February 2008 establishes that member states shall take measures to ensure that the conditions under which the USO is entrusted follow transparency, non-discrimination and proportionality principles. It further establishes that member states may ensure the USO by 'procuring such services in accordance with applicable public procurement rules and regulations, including . . . coordinating the procurement procedures of entities operating in the water, energy, transport and postal services, competitive dialogue or negotiated procedures'.

Public tenders, frequently involving auctions,[5] are common practice in perishable goods markets and network industries, such as electricity and electronic communications. In general, the aim associated with using auctions to designate USPs relates, beyond the guarantee to provide the USO, to the safeguarding of competition, the minimization of eventual USO net costs and resulting subsidies attributed to USPs, and the rationalization of costs' associated with the USO net costs' financing process.

In fact, auctions are used in most of the liberalized electricity markets, contributing to increasing efficiency and reducing price volatility in those markets, notwithstanding that certain auction design aspects could be improved, namely to reduce the possibility of market power abuses and to increase social welfare (Contreras, 2001; Rothkopf, 2002; Azevedo and Correia, 2006; Ciarreta and Espinosa, 2010).

In the European electronic communications sector, until 2010, eight countries represented in the BEREC[6] employed a public tender to designate the USP. This number should increase soon, since the national law of 20 European countries requires that public tenders are used to designate USPs (BEREC, 2010).

However, the practice in the postal sector seems to be subsumed to the example of the New Zealand historic operator which subcontracts by way of public tender 538 local postal operators (servicing around 600 rural routes) to provide postal services in rural areas to 130,000 customers, representing 10 percent of the annual mail volume.

Beyond consideration of the legal requirements, on the economic perspective, public tenders offer considerable advantages *vis-à-vis* USP designation methods involving 'beauty contests' or direct negotiations between entities potentially interested in providing USO. Hence, reverse auctions are gaining relevance, *vis-à-vis* the option to develop a study on the level of subsidy necessary for a given USP to accept the USO.

In Portugal, reverse auctions might gain momentum with the forthcoming privatization of the historical operator and, possibly, with the perspective of a public tender of its current USO. Privatization may contribute also to an increased perception of fairness regarding the state's intervention in an auction, since it would no longer be seen simultaneously as decision maker and bidder.

3 DESCRIPTION OF REVERSE AUCTIONS

A reverse auction is a standard way in which governments procure any good or service to provide it to the public, issuing a request for bids describing its specific needs.

The reverse auction is initiated with a given reserve price (in the case of the postal USO, a subsidy) established by the seller, and the proposals presented by the bidders must be equal to or lower than that reserve price. In the end, the winning bid is the one with the lowest price. The ultimate goal of the USP designation procedure should be to maximize the welfare resulting from the addition of expected consumer benefits and expected operators' profits subtracted from the subsidies payable to operators (Milgrom, 1996).

The auction design itself may take distinct formats: single versus multiple rounds, simultaneous versus sequential, or open versus sealed bids (Calzada et al., 2010). In a multiple-round auction, in contrast to a single-round auction, operators could learn from each other's perception of costs and profitability, calibrating their own bids and reducing the risk of an unsustainable bid. In a sequential auction, in contrast to a simultaneous auction, operators would not know if they had succeeded in winning all of the regions in which they were interested, which would impact on their estimates of costs and profitability.

While an open-bid auction, in contrast to a sealed-bid one, is perceived to facilitate collusion, it provides candidates with sensible feedback on the different values that other operators ascribe to each region under auction, thus diminishing the risk of a 'winner's curse' (Bulow and Klemperer, 2002, 1996).

In principle, auctions must be designed to minimize the chance of bidder collusion or price signaling (Stegeman et al., 2006). In parallel, according to Milgrom (1996), typically, an auction design may be considered optimal if and only if the total welfare is maximized by the choice of a given operator and if the sum of the net profit of that operator and its received subsidy is null.

An original suggestion to increase total welfare was presented by Peha (1999), who argued that a USO exchange between different electronic communications operators may augment welfare, especially when transaction costs are low (which may happen when the number of operators is not excessively high).

Each USO has two components: what must be done (for example, a target to be accomplished) and when it must be done (for example, a deadline to be met). This means that when a USP does not meet a target within a given deadline, a sanction may be applied. Peha (1999) argues that each USP should be free to negotiate with other operators the purchase, selling and exchange of targets to be accomplished and of deadlines to be met.

In the postal sector, this could mean that a USP that has difficulty in accomplishing a target related to postal delivery in a given rural area could have that obligation fulfilled by another operator with a postal network already established in that territory. Alternatively, a USP that has difficulty in installing, within a given deadline, a parcel distribution network could exchange that obligation with an operator that is more advanced in that area and that, on the other hand, is less interested in delivering letter mail in a different region. However, a situation where multiple USPs coexist in different regions of a country is not exempt from risk, as discussed in the following sections.

4 ADVANTAGES OF REVERSE AUCTIONS IN THE POSTAL USO

Reverse auctions as a method for the designation of USP show some distinct advantages.[7] One of the most relevant advantages is to improve transparency, avoiding situations of 'capture' of the state's agents responsible for subsidies related to the USO, which, according to the 'traditional' capture theory (Stigler, 1971; Laffont and Tirole, 1991) can be expected in the attribution of subsidies, restrictive licensing and price control. This could be of interest in the Portuguese scenario, in the light of alleged past regulatory capture situations, arising from 'revolving door' practices between the regulator and the USP (Soares, 2007).

According to Harstad and Crew (1999), the incumbent monopolist's incentive to attempt regulatory capture under price-cap regulation is 'automatically stymied' by franchise bidding. However, when the USO contract itself is ill defined (for instance, when the specification of QoS targets or technologies to be used on postal distribution is ambiguous), bidders who master the political process, and have the capacity to appropriate the resulting pecuniary advantages, still have incentives to capture the regulator after the auctioning procedure is completed. This draws attention to the difficulty in detailing contractual specifications when there is a long-term designation period for the USP (Jaag and Trinkner, 2009), particularly when there is reasonable uncertainty regarding the evolution of the substitutability between postal services and other platforms and when, due to the current economic scenario, it is challenging to make credible estimations about the future demand of postal services by business users.

A second advantage is that as (a) a wide number of targets (related to QoS, price, geographical and population coverage) are defined at an early stage of the auctioning procedures, (b) there are usually sanctions associated with the non-fulfillment of those targets, and (c) the obligation of periodical reports is usually enshrined in the contract of the successful bidder, then this contributes to increasing the monitoring capability of the government and the regulator.

Third, economic and competitive distortions tend to be reduced, since the bidder with the lowest cost is chosen and the least possible compensation is paid[8] (ibid.), which is even more appealing given the current state of public finances in a number of European countries. This advantage seems especially relevant when auctions to designate USP are repeated, allowing the correction of eventual mistakes, for instance, in the establishment of reserve prices for the subsidies or with regard to the QoS ensured by the USP.

On the other hand, it is also clear that if the auctions are repeated periodically, the USP designation period should be long enough to allow an adequate remuneration of the investment and costs related to the USO. According to Williamson (1976), a prime reason for making the contract long term is to provide the supplier with incentives to install long-lasting assets.

When discussing the length of the USP designation period, the issue of property rights over the postal infrastructure should be taken into consideration. In fact, it is a different matter to auction the USO in a scenario where the postal infrastructure is a priori the property of the bidders and in a scenario when the property rights over the postal infrastructure are being auctioned simultaneously.

In the first scenario (with a higher possibility in some urban areas, where the networks of alternative operators are ubiquitous) there is actually no need to establish a transfer price for the infrastructure supporting the provision of the USO. The winner would use its own infrastructure to provide the USO and the losers would continue to use their own infrastructure to do business as usual.

In this case, for the purpose of designing a network which fits the USO established in the reverse auction, the definition of the USP designation period should reflect a reasonable payback period for incremental investments that potential bidders incur. The estimation of that payback period may involve additional complexity where the USO is supported by different networks and technological mixes (for example, when using to hybrid mail). However, with regard to the irreversible costs already incurred by the Portuguese historical operator (for instance, in the recent modernization of the fleet, the construction of new sorting centers, human resources training or the adoption of new technologies – for example, Radio Frequency IDentification (RFID) and optical readers), its payback period would be significantly shorter compared to alternative operators, resulting in visible advantages in a reverse auction.

In the second scenario, besides the diversity of legal aspects and of the associated human resources management issues, it is a complex matter to evaluate the transfer price at which the property rights over the postal infrastructure may be conceded to the future winner of a repeated auction, in the event that the current USP fails to win renewal. If that transfer price is not adequately established and the designation period of the USP is not appropriate, incentives to invest in the maintenance of or improvements in the postal infrastructure may be scarce and transaction costs may be significant.

In this case, failure to estimate a reasonable payback period would probably result, like other network industries,[9] in considerable 'hold-up' problems due to the asset specificity and sunk costs of equipment (such as, for instance, sorting machines), of sorting facilities and of the postal fleet.[10] Nevertheless, Harstad and Crew (1999) suggest that the impact of those problems may be reduced through a correct definition of the auction rules, including the design of a transfer function.

A fourth advantage is that reverse auctions tend to address adequately the target population (to the extent that the bids commonly include a well-defined list of localities, covered as well as coverage characteristics). In the postal sector, this could also translate into the specification of different QoS levels and conditions to different categories of localities (classified, for instance, according to the population and or number of business users).

Reverse auctions also involve private initiatives in the investment of rural and peripheral regions. The OECD (2004) highlights that in a number of Latin American countries, even a small subsidy attracts significant private investment to the electronic communications sector.[11] In the more traditional and declining postal market, however, it is doubtful whether the capacity to attract private investment when employing reverse auctions would be as high as in other network industries.

A sixth advantage is that when reverse auctions are employed, the calculation of USO net costs can be avoided, which most of the time can only be done with incomplete information, generally in a rather imprecise manner and in a lengthy and often opaque process. This also helps to avoid cumbersome discussions concerning the methodology to assess USO net costs and the USO net cost levels, particularly when there are significant differences between regulator and operator evaluations[12] (as is the case, typically, of the

USO in electronic communications). This advantage is mitigated by the fact that the government or the regulator usually establishes a reserve price for the reverse auction, which has to be worked out in considerable detail.

Another important advantage is that reverse auctions 'discipline' the government and or the regulator, thus rendering less probable their use of coercive power over the historical operator, demanding exorbitant combinations of excessively low prices with excessively high QoS levels. In the words of Harstad and Crew (1999, p. 144), 'franchise bidding is not attractive to lawmakers and regulators in part because it reduces significantly their flexibility in using the regulatory process to achieve their own "social agenda"'.

Finally, Weller (1999) and Milgrom et al. (2009) add that – where USO funds are disbursed without previous auctions – the allocation of subsidies is an extremely lengthy process, given that companies have to complete complex proposals, which are then revised by governmental entities. Nevertheless, the adequate preparation of reverse auctions also takes a reasonable amount of time. For instance, the 3G frequencies' auction in the UK was prepared three years in advance (Binmore and Klemperer, 2002) and there were similar preparation periods in Portugal and other countries. Hence, the time needed for its preparation should not be seen as a real advantage of reverse auctions.

5 DISADVANTAGES OF REVERSE AUCTIONS FOR THE USO

Besides the previously mentioned advantages, there are also some recognized disadvantages when using to reverse auctions to designate the USP.

First, where the process results are multiple USPs in the same country, there is a risk that some of the USPs (that is, those with less experience or fewer resources) might deliver QoS levels considerably below those established in their contractual obligations.

This might result in time-consuming dispute resolution procedures (Borrmann, 2004), if interconnection deficiencies, especially between USPs (which may have few incentives to deliver, with appropriate QoS levels, letter mail and parcels to more costly constituents, including incoming mail and parcels from other USPs), are alleged to justify compliance failures with the aforementioned obligations. In addition, disputes can easily arise because – since the attribution of exclusive rights to USPs is evidently impossible under FMO – multiple operators (including operators acting as USPs in other regions) may be competing for customers in the same region. Suboptimal coordination between the networks of different USPs could also adversely affect efforts to reduce the carbon footprint, impacting negatively upon costs and the reputation of the USPs. Ultimately, persistent interconnection failures could result in deprivation of access to postal services by the population (not) served by the USP which is failing to meet its obligations.

On the other hand, it is possible to consider a more benevolent result, where those risks are minimized by a good design of the auctioning process and litigation between USPs can eventually be transcended. This seems to be the case, for instance, of the electronic communications markets where interconnection typically gives rise to complex litigation procedures between service providers (for example, related to interconnection prices and QoS conditions), often with judicial and regulatory intervention, but where it is relatively rare that those litigations adversely affect the end user directly. This is also without prejudice to the fact that in some electronic communications markets there are already a number of operators who have been competing for years in a given geographical market, while in the postal sector it is more difficult to see competition develop for most of the scope of the USO.

Ultimately, a structural solution to eliminate or strongly reduce interconnection problems and non-price discrimination between different USPs could involve a vertical separation of the postal network supporting the USO. In this context, there could be different types of USO reverse auctions. The first would attribute the management of the postal network to a single entity up to a certain network separation point (say, for instance, the delivery office). The second would attribute the USO to a number of regional USPs that would ensure all activities beyond that network separation point.

Although vertical separation is a solution found with some frequency in other network industries (especially in electronic communications, energy and railways), neither the theoretical nor the empirical results seem consistent.[13] Moreover, it is a solution that has not been fully tested in the postal sector, thus giving rise to numerous time-consuming problems that have to be solved before implementation. Several of those problems have been underlined by Borrmann (2004). For example, when an automated walk-sequencing of mail is undertaken by the historical operator (which is typically the case in urban areas in Portugal and in the majority of developed countries), without vertical integration, delivery is significantly more costly than with vertical integration and QoS levels are also expected to be worse.

Second, it is difficult to ensure that there are enough participants to bid against the historical operator, for two reasons. In the first place, in many cases, entrants would have to use an extensive alternative postal infrastructure or to acquire the infrastructure of the historical operator, with the exception of the means of transportation, which can be more easily subcontracted. In addition, asymmetry of information between the historical operator and the new entrants is significant, for instance, in relation to the costs and benefits of serving end users (for example, in rural areas where alternative operators are mostly absent). Even small asymmetries can have a major impact in terms of the final result of the bidding. According to Klemperer (1998), this would incentivize companies with information advantages to bid more aggressively than the remaining operators, which, even if they could win, would eventually face an accrued operational risk.[14]

As for the postal sector, the extent to which access to a customer database and to information regarding consumption patterns is important to disadvantage competitors very much depends on the present extent of competition and of the range of competitive services (since alternative operators may have had time to consolidate related databases), but also on the utility of those databases for the purpose of providing services capable of generating high value, such as direct mail, segmented advertising, and so on.

It should be underlined that, beyond publicly available information, all the bidders (historic and alternative) may try to acquire private information on the object of the auction. According to Persico (2000), incentives to acquire private information would be higher on a first-price auction (where the difference between the price presented by the winner and by the bidder placed second is important) than in a second-price auction (where the aforementioned difference is irrelevant).[15]

In the context of USO reverse first-price auctions in the postal sector, this could mean that the bidders would be willing to spend money investigating issues such as the actual capacity of the regulator or government to monitor and enforce the fulfillment of the USO or the predisposition of postal unions to proceed with 'punitive actions' if the successful bidder intends to review wage or other labor conditions.

One way to minimize the (information asymmetry and infrastructure) disadvantage of the remaining bidders *vis-à-vis* the historical operator would be to facilitate the access to the network of that operator, especially in rural areas, possibly in conjunction with the bidding process itself. Another, more extreme measure (somewhat dubious in terms of its proportionality), would be not to allow the historical operator to bid for certain regions.[16] Another approach to reduce the relevance of asymmetries among bidders, according to Klemperer (2002), would be to design a sealed-bid auction, where each bidder independently makes its final and best offer and where the bidder with the lowest requested subsidy wins. Thus, the bidders would have no way to calibrate their proposals with their expectations relative to the behavior of their opponents, nor would they have any incentive to continue bidding indefinitely until their opponents quit.

Binmore and Klemperer (2002) present an auction variant ('Anglo-Dutch') that attempts to reconcile the transparency advantages of the open-bid auctions with the already mentioned advantages of the sealed-bid auction. In a reverse Anglo-Dutch auction, the value of the subsidy would diminish until only two bidders remain. Those two would then present their best and final offers in a sealed bid.

It must also be taken into account that when a reverse auction happen at a national level, its preparation tends to take longer (Hoernig and Valletti, 2002) and the organization of the process, as well as the preparation of the human resources involved must be optimized, in order to enhance effectiveness. Nevertheless, it is possible to conceive that as a number of regulators (including the Portuguese regulator) already have extensive experience dealing with complex issues related to spectrum auctions, some economies of learning might facilitate reverse auctions with regard to the postal sector. On the other hand, the strict adherence to solutions applied in other markets might also be evidence of 'path dependence'[17] and adversely impact upon the reverse auction design and upon the auctions' results in the postal sector.

Another possible disadvantage of reverse auctions with multiple geographical areas has to do with the complexity of delineating relatively homogeneous regions to be auctioned. If that is not successfully achieved, the USP may be tempted to serve only the low-cost customers (Milgrom, 1996). If the regions are small, the demand patterns are likely to be more homogeneous and potential bidders can more easily estimate profitability and benchmark competitors (Calzada et al., 2010). Furthermore, bidders winning multiple regions would still be able to achieve some economies of scale, mostly – due to the logistics of postal services – in cases where those regions are contiguous. This seems to suggest that if the size of the geographical areas to be auctioned for the USO is small, combinatorial reverse auctions (for example, allowing the interested providers to bid for groups of geographical areas) would be more appropriate in the postal sector. This is without prejudice to the fact that, in principle, larger geographical areas would have more capacity to facilitate economies of scale and to lower the administrative costs related to the auction preparation.[18]

In any case, the EC seems to understand – at least in the scope of electronic communications services – that a USP designation mechanism that demands a national coverage by a single USP and/or demands that a single USP aggregates several of the services included in the USO does not satisfy the non-discrimination principle (Michou, 2008). This is because it is understood that a designation mechanism that demands national coverage by a single USP or that demands that a single USP aggregates several services included in the USO would not provide a fair opportunity for the alternative operators (operating at a regional level or offering only a limited range of services) to bid successfully for the provision of the USO (in particular, when the historical operator is, as is the case in Portugal, the only entity to ensure currently a full national coverage and a complete range of postal services).[19]

The above-mentioned factors seem to suggest that each of the regions to be put under an eventual reverse auction to designate the USP should reflect a reasonable compromise in terms of its size and a delicate balance between rural and urban areas. In the interest of simplicity of the process it could be considered that the envisaged solution approaches some administrative boundaries, such as, for instance, NUTS 2.[20]

As for the concern with the level of aggregation of the services covered by the USO, one should consider whether the USP should be designated to provide the full range of services encompassed in the USO scope (for example, letter mail and parcels) or for each of the services that is included.

To launch separate auctions for the designation of USP for letter mail and for the parcels components of the USO could be preferable considering the promotion of competition, since the historical operator is facing real competition in the small parcels market, while the letter mail market is less competitive.

On the other hand, the joint provision of the letter mail and small parcels components of the USO can account for a fair amount of scale and scope economies, contributing to the reduction of USO net costs. This, in turn, would reduce the eventual contributions of alternative operators towards a USO fund, thus safeguarding healthy competition in the markets (since the alternative operators, paying lower contributions to the USO fund, would enjoy more liberty to compete effectively in the postal markets where their presence is active).

As for the auction design, given the huge differences in scale between the historical operator and the other entities' operations in the Portuguese market, a single-round auction could help to preclude the possibility that the historical operator would continue bidding 'forever' until every bid from alternative operators is beaten.

Finally, another disadvantage may arise when the amount of subsidy requested by the winning bid is too low, resulting in a systematic underfunding of the USO. This, in turn, may result in lengthy and intricate negotiations to renegotiate the contract, where it is not certain that the final result may not be even worse compared with the outcome of an eventual direct negotiation *ab initio*.

6 CONCLUSION

Historically, the USO in Portugal has guaranteed the provision of affordable postal services with an appropriate level of QoS in the whole of the territory, despite the significant and persistent differences between rural and urban areas, namely in terms of income per capita, population density, mix between business and non-business clients and volume of postal traffic *per capita*.

In order to continue providing the USO in a fully liberalized environment – while promoting healthy competition in the postal markets and also accounting for the significant differences between rural and urban areas – the use, when feasible, of reverse auctions to designate the USPs seems to offer (in spite of some recognized disadvantages) relevant potential advantages over 'traditional' designation methods: increased transparency; diminished opportunities to 'capture' the state's agents; augmented monitoring capability of the government and the regulator; emergence of the possibility, in the case that the reverse auction is repeated over time, of iterative corrections of mistakes associated with its initial assumptions; more competitive and rational use of public and private funds; avoidance of often lengthy, opaque and cumbersome calculations of US net costs; and the mitigation of the government's 'coercive' power over the USP.

However, the predicted impact of a number of potentially adverse factors – namely interconnection problems, QoS deterioration, time-consuming dispute resolution, limited number of operators to bid against the historical operator, information asymmetries between the historical operator and competitors, difficulties in defining homogeneous regions, loss of economies of scale and scope, and USO sustainability – suggest that there are strong reasons to doubt whether it will be desirable to implement reverse auctions to designate the USP.

Hence, in practical terms reverse auctions (with the possible and limited exception of New Zealand) are not a reality in the postal sector, contrary to what happens frequently in the perishable goods markets and network industries, in particular in the electricity and electronic communications markets.

Finally, if reverse auctions for the designation of the postal USP is considered an appropriate measure for the Portuguese market, some outstanding issues will demand a thorough analysis, especially concerning the definition of the exact size and frontiers of the regions to be auctioned, the concrete range of services to be auctioned, the specifics of the auction design and, notably, the interconnection of the networks of USPs acting in different geographical areas.

NOTES

* The ideas and opinions expressed in this chapter do not necessarily reflect those of ICP-ANACOM.

1. The USP is required to deliver mail with the same delay in urban areas and in rural areas. For Portugal mainland, the minimum target level for D+1 is 93.5 percent and the objective level is 94.5 percent (with a non-audited level of 94.7 percent for 2010).
2. Historically, the concern with generating states' income gave rise to concerns with price affordability and fairness. In the twentieth century, postal prices were fixed by administrative order until 1993. After that, price-cap regulation was applied to the USP, associated (from 1995) with a deduction to the price cap in case of non-compliance with QoS target levels (Castro and Franco, 2006).
3. Urban areas, when compared to rural areas, have a higher average number of inhabitants per postal establishment, a higher density of postal establishments per km^2 and generate more postal traffic. In addition, urban and rural areas (accounting, respectively, for 53 and 47 percent of Portugal mainland territory) have significant differences in terms of overall population (with only 42 percent of the Portugal mainland population living in rural areas), housing (more dispersed in rural areas), income per capita (much higher in urban areas) and enterprise location (with most of the enterprises located in urban areas).
4. Besides the selection of USPs, a reverse auction can simultaneously determine the price charged to consumers (Harstad and Crew, 1999). However, in practical terms, usually the determination of the price that is considered affordable is left in the hands of a 'social planner' (for example, the government or regulator), which considers a range of economic and social aspects. In addition, Williamson (1976), while

recognizing its impracticality, supports Richard Posner's (1969) proposal to define the QoS level in an (initial) stage of the auctioning procedure, based upon commitments from potential subscribers, on the grounds that this would both relieve the QoS level to be fixed by a political body and reduce uncertainty derived from the choice between different price and QoS combinations.

5. Auctions can be considered, in conformity with the definition of McAfee and McMillan (1987), market institutions with an explicit set of rules determining the allocation of resources and prices supported by bids of the market participants.
6. The Body of European Regulators for Electronic Communications (BEREC) was created within the recent reform of the EU Telecom rules to improve the consistent implementation of the EU regulatory framework.
7. See Milgrom (1996); Harstad and Crew (1999); Weller (1999); Binmore and Klemperer (2002); Hoernig and Valletti (2002); Intven and Howard (2004); OECD (2004); Milgrom et al. (2009); Muente-Kunigami and Navas-Sabater (2009).
8. For instance, the OECD (2004) underlines that in five Latin American countries (Chile, Peru, Guatemala, Colombia and Dominican Republic) which used reverse auctions to designate USPs in electronic communications, the subsidies attributed were substantially below the reserve price established.
9. An interesting analysis regarding the periodical re-auction of a water monopoly concession is presented by Meister (2005), showing that hold-up problems arise 'if the life-time of specific assets such as water pipes exceeds the contract length and transferring the ownership of assets is difficult'.
10. Which can, however, be considered moderate comparing to other network industries.
11. For example, in Peru and Chile, each USD of subsidy attracted, respectively, two and six USD of private investment.
12. On a related issue, Harstad and Crew (1999) add that the primary benefit of franchise bidding over price-cap regulation is that it has superior efficiency properties, because of the information advantage of the firm over the regulator under price-cap regulation.
13. For an extensive discussion, at the light of the specific conditions of the Portuguese market, see Oxera-Ellare (2009).
14. For instance, in the case of an auction for frequencies in Los Angeles (USA), the Pacific Telephone Company had minor but distinctive advantages, insofar as it had a database with potential clients for new services, as it was bidding in a region where its brand awareness was already high and where its operational management was already familiar with local conditions.
15. Vickrey (1961) seems to share this perspective, maintaining that in a second-price auction each bidder may confine its efforts and attention to the assessment of the value that the object of each auction would assume in its own hands, thus avoiding mental stress and possibly expenses related to the collection of additional information on its competitors. *Prima facie*, this seems good for the bidders, but ultimately, it could be better even for the seller, since a higher number of bidders tend to participate in the auction, contributing to better results.
16. In the electronic communications sector, a contribution to a 'level playing field' has been accomplished, for instance, by auctioning spectrum at a lower reserve price in less densely populated areas, such as was done, for example, in Portugal regarding the BWA frequencies two-stage closed-bid auction initiated in 2009. In parallel, in the first stage of the auction, participation was permitted only to entities that were not mobile operators, or broadband service providers or companies that already owned usage rights in the relevant frequency bands.
17. That is, perpetuates conditions that were adopted in the past, given a specific economic and public policy context, but may no longer be efficient or even reasonable in the present.
18. Calzada et al. (2010) suggest that larger geographical areas could also facilitate economies of scope, since a postman could simultaneously distribute correspondence and offer financial services. However, we fail to see why these economies of scope could not also be achieved in smaller geographical areas.
19. According to data published by ICP-ANACOM (2011), in the 3rd quarter of 2010 there were 58 service providers active in the postal sector. Of those, only 10 had full national coverage for all the liberalized market segments (and will probably show little interest in delivering the low-end market segments of the postal market once FMO is completed) and the operators that were active only in some regions of the country were mostly concentrated in the urban areas of Lisbon and Oporto. Of the 12 major service providers in terms of revenues, only the historical operator and one other operator were not providing exclusively express mail services.
20. Nomenclature of Units for Territorial Statistics – geocode standard adopted by Eurostat to divide the EU member states for statistical purposes.

REFERENCES

Azevedo, Erick and Paulo Correia (2006), 'Bidding strategies in Brazilian electricity auctions', *Electrical Power and Energy Systems*, **28**(5), 309–14.

BEREC (2010), 'BEREC Report on Universal Service – Reflections for the Future', Body of European Regulators for Electronic Communications Brussels.

Binmore, Ken and Paul D. Klemperer (2002), 'The biggest auction ever: the sale of the British 3G telecom licenses', *Economic Journal*, **112**(478), 74–96.

Borrmann, Jörg (2004), 'Franchise bidding for postal services in rural regions', *Topics in Economic Analysis & Policy*, **4**(1), Article 10.

Bulow, Jeremy and Paul Klemperer (1996), 'Auctions versus negotiations', *American Economic Review*, **86**(1), 180–94.

Bulow, Jeremy and Paul Klemperer (2002), 'Prices and the winner's curse', *The Rand Journal of Economics*, **33**(1), 1–21.

Calzada, Joan, Urs Trinkner and Christian Jaag (2010), 'Universal service auctions in liberalized postal markets', in Michael Crew and Paul Kleindorfer (eds), *Heightening Competition in the Postal and Delivery Sector*, Cheltenham, UK and Northampton, MA, USA: Edward Elgar.

Castro, João and Agostinho Franco (2009), 'Price and quality of service regulation in Portugal', in Michael Crew and Paul Kleindorfer (eds), *Progress in the Competitive Agenda in the Postal and Delivery Sector*, Cheltenham, UK and Northampton, MA, USA: Edward Elgar.

Ciarreta, Aitor and Maria Espinosa (2010), 'Market power in the Spanish electricity auction', *Journal of Regulatory Economics*, **37**, 42–69.

Contreras, Javier (2001), 'Auction design in day-ahead electricity markets', *IEEE Transactions on Power Systems*, **16**(3), August, 409–17.

Harstad, Ronald and Michael Crew (1999), 'Franchise bidding without holdups: utility regulation with efficient pricing and choice of provider', *Journal of Regulatory Economics*, **15**(2), 141–63.

Hoernig, S. and T. Valletti (2002), 'The interplay between regulation and competition: the case of universal service obligations', CESifo Working Paper No. 682, Munich.

ICP-ANACOM (2011), 'Os desafios do sector postal face à liberalização total', Report.

Intven, Hank and Curt Howard (2004), 'Least-cost subsidy auctions for universal access telecom projects: a practical implementation guide'.

Jaag, Christian and Urs Trinkner (2009), 'Tendering universal service obligations in liberalized network industries', Swiss Economics Working Paper 0013, Zurich.

Klemperer, P.D. (1998), 'Auctions with almost common values: the "wallet game" and its applications', *European Economic Review*, **42**, 757–69.

Klemperer, P.D. (2002), 'What really matters in auction design', *Journal of Economic Perspectives*, **16**(1), 169–89.

Laffont, Jean-Jacques and Jean Tirole (1991), 'The politics of government decision making: a theory of regulatory capture', *Quarterly Journal of Economics*, **106**(4), 1089–127.

McAfee, R. and John McMillan, 'Auctions and bidding', *Journal of Economic Literature*, **XXV**(2), June, 699–738.

Meister, Urs (2005), 'Franchise bidding in the water industry – auction schemes and investment incentives', Working Paper 33, Institute for Strategy and Business Economics, University of Zurich.

Michou, Paraskevi (2008), 'Universal service and protection of communication services' users', available at: http://www.anacom.pt/render.jsp?categoryId=291135 (accessed April 2011).

Milgrom, P.R. (1996), 'Procuring universal service: putting auction theory to work', Lecture at the Royal Swedish Academy of Sciences, Stockholm, 9 December.

Milgrom, P.R. et al. (2009), 'Using procurement auctions to allocate broadband stimulus grants', Comments of 71 economists submitted to the NTIA and RUS.

Muente-Kunigami, Arturo and Juan Navas-Sabater (2009), 'Options to increase access to telecommunications services in rural and low-income areas', World Bank Paper 178, Washington, DC.

OECD (2004), 'Leveraging telecommunication policies for pro-poor growth: Universal access funds with minimum-subsidy auctions', OECD, Paris.

Oxera-Ellare (2009), 'Vertical functional separation in the electronic communications sector: what are its implications for the Portuguese market?' Study.

Peha, Jon M. (1999), 'Tradable universal service obligations', *Telecommunications Policy*, **23**(5), July 21, 363–74.

Persico, Nicola (2000), 'Information acquisition in auctions', *Econometrica*, **68**(1), 135–48.

Posner, Richard (1969), 'Natural monopoly and its regulation', *Stanford Law Review*, **21**(February), 548–643.

Rothkopf, Michael (2002), 'Control of market power in electricity auctions', *Electricity Journal*, **15**(8), 15–24.

Soares, José (2007), 'Teorias Económicas de Regulação – Grupos de Interesse', Procura de Renda e Aprisionamento, Instituto Piaget, Lisboa.

Stegeman, James, Steve Parsons, Robert Frieden and Mike Wilson (2006), 'Controlling universal service funding and promoting competition through reverse auctions', Working Paper.

Stigler, George J. (1971), 'The theory of economic regulation', *Bell Journal of Economics and Management Science*, **2**(1), 3–21.

Vickrey, William (1961), 'Counter speculation, auctions and competitive sealed tenders', *Journal of Finance*, **16**(1), (March), 8–37.

Weller, D. (1999), 'Auctions for Universal Service Obligations', *Telecommunications Policy*, **23**(9), 645–74.

Williamson, Oliver (1976), 'Franchise bidding for natural monopolies – in general and with respect to CATV', *Bell Journal of Economics*, **7**(1), 73–104.

22. Priority and Non-Priority services: returning to the origins?*

Filipa Silva[†]

1 INTRODUCTION

The postal sector is a traditional yet innovative industry. It has developed new products and services, responding to technological, demand and regulatory changes. Although the universal service providers (USPs) in the 27 European Union member states (EU27) are in different stages of development, they share common challenges such as full market opening (FMO).

This chapter analyzes the commercial strategy of USPs, specifically in the key market segment of domestic standard letter mail, be it Priority or Non-Priority, when available. In 2010, all EU27 countries had a Priority service (next-day delivery) for the domestic standard[1] letter mail, and roughly half also had a Non-Priority service. In a two-tier system, postal operators sort Priority letter mail in the peak hour, while the Non-Priority letter mail is sorted in the off-peak hour, ensuring that Priority mail is delivered the next day at a price premium and Non-Priority letter mail is generally delivered in two or three days as an economic service, at a lower price.

The first European country to adopt a two-tier system in the domestic standard letter mail was, to our knowledge, the United Kingdom, in 1968. Since then, other countries have also adopted this strategy. The latest adopters were Romania (2009), and Latvia and Lithuania (2007). Two countries temporarily adopted[2] a two-tier system for domestic standard letter mail – Italy, from 1999 to 2006, and Belgium, from 2003 to 2006. These cases suggest that the two-tier system might be used by USPs in different conditions, for different purposes.

The two-tier system, or rather its absence, raises competition concerns, since changes in quality of service and price are not evident to support the differences between the offer of Priority and Non-Priority standard letters. Moreover, the evolution of competition among postal operators (POs) will also lead to investments in customers' knowledge and needs, development of segmentation strategies, and increasing customized offers.

This chapter analyzes the evolution of the domestic standard letter mail segmentation into Priority and Non-Priority, adopted by USPs in the EU27. The approach adopted is based on the analysis of specific European country cases, including the United Kingdom, Italy and Belgium, and on the analysis of prices and quality of Priority and Non-Priority standard letter mail at the domestic level, for the EU27, in order to estimate the impact of the two-tier system on those benchmarking indicators.

† Senior Expert, ANACOM.

A questionnaire was sent to the EU27 national regulatory authorities (NRAs), plus Croatia and Norway, in order to gather information about Priority and Non-Priority standard letter mail. The questionnaire included quantitative information regarding prices, volumes and quality indicators (targets and performances), and qualitative information regarding the motives for the adoption of the two-tier system or its discontinuity. About half of the NRAs answered the survey. Additional information was gathered from Wik (2009), ANACOM (2011) and from the USP annual reports.

Section 2 provides the literature review. Section includes the analysis of the adoption of the two-tier system by some USPs, in the EU27. It presents the motives for the adoption, or not, of the two-tier system, as presented by the NRAs. The level of demand of the Priority and Non-Priority services in the EU27 countries is also presented in Section 3. Section 4 includes the analysis of the two-tier system in the context of the quality indicators and Section 5 presents the averages prices of a domestic standard letter in countries with and without the two-tier system. Conclusions are discussed in Section 6.

2 LITERATURE REVIEW

Crew et al. (1990) analyze the separation of postal letter mail into First and Second Class and its price differential. According to these authors, the main motives for the adoption of the two-tier system are due to the management of the peak-hour traffic during a period of postal letter mail traffic growth. The authors demonstrate that this disaggregation does not entirely eliminate the peak-hour traffic and that, with the increasing mechanization of the technology peak-load model, the price differential between these services would tend to increase.

Calzada (2008) considers that the automation of the postal industry has increased the peak hour at the sorting process, reducing costs and gaining in quality of service. The author develops a model to estimate the demand for Priority and Non-Priority letter mail, for the USP and competitors, as well as the access charges for these two services and their optimal quality. The author concludes that the optimal access price for each of the services depends on the level of the product differentiation (which includes the quality of each service). In the context of the regulation of access charges in a liberalized postal market, according to Calzada, new POs invest in Non-Priority services, obligating the postal incumbent to adopt new measures in order to protect its market share.

NERA (2004) points out economies of scope in the offer of Priority and Non-Priority services, due to the sorting process in the same network. Other authors have also found that new competitors are more attracted to Non-Priority services, since it requires less liability, it permits operators to minimize distribution costs (Ecorys, 2005, 2008 and Wik, 2009), allows new entrants to have low-cost models and to avoid regulated prices of the First Class mail (Capgemini, 2007) and because it permits a recapture of customers with high price sensitivity (Kleindorfer and Szirmay, 2009). Ecorys (2008) adds that demand substitution from Priority service to Non-Priority, contributed to the main financial issues of Royal Mail from 2006 to 2008.

Wik (2006) mentions the existence of a substitution trend from First Class to Second

Table 22.1 Distribution of the EU27 by two-tier system in domestic standard letter mail

Only with Priority service	With Priority and Non-Priority services
Austria (EU15)	Bulgaria
Belgium (EU15)	Denmark (EU15)
Cyprus	Finland (EU15)
Czech Republic	France (EU15)
Estonia	Greece (EU15)
Germany (EU15)	Hungary
Ireland (EU15)	Latvia
Italy (EU15)	Lithuania
Luxembourg	Poland
Malta	Portugal
Slovenia	Romania
Spain (EU15)	Slovakia
Netherlands (EU15)	Sweden (EU15)
	United Kingdom (EU15)

Source: Based on postal NRA and USP information.

Class mail, where this service is available and Capgemini (2007) adds the electronic substitution to the equation, noting that it contributes to less valuation of the urgency characteristic of Priority mail. In addition, since the business consumers, responsible for most of the mail sent are more price sensitive, Capgemini estimates that more than 85 percent of mail would be suitable for Second Class services.

Copenhagen Economics (2010) reports that, in a list of 31 European countries, two-thirds intend to provide Priority and Non-Priority letters in the Universal Service Obligation (USO) while the other third provide Priority letters only. However, Ecorys (2008) recognizes that including a First Class service in the USO may be too ambitious, especially considering the costs for its achievement in the rural areas.

Last but not least, Wik (2009) found that the two-tier system may explain the differences in the price of the Priority letters up to 20 grams among European countries, in addition to regulatory conditions, the value-added tax (VAT) exemption and different costs related to distribution (such as pensions). However, it makes no reference to the price of the Non-Priority mail, or to the quality of the Priority service in countries with and without the two-tier system.

3 ADOPTION OF A TWO-TIER SYSTEM IN EUROPEAN COUNTRIES

In 2010, nearly half of the EU27 had a two-tier system for the national standard letter mail (Table 22.1).

Motivation for the Adoption of the Two-tier System

This section presents the cases of the USPs of the United Kingdom, Italy, Belgium, Croatia, Hungary, Latvia Poland and Romania and their experience in the adoption of the two-tier system.

It can be ascertained that the historical or the first main motivation for the adoption of the two-tier system was related to the peak traffic hour.

In 1968, the *UK Post Office* (nowadays, Royal Mail) adopted the two-tier system, citing that the main reasons were the growing problem of the peak hours (which was affecting the First Class service quality), the improvement of distribution standardization and efficiency and the offer of differentiated products to the consumer. At that time, the postal volume was still growing. Over the last decade, the price of the Priority service for a national standard letter mail increased more slowly than the price of the Non-Priority service (respectively, 52 and 68 percent) for a domestic standard letter, resulting in a reduction of the price differential between both services, from 42 to 28 percent.[3] Other countries have adopted the two-tier system for other reasons. Two interesting cases are Poste Italiane and De Poste/La Poste, because both adopted the two-tier system only temporarily.

In 1999, *Poste Italiane* introduced the Priority service and in 2006 the Non-Priority service was discontinued. A two-tier system was thus short-lived (1999 to 2006). This change was made in order to comply with quality standards introduced by the Ministry of Communications regarding the universal service.[4] According to the annual report from 2005 of that PO, 88 percent of the non-registered mail was sent by Non-Priority service, representing 80 percent of the unregistered mail revenues. Therefore, the adoption of the two-tier system seems to have been a temporary measure that allowed the Non-Priority service to be replaced by the Priority service for domestic standard letters, even though most of the domestic standard letters were, at that time, sent by Non-Priority service. Other USPs have recently made this change without having a temporary two-tier system, For example, the Slovenian USP, in 2004.

In Belgium, *De Post/La Poste* had a two-tier system for the standard domestic letter from 2002 to 2005. In 2002, the existent service was the Priority service and with the introduction of the two-tier system in that year, the price of the Priority service increased from €0.42 to €0.49. Nevertheless, according to the USP, about 60 percent of users maintained the use of the Priority service. According to the annual report of the USP, the two-tier system was implemented to modernize its business and to improve the quality performance of the Priority service (in 2002, the quality performance was 82.7 percent). In 2005, its service quality performance reached 91 percent and the Non-Priority service was discontinued, thus ending the two-tier system experience.

As for the quality indicators, countries such as Malta and Slovenia already have a quality performance above 95 percent for the national Priority letter mail without adopting a temporary two-tier system, while at the beginning of the decade both countries had a quality performance below 90 percent.

Poczta Polska, the Polish USP, adopted the two-tier system for domestic standard letters in 2002, with the introduction of the Priority service. The reasons by the NRA for the adoption were: market demand, and the need to increase volumes and achieve quality requirements. However, in 2009, the quality of the Priority service was still very low (53 percent). According to estimates of the Polish NRA, only 10 percent of the standard letters were sent though Priority mail. From 2002 to 2010, the price differential decreased from 64 to 26 percent. This was due to a higher increase of the Non-Priority price – 41 percent – while the Priority service price increase was 8 percent.[5]

The most recent country to adopt a two-tier system for domestic mail was *Posta Romana*, the Romanian USP, in 2009. The two-tier system was implemented because of the demand and for commercial purposes. It should be noted that in 2009, the quality of this service at the national level was low, with a performance of 46 percent.

Other countries also adopted the two-tier system in standard domestic letters following the adoption of the Postal Directive and its definition relating to the quality of the Priority service: *Magyar Posta*, the Hungarian incumbent (2004), *Hrvatska Posta*, the Croatian incumbent (2006) and *Latvijas Pasts*, the Latvian incumbent (2006).

Both the Hungarian and Croatian NRAs estimate that the domestic standard letter volume sent by Priority service is small compared with the volume of that service sent by Non-Priority service. However, the price differential evolution is different in both countries. In Hungary it decreased from 88 to 39 percent, from 2004 to 2010, while in Croatia it increased from 17 to 48 percent, from 2006 to 2010, due to an increase in the Priority standard letter mail price and a decrease in the price of Non-Priority mail, in 2010.

In Latvia the demand for Priority standard letter mail represented, according to estimates from the Latvian NRA, one-third of the standard letter mail volume at the national level. In 2010, the price differential between Priority and Non-Priority at the national level was 14 percent.

Finally, by the end of 2010, six countries of the EU27 had opened up their postal market and half of those had a two-tier system. Thus, a relation between the adoption, or not, of the two-tier system, and the FMO cannot be assumed.

Motivation for the Non-adoption of the Two-tier System

The NRAs' answers to the survey provided a number of reasons for the non-adoption of the two-tier system. These include the high costs of disaggregating the postal network, the low demand for one of the services, the fact that the only service available already was of a very good quality and, in one case, the short distances involved do not justify the multiple categories of mail delivery.

Although it was not mentioned by the NRAs, it is questionable whether the privatization of the USP[6] may also be related to the non-adoption of the two-tier system since, at the end of 2010, in seven countries of the EU27 that had privatized their USP, totally or partially, only Greece, which has the highest percentage of state ownership (90 percent), had a two-tier system for the domestic service.

This may be explained by the assumption that, according to the answers of some of the NRAs in countries without the two-tier system, its adoption might generate higher costs, and privatized USPs might be more profit oriented than public USPs, which have additional social concerns.

To some extent, the non-adoption of the Non-Priority service might be regarded as a measure to minimize the entry of new postal operators in the postal market since, as noted in Section 2, new entrants usually invest in Non-Priority services and if the USP provides a Non-Priority service, it probably would have to make a wholesale offer to new entrants.

The Demand for Priority and Non-Priority Domestic Standard Letters

From the questionnaire to the NRA, it was possible to collect the standard letter volumes disaggregated by Priority and Non-Priority services for only five countries:[7] Croatia, Greece, Poland, Portugal and the United Kingdom. Information for Finland and Sweden was collected from the annual reports of the USP.

In 2010, standard domestic mail mainly comprised Non-Priority service in Croatia, Poland and Portugal. In Greece it mainly comprised Priority service. In Finland, Sweden and the United Kingdom, around 50 percent of the domestic standard letters comprised Priority service due to the substitution by the Non-Priority standard letter.

Finally, in 2009, a survey was conducted by the Irish NRA (ComReg) to the business and residential markets in Ireland (a country with only Priority or First Class service). For each group, residential and business, the desire for a Second Class service was questioned. The results for the business sector revealed that if a Second Class Service were to be offered, almost half of the companies would send at least half of its mail by that service while almost one-third would continue to send all its mail by First Class. With regard to the residential sector, two-fifths stated that they would send most of their mail by Second Class, while nearly one-quarter claimed it would send no mail using a Second Class service, even if it were available. Therefore, it seems that, at least in Ireland, there is a demand for a Second Class service.

QUALITY OF THE NATIONAL STANDARD PRIORITY SERVICE

As a general assumption, it might be expected that a country with a two-tier system would have a quality performance for Priority service at least as good as the quality of that service in a country without the disaggregation. Countries that have recently adopted the two-tier system as a result of the 97/67/EC Postal Directive and the quality targets for the national letter mail may be seen as exceptions.

In 2009, quality performances for priority domestic letter mail in the EU27 ranged from 46 percent (in Romania) to 98 percent (in Luxembourg). More than a quarter of the countries had a quality performance above 95 percent and more than half had a quality performance above 90 percent (Table 22.2).

To analyze the relation between the adoption of a two-tier system and the quality performance of the USP in the EU27, the average values and standard deviations for the quality indicators were obtained for countries with and without the two-tier system (Table 22.3). Notably, the average values of the quality targets and performances are higher in countries without the two-tier system, although statistically there is only significance at the 10 percent level.

In the same analysis for the EU15, there are no statistical differences between quality targets and performances in countries with and without the two-tier system, meaning that the previous differences were due to the results of new EU27 members that decided to implement the two-tier system because of the Postal Directive (Table 22.4).

Table 22.2 Quality targets and performances of the Priority domestic standard letter mail in the EU 26 (without Germany), 2009

Country	EU15	Two-tier system	Quality target (%)	Quality performance (%)
Romania	No	Yes	85.0	46.2
Poland	No	Yes	82.0	52.7
Lithuania	No	Yes	85.0	75.0
Greece	Yes	Yes	87.0	81.5
Bulgaria	No	No	80.0	84.2
France	Yes	Yes	84.0	84.7
Ireland	Yes	No	94.0	85.0
United Kingdom	Yes	Yes	93.0	87.9
Cyprus	No	No	90.0	89.4
Italy	Yes	No	89.0	90.7
Chech Republic	No	No	91.0	92.1
Spain	Yes	No	92.0	92.5
Hungary	No	Yes	85.0	93.1
Belgium	Yes	No	90.0	93.2
Estónia	No	No	90.0	93.8
Finland	Yes	Yes	85.0	94.0
Portugal	Yes	Yes	94.5	94.6
Sweden	Yes	Yes	85.0	94.8
Slovenia	No	No	95.0	95.0
Malta	No	No	93.0	95.1
Netherlands	Yes	No	95.0	95.2
Denmark	Yes	Yes	93.0	95.7
Austria	Yes	No	95.0	96.0
Latvia	No	Yes	97.0	96.3
Slovakia	No	Yes	96.0	96.8
Luxembourg	Yes	No	95.0	97.7

Sources: NRAs and Copenhagen Economics (2010).

Also, the stability obtained for the quality performances in the last five years in some of the EU27, does not seem to be related to the adoption of the two-tier system (confirmed by the Spearman test, with a p-value of 0.849).

In short, two conclusions can be drawn from this analysis. The first is that the two-tier system does not seem to be related to a higher quality of the Priority standard domestic letters, as would be expected. The second is that it is possible to achieve a good quality for that service, without having to adopt a two-tier system.

PRICES OF THE NATIONAL STANDARD MAIL

This section aims to relate the price of a domestic standard letter to the existence, or not, of a Non-Priority service, in each of the EU27 countries.

As cited by Wik (2006), the exclusive comparison of the price of a 20g First Class

Table 22.3 Average and standard deviation for the quality targets and performances, with and without the two-tier system, EU27

Two-tier system	Average		Std dev.	
	Quality target (%)	Quality performance** (%)	Quality target	Quality performance**
Yes	88.0	84.2	0.06	0.16
No	91.5	93.0	0.04	0.04
Significance*	0.081	0.068	0.062	0.009

Notes:
* 95% confidence interval *t*-test for equality of means and standard deviations, between the group of countries with the two-tier system and the group of countries without that system.
** No information for Germany.

Source: Author.

Table 22.4 Average and standard deviation for the quality targets and performances, with and without the two-tier system, EU15

Two-tier system	Average		Std dev.	
	Quality target (%)	Quality performance** (%)	Quality target	Quality performance**
Yes	88.9	90.7	0.05	0.06
No	91.3	92.9	0.05	0.04
Significance*	0.363	0.422	0.747	0.153

Notes:
* 95% confidence interval *t*-test for equality of means and standard deviations, between the group of countries with the two-tier system and the group of countries without that system.
** No information for Germany.

Source: Author.

standard letter would be an incomplete analysis, since in some countries it is possible to choose an alternative Second Class service. In addition, in some countries with both First and Second Class mail, the service mostly used is Second Class.

This section compares prices, in euros, with and without purchasing power parity (PPP), for a domestic standard letter, sent by Priority and by Non-Priority services, in the EU27. Nominal prices for 2010 were obtained by ANACOM (2011) and prices with PPP (EU27 = 100) came from Eurostat. In countries where VAT was charged, the price presented includes VAT, because it was the final price paid by the consumer.

Sorting Priority services prices in PPP, in descending order, it can be seen that the six countries with the highest price have a two-tier system and, considering that Belgium and Italy had that system in the recent past, it can be assumed that for the 12 countries with the highest Priority price in PPP, there is a relationship with a two-tier system (Table 22.5).

Table 22.5 Price, nominal and in PPP, in 2010, EU27 (€)

	Country	EU15	Price in PPP (EU27)		Nominal Price	
			Priority service	Non-Priority service	Priority service	Non-Priority service
MT	Malta	No	0.23	N	0.19	N
SI	Slovenia*	No	0.34	N	0.29	N
ES	Spain	Yes	0.35	N	0.34	N
CY	Cyprus	No	0.37	N	0.34	N
NL	Netherlands	Yes	0.41	N	0.44	N
IE	Ireland	Yes	0.44	N	0.55	N
EE	Estonia	No	0.47	N	0.35	N
LU	Luxembourg	Yes	0.49	N	0.60	N
FR	France	Yes	0.51	0.46	0.58	0.53
AT	Austria	Yes	0.51	N	0.55	N
DK	Denmark	Yes	0.51	0.46	0.74	0.67
GB	United Kingdom	Yes	0.52	0.40	0.48	0.37
DE	Germany	Yes	0.52	N	0.55	N
PT	Portugal	Yes	0.53	0.36	0.47	0.32
CZ	Czech Republic	No	0.56	N	0.39	N
IT	Italy	Yes	0.56	N	0.60	N
HU	Hungary	No	0.58	0.44	0.38	0.29
FI	Finland*	Yes	0.59	0.47	0.75	0.60
GR	Greece	Yes	0.60	0.54	0.58	0.53
LT	Lithuania	No	0.60	0.52	0.45	0.39
BE	Belgium	Yes	0.61	N	0.69	N
RO	Romania	No	0.67	0.42	0.38	0.24
SE	Sweden*	Yes	0.72	0.66	0.78	0.71
SK	Slovakia	No	0.81	0.54	0.60	0.40
PL	Poland	No	0.83	0.66	0.49	0.39
LV	Latvia	No	0.83	0.73	0.56	0.49
BG	Bulgaria	No	0.97	0.63	0.51	0.33

Note: * Prices with VAT.

Source: ANACOM (2011).

Specifically with regard to the price of the Non-Priority service, it could be argued that in countries with the two-tier system, on average, this should be cheaper than the price of the Priority service in countries where the Non Priority service is not offered. Table 22.6 presents a comparison of the average prices of Priority and Non Priority services in countries with and without the two-tier system.

The average price for sending a domestic standard letter by Priority service is statistically higher in countries with the two-tier system. This may be because, in some cases, such as Poland, Portugal, Sweden and, more recently, Croatia, Latvia and Romania, when the PO adopted the two-tier system, the price adopted for the Non-Priority service was similar to that of the already existing service, while the price adopted for the Priority service was higher.

Table 22.6 Average prices and standard deviations for domestic standard letter mail, in Priority and Non-Priority services, for the EU27, with and without the two-tier system, 2010

	PPP			Nominal		
	N	Priority	Non-Priority	*N*	Priority	Non-Priority
Average						
With two-tier	14	0.66	0.52	14	€0.55	€0.45
Without	13	0.45		13	€0.45	
Sig.*		0.000	0.111		0.070	0.928
Standard error						
With two-tier	14	0.15	0.11	14	€0.15	€0.14
Without	13	0.11	–	13	€0.13	–
Sig.*		0.178	0.864		0.368	0.820

Note: * A 95% confidence interval *t*-test was applied to compare: (a) the means of the Priority service in countries with and without the two-tier system; and (b) the means of the Non-Priority service in countries with the two-tier system and the price of the only service in countries without it.

Source: Author.

There is no statistical difference between the average price of the Non-Priority service, in PPP, in countries with the two-tier, and the average price of sending a letter by the Priority Service in countries without the two-tier, even though it would be expected that the price of the Non-Priority service would be, on average, cheaper.

Apart from the above explanation, which may partially explain this result, in the 14 countries of the EU27 that have a two-tier system, there was a decrease of the price differential between Priority and Non-Priority services, as a result of a higher growth of the price of the Non-Priority service; however, when compared with the price of the Priority service in only two countries (Finland and Denmark), there was a price differential increase.

One reason that may explain the decrease of the price differential might be the increase of the quality of the postal services in some European countries. The second reason is profitability. With the decrease of the postal traffic and the substitution of the Priority services by Non-Priority, to achieve better financial performance, it is possible that operators, *ceteris paribus*, prefer to increase the price of the service where the demand is higher.

6 CONCLUSIONS

In the aftermath of the FMO, approximately half of the USPs in the EU27 offer a two-tier domestic mail service. While, historically, some USPs adopted this approach to reduce the peak-hour traffic, more recently other USPs have used this strategy to fulfill demand requests and to ensure a better quality of their Priority service. In some cases, this strategy has been temporarily implemented to overcome quality issues.

In addition, some of the new countries of the EU27 adopted the two-tier system in order to harmonize their services with the Postal Directive and related postal quality indicators.

In countries with only a Priority service at the domestic level, the main reasons mentioned by the NRAs for the non-adoption of the two-tier system were the costs related to the implementation of the two-tier system and the low demand for one of the services.

Although none of the NRAs mentioned the privatization of the USP as a reason for non-adoption of the two-tier system, the privatization of the USP and the non-existence of the two-tier system seem to be related. In fact, six countries of the EU27 have totally or partially privatized the USP and in only one of those six countries is there a two-tier system for domestic standard letters. This apparent relationship between privatization and non-adoption of a two-tier system may occur for two reasons: first, because privatized operators tend to be more cost oriented than public operators (and the latter may also have more salient social objectives), in a context where, according to some NRAs, the two-tier system is perceived to be related to higher costs; and second, because the USP may intend to deter the entry of new operators in the postal market. In fact, new entrants usually invest in Non-Priority services and if the USP has a two-tier system, it may be under obligation to offer its competitors workshare agreements for the Non-Priority service if it offers such a service. The issue is, of course, not completely clear-cut since product differentiation and an increase in product variety could also deter entrants.

Countries with a two-tier system do not seem to have higher quality performance than countries without such a system, especially with regard to the EU15, suggesting that, to achieve better quality, a country does not need to have a two-tier system.

With regard to prices, there does not seem to be a difference between the price of the Non-Priority service and the price of the only service (Priority) in countries without the two-tier system. This similarity between prices may be because, at the time of the introduction of the two-tier system, the price of the existing service typically became the price of the Non-Priority service. Additionally, in recent years, there seems to be a tendency to reduce the price differential when the quality targets of the Priority service are achieved, a reduction that is usually made by increasing the price of the Non-Priority service in a greater proportion than the increase in the price of the Priority service.

If the differences in cost between Priority and Non-Priority Services become less significant, the result may be the reduction of their price differential and, in the medium term, the discontinuation of one of the services. However, the information gathered in this study was not sufficient to allow an assessment of the costs, or the differential in costs, of Priority and Non-Priority services.

In order to develop these ideas further, it would be necessary to collect additional information. For instance, it would be interesting to know the proportion of Priority and Non Priority mail in domestic standard letter mail for all the countries of the EU27. In addition, the costs allocated to each service would provide some insights into the incentives to adopt the two-tier system under FMO. These and other questions await further research on the continuing development of two-tier pricing in the postal sector.

NOTES

* The opinions expressed are those of the author and do not necessarily reflect the views of ANACOM.

1. In Austria, Bulgaria, Cyprus, France, Germany, Greece, Hungary, Italy, Latvia, Lithuania, Luxembourg, Portugal, Romania, Slovenia, Spain, Sweden and the Netherlands, a standard letter weighs 20g, in Belgium, the Czech Republic, Denmark, Estonia, Finland, Ireland, Malta, Poland and Slovakia it weighs 50g and in the United Kingdom it weighs 100g.
2. A temporary adoption of the two-tier system also occurred for cross-border mail. For instance, the Netherlands had a temporary two-tier system from 1998 to 2010.
3. In 2000, the prices for standard domestic Priority and Non-Priority services were, respectively, 27p and 19p, whereas in 2010 they were 41p and 32p.
4. For more details, see 'Regulations for mail delivery within the scope of the Universal Postal Service. Tariffs and prices for domestic and overseas mail delivery', available at: http://www.poste.it/azienda/ass_consumatori/carta_qualita_24_06_08.pdf (accessed 19 April 2011).
5. In 2002 the price (in PNL) of Priority and Non-Priority mail was, respectively, 1.80 and 1.10 while in 2010 it was 1.95 and 1.55.
6. Countries where the USP has been privatized and its percentage state ownership are: Austria (52.83%), Belgium (50% + 1 share), Germany (30.5%), Greece (90%), Italy (65%), Malta (0%) and the Netherlands (0%). Information from Copenhagen Economics (2010),
7. Some NRAs did not respond to the questionnaire, and in the group that did respond, some do not collect information disaggregated by Priority and Non-Priority service or this information is confidential.

REFERENCES

ANACOM (2011), 'Comparisons of Prices of Universal Postal Service Providers in the European Union in 2010', available at: http://www.anacom.pt/render.jsp?contentId=1066054 (accessed 17 January 2011).

Calzada, Joan (2008), 'Access charges under two-tier pricing', *Journal of Regulatory Economics*, **35** (3), 296–311.

Capgemini (2007), 'European Postal Perspective, facing the challenge from low-cost post', available at: http://www.capgemini.com/insights-and-resources/by-publication/european_postal_perspective/ (accessed 27 January 2011).

ComReg (2009), '2009 Postal Market Business and Residential Surveys', available at: http://www.comreg.ie/publications/2009_postal_market_residential_survey.597.103533.p.html (accessed 3 May 2010).

Copenhagen Economics (2010), 'Main developments in the postal sector (2008–2010)', study for DG Internal Market and Services, European Commission, available at: http://ec.europa.eu/internal_market/post/studies_en.htm (accessed 14 December 2010).

Crew, Michael A., Paul R. Kleindorfer and Marc A. Smith (1990), 'Peak-load pricing in postal services', *Economic Journal*, **100** (September), 793–807.

De Post/La Poste (2004), 'Rapport annuel 2003', available at: http://www.bpost.be/site/fr/postgroup/prestations/annual_reports/ (accessed 26 March 2011).

De Post/La Poste (2008), 'Annual report 2007', available at: http://www.bpost.be/site/fr/postgroup/prestations/annual_reports/ (accessed 26 March 2011).

Ecorys (2005), 'Development Competition in European Postal Sector', available at: http://ec.europa.eu/internal_market/post/studies_en.htm (accessed 16 June 2010).

Ecorys (2008), 'Main Developments in the Postal Sector (2006–2008)', available at: http://ec.europa.eu/internal_market/post/studies_en.htm (accessed 15 December 2009).

Kleindorfer, Paul R. and Zoltan Szirmay (2009), 'Pricing practice in the postal industry', *Social Science Research Network*, available at: http://papers.ssrn.com/sol3/papers.cfm?abstract_id=1414308 (accessed 11 February 2011).

Magyar Posta (2008), 'Annual report 2007', available at: http://www.ipc.be/~/media/Documents/PUBLIC/Annual%20Reports/Member%20Reports/2007/Magyar%20Posta%202007.ashx (accessed 13 April 2011).

NERA (2004), 'Economics of Postal Services, Final Report', available at: http://ec.europa.eu/internal_market/post/studies_en.htm (accessed 15 February 2011).
Post Italiane (2006), 'Annual report 2005', available at: http://www.poste.it/en/azienda/chi_siamo/bilanci.shtml (accessed 13 December 2010).
Post Italiane (2007), 'Annual report 2006', available at: http://www.poste.it/en/azienda/chi_siamo/bilanci.shtml (accessed 13 December 2010).
Post Italiane (2010), 'Annual report 2009', available at: http://www.poste.it/en/azienda/chi_siamo/bilanci.shtml (accessed 11 May 2011).
Postcomm (2010), '2009 Customer Survey, Report of Findings from Research with Residential Customers and SMEs', available at: http://www.psc.gov.uk/documents/92.pdf (accessed 11 February 2011).
Wik (2006), 'Main developments in the postal sector (2004–2006)', available at: http://ec.europa.eu/internal_market/post/studies_en.htm (accessed 15 February 2011).
Wik (2009), 'The Evolution of the European Postal Market since 1997', available at: http://ec.europa.eu/internal_market/post/studies_en.htm (accessed 15 December 2009).

23. Understanding consumer preferences for paper and digital marketing channels

Kari Elkelä[†]

1 INTRODUCTION

Marketing is an essential part of the communications market. We encounter it both in the form of separate marketing messages and in many channels related to information and entertainment. The rapid development of mobile phones and Internet services is changing the character of marketing and challenging the traditionally strong paper channels. Numerous studies in many countries have been carried out targeted at only one or two new digital channels. However, an overall view of consumer preferences for alternative marketing channels, and the demographic and other factors influencing these, has yet to appear. Is paper marketing still the dominant form? How widely is digital marketing accepted? What are consumer preferences for each channel? Why are certain channels preferred by certain consumers? Answers to these questions are important both for marketing enterprises and for operators providing traditional and digital delivery services. This chapter presents a framework for analyzing these questions, together with some results based on survey data gathered over the last five years in Finland.

Two quite large sets of quantitative cross-sectional data were used for this research. The change follow-up and segmentation data, which consisted of 1,180 responses, was collected in June 2010 (Elkelä, 2010). The channel preference explanation data, with 1,397 responses, was collected in October 2010 (Elkelä, 2011). Both sets of data are representative samples of Finns aged over 15 years. This research can also be viewed as following, enlarging on and deepening my earlier study 'Paper or electronic?' (Elkelä, 2005), which covered just four channels and presented only a preliminary discussion of reasons for channel preference.

The chapter proceeds as follows. Section 2 presents four ways of grouping and classifying marketing communication channels. Furthermore, the formation of consumers' channel preferences is structured as a continuous process. Section 3 describes channel preferences for marketing communication in Finland. Consumer preferences from 2010 are compared with the situation in 2006. Because different consumers prefer different channels, consumers are segmented on the basis of their channel preferences, whereby the main dimensions behind this segmentation are examined. Section 4 presents an explanatory model in which channel preferences are explained on the basis of expected utilities of marketing channels evaluated by consumers. Section 5 is devoted to conclusions and recommendations.

[†] Research Manager, Itella Corporation.

2 MARKETING COMMUNICATION CHANNELS AND THEIR PREFERENCE FORMATION

By definition, marketing communication is used to 'inform, persuade, reinforce and build images to differentiate a product or service' (Fill, 2009, p. 9). In practice this is done by using a wide selection of marketing communication channels, of which the most important are compared in this study. In order to better analyze this wide range of channels it would be reasonable to group and classify them. This can be achieved in several ways, which complement one another.

First, according to Finnish marketing statistics, marketing communication can be divided into media advertising and direct marketing, and their channels are comprehensively compared in this study. The third area of marketing communication found in the statistics is sales promotion, but this has been left out of the study because its forms cannot be considered as communication channels. Media advertising channels include the following examined in this research: newspapers, magazines, Internet advertising, radio, television and outdoor advertising. Catalogs and leaflets, addressed and unaddressed letters, phone calls, text messages and emails are classified as direct marketing. Various ways of categorizing marketing communication channels are shown in Table 23.1.

Second, marketing channels can be divided according to their age group. The paper channels, to which letters, newspapers, magazines and other paper publications belong, are the oldest. The traditional electronic channels – phone calls, radio and television – which have already long been in use, are placed in the second age group. The most recent group, the new digital channels, consists of email and text messaging, as well as all the Internet channels. Outdoor advertisements, which can be either paper or electronic and door-to-door selling, which is neither, fall outside this classification.

Third, channels can be grouped into targeted and mass communication. Targeted messaging is addressed to or otherwise directed at a certain individual. Targeted messaging channels are the addressed letter, email, text message, sales call and door-to-door selling. In mass communication the individual targeted person is not identified, rather messages are directed at large public groups. Mass communication can be further divided into advertising and journalistic mass communication.

Advertising mass communication contains mainly marketing material. Pure advertising mass communication channels are the unaddressed letter and outdoor advertising. Furthermore, catalogs and leaflets are classified as advertising mass communication here even though some are sent addressed. Also, Internet search services can be classified as advertising mass communication because information is searched for purchasing, and the obtained search results come primarily from sellers. In journalistic mass communication the marketing material is included with the journalistic main content. This also affects the evaluation of the channel as a marketing channel. Journalistic mass communication channels are the newspaper, magazine, radio, television and Internet news pages. Also, the social media can be placed in this group even though the principal producers of content are other consumers. However, the content has been delivered to the whole so-called 'circle of friends' and not just certain individuals.

Fourth, a division into search channels and reception channels can be made. It is typical of information search channels to contain plenty of available product and service

Table 23.1 Classification of surveyed marketing communication channels according to main characteristics

Marketing communication channels	Media or direct marketing	Channel age group: paper – electronic – digital	Targeted or mass com, journalistic or only advertising	Search or reception channel
Newspaper	Media	Paper	Journalistic mass com	Information search channel
Magazine	Media	Paper	Journalistic mass com	
Catalog or leaflet	Direct	Paper	Advertising mass com	
Internet search services	Media	New digital	Advertising mass com	
Internet in newspages	Media	New digital	Journalistic mass com	Reception channel
Social media	Media	New digital	Journalistic mass com	
Addressed letter	Direct	Paper	Targeted messaging	
Unaddressed letter	Direct	Paper	Advertising mass com	
Radio	Media	Traditional electronic	Journalistic mass com	
Television	Media	Traditional electronic	Journalistic mass com	
Phone call	Direct	Traditional electronic	Targeted messaging	
Text message	Direct	New digital	Targeted messaging	
Email	Direct	New digital	Targeted messaging	
Outdoor ad	Media	Paper and electronic	Advertising mass com	
Door-to-door selling	Neither	Neither	Targeted messaging	

alternatives and to provide an opportunity for target-oriented search and a pleasurable experience because of the versatility of the alternatives. Catalogs and leaflets, newspapers, magazines, and Internet search services can be classified as search channels. Other channels can be classified mainly as reception channels in which the seller feeds or pushes one or several alternatives and the consumer is in a take it or leave it choice situation of the marketing message. However, these main classifications are not unambiguous but, for example, the channel, which has been classified here as a reception channel, can also be used as a search channel.

From the meta-theoretical point of view this study is based on the theoretical idea according to which the independently acting human being establishes his/her behavior based on a subjective perception of the environment, makes choices actively, and is able to anticipate future situations (Hartmann, 2009a, pp. 4–5). This starting point creates a good base for measuring, analyzing and explaining channel preferences. Prior to this, it is useful to structure the process in which preferences are formed.

Figure 23.1 illustrates the formation of channel preferences for communication in general and especially for marketing communication. Consumers have some understanding of the various communication channels and the utilities received through them. On

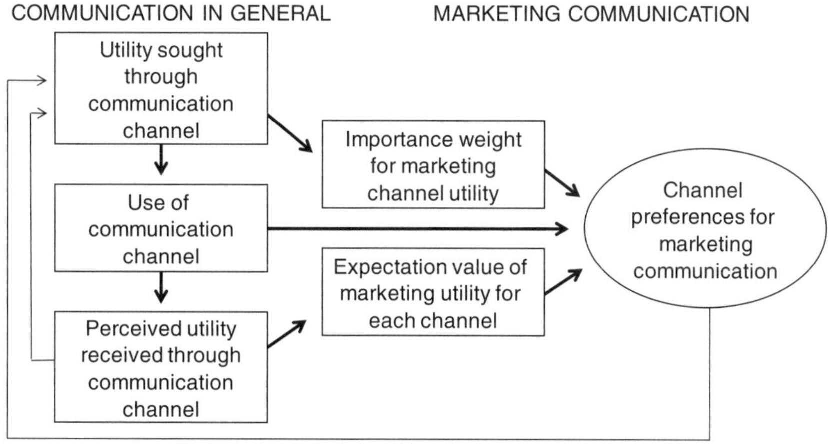

Figure 23.1 Channel preferences as expectation values of utilities

the basis of this, the consumer mainly has to decide whether to begin or continue to use each channel. Over time the use tends to become a routine, in addition to which the individual choice is influenced by chance, and various situational factors. Use of channels produces perceptions of their utility (for utility concept in media choice, see, for example, Hastall, 2009, pp. 152–3). Positive perceptions may maintain and even increase channel use. For example, Facebook's social media usage may be evaluated as 'more convenient' than phone calls, text messages and emails, with the result that the use of these old channels decreases. When the range of communication channels rapidly diversifies such an evaluation circle is emphasized.

A perception of the total utility from communication channels is a background process for the evaluation of channel preferences for marketing communication channels. According to the Expectation Value Model for the media (McQuail, 2010, pp. 426–7) the complete gratification sought from the media object is the sum of the expected perceived gratifications weighted with its importance to the consumer. Accordingly, channel preference for marketing communication can be calculated as a sum of the expected utilities weighted with their importance to the consumer. The importance of these utilities can be assumed to be relatively stable and independent of the channel, although in actual choice situations, of course, variation also occurs. On the other hand, the expected values of utilities are usually channel specific, which explains why channels are preferred for different reasons.

The use of various communication channels has a direct effect on the channel preferences of marketing communication, mainly as a routine or habituation. Also the channel preferences have a feedback effect on utilities sought from communication channels and thus on their use. These kinds of processes, which reinforce, debilitate and maintain channel preferences, are in continuous motion. However, in this research which uses cross-section data, this process and these feedback effects are not studied.

3 PREFERENCE CHANGES AND CONSUMER SEGMENTS

Two cross-sectional data collections were performed in 2006 and 2010 in order to identify the change of preferences and to segment consumers. The channel preferences were measured on a 3-point ordinal scale; preferred, (other) accepted, and disfavored. Respondents were first asked to name three of their favorite channels and after that they were able to choose from the rest those channels they do not want to use at all. The results for 13 channels in 2006 and 2010 are presented in Figure 23.2 (Elkelä, 2007 and 2010).

The product catalog and newspaper were the most favored marketing communication channels for Finnish consumers in both years. The Internet has accelerated the introduction of a third. The most obvious strength of all these channels is that one can easily become acquainted with them and exactly in the way one wishes. Furthermore, they are informative and provide excellent opportunities to search for information.

The fourth place is occupied by the addressed letter, the popularity of which has dropped most of all. The addressed advertising letter which, in 2006, was accepted by most consumers has now diminished radically in popularity and opinions are divided distinctly. For some it continues to be favored because it symbolizes the individual's identity. However, for others the advertising letter is intrusive, not ecological and causes unnecessary litter. Yet, the addressed letter is the only marketing channel that is regarded as really personal and targeted, meant exactly for that recipient who is expecting it.

Email is another opinion-separating channel toward which a conflicting attitude exists. On the one hand it can be read anytime, anywhere, one can get additional information through the links and it is easy to destroy an unsolicited message. On the other hand, some recipients would like to restrict email messages to personal matters or do not read them at all. The difference compared to the addressed paper letter is that of those who favor email, only a few feel that they have been approached personally.

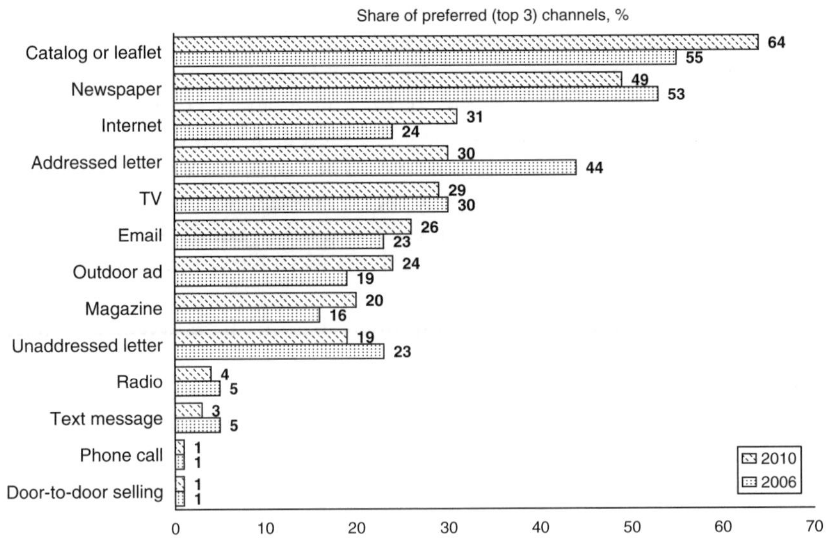

Figure 23.2 Marketing communication channel preferences in Finland, 2006 and 2010

Consumer attitudes to radio, television, magazines and outdoor advertising are of neutral acceptance. Yet, a clear majority of consumers consider door-to door selling, sales calls and text messages as the most disfavored channels which are all regarded as an intrusive encroachment on their personal time.

Cluster analysis classifies consumers according to their channel preferences into groups which are as homogeneous as possible internally but as heterogeneous as possible compared to other groups. The analysis was made using the *k*-means clusters method, which is well suited to analyzing extensive data. The best cluster solution is presented in Table 23.2 and includes five clusters. The solution can be considered good in the sense that all clusters were big enough and of approximately the same size, consumer shares varying from 15 to 24 percent.

Consumer preference segments have been arranged in Table 23.2 from the most broad-minded attitudes toward marketing channels to the most restricting. The anonymous channel limiters have the strictest definition of preferences, whereas the targeting acceptors are the most 'omnivorous', and willing to use the broadest range of channels. The paper supporter's attitude is the second most restricting. Both web and traditional mass media supporters are ready to use a range of channels that are a little broader than average.

The channel group averages supporting this interpretation are shown below the primary cluster solution in Table 23.2. Generally the greatest difference between the groups is in the attitude to the opinion-separating channels and to the new digital channels and targeted messaging. The groups differ least in the attitude to the search channels and to journalistic mass communication, in both of which a distinctly more positive average attitude to marketing prevails. A fairly positive attitude to product catalogs and newspapers prevails in all five segments. On the other hand, the attitude to door-to-door selling is clearly negative in all segments.

- *Anonymous channel limiters* do not want to give their name and address information to marketeters. They welcome marketing through newspapers, product catalogs, and outdoor advertisements, which are all unaddressed channels. However, they want to avoid all targeted channels: letters, email, SMS, phone call, and door-to-door selling. Of the new electronic channels they only accept the Internet, which is not seen so much as a marketing messages reception channel, but rather as a channel for product information search.
- *Paper supporters* prefer to receive their marketing through catalogs, newspapers and paper letters. Their most negative attitude concerns sales calls, text messages and email advertising. In addition, they dislike Internet marketing.
- *Traditional mass media supporters* feel most positively toward television and newspaper advertising, and product catalogs. This segment also prefers traditional electronic channels more than any other group. They have a negative attitude to sales calls and text messages, as well as a rather negative attitude toward email advertising.
- *Web supporters* clearly favor Internet and email as marketing channels, but they also read catalogs with great enthusiasm. They have a negative attitude to sales calls and text messages, and their disposition toward paper letters is also one of doubt. This group can be looked upon as the antithesis of paper supporters, because this

Table 23.2 Consumer preference segments for receiving marketing communication

	Clusters and cluster means					Mean	Std dev.
	Anonymous channel limitators	Paper supporters	Traditional mass media supporters	Web supporters	Targeting acceptors		
Marketing communication channels							
Catalog or leaflet	2.5	2.8	2.5	2.4	2.7	2.6	0.59
Newspaper	2.7	2.7	2.6	2.3	2.2	2.5	0.55
Internet	2.1	1.8	1.9	2.8	2.1	2.2	0.65
Magazine	2.3	2.2	2.2	2.0	2.1	2.1	0.47
TV	2.3	1.8	3.0	2.1	2.0	2.2	0.58
Outdoor ad	2.4	2.2	2.1	2.1	2.1	2.2	0.55
Radio	1.8	1.8	2.0	1.9	1.9	1.9	0.42
Addressed letter	1.0	2.3	2.1	1.8	2.7	2.0	0.75
Unaddressed letter	1.2	2.4	2.1	1.8	2.1	2.0	0.65
Email	1.2	1.4	1.6	2.6	2.5	1.9	0.78
Text message	1.1	1.1	1.3	1.4	1.7	1.3	0.53
Phone call	1.1	1.1	1.3	1.2	1.5	1.2	0.45
Door-to-door selling	1.1	1.1	1.1	1.1	1.2	1.1	0.34
Share of consumers, %	17	24	15	23	22	100	
Channel groupings							
Paper channels	1.9	2.5	2.3	2.1	2.4	2.2	0.29
Traditional electronic channels	1.7	1.6	2.1	1.7	1.8	1.8	0.32
New digital channels	1.4	1.4	1.6	2.3	2.1	1.8	0.46
Targeted messaging	1.1	1.4	1.5	1.6	1.9	1.5	0.34
Advertising mass com	2.0	2.5	2.2	2.1	2.3	2.2	0.36
Journalistic mass com	2.2	2.1	2.3	2.2	2.1	2.2	0.23
Search channels	2.4	2.4	2.3	2.4	2.3	2.3	0.24
Reception channels	1.5	1.7	1.8	1.8	2.0	1.8	0.23
Most preferred channels	2.6	2.7	2.5	2.3	2.4	2.5	0.39
Neutrally accepted channels	2.2	2.0	2.2	2.2	2.1	2.1	0.25
Opinions separating channels	1.1	2.0	1.9	2.1	2.4	2.0	0.49
Least preferred channels	1.1	1.1	1.2	1.2	1.5	1.2	0.32
Mean, all channels	1.7	1.9	2.0	2.0	2.1	1.9	

Note: Scale: 1 = Not favored, 2 = Accepted, 3 = Preferred (top 3).

segment is the least willing to receive ads on paper, and situates the Internet well ahead of newspaper advertising.

- *Targeting acceptors* prefer the addressed letter, email and product catalogs. This group has been characterized to some extent as having a positive attitude toward all channels. They clearly have a more tolerant attitude than any other group even

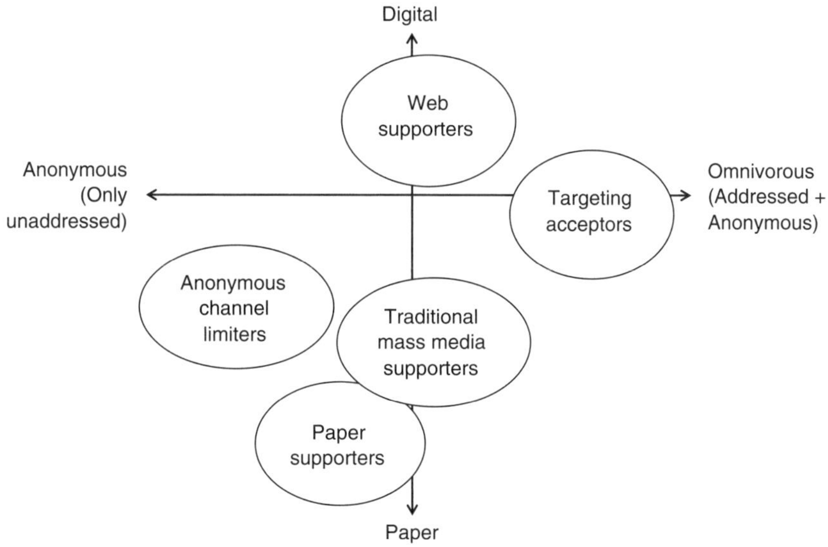

Figure 23.3 *Consumer attitudes to marketing communication channels: segments and main dimensions*

toward the most disfavored channels, the text message and sales call. Still, this group can be seen as the clearest opposite to the anonymous channel limiters.

With the support of cluster analysis and channel groupings it is possible to define two main dimensions behind consumer channel preferences, and consumer preference segments can be placed according to these dimensions. The first of those two main dimensions is *anonymous versus omnivorous*. At the anonymous end of the dimension is strict limitation to unaddressed channels, in which consumers' channel preferences emphasize mass communication and spontaneous information search. At the omnivorous end of the dimension targeted media is accepted and consumers are ready to receive both addressed and unaddressed messages through any channel.

The second main dimension of *digital versus paper* describes orientation toward either new digital network communication or traditional paper communication. Network communication is especially favored by those under 35 years, and traditional paper communication by those over 60 years. In the future, this confrontation may become even more critical. The older age groups which are more familiar with and feel more at ease with paper may wish to exercise their right to paper advertising ever more determinedly in the future. On the other hand, in those age classes which grew up in a network communication environment, paper advertising may be more actively opposed in the future and viewed as a way of evading environmental responsibility.

We can also see from Figure 23.3 that paper marketing is preferred by the majority of consumers, because most of the segments on the digital versus paper dimension are placed on the paper side of the scale and only web supporters would like to receive their marketing communications messages mainly digitally. However, among the other groups targeting acceptors have a somewhat positive attitude toward new digital marketing communication, which group in fact very warmly welcomes all marketing channels and is the only group to be placed clearly at the omnivorous end of the scale. The anonymous channel limiters are naturally situated at the anonymous end, but the paper supporters are to be found quite close, because their negative attitude toward digital channels reduces the number of channels they accept. A little more than the average number of channels is suitable for web supporters and traditional mass media supporters.

If we compare this 2010 cluster solution and the two main dimensions model based on it with the 2006 segmentation data (Elkelä, 2009, p. 49), it can be seen that a clear digital versus paper dimension did not emerge in the earlier data. The main reason for this is that in the course of four years the addressed letter lost much of its popularity and changed from one of the most preferred channels to an opinion-separating channel, and as a counterbalance to this the Internet and email are now viewed in a more positive light.

The changes in the background to this development appear to be related to an increased offering of Internet services and improved use skills, and on the other hand increased criticism of paper use from an environmental perspective. In 2006, the addressed letter was still so popular that it was disfavored only by anonymous channel limiters. At that time, the paper versus digital confrontation did not produce results, because even those who took the most positive attitude toward the Internet were also willing to receive addressed marketing letters. The situation is manifestly different in the 2010 results.

4 EXPLANATORY MODEL FOR CHANNEL PREFERENCES

The consumer data (Elkelä, 2011) including utility evaluations for each channel were used to estimate linear regression models which explain channel preferences for marketing communication. The expected utilities form the core of the explanation model of channel preferences. Utilities are the perceived properties of the channels, in other words the reasons to use channels. The first four groups of utilities, *informative*, *entertaining*, *personal*, and *interactive* are based on earlier studies on the Uses and Gratifications Approach (McQuail, 1983, pp. 82–3). Because consumers now have available many more alternative marketing channels than earlier, they are becoming more and more selective in their choices. So, *controllability,* which has been found to be a new important factor in my own preliminary studies, has been measured empirically in Australia (Danaher and Rossiter, 2005, p. 46) and this type of factor is also a central explanatory variable in the Theory of Planned Behavior (Hartmann, 2009b, pp. 33–5). *Environmental responsibility* is an emergent value which affects consumer choice more and more.

The explanatory model is shown in Figure 23.4 and its equation form is the following:

$$p_k = a + c_1(b_{1k}w_1) + c_2(b_{2k}w_2) + c_3(b_{3k}w_3) + c_4(b_{4k}w_4) + c_5(b_{5k}w_5) + c_6(b_{6k}w_6)$$

$$+ c_7 x_{7k} + c_8 x_8 + \ldots + c_n x_n,$$

Where:

p_k preference for channel k, $k = 1, \ldots, 12$ (alternatively all channels or channel group);

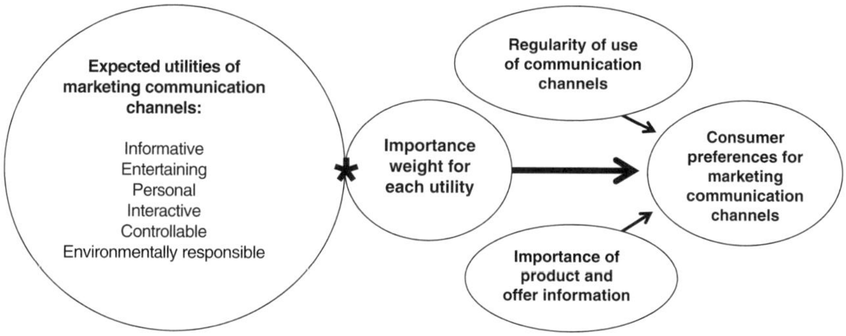

Figure 23.4 Explanatory model of consumer preferences for marketing communication channels

a constant to be estimated;
c_j coefficient of the explanatory variable, $j = 1, \ldots, n$;
b_i estimate of how well utility, property or use reason *i* is verified in channel *k*, $i = 1, \ldots, 6$;
w_i weight of how important utility, property or use reason is considered in *i*, $i = 1, \ldots, 6$;
$b_i\, w_i$ estimated utility of property *i* weighted according to its importance;
x_{7k} regularity of use of communication channel, product group $k = 1, \ldots, 12$;
x_8 importance of product and offer information, average 10 product groups; and
x_i other possible explanatory variables, for example, demographic variable.

In the data collection channel preferences, the expected utilities of each channel, and the importance weights of each utility were measured on the 11-point Likert-type scale, in which a respondent was able to move the pointer from the center in the desired direction according to his or her opinion. The ends of the scale were: for channel preferences 'preferred' or 'disfavored', for expected realization attributes 'describes very well' or 'describes very badly', and for importance evaluations 'very important' or 'not at all important'.

The explanatory model for channel preferences of marketing communication can be estimated for all channels, a group of certain types of channel or each individual marketing communication channel. The six utility groups for marketing communication channels are operationalized using the 17 utility indicators in Table 23.3. In the calculations, each channel-specific utility is weighted with the general importance of this utility in the case of the interviewee in question, and the averages of these products have become the explanatory utility variables for the model.

Because consumers use many communication channels mainly for reasons other than reception of marketing messages, the regularity of using the communication channel in question is included in the model as the explanator of the preferences of each marketing communication channel. Because the model explains the channel preferences of marketing communication, the significant influencing factor is the consumer-specific importance of product and offer information which has been calculated as an average of interests in 10 ordinary product groups.

The estimated general explanation model of channel preferences is based on a total of

Table 23.3 Indicators for the importance weights and expected values of utility

Indicators	
Informative	Interactive
1 Gives reliable information	10 Provides subjects for discussion
2 Is up to date	11 Easy ask and search for information
3 Helps with purchasing decisions	12 Is part of my life
Entertaining	Controllable
4 Entertains and relaxes	13 I can look at it when I wish
5 Nice to read, look at and listen to	14 Easy to reject if not interested
6 Helps to escape daily routines	15 Does not seem annoying
	16 Does not distract from other matters
Personal	Environmentally responsible
7 Meant just for me	17 Does not significantly waste natural resources
8 Arouses my interest	
9 Takes my needs into consideration	

7,011 consumer evaluations of 12 marketing communication channels. The percentage of variation in the data explained by the model is a reasonable 33 percent. All six utility groups of marketing communication channels, use of each communicational channel, and importance of product and offer information are included in the model with statistically significant *t*-values, and there is no disturbing multicollinearity problem between the explanatory variables. The beta coefficients of this all channels model are presented in the bottom row of Table 23.4.

The model was generated with a stepwise regression analysis in which the first four variables selected were in the following order: personal, controllable, use of each channel and entertaining. However, in the final model it will be observed from the standardized beta coefficients that the most effective variable is controllable and the second best is the regular use of each communicational channel. The third-best explanatory variable is entertaining. On the other hand, person-related feelings, which were introduced into the model first, are only the fourth most significant explanatory variable. The fifth and not so effective variable is environmental responsibility which differs from the others because of its negative coefficient. The result can be interpreted in such a way that those who stress environmental values do not want to receive marketing communication at all, because they consider it a waste of natural resources. Other less effective variables included in the model are informative, interactive and the importance of product and offer information.

A model which covers all marketing communication channels explains which factors usually affect channel preferences. The channel group model explains which factors have an effect on preferences within a channel group of, for example, paper channels. The channel-specific model in turn explains which factors are influential, how preferred or undesirable a particular channel, for example, newspaper, in the reception of marketing communication.

The channel group models were also estimated using stepwise regression analysis. Beta coefficients of these models are shown in Table 23.4. Explanation percentages vary from 30 to 36 percent. Some of the general model variables were not included in the channel group models, because the *t*-values were below the statistical significance criteria. Each channel group model includes utilities: controllable, entertaining and personal.

Table 25.4 Preference models for marketing communication channel groups

Marketing communication channel groups	R^2 %	Standardized beta coefficients							
		Informative	Entertaining	Personal	Interactive	Controllable	Environmentally responsible	Use of each messaging channel	Importance of product and offer information
Paper messaging	36.3	0.236	0.107	0.070		0.089		0.233	0.128
Traditional electronic	34.0	0.069	0.248	0.130		0.134	–0.082	0.166	0.072
New digital	32.0		0.093	0.107	0.180	0.167	–0.038	0.196	0.050
Targeted messaging	29.9		0.237	0.111	0.116	0.147	–0.073	0.041	0.072
Advertising mass comm.	33.5	0.163		0.179		0.242	–0.073	0.151	0.098
Journalistic mass comm.	33.8	0.093	0.100	0.112	0.056	0.113	–0.063	0.289	0.105
Search	31.9	0.200		0.146		0.155	–0.039	0.200	0.124
Reception	31.2	0.038	0.193	0.115	0.097	0.112	–0.060	0.172	0.075
All channels	33.4	0.091	0.153	0.118	0.051	0.200	–0.093	0.164	0.071

Furthermore, environmentally responsible with a negative coefficient is involved in all other models except that of paper communication. Regular use of the communication channel and the importance of product and offer information are included in all models.

Marketing communication channels seem to carry their history with them. Paper channels are preferred mainly as informative, traditional electronic channels are preferred principally for their ability to entertain, and digital channels are preferred especially if they are considered interactive. Besides being informative, when preferences for paper channels are explained, the regular use of each channel is emphasized. In channel-specific models the utility of informativeness is emphasized in newspapers and magazines and in product catalogs and leaflets. On the other hand, the most important criterion for preferring the addressed letter is its perception as interactive, which is evident from the fact that those who dislike it stress the non-interactivity of the addressed letter.

In traditional electronic communication, channel preferences are mainly based on channels' ability to entertain. This is emphasized in sales calls, which only a few consumers actually consider entertaining. In new digital communication the best explanatory variables are, besides interactive, the controllable and regular use of the channel. Interactivity is emphasized in the Internet news pages and controllability in net search services. For marketing in the social media the most important factor is whether the channel in question is usually in active use or not.

The channel preferences of targeted messaging are best explained by their entertainmental value, and it should be further observed that other use of the communication channel in question has an exceptionally small effect. For example, a person who frequently receives phone calls does not usually want to receive sales calls. In pure advertising mass communication the strongest explanatory variable for marketing channel preferences is controllability, meaning that the consumer can, for example, read a product catalog whenever and wherever according (s)he desires. In connection with journalistic mass communication, marketing is preferred especially because it has been customary to use these communication channels for the reception of all kinds of messages and there is also a need to ensure their use in the future. Preference for search channels is best explained by their perceived informativeness. Conversely, the reception channels are expected to be entertaining or at least not annoying.

5 CONCLUSIONS AND RECOMMENDATIONS

The implementation opportunities for marketing communication have diversified considerably in recent decades. The development of the Internet and mobile communication has brought and will continue to bring to our use new channels and new reception devices. Thus, consumer channel preferences will also change. The main trend will be for paper communication to gradually lose its traditionally strong role in marketing. Especially younger consumers can be expected to switch to the digital media, which they consider to be more convenient to use and environmentally more acceptable.

Although the main trend seems to be clear, there are also many differences between countries. In Finland particularly, preference for the addressed letter fell by 14 percentage points from 2006 to 2010. This contrasts sharply with countries such as Australia, where the popularity of letter mail marketing remained roughly unchanged from 2003 through

2008 (TNS Australia, 2003 and Open Mind Research Group, 2008). On the other hand, although during those periods the popularity of email marketing grew by 15 percentage points in Australia, it grew by only 3 percentage points in Finland. There are historical and cultural factors behind the underlying differences between the two countries: for example, in Finland there was an insignificant use of email marketing solutions. These differences between countries are a good reason for conducting channel-preference studies of this kind in different countries, preferably research comparing several countries at the same time.

It is important to note that different consumers groups prefer different marketing channels. For example, opposite to the targeting acceptors are the anonymous channel limiters, who do not want to give their name or any other personal information to marketers, but wish to search for the necessary marketing information themselves through the mass communication channels. In extreme cases, they also enroll in telemarketing and direct marketing not-to-be-disturbed banning registers. From the perspective of marketing efficiency it would be important for various consumer channel preferences to be identified and for marketers to comply with these wishes. Consumers are actively able to convey only some of their channel preferences to marketers and delivery operators, who for this reason have to rely increasingly on surveys, data mining and other methods for obtaining the necessary information concerning changing preferences.

Targeting is often seen as the best marketing solution for the future. However, in Finland only about one-fifth of consumers prefer marketing of this kind and most of these people are not those that marketers are interested in. The problem is that almost all message targeting marketers bombard the wealthy, for which reason they are on the verge of losing their faith in targeted marketing. To really succeed in targeting and earn the acceptance of consumers, marketers should better utilize existing data on customer purchasing behavior, phase of life and other features, leading to a better match between the contents, channels and timings of messages and the conscious and unconscious expectations of customers. There is business potential in this area for delivery operators if they are prepared to help marketing organizations with their targeting, for example, by offering them customer analytics combined with a set of physical and digital delivery services.

The results of the study reported here suggested that marketing communication channel preferences are best explained by perceived controllability. This controllability means the possibility of using marketing communication when one wishes, together with the ease of rejecting it if not interested. Further, the channel should not distract from other activities or seem annoying. The growth in possibilities of channel choice seems to emphasize the importance of controllability, which is particularly true in the case of the evaluation of the purely advertising channels of the mass media. On the other hand, marketing in conjunction with journalistic communication can be considered less problematic and very often a good opportunity to receive information and special offers. These possibilities, and the rapidly developing technologies underlying them, suggest continuing changes in channel preferences for marketing media in the years ahead. These changes can be expected to be of fundamental importance for the future of advertising, and for the continuing evolution of paper versus digital channel preferences of consumers.

REFERENCES

Danaher, Peter and John Rossiter (2006), 'A comparison of the effectiveness of marketing communication channels: perspectives from both receivers and senders', available at: http://www.mailmarketing.com.au/files/AuspostDanahersFullReport_1_.pdf (accessed 15 July 2011).

Elkelä, Kari (2005), 'Paper or electronic? Preferred and disfavored reception channels for direct marketing', in Michael Crew and Paul Kleindorfer (eds), *Regulatory and Economic Challenges in the Postal and Delivery Sector*, Boston, MA: Kluwer Academic Publishers, pp. 333–54.

Elkelä, Kari (2007), 'Kuluttajamainonnan vastaanoton kanavapreferenssit. 13 tärkeimmän kanavan valinnat ja torjunnat', Finland Post Corp. Research series 23/2007.

Elkelä, Kari (2009), 'Halutaanko markkinointiviestintä sähköisesti vai paperilla?', in Liisa Uusitalo and Mirella Lähteenmäki (eds), *Kuluttaja ja media tietotaloudessa*, Helsinki School of Economics B-113.

Elkelä, Kari (2010), 'Kuluttajien suhtautuminen markkinointiviestintäkanaviin' (Consumer attitude to marketing communication channels), Itella Corp. Research series 21/2010.

Elkelä, Kari (2011), 'Mikä markkinointikanavissa miellyttää? Ominaisuudet kanavapreferenssien selittäjinä', Itella Corp. Research series 4/2011.

Fill, Chris (2009), *Marketing Communications: Interactivity, Communities and Content*, 5th edn, Harlow: Prentice-Hall.

Hartmann, Tilo (2009a), 'A brief introduction to media choice', in Hartmann (ed.), *Media Choice: A Theoretical and Empirical Overview*, New York: Routledge, pp. 1–9.

Hartmann, Tilo (2009b), 'Action theory, theory of planned behavior and media choice', in Tilo Hartmann (ed.), *Media Choice: A Theoretical and Empirical Overview*, New York: Routledge, pp. 32–52.

Hastall, Matthias (2009), 'Informational utility as a determinant of media choice', in Tilo Hartmann (ed.), *Media Choice: A Theoretical and Empirical Overview*, New York: Routledge, pp. 149–66.

McQuail, Denis (1983), *Mass Communication Theory: An Introduction*, London: Sage.

McQuail, Denis (2010), *McQuail's Mass Communication Theory*, 6th edn, London: Sage.

Open Mind Research Group (2008), 'Which flavor do your customers prefer? Reaching consumers 2008. A study of media preferences', available at: http://www.transpromo.com.au/media/pdfs/Reaching_Consumers_A_Study_Of_Media_Preferences_(2008).pdf (accessed 15 July 2011).

TNS Australia (2003), 'Reaching consumers in the information age. How Australian consumers prefer organizations to communicate with them', available at: http://www.ourcommunity.com.au/files/Reachingconsumers.pdf (accessed 15 July 2011).

24. Accounting for behavioral biases for non-biased demand estimations*

Meloria Meschi[†] and Carla Pace[‡]

1 INTRODUCTION

Behavioral economics combines insights from psychology and traditional economic models to represent the process by which economic agents make decisions. As recently as 20 years ago, it was on the fringe of the discipline. During the past few years, however, the study of how people make choices has helped explain why human behavior appears sometimes to be at odds with mainstream economic predictions. It has also shown how 'choice architectures' can be established to nudge individuals in beneficial directions without restricting freedom of choice. With the institution of a 'nudge' Unit[1] in the Cabinet of the British Prime Minister David Cameron, understanding how people actually make choices has also officially become an important step in designing policy and regulatory measures aimed at 'nudging' them in the desired direction.

The standard economic model of human behavior is *Homo economicus*, a self-interested and rational being with perfect knowledge, a dislike of work and a love of wealth. *Homo economicus* makes decisions by weighing costs against benefits, and maximizes value and profit to himself. He is quite capable of perfect self-regulation when pursuing his future goals, a quality known as 'time consistency'. The standard theory has only one flaw: *Homo economicus* is allegedly hard to find.

Behavioral economics looks to *Homo sapiens* instead. This individual shows a lack of processing power (known as 'bounded rationality', a term coined by Nobel laureate Herbert Simon to characterize an intendedly rational actor that was subject to mistakes and biases because of information-processing limitations of human decision makers) and a preference for framing. He is time inconsistent and, finally, averse to losses. These behavioral characteristics require that economists find a way to take them into account when modeling economic behavior. The debate about who are right – neoclassical or behavioral economists – has been raging for years. In the meantime, the discipline has progressed and expanded.

Seen in this perspective, and to paraphrase Conlisk (1996), the failure to include bounded rationality in economic models is not a failure of economic models, it is bad economics: since brainpower and time are limited resources we cannot expect difficult problems to be solved optimally. In the presence of such constraints, the most rational thing for people to do is to use rules of thumb to economize on cognitive faculties, a

† Director, FTI Consulting.
‡ Senior Economic Intelligence Expert, bpost.

fact that can be worked into economic models. By the same token, individuals may be time inconsistent not because they lack the rational ability to make long-term plans (for example, plans to stop smoking, drinking, or eating too much), but because they lack the self-control to carry these plans through, given the high short-term costs that these plans involve.[2]

Some behavioral biases have been successfully worked into economic models, and the recent interest in behavioral economics has produced a critical mass of empirical research aimed at explaining unexpected reactions by economic agents. In this chapter, we focus on (i) how consumers process price information and formulate their price responses, (ii) what this implies for traditional demand analysis and (iii) how empirical research could check and take into account behavioral biases in the postal sector.

In Section 2, we discuss traditional demand analysis from a theoretical perspective, and in Section 3 we describe how traditional empirical demand models are derived. In Section 4, we discuss behavioral biases how they may affect demand. In Section 5 we suggest ways in which traditional estimates of demand of postal services could fail to give a correct representation of how consumers react to price changes, and how these estimates could be improved by modelling behavioral biases. Section 6 concludes.

2 TRADITIONAL DEMAND ANALYSIS

According to traditional economic theory, *Homo economicus* derives utility from consumption and leisure, thereby facing the first of many tradeoffs: because consumption costs money, to consume more *Homo economicus* has to give up some leisure – he has to work. He makes decisions about whether and how much to consume rationally, and based on comparisons between market prices and reservation prices, conditional on his income, or budget constraint.

The reservation price for a certain amount of a good is nothing but the maximum willingness to pay for that amount of the good. The larger the amount, the lower the reservation price, because individuals derive less utility for additional consumption of the same good.[3] Aggregated over all consumers, the demand curve shows how much buyers are willing to pay (what is the reservation price) for different quantities of the good. An individual consumer will not buy anything if the market price is higher than his or her willingness to pay.

For *Homo Economicus*, preferences are stable and in the presence of a budget constraint, prices measure how much of one good[4] has to be forgone in order to consume more of another. Thus, the (maximum) willingness to pay for a certain good is *independent* of the prices observed by the individual. It is the *quantity* that individuals want to buy that depends on the prices they face, as well as on other variables such as their income (the budget constraint), expectations about future market prices, the prices of related goods (substitute and complement goods), and their tastes[5] (including their time preference, that is, the value they place on consuming now): these are the so-called 'demand shifters'.

Any business knows that the lower the price, the higher the quantity it can sell, at least until the point where the consumer's demand is 'exhausted'. Traditional economic theory suggests the following: (i) for given levels of demand shifters, demand falls as the asked

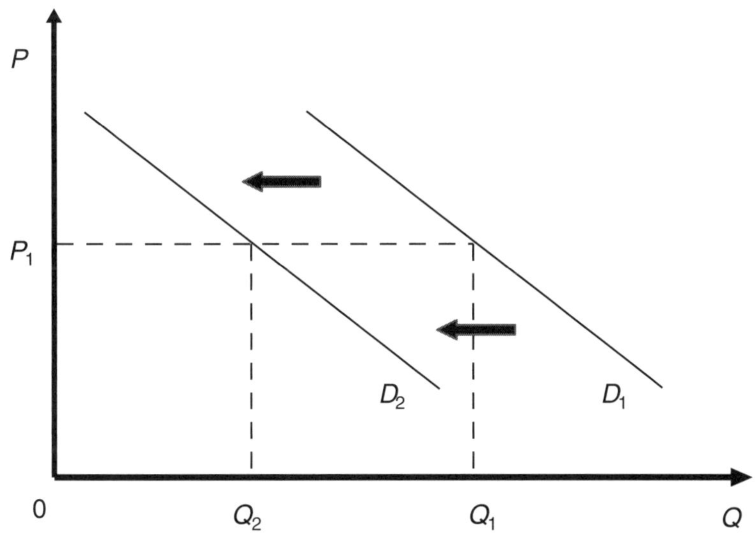

Figure 24.1 *Example of shift in demand due to a change in demand shifters*

price increases; (ii) for a given price level, a change in demand shifters causes a shift of the demand curve (see Figure 24.1). To use an example relevant to the postal sector, when broadband prices drop, the demand for letter mail would fall at any given mail price: when price is P_1, the quantity demanded would fall from Q_1 to Q_2. In this example, the slope of the demand does not change when the curve shifts.

According to traditional economic theory, therefore, the willingness to pay of individual consumers reflects their underlying rational preferences and does not depend on, or change with observed prices.

This framework has particular consequences for modeling the demand by *Homo economicus*, not only in terms of what drives demand, but also in terms of how these drivers actually affect the quantities *Homo economicus* wants to buy and the value he derives from what he is buying. We discuss below how these prescriptions can be translated into empirical models of demand.[6]

3 EMPIRICAL TESTING BASED ON TRADITIONAL DEMAND ANALYSIS

Homo Economicus and Reservation Prices

The process by which rational consumers decide whether and how much to purchase of any given good is quite straightforward: they compare the market price[7] to their reservation price and only buy the good if its price is lower than or equal to[8] the reservation price.

The modeling of consumer demand for empirical testing takes different forms according to: (i) the type of data available: these range from records on individual consumers' expenditures for one (cross-section) or more time periods (panel data) to aggregate data by product or by country, generally available over a number of periods; (ii) whether some consumers are constrained in their choice: there are products, for instance mortgages, that some consumers may not be able to buy even if they are prepared to pay the market price for them. The estimation and data-gathering methodologies need to be adjusted to account for this possibility. This is not the case of postal services, which are guaranteed through the Universal Service Obligation (USO); and (iii) whether the good being studied is homogeneous (for example, a commodity) or differentiated. Branded goods are a typical example of differentiated goods. Products with different qualitative attributes can also be thought of as differentiated: for example, a First Class and a Second Class stamp are differentiated products.

The degree to which demand reacts to changes in prices and income (elasticity of demand with respect to own price, cross-price elasticity of demand, and income elasticity of demand) can all be measured based on observable data: it is not necessary to gather data on reservation prices in order to estimate demand models. Observed prices and quantities are sufficient for the purpose: if a consumer is buying a quantity x when the price is y, its reservation price has to be below or equal to y – everything else being the same.

Moreover, when dealing with differentiated goods, traditional economic theory allows the estimation of the weight that consumers place on each characteristic; of the tradeoff (the marginal rate of substitution) between characteristics, including price; and of the value that each consumer places on changes in each characteristic.[9] Again, the underlying assumption here is that for certain levels of each characteristic, the willingness to pay does not change with observed prices.

Knowing the way each demand driver affects consumer demand provides invaluable information to a business. Rational consumers respond to incentives, and developing a demand taxonomy can provide businesses with profit-maximizing marketing strategies. This is particularly useful when products have qualitative dimensions that are valued by customers, who are willing to pay higher prices for products that are differentiated along these dimensions.

For example, speed of delivery, traceability and security are qualitative attributes of mail products which are valued by customers. Delivery at places other than the customer's home is becoming increasingly important as e-commerce expands and fewer and fewer people are at home during working hours. Knowing how much tracking their mail is worth to customers allows optimal pricing of track and trace products; it also allows businesses to forecast, for different price levels, how many customers would buy the service.

Businesses that are able to measure the value that consumers place on different attributes of their products and that succeed in segmenting consumers into groups paying different prices for different, adapted versions of individual products, could succeed in stimulating the demand and generating additional value.

Finally, having a detailed knowledge of what customers want would allow for the optimal provision of the USO by balancing the value that consumers place on its fundamental elements (such as, for example, the number of deliveries per week) and a combination of elements (for example, speed and frequency of delivery) with the cost of providing them.

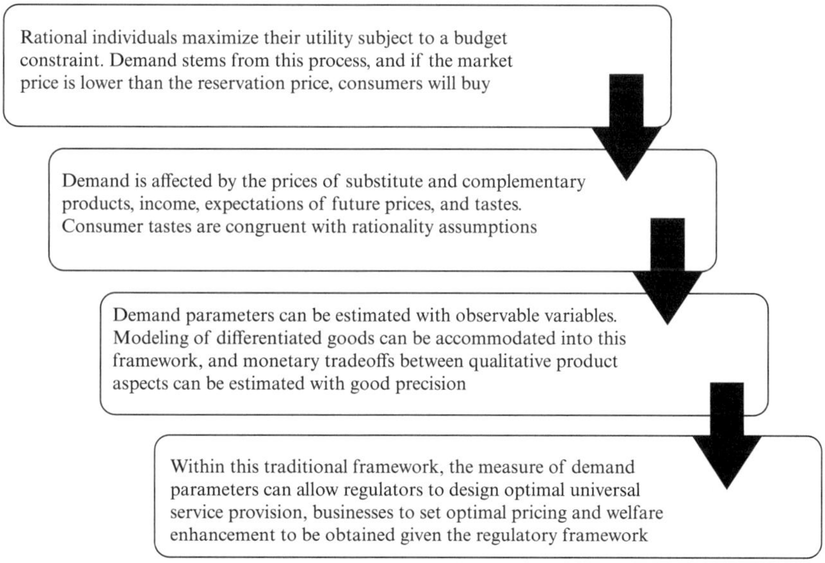

Figure 24.2 Development of traditional demand models

Figure 24.2 summarizes how traditional demand models have developed.

In sum, traditional economic theory assumes that consumers consider the observed price of a product, as well as the prices of substitute and complementary products, their income and expectations, given their tastes, as the relevant decision variables when deciding whether buy to a specific good. When the good is differentiated, consumers also take non-price characteristics into account when making a decision.

Consumers compare observed prices with reservation prices, where reservation prices do not depend on, or vary with, observed prices. Based on these assumptions, econometric analysis can be conducted using data on the quantities bought of a certain product, its price, the prices of substitute and complementary products, income or expenditure, and other relevant variables that cause changes in tastes for the product. Such data can be collected for samples of individuals, stores, regions or countries for a single period (cross-section) or multiple periods (time-series or panel data).

The information thus collected can then be used to estimate, among other things: (i) how consumers respond to a change in the price of a particular product, assuming that all other demand drivers do not change (elasticity of demand); for example, is the elasticity of demand constant, or does it vary with price, and according to what rule; (ii) how contemporaneous changes in more than one driver affect demand – for example, what happens if the price of a product decreases and that of its main substitute decreases as well; (iii) what happens if events take place that change consumers' tastes (environmental preferences, for example), or if new products enter the market; (iv) what are the pricing policies, and price–quality combinations, that maximize revenues under a number of scenarios; and (v) what is the optimal design of services such as the USO.

Homo Sapiens and Reference Prices

While the traditional *Homo economicus* is assumed to have a reservation price based on objective and rational observation, consumers seem to go through a subjective encoding of prices when making buying choices: their reaction to market prices and price changes seem to depend on the way they encode prices, rather than on comparisons between reservation and market prices.[10] There are a number of reasons why this may be the case, known as behavioral biases, including anchoring, framing, loss aversion and the 'bandwagon effect':

- *Anchoring* (Tversky and Kahneman, 1974): individuals tend to anchor their decisions to a particular piece of information when making decisions. For example, when making buying decisions, such a piece of information may be the actual price distribution or a past price; buyers may use this price information as the benchmark against which they decide whether to buy or not.
- *Framing* (Tversky and Kahneman, 1981): individuals make different decisions depending on the way a choice is framed. Because individuals are risk averse, when choices involve risk, presenting an option as a 'sure gain' will induce buyers to choose that option.[11] In a more traditional marketing setting, individual choices and willingness to pay for differentiated products can be influenced by framing attribute information (Levin and Gaeth, 1988) – for example, 'this service is x% faster than that service' versus 'that service is y% slower than this service'.
- *Loss aversion*: for an individual, 'the disutility of giving up an object is greater than the utility associated with acquiring it' (Kahneman et al., 1991, p. 194); by offering rebates and trial periods businesses can acquire customers who will then be less prone to leave when the rebate is removed or the trial period ends (that is, when the price increases).
- Finally, the *bandwagon effect* (Leibenstein, 1950): individuals' preferences for a product may increase the more people buy that product.[12]

Several reasons have been put forward for why behavioral biases arise, including bounded rationality (Simon, 1957 and Williamson, 1981), where individuals' ability to make optimal decisions is limited by the time, information and cognitive ability that they have. For the purpose of this chapter, what is important is that when some behavioral biases are present, an individual willingness to pay may be based on a *reference price* rather than, or in addition to, being equal to the reservation price described above.

Behavioral economics considers the reference price as the benchmark price to which an individual compares the observed price of a product in deciding whether to buy.[13] The mechanics of the comparison are the same as those described by the traditional approach for the reservation price: when the reference price is higher than the product price, the individual perceives a gain, which will positively affect demand, whereas when the reference price is lower than the product price, the individual perceives a loss and does not buy.

4 NEGLECTING BEHAVIOURAL EFFECTS CAN LEAD TO BIASED TRADITIONAL DEMAND ESTIMATES

What makes the reference price different from the reservation price is that it depends on prices through the effect of behavioral biases.[14] If individual consumers are price takers, then reference prices depend on supply, and this makes traditional demand estimation biased. In particular, traditional analysis can misestimate the elasticity of demand with respect to the product price and suggest price hikes that are too high or too low and result in revenue losses with respect to an optimal situation. To understand why this is the case, consider first Figure 24.3.

Demand (D_1) and supply (S_1) of a product are in equilibrium at price A. Consider a situation where the quantity supplied decreases at any given price, because for example the price of a production input increases. The whole supply curve shifts upwards, from S_1 to S_2. Because no demand shifters have changed (either the prices of related goods, or consumers' income/expenditure, expectations or tastes), traditional economic theory predicts that demand does not move: it is still D_1. The new market equilibrium will be at point B, where D_1 and S_2 meet. In the absence of any further changes, this is a long-run equilibrium.

Suppose now that there is some kind of bias in consumers' behavior. In experiments conducted by Mazar et al. (2009), for example, consumers do not know the price distribution prior to the experiments, and they form their reservation price based on observed prices: when observed prices are higher, so is the reservation price. Following their results, point B in Figure 24.3 could not be an equilibrium; consumers adapted to the changed environment and their demand shifted out to D_2 – even though none of the traditional demand shifters has changed. The new equilibrium will be at point C.

Empirical analysis based on traditional economic theory will not be able to account for this shift in demand (because there is no variable in the traditional model that accounts

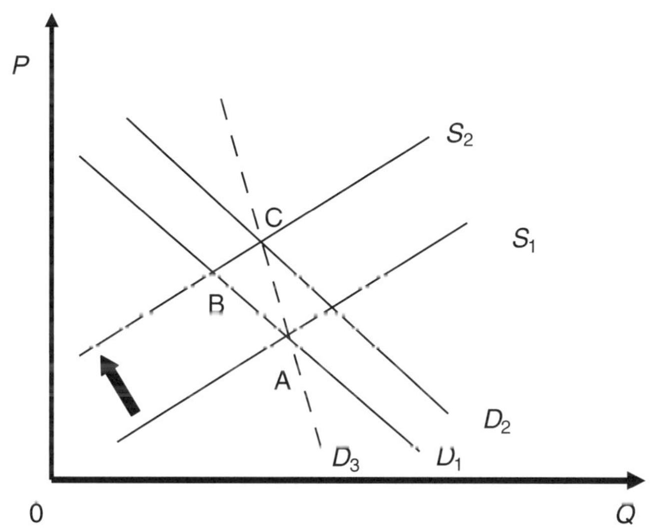

Figure 24.3 Example of underestimation of demand elasticity

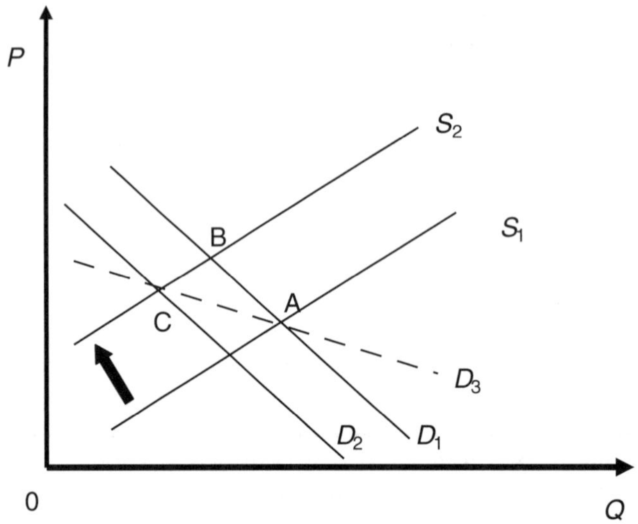

Figure 24.4 Example of overestimation of demand elasticity

for the reference-price effect). As a result, faced with points A and C it will predict that the demand curve is one, and one only, and that it is D_3. The resulting elasticity of demand at C will be lower than the true elasticity, with negative consequences for future pricing decisions.

The situation depicted above is one where consumers do not know the prices of what they buy in advance, and it was developed within an experimental approach aimed at assessing the effects of external price stimuli on the formation of consumers' internal reference price and price judgment.[15]

There are many instances, however, where consumers buy the same product repeatedly (firms buying Direct Mail services from postal operators could be a good example). In this case, they use their past shopping experience to build a reference price (Greenleaf, 1995, Kopalle and Winer, 1996, and Kopalle et al., 1996 all discuss the literature on reference-price modeling). Individuals observe prices regularly and use these prices to form their reference price, which is not only an internal price, but also assumes some 'fair price' connotation. This anchor price is used when making purchasing decisions: moreover, when prices increase, loss aversion causes a larger reaction than that which follows a price decrease.

This kind of behavioral bias is shown in Figure 24.4.

Here again, the demand (D_1) and supply (S_1) are in equilibrium at price A. The quantity supplied decreases at any given price, following the increase in the price of a production input. The whole supply curve shifts upwards, from S_1 to S_2, and traditional economic theory predicts that demand remains D_1, with new market equilibrium at point B.

However, in this example consumers use their past shopping experience to build a reference price. They adapt to the shock and their demand shifts out to D_2 – even though none of the traditional demand shifters has changed: the new equilibrium is actually in C.

Empirical analysis based on traditional economic theory will not be able to account for this shift in demand due to the reference price effect. As a result, faced with observed points A and C it will predict that the demand curve is D_3. In this case, the estimated elasticity of demand will be higher than the true elasticity.

The analysis of Fibich et al. 2005 presents evidence of this kind of misestimation in traditional demand analysis. The authors derive different formulae for short-run and long-term elasticities in the presence of reference-price effects.[16] They find that the short term price elasticity is higher than the long-term price elasticity. This is because the reference-price effect is highest immediately after a price change, because consumers have had no time to adapt to the change itself. This runs counter to prediction by economic theory, where demand is more elastic in the long run. The authors also find that the elasticity is larger following a price increase (loss aversion) than a decrease in the price, instead of being symmetric.

The combined effects of these two behavioral biases (anchoring and loss aversion) have been considered extensively in the marketing literature, and in particular with respect to grocery products. Mazumdar et al. 2005 summarize the main findings of this literature. Marketing managers have been able to use these findings in their day-to-day work, making predictions concerned with the timing and size of price changes and the use of promotions, rebates and staggered price changes.

In addition, in this case, not accounting for these phenomena in empirical work would result in biased estimates of consumers' reaction (price elasticities). In particular here, the impact of asymmetry in customers' reactions to increase and decrease in prices would be missed.

5 IMPLICATIONS FOR POSTAL DEMAND ESTIMATIONS AND FUTURE DIRECTIONS OF RESEARCH

Traditional economic analyses of demand may yield biased results because they do not incorporate the effects of behavioral biases. Similarly, a purely behavioral approach may yield biased results because it does not fully account for the effect of relevant economic and individual factors. What is necessary at this juncture is a better convergence between these two large areas of research, and an extension of this research beyond traditional 'supermarket-type' products.

As more data becomes available, marketing and economic models should be increasingly pooled together to account for how shifters such as income/expenditure constraints, tastes and the prices of related goods, affect consumer demand. Advances have already been made to account for the impact of consumer heterogeneity on the estimation of demand parameters, with the use of panel data (Bell and Lattin, 2000), and the analysis of consumer survey data, or scanner panel data has proved a popular and fruitful avenue of research. An additional effort should be made to incorporate price-reference effects in traditional demand modeling. This would be particularly useful in postal economics, where pricing is evolving in a more and more competitive environment.

For example, a rationalization of pricing grids that group two contiguous weight classes in a single class with price equal to the former heavier class could have a stronger effect than foreseen by traditional demand analysis. Customers previously buying the lighter product could perceive the price increase as unfair, because they are anchored to the historical price levels of a weight category no longer available. Their reaction could be far more negative than expected by just looking at the relative price increase.

Even changes in the range of products offered could have effects stronger than expected under traditional demand analysis. Withdrawing the economy class, for example, could cause a higher fall in volumes from that which would be expected by simply considering the de facto price increase. Customers could continue to be anchored to the historical price of the economy class, without regard to the fact that they are now buying a *different* product, with improved features.

It would be interesting to test whether the switching behavior of postal customers differs in response to price increases and price decreases. For example, Dawes (2004) analyzed the relationship between changes in car insurance premiums and customer switching in Australia. He found that the impact of price decreases on defection rates was reduced compared to the impact of price increases.

The effect that these types of behavior have on consumers' demand requires adjustments to be made to the econometric specification of demand models (for example, by allowing for the estimation of asymmetrical price effects) as well as to the design of surveys that are meant to capture consumer preferences and help quantify tradeoffs between qualitative and quantitative attributes of a product.

6 CONCLUSIONS

Behavioral economics combines insights from psychology and traditional economics to represent the process by which economic agents make decisions.

In traditional demand analysis, the reservation price for a certain amount of a good is the maximum willingness to pay for that amount. *Homo economicus*, at the center of traditional demand analysis, has stable preferences, a budget constraint, and faces prices that measure how much of one good he must forgo in order to consume more of another. This implies that reservation prices are *independent* of the prices observed by the individual.

Instead, the *Homo sapiens* observation unit of behavioral economics suffers from a series of biases. Under them, an individual's willingness to pay may be based on a reference price rather than, or in addition to, the reservation price. The reference price can generally be defined as the benchmark price to which an individual compares the observed price of a product in deciding whether to buy. What makes the reference price different from the reservation price is that it depends on observed prices, either current or past.

Estimation of demand based only on a traditional economic approach may yield biased results because it does not account for the effect of behavioral biases, especially those linking buying decisions to past prices, or to price comparison with competing products. A purely behavioral approach in turn may yield biased estimations too, because it does not fully account for the effect of other relevant economic and individual factors.

The behavior of end consumers in postal markets could be better understood by incorporating the lessons learned from behavioral economics to the modeling of consumer demand in order to better understand the sensitivity of different consumers to price variations, useful both for firms and regulators.

Although the focus of our review has been on consumer demand, we note that businesses are run by people who may behave as *Homo sapiens* rather than as *Homo economicus*: bounded rationality is not limited to consumption decisions. There is scope to use insights from behavioral models of firm behavior which refute the paradigm of profit maximization, to analyze the behavior of businesses that buy postal services. Reference can be made to the large body of behavioral literature applied to corporate finance, investment theory, marketing and industrial strategy, among others.[17]

The field of postal economics could benefit from the application of the precepts of behavioral economics, especially in devising empirical models of customer behavior that could be used for marketing and strategy purposes. In particular, it would be important to understand the extent to which behavioral biases such as anchoring, loss aversion and bandwagon effects may affect the purchasing of services – such as direct mail services – by very small businesses and small and medium-sized enterprises.

Further research in this direction would shed light on the effectiveness of marketing tools such as promotions, rebates and staggered prices on business purchasers, and help design optimal pricing policies.

NOTES

* The views expressed in this chapter are those of the authors and do not necessarily reflect the views of FTI Consulting or bpost.
1. The Unit, formally known as the Behavioural Insight Team, is advised by Richard Thaler, the Chicago professor who co-authored with Cass Sunstein '*Nudge*', the business best seller that shows how a thoughtful '*choice architecture*' can be established to nudge individuals in beneficial directions without restricting freedom of choice.
2. Gruber (2010). This is the concept of hyperbolic discounting, one of many behavioral biases *Homo sapiens* can have.
3. In other words, marginal utility is decreasing.
4. Often this is modeled as a 'composite' good, so that the choice problem is reduced to a simple alternative.
5. Consumer tastes may and do change over time; they may also vary with cultural, demographic and educational characteristics. However, they are developed within the preference structure that characterizes *Homo economicus*. This individual has preferences that are complete, reflexive, transitive and continuous. Also, they are (weakly or strongly) monotonic, exhibit local non-satiation and are convex (see, for example, Varian, 1992).
6. From a theoretical perspective, passing from individual demand to aggregate demand (either by a group of consumers or by all consumers) requires the application of another set of assumptions. The discussion of these goes beyond the scope of this chapter. Whether we talk about empirical models based on individual or aggregate data, we assume that they are compliant with economic theory.
7. The implied assumption here is that the market price is independent (exogenous) of the quantity sold. Were this not the case, the model could be adjusted using the appropriate methodology.
8. Technically, when reservation and market prices are the same, the consumer is indifferent between buying and not buying.
9. This is what is done with discrete choice modelling (using, for example, multinomial or nested logit models). Daniel McFadden (1973, also see 1980) was the first to develop such models to help design public transport systems. He was awarded the Nobel Prize in Economics in 2000 for his research on the topic.
10. See, for example, Winer (1986), Lichtenstein et al. (1991), Hardie et al. (1993), Briesch et al. (1997).
11. This type of bias, incorporated in prospect theory, is particularly relevant to analyzing the behavior of agents operating in financial markets. Daniel Kahneman won the Nobel Prize in Economics in 2002 for his work in this field.
12. This is different from the network effect, which is a rational effect that takes place because the more people are on a network, the higher is the utility from joining (there is no point having a phone if one can call no-one!).
13. Monroe (1973); Winer (1986); Kalwani et al. (1990), Mayhew and Winer (1992).

14. Recent experiments by Mazar et al. (2009) have shown, for example, that even without a clear price distribution to use as an anchor or reference price, and in controlled experiments that eliminated the possibility of framing and loss effects, the willingness to pay depends on the actual distribution of product prices rather than on independent reservation prices.
15. Pioneering work in this field can be found in Urbany et al. (1988) and Alba et al. (1999) and is reviewed in Mazumdar et al. (2005). We note that these experiments fit products that are bought infrequently better than other products.
16. The authors consider the cases where the product being investigated is sold by a monopolist, or in a more competitive market.
17. An early reference can be found in Kleindorfer et al. (1993). Firms are seen as heterogeneous entities with bounded rationality in an uncertain environment gathering information by search activity (Cyert and March, 1963). Kahneman and Tversky (1979) presented a critique of expected utility theory and developed an alternative model for decision making under risk: the prospect theory. Under the prospect theory, firms' decision makers are allowed to be loss-averse, risk seekers for a possible gain and risk-averse towards losses. In their investment decisions managers can fall under the sunk cost fallacy (especially when they feel responsible for a bad investment) or be overly optimistic on returns (Brockner, 1992; Whyte, 1993). Firms' decision makers can show time-inconsistent preferences, which have been modeled by hyperbolic discounting (Loewenstein and Prelec, 1992). The functioning of financial markets has been deeply investigated by behavioral finance: reluctance to depart from the status quo (Samuelson and Zeckhauser, 1988); managers' overconfidence (Malmendier and Tate, 2005); earnings' management (Degeorge et al. 1999); 'torpedo effect' (Skinner and Sloan, 2002); and returns associated with meeting or beating expectations (Bartov et al., 2002). Finally, the relevance of behavioral biases in economic activity and human decision making is also recognized by policy makers. Many public policy analyses take into account behavioral biases: health care and well-being (Thaler and Sunstein, 2008), financial regulation (Akerlof and Schiller, 2009), poverty (Bertrand et al., 2004), and saving and pension funds (Thaler and Benartzi, 2004).

REFERENCES

Akerlof, G. and R. Schiller (2009), *Animal Spirits: How Human Psychology Drives the Economy, and Why It Matters for Global Capitalism*, Princeton, NJ: Princeton University Press.

Alba, J.W., C.F. Mela, T.A. Shimp and J.E. Urbany (1999), The effect of discount frequency and depth on consumer price judgments, *Journal of Consumer Research*, **26**, 99–114.

Bartov, Eli, D. Givoli and C. Hayn (2002), 'The rewards to meeting or beating earnings expectations', *Journal of Accounting and Economics*, **33**, 173–204.

Bell, D.L. and J.M. Lattin (2000), 'Looking for loss aversion in scanner panel data: the confounding effect of price response heterogeneity', *Marketing Science*, **19**, 185–200.

Bertrand, M., S. Mullainathan and E. Shafir (2004), 'A behavioral economics view of poverty', *American Economic Review*, **94**(2), 419–23.

Briesch, R.A., Lakshman Krishnamurthi, Tridib Mazumdar and S.P. Raj (1997), 'A comparative analysis of reference price models', *Journal of Consumer Research*, **24**, 202–14.

Brockner, J. (1992), 'The escalation of commitment to a failing course of action: toward theoretical progress', *Academy of Management Review*, **17**(1), 39–61.

Conlisk, J. (1996), 'Why bounded rationality?', *Journal of Economic Literature*, **34**(2), 669–700.

Cyert, R.M. and J.G. March (1963), '*A Behavioral Theory of the Firm*', Englewood Cliffs NJ: Prentice-Hall.

Dawes, J. (2004), 'Price changes and defection levels in a subscription-type market: can an estimation model really predict defection levels?', *Journal of Services Marketing*, **18**(1), 35–44.

Degeorge, F., J.S. Patel and R.J. Zeckhauser (1999), 'Earnings management to exceed thresholds', *Journal of Business*, **72**(1), 1–33.

Fibich, G., A. Gavious and O. Lowengart (2005), 'The dynamics of price elasticity of demand in the presence of reference price', *Academy of Marketing Science Journal*, **33**, ABI/INFORM Global, 66.

Greenleaf, E.A. (1995), 'The impact of reference price effects on the profitability of price promotions', *Marketing Science*, **14**, 82–104.

Gruber, J. (2010), 'Commentary', in *Dimensions of Tax Design: The Myrlees Review*, Institute for Fiscal Studies, London.
Hardie, B.G.S., E.J. Johnson and P.S. Fader (1993), 'Modeling loss aversion and reference dependence effects on brand choice', *Marketing Science*, **12,** 378–94.
Kahneman, D., J.L. Knetsch and R.H. Thaler (1991), 'Anomalies: the endowment effect, loss aversion, and status quo bias', *Journal of Economic Perspectives,* **5**, 193–206.
Kahneman, D. and A. Tversky (1979), 'Prospect theory: an analysis of decision under risk', *Econometrica*, **47**(2), 263–92.
Kalwani, M.U., J.H. Rinne and Yoshi Sugita (1990), 'A price expectations model of customer brand choice', *Journal of Marketing Research*, **27**, 251–62.
Kleindorfer, P., H. Kunreuther and P.J.H. Schoemaker (1993), *Decision Sciences: An Integrative Perspective*, Cambridge: Cambridge University Press.
Kopalle, P.K., Ambar G. Rao and João L. Assunção (1996), 'Asymmetric reference price effects and dynamic pricing policies', *Marketing Science*, **15**, 60–85.
Kopalle, P.K. and R.S. Winer (1996), 'A dynamic model of reference price and expected quality', *Marketing Letters*, **7**, 41–52.
Leibenstein, H. (1950), 'Bandwagon, snob, and Veblen effects in the theory of consumers' demand', *Quarterly Journal of Economics*, **64**, 183–207.
Levin, I.P. and G.J. Gaeth (1988), 'How consumers are affected by the framing of attribute information before and after consuming the product', *Journal of Consumer Research*, **15**, 374–8.
Lichtenstein, D.R., S. Burton and E.J. Karson (1991), 'The effect of semantic cues on consumer perceptions of reference price ads', *Journal of Consumer Research*, **18**, 380–91.
Loewenstein, G. and D. Prelec (1992), 'Anomalies in intertemporal choice: evidence and an Interpretation', *Quarterly Journal of Economics*, **107**, 573–97.
Malmendier, U. and G. Tate (2005), 'CEO overconfidence and corporate investment', *Journal of Finance*, **60**(6), 2661–700.
Mayhew, G.E. and R.S. Winer (1992), 'An empirical analysis of internal and external reference prices using scanner data', *Journal of Consumer Research*, **19**, 62–70.
Mazar, N., B. Koszegi and D. Arieli (2009), 'Price sensitive preferences', Berkeley, CA, available at: http://elsa.berkeley.edu/~botond/PriceSensitivePreferences.pdf (accessed 28 August 2011).
Mazumdar T., S.P. Raj and I. Sinha (2005), 'Reference price research: review and propositions', *Journal of Marketing*, **69**(October), 84–102.
McFadden, D. (1973), 'Conditional logit analysis of qualitative choice behaviour', in P. Zarembka (ed.), *Frontiers in Econometrics*, New York: Academic Press.
Mc Fadden, D. (1980), 'Econometric models for probabilistic choice among products', *Journal of Business*, **53**, S13–S29.
Monroe, K.B. (1973), 'Buyers' subjective perceptions of price', *Journal of Marketing Research*, **10** (February), 70–80.
Samuelson, W. and R. Zeckhauser (1988), '*Status quo* bias in decision making', *Journal of Risk and Uncertainty*, 1, 7–59.
Simon, H. (1957), 'A behavioral model of rational choice', in *Models of Man, Social and Rational: Mathematical Essays on Rational Human Behavior in a Social Setting*, New York: Wiley.
Skinner, D.J. and R.G. Sloan (2002), 'Earnings surprises, growth expectations, and stock returns: don't let an earnings torpedo sink your portfolio', *Review of Accounting Studies*, 7, 289–312.
Thaler R.H. and S. Benartzi (2004), 'Save more tomorrow: using behavioral economics to increase employee saving', *Journal of Political Economy*, **112**(1), S164–S187.
Thaler R.H. and C. Sunstein (2008), *Nudge: Improving Decisions about Health, Wealth, and Happiness*, New Haven, CT: Yale University Press.
Tversky, A. and D. Kahneman (1974), 'Judgment under uncertainty: heuristics and biases', *Science*, **185**, 1124–30.
Tversky, A. and D. Kahneman (1981), 'The framing of decisions and the psychology of choice', *Science*, **211**, 453–8.
Urbany, J.E., W.O. Bearden and D.C. Weilbaker (1988), 'The effect of plausible and exaggerated

reference price on consumer perceptions and price search', *Journal of Consumer Research*, **15**, 95–110.
Varian, H.R. (1992), '*Microeconomic Analysis*', New York: Norton.
Whyte, G. (1993), 'Escalating commitment in individual and group decision making: a prospect theory approach', *Organizational Behavior and Human Decision Processes*, **54**(3), 430–55.
Williamson, O.E. (1981), 'The economics of organization: the transaction cost approach', *American Journal of Sociology*, **87**, 548–77.
Winer, R.S. (1986), 'A reference price model of brand choice for frequently purchased products', *Journal of Consumer Research*, **13**(2), 250–56.